MORAL REASONING

A Philosophic Approach to Applied Ethics

Richard M. Fox
Joseph P. DeMarco
Cleveland State University

HOLT, RINEHART and WINSTON, INC.

Fort Worth   Chicago   San Francisco   Philadelphia   Montreal   Toronto   London   Sydney   Tokyo

Publisher	**Ted Buchholz**
Acquisitions Editor	**Jo-Anne Weaver**
Project Editor	**Michele Tomiak**
Manager of Art and Design	**Guy Jacobs**
Production Manager	**Ken Dunaway**
Copy Editor	**Ann Burns Moyer**
Interior Design	**Tom Dawson/DUO Design Group**
Cover Design	**Rhonda Campbell**

Library of Congress Cataloging-in-Publication Data

Fox, Richard M. (Richard Milan)
    Moral reasoning : a philosophic approach to applied ethics /
Richard M. Fox, Joseph P. DeMarco.
        p.   cm.
    Includes bibliographical references.
    ISBN 0-03-026594-0
    1. Ethics.   I. DeMarco, Joseph P., 1943-   . II. Title.
BJ1012.F67   1989   89-48247
170—dc20   CIP

Copyright © 1990 by Holt, Rinehart and Winston, Inc.

Requests for permission to make copies of any part of the work should be mailed to: Copyrights and Permissions Department, Holt, Rinehart and Winston, Inc., Orlando, Florida 32887.

Address editorial correspondence to: 301 Commerce Street, Fort Worth, Texas 76102.

Address orders to: 6277 Sea Harbor Drive, Orlando, Florida 32887, 1-800-782-4479, or 1-800-433-0001 (in Florida).

Printed in the United States of America

ISBN 0-03-026594-0

 0 1 2 090 9 8 7 6 5 4 3 2

Holt, Rinehart and Winston, Inc.
The Dryden Press
Saunders College Publishing

MORAL REASONING: A Philosophical Approach to Applied Ethics provides an analysis of the principles and techniques required for rational decision-making in ethics. It develops reasoning skills needed to understand and apply ethical theories. As the title indicates, the emphasis is on reasoning, on how reasoning can be used to apply moral principles and rules to the solution of moral problems. It is also a *philosophical* book, for it approaches ethics from a philosophical point of view and develops a theory of applied ethics.

The book is intended to be used as a primary text in philosophy courses on moral reasoning and applied ethics. It may be used in conjunction with a supplementary book of readings, for it shows how the insights and techniques developed by philosophers can help illumine and resolve moral issues. It also includes a large number of examples, many in the form of exercises and case studies, which include topics covered in readings courses.

In writing this text, the authors were motivated by the conviction that a philosophy course in moral reasoning, or in applied ethics, should be philosophical. It should engage the student in philosophical inquiry and not simply teach the *results* of philosophical investigation, in the form of ethical theories, or by simply exposing opposing views on controversial issues. Such a course would teach students about philosophical questions and modes of inquiry, and it would develop an appreciation of and skill in logical argumentation—the chief tool of philosophical investigation. As a course in applied ethics, it should show how philosophical inquiry can contribute to the solution of practical problems.

Mainly the authors feel that philosophy and philosophers have a great deal to teach on the subject of ethics and that, in existing courses, a vast amount of this information is simply being passed over, in an attempt, perhaps, to find something simple to say about lower-level issues. However, over the centuries, philosophers have found in ethics a complex subject matter worthy of serious investigation, and they have learned a great deal about it. Just what they have learned, or what they have to teach, is itself a matter of investigation. It is the subject matter of this book.

We believe that many instructors will recognize that a book of this kind is urgently needed. Many realize that we can no longer simply present ethical theories as if they were, all by themselves, an adequate means of solving moral problems. Yet, as philosophers, we believe that such theories are relevant. This text is therefore meant to fill the gap which now exists between theory and practice, by showing how theory and practice are related.

Other texts on applied ethics tend to omit analyses of both ethical reasoning and philosophical reasoning. The general practice is to offer a few abstract moral theories, or a small number of principles, and then assume that these theories or principles will be applied to a wide variety of moral problems. Following a discussion of theories or principles, the usual text presents a variety of articles on contemporary moral issues and then leaves the reader to apply the theories or principles—or to abandon them—as he or she sees fit. Little instruction is given on how to apply theories or principles, on how to choose from among them, or on whether the theories can be applied at all.

At this point in the development of applied ethics, this is not a very effective procedure. Those familiar with ethical theories understand that it is often difficult and sometimes impossible to apply theories directly to moral issues. They also understand that some of the most difficult questions of ethics have to do with evaluating theories. Our text meets these issues head on, by developing reasoning skills and strategies, by clarifying the place and function of principles and rules in reasoning, and by showing how principles and rules can be modified in the process of application.

The book is divided into four major sections. Part One, including Chapters I through IV, covers preliminary information regarding the nature of morality, the logic of moral reasoning, the levels of moral reasoning, and obstacles to moral reasoning. Part Two, consisting of Chapters V through VII, explains and critiques a number of moral theories, including Kantianism and utilitarianism, self-realization theory, natural law theory, contractarianism, formalism, pragmatism and existentialism. All these theories, and the logical structures explained in Part One, are used in Part Three to develop and apply a set of moral principles. Thus, in Part Three, there are chapters on developing and applying moral principles, on the need for subordinate rules and the critique of social institutions, and on judging individual acts. In Part Four, the system developed in Part Three is applied to cases taken from personal ethics, business ethics, and medical ethics.

The features of the book include, in Part One, an extensive treatment of questions *about* ethics: the nature of morality, the forms and levels of moral reasoning, and the very possibility of finding solutions to moral problems by rational means. Part Two includes a much more extensive treatment of moral theories than other applied ethics texts. The point of analyzing the theories is to learn something about moral reasoning on this level, about the kinds of reasons that may be offered in support of principles, and about how theories themselves can be criticized. Thus the chapters on theory present reasons for rejecting certain theoretical claims, but they also seek to retain insights which may be included in a more comprehensive theoretical view. Part Three then attempts to incorporate these insights into a system of principles and rules and shows how these can be applied to social practices and particular acts. Exercises are included throughout, to illustrate specific points in the text, but the last section, on case studies, provides practice in using the system as a whole.

A glossary is included at the end of the book to aid students in understanding technical terms, and there is a list of selected readings at the end of each chapter. There are short box quotations at various places in the text to give students examples of philosophical writings related to subjects being discussed, and to illustrate points being made. The instructor may wish to suggest that the students read the boxed quotations as they appear in the text, so they can reflect on this material as it relates to the topic at hand. As an alternative, the students may be asked to skip the boxed quotations to facilitate reading; the instructor may then call attention to quotations he or she wants to discuss in class.

Instructors can adapt the book to their specific needs. In a course dedicated to moral reasoning, the instructor may wish to assign all of the chapters in the order in which they appear, but some chapters may be assigned for reading only and others for discussion in class. The chapters on logic may even be omitted if students have had a logic course. In any case, it is doubtful that all of the material can be covered in less than a full semester, so persons who teach on the quarter system may need to be selective.

In a contemporary issues course, instructors will probably find Parts Three and Four most useful, for the material in these sections can be applied directly to issues discussed in class. Although, in an issues course, the chapters on theory may be assigned as background reading, instructors may wish to spend less time on them in class. However, the introductory chapters of the book should prove valuable in helping students develop skills in argumentation and an appreciation of the value of logic, while at the same time helping to ward off the kinds of premature skeptical objections that tend to disrupt discussions.

There is some redundancy in the presentation of a number of points made throughout the book. The authors believe that such repetition is important to learning, and to understanding how ideas carry over from one subject to the next. Also, because instructors may choose not to assign all of the chapters, or not assign them in the order presented, students may not have read any or all of the preceding material.

Of course, we do not expect every instructor, or every student, to agree with every point in the book. Indeed, we would be happy to receive suggestions for improvement. But we do hope that, by writing this book, we will be able to help readers gain a better understanding of the many factors involved in moral decision making. Given practice, this should lead to greater ability in resolving moral disputes.

We would like to thank the people who have assisted us in preparing the manuscript for publication: especially Cindy Bellinger, who typed and retyped the original drafts; Brenda Kohout, who helped put together the final versions; and Charlotte Pressler, who helped with the glossaries and bibliographies. We would like to thank our wives, Patricia Fox and Bonnie DeMarco, for lending their minds out to us in a discussion of the quality of our writings and our views. Finally, we would like to thank the editors of Holt, Rinehart and Winston for their support and assistance in bringing this book to press. None of these people are responsible for our errors. The responsibility for the ideas and writing of the book is equally shared by us.

Richard M. Fox
Joseph P. Demarco

CONTENTS

PART ONE

DEFINITION, FORMS, AND FALLACIES OF MORAL REASONING

THE NATURE OF MORALITY

It seems appropriate to begin by trying to define "moral reasoning." Almost everyone knows something about moral reasoning, for we engage in it whenever we argue about how we should act or whenever we give reasons to justify or criticize behavior.

For example, if a person condemns a social practice such as a home foreclosure or eviction of the poor on the ground that it causes suffering, that person not only judges the practice wrong but also gives a reason to support that judgment. The reason is offered to show why that kind of action is believed to be wrong or why that judgment is thought to be correct. Someone may disagree, arguing that the practice is fair, because foreclosure laws apply in the same way to everyone who defaults on mortgage payments or rent. The second person would then be giving a reason for holding a different opinion on the same subject.

Thus, moral reasoning involves offering reasons for or against moral beliefs in an attempt to show that those beliefs are either correct or mistaken. The purpose of this book is to examine such reasoning, to see whether the reasons offered in moral arguments are true or plausible, and to see whether the conclusions drawn are supported by those reasons. The practical aim of the book is to help readers become better moral reasoners by means of such analysis and by practice gained in working through moral arguments. The reader will learn how to avoid various obstacles and fallacies in moral reasoning, on the one hand, and to apply moral principles and rules to practical issues, on the other.

WHAT IS MORALITY?

In reasoning, we are frequently trying to answer questions. The detective reasons in order to answer the question "Who done it?" and a jury reasons in order to answer the question "Is the defendant guilty?" Scientists reason to answer the question "What is the best explanation of this phenomenon?" and parents often reason in an attempt to find out "How should we raise our children?"

In this sense, reasoning is a problem-solving activity, a way of trying to find answers, or a way of critiquing answers to see whether they are correct. Reasoning is not limited to a defense of positions we already hold or to an attack upon positions we oppose—although it may sometimes be used for these purposes. The primary intellectual and presumably moral purpose of reasoning is to discover truth and not to win arguments or defeat other people.

When we look at opposing positions, we will try to see whether there is adequate reason to agree with one or the other side. But we will also want to see whether there is a more reasonable view. In this respect, we shall be concerned not only with defending or criticizing positions we now hold—or where it is we now take our stand—but also with how we can move from where we are toward a resolution of the problems we face.

THE RESOLUTION OF OPPOSING VIEWS

Opposing views cannot always be reconciled. Sometimes one is right and the other is wrong, and that is all there is to it. However, many views are exaggerated because, among other things, they are based on limited information, and because it is easier to learn, remember, and apply simple ideas than it is more complicated ones. We all tend to express our ideas in the form of slogans and clichés. We also tend to become emotional and defensive when discussing ideas that are important to us, and we are resistant to criticism. We thus tend to exaggerate by claiming that something is *always* the case or that it *never* is, when in point of fact it sometimes is and sometimes is not.

For example, when a child is late for dinner, a brother or sister may say, "Oh, you're always late!" The accused child will probably reply by saying, "No, I'm not." The truth of the matter may be that the accused is sometimes late, even frequently late, but not always so. So, because of the exaggeration, the person making the accusation loses an otherwise valid point.

Likewise, one person may say that a particular kind of act is always wrong and another that it is always right, when a more reasonable view would be that it is sometimes wrong and sometimes right. Many pacifists, for instance, start off holding that persons should never fight under any circumstances but are then forced to modify their position when confronted with cases of extreme cruelty or injustice to themselves or others. They may be correct in thinking that it would be wrong to fight under normal conditions, but their position may be wrong in extreme cases.

We also know that parents frequently tell their children never to lie while, as children learn, they are sometimes expected to lie. Presumably lying is wrong, but it may not always be wrong, for there may be times when lies are justified. Realizing this, we may then be able to move from an extreme position to a middle ground and begin to question when it is wrong to lie and even why it is. Such questioning involves us in a closer examination of the reasons for and against alternative courses of action.

In attempting to answer the question "What is morality?" then, we will consider (1) various positions which can be taken on this subject, (2) objections to these positions, and (3) what appears to be a reasonable resolution of these views. The reader may not always agree with our analysis or our conclusions, but the factors we take into account should lead to a more sophisticated understanding of the nature of morality and the problems it raises.

Because our first attempts to define morality will not take into account all aspects of the subject, we will need to modify our position as we consider more information. In this way, our original highly abstract conceptions of the subject will also tend to become more detailed and concrete, approaching more and more closely the complexity of moral reasoning itself.

Notice that in qualifying our original position, we are not seeking a compromise in the usual sense of the term. We hope to retain what is true and to reject only what is false on the basis of the reasons offered.

THE PROBLEMATIC NATURE OF MORALITY

How is moral reasoning different from other kinds of reasoning? Indeed, what is morality? The question poses a problem because there seem to be several plausible answers, and yet there are reasons for rejecting each of the answers. The solution seems to lie in reconciling opposing views, accepting each insofar as it is true, and rejecting in each whatever seems false.

One's view of the nature of morality is likely to affect one's judgment of particular moral issues. It will at least determine what one considers to be a moral issue and what sorts of things one thinks people should be concerned about as human beings. If, for example, one had a very narrow view of morality, thinking that morality is concerned only with matters of human sexuality, one would thereby exclude from the domain of moral concern matters of war, say, or of economic injustice. In our definition, therefore, we will try to avoid an overly narrow view, one which leaves out important human concerns or prejudges important moral issues.

A narrow view of morality leaves out issues other people find significant. Given the wide variety of human concerns, ranging from issues of nuclear war to cheating on tests, a narrow view of morality prematurely closes human inquiry by declaring, in effect, that some human interests should not be taken seriously. But we cannot determine the significance of acts by simple declaration or by simply excluding them from our definition. Whatever else morality may be, it must include important human concerns, at least the most important concerns, and hence take priority over all other issues.

The position we develop, then, will express a broad conception of morality, for we will conclude that any human act can have moral significance if viewed from a moral point of view. *To view an act from a moral point of view, we shall maintain, is to consider its effect upon persons, according to moral principles*

5

and rules. However, in this chapter, we do not argue in favor of any particular set of principles or rules, or that any particular actions are right or wrong according to those rules. Mainly, we hope to show that other views of the nature of morality err by being overly narrow or by being vague, inconsistent, or incomplete.

MORALLY SIGNIFICANT VERSUS MORALLY RIGHT

We need to distinguish between the question "What is morality?" and the question "What is morally right?" or "What is morally wrong?" That is, we want to distinguish the kinds of questions that are morally relevant from the correct answers to those questions. The domain of morally relevant acts involves both morally good acts and morally bad acts.

The terms "moral" and "ethical" are somewhat ambiguous because they sometimes distinguish subjects of moral concern from subjects where morality is not an issue, and they sometimes distinguish morally good behavior from morally bad behavior. "That's moral" sometimes means "That's morally good" or "That's morally right," and "That's immoral" means wrong or bad. However, "That is a moral issue" may mean simply that the issue is a matter about which ethical deliberation is appropriate.

In defining morality, we mean to distinguish matters of moral concern from matters that are not of moral concern. We are not *now* interested in distinguishing morally right acts from morally wrong acts. Much of the remainder of this book, however, is concerned with determining the rightness or wrongness of acts. *That,* of course, is the main point of reasoning in ethics.

ETHICS AND MORALITY

As we have seen, one of the difficulties in trying to define the term "morality" is that words can have many different meanings. The words "ethics" and "morality," for instance, are sometimes used interchangeably to mean the same thing, but they are sometimes used differently. For example, the word "morality" is sometimes used to refer to the customs or practices of a person or group, whereas the word "ethics" is used to refer to the rules or principles explicitly held or stated by that person or group. We say that doctors and lawyers have codes of ethics because, presumably, the standards of these professions are explicitly stated; we may then say that some of the members of these groups are immoral because they do not live up to these standards.

Other distinctions can be made between "ethics" and "morality." However, to avoid the complication of constantly specifying different senses or meanings, we will simply adopt the convention of using these terms interchangeably.

A PRELIMINARY DEFINITION

Let us begin by proposing a simple preliminary definition of morality, the kind you are likely to find in any dictionary.

Morality is the evaluation of human conduct.

It seems that few people would disagree with the truth of this statement, for morality seems to be obviously concerned with conduct and with evaluating conduct as good or bad, right or wrong.

One might say that morality is concerned with the evaluation of *all* human action, including not only whether a person ought to lie or steal, say, but also whether one should go to college, break an engagement, or support a boycott. Parents tell their children not to waste food, and this certainly seems like moral advice, although it may be backed by a reason most children find incomprehensible—"because there are starving people in India!"

However, this definition appears too broad, for it seems to cover actions and evaluations of actions that are not moral evaluations. A teacher may say to a student that he or she has arrived at the wrong answer in arithmetic, or a coach may tell a football player that he has blocked his opponent in the wrong way, without anyone supposing that these are *moral* evaluations. The former, one might say, is a mathematical evaluation, and the latter seems to be technical, in the sense that it is concerned with correcting technique. There also appear to be aesthetic evaluations and even matters of etiquette, say, which are not matters of moral concern.

Indeed, one might argue that the definition is not only too broad but also too narrow, because there are matters of moral concern that are not actions. That is, morality seems to include the evaluation of the character of persons and the quality of institutions, and these are not actions. We may say of someone, for example, that "Jim is kind," or "Alice is fair," or "Kim is ambitious." In so doing we are calling attention to the virtues or vices of persons and not to the rightness or wrongness of acts. Further, we may also judge the quality of institutions, such as the government or a business corporation, as if these were individuals.

The original definition, therefore, seems false as it stands. The definition will not be accurate, it seems, unless moral acts are distinguished from nonmoral acts, and unless it also takes into account the character of persons. On the other hand, moral acts may not be different from other acts; the difference may lie only in the way acts are considered. That is, morality may represent a distinct point of view or a different basis of evaluation.

EXERCISES

1. Try to think up examples of opposing views stated in an "all or nothing" form. In which cases do you think the truth lies somewhere in between?

2. Do you think there is any kind of act that is always right or wrong? Note how acts described in moral terms, such as "murder" or "stealing," are different from acts given morally neutral descriptions, such as "killing" or "taking money."

MORALITY AS CUSTOM OR PRACTICE

In trying to identify morally significant acts, it may be helpful to see how people have tried to make these distinctions. From the standpoint of the social sciences, morality is looked upon as the customs, mores, or practices of a nation or group. Indeed, customs do seem to guide behavior more than anything else. People usually believe that their own customs or practices are morally right. Sometimes they do not even question them. Their customs allow them to "get by" and even "get along" with others, especially when those customs are shared. Customs also provide a basis for predicting the behavior of other people. Without customs, it would seem difficult to conduct even the most trivial affairs. Because customs tend to determine expectations, they also seem to create moral obligations.

CULTURAL RELATIVITY

Anthropologists have emphasized the fact that people of different cultures have different customs, and hence that what is considered appropriate at one place or time may not be considered appropriate at another. This is a purely factual claim which does not, by itself, have any philosophical implications. However, some philosophers have argued that all knowledge is culturally relative, and others have concluded that ethics is culturally relative, meaning that there are no universal moral standards or absolute moral truth.

One objection to cultural relativity in ethics, however, is that the approach of the social sciences is *descriptive* and not *prescriptive*. Social scientists can tell us what people *do* believe, or how people do in fact act, or even what the practices or rules of their culture happen to be, but they cannot tell us, based upon scientific findings alone, how people *ought* to act. To say that people do certain things is quite different from saying that they ought to do them. For example, drinking to the point of intoxication may be the practice in a given society, but such drinking may also be wrong.

GRAHAM SUMNER
(1840–1910)
On Ethical Relativity

The folkways are the "right" ways to satisfy all interests, because they are traditional, and exist in fact. They extend over the whole of life. There is a right way to catch game, to win a wife, to make one's self appear, to cure disease, to honor ghosts, to treat comrades or strangers, to behave when a child is born, on the warpath, in council, and so on in all cases which can arise. . . . The tradition is its own warrant. It is not held subject to verification by experience. The notion of right is in the folkways. It is not outside of them, of independent origin, and brought to them to test them. In the folkways, whatever is, is right. . . .

From: *Folkways*. W. G. Sumner. Boston: Ginn and Co., 1907.

PRESCRIPTION AND DESCRIPTION

This distinction between prescription and description can be observed by noting the discrepancy between what people believe they should do and their actual behavior. People do not always live up to their own beliefs or expectations. Indeed, one of the aims of moral reasoning is the reconciliation of beliefs and actions. As long as we act in ways that do not conform to our beliefs about how we ought to act, there is a practical contradiction or inconsistency in our lives. One can question whether one really believes what one says if one is not willing to act upon that belief. For example, representatives of the nuclear power industry argue that nuclear power plants are safe, yet they also lobby in congress for laws limiting their liability in case of nuclear disaster. Part of the job of moral reasoning is to evaluate the consistency of such beliefs and actions.

Even anthropologists face the problem of determining what they should accept as evidence, because they too will observe this discrepancy between what people do and what they think they ought to do. The problem is complicated by the fact that practices, customs, or mores are supposed to have normative or prescriptive force. As we have said, customs or habits serve to determine "what is expected," and "what is expected," or "the done thing," is often what people understand by moral obligation. If someone asks why you are planning to attend a wedding, you might say, "Because I have an obligation," meaning, "I am expected to attend," or, "That is the custom." So, while it does not follow directly from the fact that people do act a certain way that they ought to act that way, it seems to be true that the existence of a practice may be a relevant and even important consideration in determining how persons ought to act.

The Complexity of Customs

There are also many groups and cultures. For this reason, it is often difficult to know which practices to follow. It is not enough to say that one should follow the rules of one's group if one does not know which group has authority or jurisdiction, or if one has reason to question the authority of a group or the reasonableness of its rules. Ultimately, one wants to be able to ask of any group or culture whether its rules or practices are justified, morally speaking, and it seems that one could not do this simply by referring to those same rules or practices. This consideration alone has led many philosophers to the conclusion that there must be rules or principles which transcend particular groups or nations or that there must be principles which are universal in the sense of being intersubjective, international, and applicable to all.

Morality Is Not Simply Custom

The belief that morality is defined by customs seems much too limited. Even if all actions were subject to moral evaluation by cultural rules or practices, the culture and its norms would still be open to evaluation. Because we do question cultural practices and because so many of the really interesting moral problems are a result of conflicts within and among cultures, the limitation of morality to customs alone is highly questionable. There may be many cases in which the customs of society should be followed, but there are also many cases in which they should not. The difference between these two types of cases cannot be explained, it appears, unless there are norms which apply across cultures.

Whether there are universal rules or principles is one of the questions

9

considered in subsequent chapters. However, we cannot legitimately conclude that there are no such principles simply because rules and practices differ from one society to another. Even if all the rules and practices of societies happened to differ, it would not follow that there are no universal principles, for it is possible that different rules follow from the same principle under different conditions. For example, one moral principle might enjoin us to sustain life, but what it takes to sustain life may differ from place to place or time to time. On a warm, South Seas island, there may be little need to preserve food, but on a cold, rocky, north Atlantic island, it may be necessary to preserve food for long winters.

People can also make mistakes in applying principles or apply them without having correct factual information. People in a primitive culture may not understand how to care for their soil because they see no connection between what they do one year and what happens the next. Even in modern society we seem to be polluting our air and water and destroying our forests and arable land with little concern for future generations. So it seems highly doubtful that our practices are self-justifying or, in some cases, justifiable at all. It is logically possible for groups and cultures which have different rules to all be right, but it is also possible that, on at least some issues, some or all of them are wrong. The point is that no rules could be wrong unless there were criteria for evaluating rules.

INTERNATIONAL PRACTICES

But, of course, there are many rules and practices that the people of the world share. In fact, in recent years, the world has grown much smaller in the sense that global communication and transportation have greatly improved. World trade is enormously important, even to a large economy like that of the United States. Problems of population, environmental pollution, and warfare have become problems that all people face. If the theory of cultural relativity were true, these problems would seem to be insoluble, unless perchance an international community were formed. In fact, international problems are sometimes dealt with by international bodies such as the United Nations. Such organizations reveal that there are not only national but international rules. Global problems also suggest that there are common criteria by which all people can recognize what is or is not a moral concern.

WHICH CUSTOMS ARE MORAL?

If morality could be defined as the practices or customs of society, we would still need to determine which customs or practices are moral customs, for, presumably, there are many customs or practices that are not moral. Science, religion, law, art, and etiquette, for example, also seem to be governed by customs or practices, yet each of these seems different from morality.

How, then, are they different from morality, or how is morality different from them? As we shall see, these distinctions are difficult to draw because any action or activity may be a matter of moral concern, and hence subject to moral judgment or evaluation. And any consideration, including matters of law, art, or etiquette, may have a bearing upon moral judgments or evaluations. Indeed, morality cannot differ from other subjects by being wholly separate from them. *Any practical issue may become a moral issue when looked at from a moral point of view.*

The conclusion in this section is not that social customs are unimportant in life or that they should not be taken into account in moral reasoning. On the contrary, we maintain that customs occupy an important place in morality. However, customs alone are not sufficient to account for all aspects of morality. Although customs sometimes provide a decisive reason for or against an action, there are other occasions when cultural practices do not provide clear guidance or when they are simply wrong. Even when customs provide a correct answer, we cannot claim that an action is right or wrong merely because it is approved or disapproved by custom. If we accepted the definition of morality as custom or practice, we would then be declaring in effect that no other reasons count or that customs or practices are not subject to criticism, and it is this view, we have argued, that is false.

EXERCISES

1. Give examples of acts that may be viewed from both a moral and a nonmoral point of view. How, then, do these acts differ? Consider, for example, horror movies about mad scientists. If they are really working in the interests of science, why do we consider these scientists mad?

2. Society's rules have sometimes been compared with game rules. Are all actions within a game justified by the rules of the game? Can we criticize actions within a game on external grounds?

3. List customs or practices that are usually good but sometimes bad, morally speaking. Perhaps you can think of others that are almost always bad—or at least bad under present conditions.

   People are currently arguing about giving condoms to teens, and this is certainly a change in recent social practice. This change in practice is apparently due to changes in teen sexual behavior. What would you say to someone who said that extramarital sex is wrong: that therefore, teens should not be given condoms?

4. If something is against the law in the United States but not in another country, it is wrong here, legally speaking, and right there. In this sense, it seems, legal relativity is true. Give some examples of comparable moral relativity.

5. From your reading of the text, can you think of any reasons why it seems wrong to accept the relativist view of morality, even though moral rules do seem to change from place to place?

MORALITY AND LANGUAGE

Some philosophers have attempted to distinguish moral issues from non-moral issues by paying attention to the concepts, types of sentences, and arguments used in morality, and by trying to distinguish them from language used in other subjects. We have already noted that, in morality, we often use words like "good" and "bad" and "right" and "wrong." We also said that the sentences used in morality seem to be prescriptive rather than descriptive. When we use a word like "ought," some philosophers have claimed that we are directing or guiding behavior, that we are not simply reporting about it.

MORAL IMPERATIVES

Indeed, according to a whole tradition in philosophy, moral sentences are taken to be imperatives. Moral rules can take the form of imperatives such as "Do this" or "Don't do that." Of course, people in positions of authority sometimes give commands to other people, as parents do to children, or as military officers do to enlisted soldiers. Thus, to say that someone ought to do something may seem to be a weaker form of command, a way of suggesting rather than ordering someone to do something. To say that an act is good may be an even weaker way of doing the same thing.

THE EMOTIVIST VIEW

In keeping with this view of language, recent philosophers called emotivists have claimed that all moral utterances are imperatival or action-guiding and not declarative or fact-stating propositions. In its extreme form, emotivism, as advocated by A. J. Ayer, holds that moral utterances are "noncognitive," that is, neither true nor false. An imperatival sentence can be neither true or false, he says, for if someone shouts, "Shut the door" or "Stand up," it makes no sense to say that the statement is either true or false. Hence, if the statement "You ought to tell the truth" is an imperative, or a weaker, disguised imperative, it would seem that it cannot have cognitive meaning. That is, if this type of emotivism were correct, it would make no sense to claim that moral statements are either true or false.

A. J. AYER
(1910–1989)
An Emotivist View

Thus if I say to someone, "You acted wrongly in stealing that money," I am not stating anything more than if I had simply said, "You stole that money." In adding that this action is wrong I am not making any further statement about it. I am simply evincing my moral disapproval of it. It is as if I had said, "You stole that money," in a peculiar tone of horror, or written it with the addition of some special exclamation marks. The tone, or the exclamation marks, adds nothing to the literal meaning of the sentence. It merely serves to show that the expression of it is attended by certain feelings in the speaker.

From: *Language, Truth and Logic*. A. J. Ayer. London: Victor Gollancz Ltd., 1936; New York: Dover Publications, Inc., 1950.

The kinds of reasons that lie behind the emotivist's position are the basis most people seem to have for distinguishing values from facts. People think of values as expressions of feelings or emotions, as the emotivists did, and not as factual reports about the world. Thus, the emotivists have also concluded that, in moral disagreement, no one is really right or wrong, but is simply expressing different feelings or attitudes.

Can Morality Be Defined by Language?

One of the above objections against the idea that customs define morality can be applied to language as well; that is, we do not use the words "good" and "bad," for example, or the words "right" and "wrong," only in morality. We use these words in other subjects as well. We can speak of the right way or the wrong way to do arithmetic, or the right way or wrong way to play football. Indeed, the ideas "good" and "bad," "right" and "wrong," apply to all subjects. There are even good ways and bad ways to proceed in science. So it seems that these words cannot be used to pick out moral statements and distinguish them from statements of other kinds.

We might also note that sentences including words like "ought" or "right" are not imperatives, strictly speaking. To call them "disguised imperatives" only emphasizes this point. Statements containing "ought" seem more like sentences described grammatically as hortatives, that is, statements expressing desires or wishes. If I say, "I think you ought to tell the truth," this is grammatically similar to "I wish you would tell the truth." In fact, sentences containing the words "good" and "bad" or "right" and "wrong" usually are, grammatically speaking, declaratives. If I say, "Killing is wrong," I have expressed a sentence of exactly the same form as "This book is red." For this very reason, some philosophers have asserted, contrary to the position of the emotivists, that there are moral facts, or at least that moral sentences do not merely express emotions.

The Role of Criteria

Criteria in medicine, mechanics, and science are subjective, as are criteria in ethics, in being related to interests, desires, or feelings. Statements in these fields are either true or false, however, as they correctly or incorrectly maintain that an object or act satisfies or fails to satisfy a criterion. Thus, given that a criterion of some sort is understood, an objective judgment can be made. If in buying a car, one wants it to be fast, the car may rightly or wrongly be described as a good car according to that criterion. In this context, "good" means "fast," and this judgment can be verified or falsified by objective tests. Some such criteria may be relative to a given culture or group, but they also may be universal with respect to the kind of judgment being made. Even science makes judgments according to assumed criteria, and when it does, its judgments are sometimes called "findings."

A conclusion we can draw from this is that moral reasoning need not be entirely subjective, just as the notion of what is or is not a good car is not entirely subjective. Once we recognize this, we may begin to see how moral judgment and reasoning can be founded upon objective considerations, as is science itself, and that the role of reasoning in ethics is not wholly

---

ALAN GEWIRTH
(1912–   )
On Normative Criteria

The point, in other words, is that disagreements can be primarily cognitive and not emotive wherever, as in the sciences which the noncognitivist philosophers would recognize, there are already agreed-upon norms, and particularly norms as to the methods by which to solve problems and resolve controversies. To decide a cognitive issue in any field requires at least two things: first, knowledge of the relevant facts, and second, agreement on criteria or norms for decision. The reason why scientific questions can be decided solely by cognitive means is that, since we . . . agree on the norms or criteria of scientific method, the chief thing that remains is to determine the facts by the use of this method, and such determination is hence a purely cognitive process. But this is also true in respect of ethical and political issues. If men agree on ethical or political norms or criteria, then they can come to agreement by considering the facts in the light of these norms, and such consideration, too, is a purely cognitive process.

From: "Positive 'Ethics' and Normative 'Science.' " Alan Gewirth. *Philosophical Review*, 69, 1960: 311–330.

different from the role of reasoning in other fields. Indeed, in considering linguistic criteria, as in considering social customs, we discover that morality has features in common with other subjects. In all subjects, as in morality, we use evaluative terms and social or cultural criteria. In morality, as in other subjects, there are both subjective and objective considerations.

In moral reasoning, we are often concerned with issues that extend beyond our own feelings and interests to include the interests and feelings of others. This is especially evident when we reason about institutional practices. We may vote to support a tax on ourselves that helps others, even though, considering our own personal interests, we would rather not pay the tax. Persons may even support their country by fighting in a war and risking their lives.

Although we cannot ignore interests or sentiments, whether our own or another's, as data to be taken into consideration, we cannot settle moral disputes on that basis alone. Our personal preferences are themselves often subject to moral criticism or censure, for we can morally condemn a preference for drugs or alcohol, say, or a preference for racial injustice. We may disapprove of violent expressions of emotion or feeling, even when they favor a just cause, because they are excessive or out of place.

EXERCISES

1. The text suggests that it is common practice to distinguish facts from values. What reasons are there for making this distinction?

2. Are values limited to morality? Is science value-neutral? Can you think of any reasons for believing that even scientific claims, or claims in other fields, involve evaluative assumptions?

THE PRINCIPLES OF MORALITY

Another way of trying to define morality is by reference to the rules or principles of morality. A whole range of principles or rules, from "Don't lie" and "Don't steal" to "Do unto others as you would have them do unto you," are used to provide moral guidance. Because these are generally acknowledged to be *moral* rules as distinct from rules of other kinds, they may also be used to distinguish morality from other subjects.

We said that we are interested in finding out what distinguishes matters of moral concern from matters not of moral concern, and not in distinguishing morally right acts from morally wrong acts. So one might object that any attempt to define morality by reference to moral rules is bound to fail, because moral rules tell us which acts are morally right or morally wrong. Moral rules do not distinguish morally significant acts from acts that are not morally significant. However, if one could know literally *all* the moral rules and thus know all the kinds of acts that are morally right or wrong, then it would seem that one could also distinguish acts that are matters of moral concern from those that are not. After all, the morally right and wrong acts covered by the rules would encompass all the morally significant acts.

THE RANGE OF PRINCIPLES AND RULES

This approach contains at least two problems. One problem is that it is difficult to know for certain that any list of rules is complete, that no rules exist other than those on the list. The second problem is that there may be matters of moral concern which are not covered by rules. Defining morality by appealing to rules and principles appears to have an advantage over defining morality by reference to customs or language because we do seem to know that, in some cases at least, certain rules are moral rules and not rules of other kinds. The approach looks less appealing when we consider that there may be moral problems not covered by any rule at all.

There are, however, differences between principles and rules that are explored more fully in the chapters that follow. One difference is that principles are usually supposed to cover more ground than rules. Another is that principles, unlike rules, are often thought to apply universally without exception. Thus, a principle such as "Do unto others" is much broader than the rules "Don't lie" and "Don't steal," and the latter in fact may be derived from the former. The latter may also have exceptions, while the former does not. If so, the domain of morality may be defined by principles more adequately than by rules. But the same problems may ultimately arise, for we still need to know that we have taken all the principles into account and that there are no matters of moral concern not covered by the principles.

If we could show that there is only one principle of morality or only a limited set of principles, the first problem might be solved. Indeed, the second problem might be solved if we could show that there could be no moral issue not covered by a given principle or principles. As we shall see, these are matters of moral philosophy that we cannot fully explore in this chapter. Some theories hold that one and only one ultimate principle of morality exists, and others hold that there are several. Some hold that all moral issues can be resolved by rules or principles, and others hold that rules and principles are not always, and perhaps never, sufficient.

The Implications of Moral Beliefs

However difficult it may be to arrive at an exhaustive list of principles or rules, one way of more adequately understanding the scope of morality is by drawing out the implications of moral beliefs. Some people claim to have a very narrow conception of morality, but when we draw out the implications of their beliefs, we are apt to discover that even they may be willing to include much more than they originally supposed. Such a narrow view may be expressed by the principles or rules a person claims to accept. But people do not always believe what they claim to believe. That is, they may have false views, even about themselves. A person may claim to believe, for example, that morality is concerned only with matters covered by the Ten Commandments, but that person may then accuse others of being immoral for causing pain. Yet no commandment says we should not cause pain. Therefore, the person really has a broader view of morality than he or she originally claimed.

It seems possible to test the range of people's beliefs about morality by seeing (1) what their beliefs not only state but also imply, (2) what they in practice praise or condemn, or what kinds of acts they encourage or try to prevent, and (3) what reasons they offer to defend themselves or criticize others. These different elements of moral reasoning and judgment may or may not always agree because people are not always consistent in their beliefs and actions, but the process of trying to render them consistent should produce a more adequate moral view.

Suppose, for example, that someone claims to be an egoist, meaning that he or she believes that everyone always acts in self-interest, or that everyone always should. Then suppose that this same person also complains when others do not take his or her interests into account. Implicitly, this person is making moral claims that do not agree with the moral theory he or she professes. Such a person may not only complain about violations of his or her own interests but also demonstrate for the rights of others, condemning, say, racial discrimination. In such a case, it seems that he or she really believes that morality includes obligations to be benevolent or altruistic. Certainly, if such a person appeals to the rights of all, or to justice, then he or she has a conception of morality that goes beyond mere egoism.

Therefore, while persons may begin an investigation of morality with a very narrow conception of the subject, they may be led to see that, even on their own view, morality includes much more than they initially thought. As in the example above, they may be led to see that their initial philosophical theory about themselves, or about their own beliefs, is mistaken. They may need to change their philosophical theory to make it coincide with their own nonphilosophical beliefs. Part of moral reasoning involves the adjustment of our more general beliefs to more specific beliefs, or vice versa, as we try to construct for ourselves a more consistent, that is, a more rational view.

16

The Moral Point of View

Even if we could know all the rules or principles and know that these principles cover the whole domain of moral concern, we would still need to know the characteristics of moral rules or principles that make them moral. Otherwise, we would simply have a list of the *kinds* of things that are included in the class of morally significant acts; we would not have a *definition* of what it means to call them moral. Squares, rectangles, and triangles, for example, are *kinds* of closed, plane figures, but they are not explanations of what we mean by "closed, plane figure." As a definition of "closed, plane figure" one might say "a two-dimensional space enclosed by one or more lines." Thus, by "morally significant act" we would want to specify an act which has some characteristic that distinguishes it from all other kinds of acts. To say that a morally significant act is one covered by moral rules or principles seems to beg the question at issue, that is, to assume the point that requires demonstration.

It may also be the case, as previously suggested, that there is no one class of acts that are moral and another class of acts that are not moral. Whether or not acts are moral may depend on how we conceive of them or on our point of view. One may find that acts not usually viewed as moral acts can become matters of moral concern when additional factors are taken into account. Take, for example, a person piloting a boat on a lake. There seems to be nothing particularly moral or immoral about such an action. But then suppose that there are swimmers nearby who may be injured by the boat. Immediately, it seems, the matter becomes one of moral concern. Or, one may think that throwing boxes of tea into the ocean is a morally neutral act, but if one sees it as starting a revolution, it takes on moral significance.

A moral act is an act looked at from a certain point of view, so we need to specify what characterizes that point of view. From the above examples, and according to our hypothesis, moral questions arise when we consider the effects of actions upon persons or other sentient beings. We view acts nonmorally, therefore, when we abstract from that consideration, or when it simply does not arise.

EXERCISES

1. Explain how it is possible for people to have mistaken beliefs about themselves, or about their own beliefs. For example, how might a person who says, "I'm an egoist" be wrong, even in reporting about his or her own moral view?

2. What, then, do you think of the popular idea that each of us has privileged access to our own mind, or that we can know ourselves in a way that no one else can? Is it possible that others may know more about us than we know about ourselves?

THE AIMS OF MORALITY

Still another way of trying to distinguish morality from other subjects is by general purpose or goal. For example, we think of people involved in different fields as being dedicated to different goals or objectives. A doctor is supposed to be dedicated to saving lives, a lawyer to defending clients, a judge to administering justice, and a scientist to trying to discover knowledge. These characterizations may be oversimplified, but they serve to make the point that we often define things teleologically, that is, by reference to the ends or purposes of action.

Artifacts are regularly defined in this way; a chair is something to sit on, a bed something to sleep in, and so on. Roles or jobs are usually so defined; it is the job of a navigator to pilot a ship or of a soldier to fight wars. Persons engaged in these activities usually evaluate their behavior as being good or bad, right or wrong, according to their degree of success in realizing these goals. And things are said to be good or bad—such as good chairs, good beds, or good cars—insofar as they are useful for doing the things they were designed to do.

ARISTOTLE
(384–322 B.C.)
On Teleology

Every art and every inquiry, and similarly every action and pursuit, is thought to aim at some good; and for this reason the good has rightly been declared to be that at which all things aim. But a certain difference is found among ends; some are activities, others are products apart from the activities that produce them. Where there are ends apart from the actions, it is the nature of the products to be better than the activities. Now, as there are many actions, arts, and sciences, their ends also are many; the end of the medical art is health, that of shipbuilding a vessel, that of strategy victory, that of economics wealth.

From: Nichomachean Ethics. W. D. Ross, trans. *The Works of Aristotle*. Oxford: The Clarendon Press, 1925.

TECHNOLOGICAL REASONING

Such types of evaluation may be said to be technological as opposed to moral, however, because they are limited to specific types of activity, determining whether actions or things are efficient or inefficient for some limited purpose, but not determining how good or bad they may be, all things considered. A good soldier, for instance, might fight in a morally bad war. A good car might waste needed resources or be capable of going too fast for safe driving.

Technological reasoning assumes some purpose or end and tries to discover the best way to reach that end, given certain constraints. If we need a bridge that can support a certain amount of traffic, we appeal to the engineer to solve the problem, keeping in mind that limited funds (a constraint) are available. But building a bridge is a complex matter. It involves more than

18

simply building the bridge with the available funds. We also need to consider how the community is affected. Will the increased traffic change patterns of life? Will it cause increased pollution? Is it aesthetically satisfying? Once the range of questions is broadened, we begin to recognize issues that are not merely technological but also moral.

Moral Reasoning

No matter what the issue, it is possible to imagine circumstances which may lead to moral inquiry. *Moral reasoning typically arises when our frame of reference is broadened. For this reason, it may be characterized as looking at actions "all things considered."* Philosophers have contrasted the notion of something's being good or bad, right or wrong, "all things considered," or "on balance," with the idea of something's being good or bad, right or wrong, in a "prima facie" sense, or "at first look," or "all things being equal."

The idea is that some acts may be supposed to be right if there are no overriding objections to them, no conflicting duties or obligations that would rule them out. Thus, some philosophers have argued that what is morally right is what is right on balance, as opposed to what is right in a prima facie sense. They have argued that moral rightness or wrongness is determined by taking all factors into account. *According to this notion of morality, moral judgment is necessarily authoritative. It is superior to and hence takes precedence over all other types of judgment.*

W. D. ROSS
(1877–1971)
On Prima Facie Duties and Actual Duties

It is necessary to say something by way of clearing up the relation between *prima facie* duties and the actual or absolute duty to do one particular act in particular circumstances. If, as almost all moralists except Kant agreed, and as most plain men think, it is sometimes right to tell a lie or break a promise, it must be maintained that there is a difference between *prima facie* duty and actual or absolute duty. . . . We have to distinguish from the characteristic of being our duty that of tending to be our duty. . . . *Being* one's duty is a toti-resultant attribute, one which belongs to an act in virtue of its whole nature and of nothing else than this. . . .

From: *The Right and The Good.* W. D. Ross. Oxford: The Clarendon Press, 1930.

Moral Criteria

Our definition of morality still does not tell us which factors, among all the factors taken into consideration, will determine what is good or bad on balance. Theories of ethics specify such criteria. Hedonism, for example, maintains that the ultimate considerations are pleasure and pain. Other philosophies maintain that the final consideration is self-realization. Still others emphasize justice or fairness. Thus, one of the issues considered in this book is whether there is any one value which serves to determine the answers to all moral questions, or whether there are several ultimate values.

Nonetheless, *most theories of ethics seem to have in common the idea that moral goods must somehow be good for persons* (and perhaps other sentient beings). Immanual Kant, for example, said that persons are always ends of human action, never means only. Aristotle asked specifically, "What is good for man?" Utilitarians have focused on the pleasures and pains of persons, but they have also allowed that animals should be taken into account. There are controversial moral issues today about who or what should be considered a person or an appropriate object of moral concern, but there is little doubt that the welfare of persons, and perhaps other beings who share some important traits of persons, is at the center of morality.

We have said that morality is concerned with evaluating human action. It is concerned with evaluating human action by looking at things from a broad or inclusive point of view and not simply a limited perspective. It is not only concerned with actions by persons but also with actions *for* persons, or how persons (including ourselves) are affected by what we do. We shall also point out as we progress that morality involves actions *with* other persons as well, for the values of our actions often depend on the ways in which, and the extent to which, we can cooperate with others in attempting to reach our goals.

The Intersection of Morality and Other Fields

If the above analysis is correct, the subject matter of morality is not different from other fields such as law or science but is inclusive of them. Other fields or activities may be said to be nonmoral only to the extent that, in focusing on them, we abstract from moral considerations, do not raise moral questions, and suspend the moral point of view.

We suppose that science is morally justified because of its pursuit of knowledge and because we also suppose that the pursuit of knowledge is a morally justified thing to do. Once we make such an assumption, we may not think much about it. We may even think that science is morally neutral. But neither science nor any other human activity can be morally neutral, although it may be thought about without specifically raising moral considerations.

Just as we may suppose that moral activity is made up of other types of activity, we may also suppose that every other type of activity has an effect upon morality. That is, how we behave scientifically, legally, and so on, has an effect upon the kinds of people we are, morally speaking. Even further, the kinds of values we realize or discover in these various activities are values to be considered in moral evaluation, for we could not look at things "all things considered" if we left them out.

What usually happens is that we engage in activities with limited goals in mind, without raising moral questions, although at other times moral questions will arise. We are limited by the fact that we cannot focus our attention on everything at once. In playing a game, for example, we may be focusing our attention on winning without ever considering whether playing that game is morally right or wrong. At other times, however, we may question the morality of a game or an action within it. For these reasons, some activities are conducted with little thought of morality, while other things we do are directly influenced by moral considerations.

CONCLUSION

In this chapter we have attempted to give a definition of morality which is neither too broad nor too narrow. However, because most proposed definitions tend to be too narrow, we have emphasized the importance of taking many considerations into account. *Thus we have defined morality broadly, saying that it deals with all human acts, and dispositions to act, insofar as these affect persons and other sentient beings.* In day-to-day life, moral issues tend to arise in specific ways, of course, because of unusual occurrences, or because of objections raised by others. The point here is that any moral issue may arise out of a variety of concerns and that an overly narrow view of morality tends to block moral reasoning and inquiry by excluding relevant and important human interests. To have a moral point of view, therefore, is simply to be concerned about how people and other animals are affected by the things that people do, and hence to take their interests into account. In this sense, human beings are not only moral agents or subjects of moral action, but also moral patients, or subjects which are acted upon and affected by what they and others do.

EXERCISES

1. Identify the conceptions of morality that seem to be expressed in the following examples. Based on the material in this section, how might these conceptions be challenged?

    a. Professor Smith, a world famous economist, tells her students that the job of an economist is to describe economic reality. In response to a student who argues that inflation should be lowered because it hurts people on fixed incomes, Professor Smith replies that there is no objective basis for such normative claims.
    b. Jim holds that recreational use of drugs is morally acceptable because he is not hurting anyone.
    c. Mr. I. Globus is working in South America for a Fortune 500 company, GPI. To get deals closed, Mr. Globus has an expense account for "gratuities" used for bribes. When questioned about the morality of such bribes, Globus responds that this is the way business works in these countries, and if he doesn't comply, he can't do business.
    d. Coach Basey tells his athletes that they have a moral responsibility to give 100 percent effort on the field, during practice, and during the games.
    e. Dr. Libo explains that it is his moral responsibility to lie to patients provided it will help them regain their health, or in some cases, when the lie will help severely ill patients suffer less.
    f. Judge Heart is opposed to capital punishment because she believes that it is morally wrong to murder. When challenged by the claim that capital punishment may deter other murders, the Judge answers that the empirical evidence shows no such deterrence power. Even if it did, this would not be a matter of moral concern, she says, because we can only control our own actions according to the moral law.

21

g. Alice does her job well, pays her taxes, and doesn't hurt anyone. She thinks of herself as leading a fine moral life. Her friend Bob objects. He says she is morally nearsighted.

h. The director of news for Channel 5 decided to air the complete video tape of a councilman's suicide, even though the tape is quite graphic. He was overheard saying that censorship of the news is un-American.

i. Allen did nice work playing a violin concerto solo, but he did make several errors. Although the audience seemed to love the solo, Allen's teacher sharply reprimanded him for making the mistakes. The teacher claims it is his responsibility to bring such errors to the attention of his students in a way that will ensure it does not happen again. When told that his remarks seriously depressed Allen, the teacher replied that such is the price a violinist must pay.

2. Explore the following.
    a. Do you think that most people have a view on what constitutes a moral issue?
    b. How do you think people arrive at their moral opinions? Via religion? The home? Peer groups? The media? Does anyone ever think up answers for themselves? If so, how?

3. Identify at least two major social issues that are currently being discussed in the media in terms of their moral dimension. Do any of the views of morality examined in this chapter dominate the viewpoint of the media?

SUPPLEMENTARY READINGS

Aristotle. *Nichomachean Ethics*, Bk. 1 (many editions).

Baier, Kurt. *The Moral Point of View*. Ithaca, N.Y.: Cornell University Press, 1958.

Brandt, Richard B. *Ethical Theory*. Englewood Cliffs, N.J.: Prentice-Hall, Inc., 1959.

Broad, C. D. *Five Types of Ethical Theory*. London: Routledge & Kegan Paul Ltd., 1930.

Ewing, Alfred C., *Ethics*. New York: Macmillan, 1953.

Frankena, William K. *Ethics*. Englewood Cliffs, N.J.: Prentice-Hall, Inc., 1963.

Hospers, John. *Human Conduct*. New York: Harcourt Brace Jovanovich, Inc., 1972.

Ladd, John. *The Structure of a Moral Code*. Cambridge: Harvard University Press, 1957.

Nowell-Smith, Patrick. *Ethics*. Baltimore: Penguin Books, 1954.

Plato. *Republic*, Bk. 1 (many editions).

Ross, Stephen David. *Moral Decision*. San Francisco: Freeman, Cooper & Company, 1972.

Shirk, Evelyn. *The Ethical Dimension*. New York: Appleton-Century-Crofts, 1965.

Thiroux, Jacques P. *Ethics: Theory and Practice*, Third Edition. New York: Macmillan, 1986.

Wall, George B. *Introduction to Ethics*. Columbus, Oh.: Charles E. Merrill Publishing Co., 1974.

Warnock, G. J. *The Object of Morality*. London: Methuen, 1971.

REASONING IN ETHICS

REASONING IN GENERAL

People often reason to prove to someone else that their beliefs are true, and when they do, they offer statements as supporting evidence. However, they also reason to find out which beliefs are true, seeking to learn something new from existing evidence or searching for new evidence. Sometimes, in fact, they reason hypothetically to see what would be true *if* certain other beliefs were true, as they look ahead, for example, in moral deliberation to consider the consequences of acting one way or another.

Suppose Sue and Fran are hiking and it is dusk. Sue says to Fran, "Should we pitch camp and bed down for the night? I'm tired and it's getting late." Fran replies, "This place is rather low and wet. We can make it to higher ground before dark." Sue agrees, "I think you're right. We'd better move on."

In this case the two campers are considering reasons for choosing between alternatives, and they are trying to influence one another. However, even if one of them were alone, she could have reviewed the same alternatives in trying to make up her mind.

MORAL REASONING

Moral reasoning is a species of reasoning in general. It is subject to the general principles and rules of reasoning that apply to all subjects. However, because morality includes other subjects, it also includes special forms of reasoning appropriate to those subjects. Morality, as stated earlier, is all embracing. Its purpose is the guidance of the day-to-day conduct of individuals and the regulation of social institutions. Moral reasoning is, therefore, at

least as important as any other type of reasoning. Indeed, we have characterized moral concerns as ultimate human concerns; moral problems are the
problems that most concern us as human beings.

HERBERT FEIGL
(1902–   )
On the Use of Logic in Ethics

Firstly, the validity of deductive or inductive inference is presupposed
in ethical argument. Reasoning in matters of morality utilizes, as any reasoning
must, principles of deductive inference when special cases are subsumed
under general (in this case, moral) rules. And in any practical issue of moral
choice, inductive inference is indispensable for the determination of the most
likely consequences of actions.

From: "Validation and Vindication." Herbert Feigl. *Readings in Ethical Theory*, Sellars and Hospers,
eds. New York: Appleton-Century-Crofts, 1952.

Moral problems can also be highly personal problems because we care
so much about them. As a result, moral disputes can also be highly charged
with emotion. Emotionality can interfere with reasoning, but reasoning can
help prevent us from holding beliefs simply on emotional grounds. Some
such beliefs may turn out to be superstitions or taboos, and others may be
counterproductive or obsolete. And, even if true, they may be only partly
true. The purpose of reasoning in ethics is to reflect upon moral beliefs to
see whether they are true.

Because morality is such an important part of life, we use moral reasoning
to gain confidence that our moral views are correct. Our personal moral
codes serve to guide our personal behavior, and our interaction with others
is usually governed by socially accepted rules. When people conflict about
which code or which rules of a code should be accepted, or when a personal
code conflicts with the code of the group, arguments usually erupt. Such
arguing is not necessarily bad, as some people believe, for it can be a way
of trying to reach agreement through reasoning. Arguing may be bad if

---

KURT BAIER
(1917–   )
On Good Reasons in Ethics

It is true that many people will come to regard this or that as a reason
for doing something because of the conventions prevailing in the group, as
when we learn to refrain from belching after meals. But there are many
reasons for or against doing something which are not conventional in this
sense at all . . . it is possible to ask the question which many people never
ask, namely, whether *what is regarded* as a good reason for doing something
really is a good reason for doing it. The most obvious need for asking this
question arises when two people give the same fact, one as a reason for,
the other as a reason against, doing one and the same thing.

From: "Good Reasons." Kurt Baier. *Philosophical Studies*, IV, 1, 1953:1–15.

---

irrational or if the persons engaged in it are unreasonable, but it can also be good if it is used to make progress in discovering moral truth. Thus, the purpose of this book is to help distinguish, in moral reasoning, good arguments from bad.

ARGUMENTATION

Logicians speak of reasoning as argumentation. By "argumentation" they do not necessarily mean fighting or even heated disagreement. They mean simply the attempt to demonstrate that some beliefs are true on the basis of the truth of other beliefs. Beliefs, in turn, are referred to by logicians as propositions. A proposition is, by definition, any statement or sentence that is either true or false. "It is raining outside" is a proposition because it either is or is not raining (even though we might not know whether it is). But "Shut the door" is not a proposition because imperatives are not literally true or false.

In argumentation, some propositions function as conclusions, for they express beliefs someone is trying to prove, and other propositions function as premises because they are used to support the conclusion. The argument "All cheating is deception" and "All deception is wrong," so "All cheating is wrong" is composed of three propositions, two of which function as premises to the argument, and one of which is the conclusion.

In this case, the word "so" indicates the conclusion and hence enables us to identify the other two propositions as premises. Other expressions used to indicate conclusions are: "therefore," "thus," "it follows that," "hence," "in conclusion," and "as a consequence." Often, however, there will be no words indicating a conclusion, but there will be words indicating premises: for example, "since," "because," "as," "whereas," and so on.

After identifying premises and conclusions, logicians have adopted the convention of placing the premises first and the conclusion last. Thus, the above argument could be stated:

All cheating is deception.

All deception is wrong.

All cheating is wrong.

In ordinary discussions, the premises and conclusions can occur in any order, however, and the order in which they appear does not affect the validity or invalidity of the argument. For instance, one might say: "All cheating is wrong because all deception is wrong and cheating is deception."

For the sake of illustration, the above argument was an artificially simple example. Real arguments are usually more complex. For instance, in 1986, the United States Armed Forces bombed Libya, presumably because Libya was supporting worldwide terrorism. But the reasoning in support of the U.S. action was quite complex.

After the incident, President Reagan appeared on television to explain what happened and to give his reasons for this action. But it is somewhat difficult to reconstruct his argument, partly because he used various rhetorical devices and emotional appeals, and partly because some of the assumptions of his argument were unstated. Indeed, even the conclusion to the argument is subject to various interpretations. He may have been trying to show, for example, that the United States action was justified by international law, or that even if not justified by law, it could be justified by moral principles, or if neither of these, that it was nonetheless in the U.S. interest.

It is important to know the conclusion to know whether the reasons being offered really support that conclusion. If, for instance, the president meant that the action was justified by international law, then it would be important to know what international law requires. If he thought it was justified by moral principles, we should want to know the moral principles involved. If, however, the action was supposed to be in the U.S. interest, whether or not it was justified by law or morality, we would want to look at the evidence that is supposed to establish this point. In other words, the supporting evidence depends on the nature of the conclusion. If, however, the act were simply an attempt to "get even," so to speak, it may not have been justified in any of these senses.

Of course, the president may have been arguing in favor of all these conclusions, for he made no clear distinctions among them. He was most probably trying to win support for his action however he could from members of his own party and the general public, and he was also trying to answer his critics.

A good way to start in attempting to reconstruct such an argument is to *find the conclusion and try to state it clearly.* The way to do this is to ask, "What is this person trying to prove?" Once we find the conclusion, we can then look for reasons to show that it is true. This may seem simple enough, but the conclusion may not be clearly stated. Indeed, it may not be stated at all, but merely implied. In such a case, the person presenting the argument may trade on its ambiguity. If you say, "Well, you did not prove that we must invade—that we did not have any alternatives," he might reply, "I didn't say that we had no alternatives. I merely meant we were justified." If you object by saying, "This is not in accord with international law," he might reply, "I was not appealing to international law." So it is very important to know, or to try to find out, exactly what the conclusion is and the reasons being offered to defend it. Otherwise, the argument will keep shifting interminably from one point to another.

After identifying the conclusion, we can then pick out the evidence offered to support it, the premises of the argument. Typically these will be a list of facts of one kind or another. The president referred to terrorist actions and incidents in which people lost their lives. He claimed that the United States tried to prevent terrorism by employing other actions such as economic boycotts. He argued that the U.S. government had evidence of Libya's involvement. But these *factual claims alone will not establish a moral conclusion.* At some point in the argument, *a general rule or principle must be introduced that links these facts to the conclusion.* Again, such principles or rules are frequently not stated, so we may need to figure out from the conclusion and the facts the sort of rule that would be needed to connect them.

Suppose we know that Libya committed terrorist acts. Nothing follows from this unless we assume that, as a general rule, whenever anybody causes terrorist acts somebody ought to do something about it. Indeed, to support the U.S. action, we need to assume that, as a general rule, the U.S. ought to do something about it, at least when nobody else will. Thus the argument might look something like this:

Libya is causing terrorist acts.

Terrorist acts ought to be stopped. (Rule)

Therefore the U.S. ought to stop them (if nobody else will).

Furthermore, if terrorist acts cannot be stopped by any other means, then bombing or force should be used. (Rule)

Other means have failed.

Therefore bombing or force should be used.

EXERCISES

Identify the implicit or explicit moral conclusion and the implicit or explicit premises in the following arguments. Which premises are factual, and which involve moral claims?

1. Jim always found a "good" reason to tell another lie. But to his friends, his lies seemed to be getting out of hand. One of his friends, Alice, a philosophy major, tried to talk sense to Jim. She quoted the philosopher Sisella Bok: "More and more lies may come to be needed; the liar always has mending to do. And the strains on him become greater each time—many have noted that it takes an excellent memory to keep one's untruths in good repair and disentangled. The sheer energy the liar has to devote to shoring them up is energy the honest man can dispose of freely." (Sisella Bok. *Lying: Moral Choice in Public and Private Life*. New York: Vintage, 1979, pp. 26–27.)

2. Mrs. Jones refuses to have a blood transfusion. Her doctor tells her she must or else face probable death. She refuses because it is against her religious beliefs.

3. A parent in Montgomery County recently objected to a book being used in kindergarten class on the ground that it inaccurately portrayed animal behavior. In short, she claimed the book was guilty of anthropomorphism because it attributed human qualities to animals. A teacher committee agreed and withdrew the book because of its misleading scientific statements. A dissenter on the committee objected that this sort of decision would lead to banning "Peter Rabbit."

4. "We ought to prohibit smoking in all public places. Smoking represents a slow form of death, whether to the smoker or to those exposed to smoke." This view was expressed by Councilman Cleaner in a recent hearing.

5. People who commit murder give up their normal rights. To say that capital punishment is a form of murder is to forget this important observation.

DEDUCTIVE VALIDITY AND SOUNDNESS

The factual claims or rules, stated or assumed, may or may not be true. In the previous example, Libya may not in fact have been causing terrorist acts. Some evidence is needed here. The argument also assumes that if no other means of stopping terrorism works, we should bomb the terrorists. But bombing may not stop them either, and other means may be effective.

Thus, two separate issues will concern us. One issue is whether the premises support the conclusion, and the other is whether the premises are true. The first issue is the question of whether the argument is valid, and the second is whether, if valid, it is also sound. As we shall see, we can always make a bad argument valid by supplying false premises. On the other hand, the argument may be invalid although only true premises are used.

Some arguments are meant to conclusively establish the truth of conclusions. In these arguments, the conclusion is supposed to be true whenever the premises are true. This kind of reasoning is called deductive reasoning. In deductive reasoning, arguments are said to be valid if the conclusion follows necessarily from the premises; that is, if the premises are true, the conclusion must be true. This means that it would be inconsistent to claim that the premises are true and at the same time that the conclusion is false.

The argument "All cheating is deception and all deception is wrong, so all cheating is wrong" is valid because the conclusion follows necessarily from the premises. Consider the argument:

All lawyers are heroes.

All heroes are saints.

All lawyers are saints.

This argument is also valid because *if* the premises were true, the conclusion would be true—because the conclusion follows from the premises. But, apparently, the premises are false, and so is the conclusion. When at least one of the premises essential to an argument is false, the argument is unsound. *A sound argument has two properties: (1) It is valid, and (2) it has true premises.*

Normally, of course, we are interested in producing not only valid arguments but also sound arguments, for we want to show that a conclusion is true and not simply that it would be true if something else were true. However, as mentioned above, in moral reasoning we are often interested in what would happen if we did one thing or another or what would be true if certain premises were made true by our acts. In moral reasoning, we are not only interested in describing the world, or in the way the world is, but also in how the world could be or in how we might change it by our actions.

A legislator, for example, might reason as follows: "If we make drug purchases a crime and jail the offenders, our jails will be overcrowded. Citizens will probably not accept a tax to pay for additional jails. Therefore, we cannot make drug purchasing a crime." In such a case, the legislator would not be reasoning about something that has happened but about what would happen if a particular alternative were chosen or rejected.

SYLLOGISMS

Syllogisms are deductive arguments. A categorical syllogism is an argument which contains as its premises and conclusions *categorical propositions,* that is, propositions which make definite assertions of truth or fact *without qualification.* Categorical propositions are distinguished from hypothetical propositions, for example, which are conditional or "iffy" and claim that something is true *if* something else is true. Categorical propositions are also distinguished from disjunctive or alternative propositions, which claim that *either* one thing is true *or* another thing is true without saying which one. Thus, "The U.S. bombed Libya" is a categorical proposition, but "If we camp here, we'll get wet" is a hypothetical or conditional proposition, and "Either we increase taxes or limit the number of prisoners" is a disjunctive or alternative proposition.

UNIVERSAL PROPOSITIONS

The categorical propositions we have been considering are also *quantified,* for they are propositions about *classes* of things in which we were talking about *all* the members. We said, for example, that "All cheating is deception." But we might also have spoken of some members of a class by using the word "some," as in "Some lawyers are heroes."

ARISTOTLE
(384–322 B.C.)
On the Syllogism and Premises

A premise then is a sentence affirming or denying one thing of another. . . . By universal I mean the statement that something belongs to all or none of something else; by particular that it belongs to some or not to some or not to all . . . a syllogistic premise without qualification will be an affirmation or denial of something concerning something else. . . .

A syllogism is a discourse in which, certain things being stated, something other than what is stated follows of necessity from their being so.

From: *Prior Analytics,* Book I, 1, 24a and 24b. A. J. Jenkinson, trans. *The Basic Works of Aristotle.* Richard McKeon, ed. New York: Random House, 1941.

The words "all" and "some" are referred to as *quantifiers,* for they indicate the number of things in the subject-class we are talking about. The subject-class is the class that functions as the subject of a proposition, and it is distinguished from the *predicate* class, which functions as the predicate of a proposition. In the proposition, "All cheating is deception," the term "cheating" is the subject term, and the term "deception" is the predicate term.

Not all categorical propositions have quantifiers, however. Sometimes the quantifiers are merely implicit, as in "Loitering is not permitted," which may be taken to mean "No loitering is permitted." In saying that no loitering is permitted we are saying that all things in the subject class are excluded from all things in the predicate class. Therefore, even if we do not say so, we are speaking *universally* of things in both the subject class and the predicate class.

Also notice that predicate terms are usually not quantified. Thus, "All cheating is deception" indicates that we are talking about all acts of cheating but not about how many acts of deception. But, by implication, we may suppose that we are talking about only *some* acts of deception, for all acts of cheating are only some of the acts of deception. All the acts of cheating are not all the acts of deception because there are acts of deception that are not acts of cheating.

SINGULAR AND PARTICULAR PROPOSITIONS

In a valid argument, not all the premises need be universal. The premises to an argument may also be singular or particular. A singular proposition refers uniquely to one and only one individual act or thing, and a particular proposition refers to part of a class of persons, acts, or things. Thus, the proposition "This act is an act of cheating" is singular because it refers to one and only one act. The proposition "Some acts of cheating are wrong" is particular because it refers to part of the class of acts called "cheating." But because one thing is also a part of a class, singular propositions are sometimes also said to be particular. Thus, consider the following argument:

All cheating is deception.

This act is an act of cheating.

This act is an act of deception.

In this argument the first premise states a universal proposition, but the second premise is a statement about an individual act. The second premise places this act in the class of cheating, and because the first premise places all cheating in the class of deception, the conclusion can assert that this act is also in the class of deception. The universal premise gives us a license or warrant to say something about all acts of cheating and hence the act of cheating referred to in the second premise. The second premise tells us that the act is covered by the universal premise or rule.

Much of scientific reasoning, legal reasoning, and ethical reasoning is like this. General statements that make up scientific theory, the law, or moral codes are rules we can apply to individual cases. In physics, for example, we learn that copper conducts electricity. When we see an object that looks like it is made of copper, we may conclude that it conducts electricity. However, we sometimes need to test such judgments, for things that look like they are made of copper may be made of some other material and hence may actually be insulators. In more complex cases, as in applying an income tax law, for instance, it may be difficult to determine whether a particular expense is an exemption and hence whether it is covered by the rule. This may be because the rule itself is not clear. For these reasons, it is important to try to clarify the rules involved.

When we examine categorical syllogisms, we discover that no conclusion follows from two particular premises. For example, consider the following syllogism:

Some lies are harmful acts.

Some harmful acts are immoral.

Therefore some lies are immoral.

This syllogism is invalid. It might be that the harmful acts that are immoral are not the same harmful acts as those committed by a lie. The problem with such syllogisms is that there is no sure tie or link between the premises.

Another way of saying this is that *at least one premise must be universal.* A valid categorical syllogism always presupposes a universal truth. Therefore, in ethical arguments that have this form, as many do, we are entitled to expect more than a list of particular facts offered in support of a conclusion. We need to see a relationship between these facts and the conclusion, and this relationship must be expressed as a rule.

EXERCISES

From the contexts of the following arguments, try to determine whether the conclusion expressed is singular, particular, or universal.

1. Venetia is the leading expert on a form of recombinant DNA research relating to lung cancer. She seems close to a breakthrough but wants to retire because she has been working for thirty-five years and is now sixty-five years old. Her colleagues believe that without her input and special knowledge, the project will take at least three years longer than it will with her help. They try to pursuade her that she has a moral obligation to stay, for perhaps two more years, so that she can adequately train someone to replace her.

2. It is wrong to bury one's talents. So Mary, a Cat Stevens fan, argues that he should give up his commitment to a religion she doesn't understand and return to a singing career.

3. Because it is wrong to pay a baseball player less than others with similar skills, many argue that the Indians ought to pay Joe Carter at least $450,000 rather than the current $250,000 figure.

4. Competition is bad. It destroys human cooperation and sets up false goals. It isn't so important to be better than someone else. What is important is doing a job well. After all, a society needs good products

and services. The Japanese are more productive partly because they stress cooperation and tradition over competition.

5. Honesty is the best policy. When we treat a customer honestly, that customer is more likely to return.

6. Roger argued that some day in the future our society will look primitive. Given the pain, degradation, waste, and consequent poor health attendant on producing, slaughtering, and eating meat, some future generation will look upon us as immoral. Eating meat is, he argues, immoral and eventually will be widely recognized as such.

DISJUNCTIVE AND HYPOTHETICAL SYLLOGISMS

The rules of science or of ethics apply to entire classes of events or actions. However, reasoning is not always based explicitly on rules. Sometimes we know or suppose that at least one of two or more facts is true. Suppose that some camp counselors are planning a picnic for the Fourth of July. They might know that:

Either we have a picnic on the Fourth or the campers will be unhappy.

An "either/or" statement like this is called a disjunctive proposition by logicians. It is a complex proposition which says that at least one of two simpler propositions is true. We say "at least one" because, as in this example, it is possible that the campers will be unhappy even if there is a picnic. It is probably clear to the counselors that if they don't have a picnic, the campers will be unhappy. But, if one thinks about it, the campers might be unhappy for other reasons as well. Suppose then, for whatever reason, the counselors also know that they cannot have the picnic. Based on these considerations, we can then construct the following argument.

Either we have a picnic on the Fourth of July or the campers will be unhappy.

We cannot have a picnic on the Fourth.

Therefore, the campers will be unhappy.

This type of argument is called a disjunctive syllogism. An argument having a different form but the same content can be stated conditionally or hypothetically:

If we do not have a picnic on the Fourth, then the campers will be unhappy.

We cannot have a picnic on the Fourth.

Therefore, the campers will be unhappy.

This latter argument is a hypothetical syllogism because, unlike the former, it has a hypothetical proposition as its main premise.

THE HYPOTHETICAL SYLLOGISM

A hypothetical syllogism contains at least one hypothetical or conditional premise. The classification of hypothetical syllogisms contains both *pure* hypothetical syllogisms and *mixed* hypothetical syllogisms. Both contain hypothetical propositions of the form: If A, then B, where A is referred to as the *antecedent* of the proposition and B as the *consequent*. A pure hypothetical syllogism has the form:

If A, then B
If B, then C
If A, then C

This form of the pure hypothetical syllogism is the only valid form, and any argument that has this form is a valid argument. Thus the following argument is valid:

If it rains, the picnic will be cancelled.
If the picnic is cancelled, the campers will be unhappy.
If it rains, the campers will be unhappy.

A mixed hypothetical syllogism has a hypothetical proposition for one premise and a categorical proposition for the other. Such a syllogism is valid only when the categorical proposition either affirms the antecedent or denies the consequent, as in the following forms:

If A, then B	If A, then B
A	not B
B	**not A**

Thus the following arguments are valid.

If there is a picnic, the campers will be happy.
There will be a picnic.
The campers will be happy.
If there is a picnic, the campers will be happy.
The campers will not be happy.
There will not be a picnic.

Again, the premises may or may not be true, but if the premises are true and the argument is valid, then the conclusion must be true.

Reasoning in ethics is often hypothetical because we often want to know what will follow from an action. Undesirable consequences may indicate that a particular action is not morally permitted. For example:

If I lie, I create mistrust.
If I create mistrust, my family will be unhappy.
So if I lie, my family will be unhappy.

This is a pure hypothetical syllogism. Because an action that produces undesirable consequences is often thought to be immoral, one might add to the above argument:

It is wrong to make my family unhappy.

Therefore, I must not lie.

This argument is clearly moral because a moral rule has been introduced: that it is wrong to make one's family unhappy. By explicitly stating such rules we can place the argument under better critical control.

THE DISJUNCTIVE SYLLOGISM

There are two kinds of disjunctive or alternative propositions, the strong and the weak, or the exclusive and the inclusive. If one says that actions are either right or wrong, we understand that they cannot be both. So this is a strong, or exclusive, disjunction. But one might say something like, "An action is either permitted or obligatory," in which case it could be both. So this latter disjunction is weak, or inclusive. In logic, we need be concerned only with the weaker, or inclusive, sense of disjunction, partly because we do not want to assume more than we know, and partly because the stronger sense can always be stated in terms of the weaker by adding "but not both."

Disjunctive syllogisms are valid only when one or the other of the disjuncts or alternatives is denied. Suppose that either the campers will have a picnic or they will be unhappy. Then, if they do not have a picnic they will be unhappy, or if they are not unhappy they will have a picnic. But if we know they will have a picnic, we cannot infer that they will or will not be unhappy, or that if they will be unhappy they will or will not have a picnic.

Ethical arguments often include a disjunctive syllogism. For example, someone may argue: "Either we vote for the tax or the hospital serving the poor will close. A vote against the tax means the hospital will close. Therefore, we must not vote against the tax."

This is an incomplete argument because it leaves out some of the premises. But it does contain a subordinate argument in the form of a disjunctive syllogism. It presents two alternatives: (1) voting against the tax and (2) closing the hospital. The argument seems to assume that one alternative is immoral. The person offering the argument seems to believe that we have a moral responsibility to aid the poor by providing basic health care. Implicitly, the author of the argument is appealing to a broadly supported ethical rule, but the rule needs to be made explicit.

Sometimes a disjunctive argument explicitly contains an ethical position. Consider the following: "Buy an American car or you will be unpatriotic." "Support the ban on contraceptive advertising or support immoral sex practices." By being told that the alternative is immoral, there is an implicit appeal to a rule.

THE DILEMMA

The hypothetical and disjunctive propositions are combined in the dilemma. In ethics we are often faced with dilemmas, for we are faced with alternatives and must choose between them. Moral deliberation is a process of reasoning by which we try to determine which of two or more alternatives we should choose. We often make such determinations on the basis of the consequences of choosing one way or another, or on the basis of moral rules. For example, a smoker may reason:

If I continue smoking, I will reduce my lifespan.
If I stop smoking, I'll be nervous and discontented.
I must either continue or stop.
Therefore, I'll either reduce my lifespan or be discontented.

The smoker might then reason:

I'd rather die early than be nervous and discontented.
Therefore, I will not stop smoking.

On the other hand, considering moral obligations:

I'd be wrong to ruin my health, die early, and neglect my responsibilities to others.
Therefore, I'd better stop smoking.

Dilemmas are particularly troublesome in ethical reasoning because, no matter what we do, we may violate a rule. In the above example, we may have a genuine responsibility to avoid becoming nervous and discontented, and simultaneously, a responsibility to extend our lifespan. No matter what action is taken, a moral rule may be violated. In moral reasoning we frequently confront such apparent conflicts of duty. Thus, in the coming chapters, we examine a variety of theories and decision procedures designed to help us resolve such dilemmas.

EXERCISES

Identify the conclusion in each of the following arguments and distinguish it from the premises. If the premises are also conclusions, show how they are supported by other premises. Then identify the form or forms of reasoning used: for example, categorical syllogism, disjunctive syllogism, hypothetical syllogism, or dilemma.

1. Joe, getting older and a little bald, decides to receive hair transplant treatments at considerable expense. His daughter tells him that given the family's financial circumstances, spending money on these treatments means there will not be enough money in the budget to send her to art school, which means that she will not be able to pursue her chosen career. She believes her father should not spend money on such frivolous things because he has a responsibility to do all he can for her education.

2. Professor Jones believes one of his colleagues is not using appropriate material in the department's deductive logic course. He thinks it is his

responsibility to bring this to the attention of the department chairperson. On the other hand, he also believes that to preserve academic freedom, instructors should control their course material. He feels he should never violate the principle of academic freedom. He seeks to resolve this problem by conferring with a colleague in the chemistry department.

3. Supporting a big military budget means less money for domestic programs, and less money for domestic programs will entail a weakening of the national fabric. On the other hand, we must choose between a strong military and susceptibility to international coercion. One way or another, the country seems to be in for hard times.

4. Jane is concerned about her oldest son, who is completing high school. He has been acting strangely; she thinks he is taking drugs. Regardless, he has been getting into trouble with the law. She is considering sending him away from home so he will not be a poor model for her younger son and daughter. But she cannot bring herself to do this; she feels it would be wrong to turn away from her own child in a time of need.

5. Mr. Truck, a leading engineer for an automobile manufacturer, faces a choice. Either oppose a crucial design flaw or be responsible for the harm it will undoubtedly produce. Being of high moral character, he knows he must blow the whistle. (Based on a news story in *The Washington Star*, June 6, 1975.)

6. A local educational T.V. station aired a program about prison life containing a variety of "four letter words." Reverend Smith claims that this is immoral. Many people in the audience, he claims, are offended by such language, and many children may be unduly influenced by such vulgarity in the public media.

7. Bob decided not to go to work today and so called in sick. He actually wanted to go to the opening day of baseball at the city stadium. His friend, Jim, argues that this is not right; it will cost the company considerable money for Bob's entertainment. This cost will ultimately be paid by the consumer. Bob says that he is rarely sick, compared with others, and that he has saved the company considerable money over the years. They "owe" him this one; anyway, sick leave is a fringe benefit meant to be used.

8. The former United States Secretary of Education, William Bennett, argues that student loans should not be subsidized by the taxpayer but should be paid at fair market interest rate. After all, college graduates make an average income of $630,000 more than nongraduates. Why should all pay for individuals who gain so much?

ANALYZING ARGUMENTS

In the material that follows, we will be analyzing arguments used in ethics. In doing so, we will need to distinguish premises from conclusions, and we will try to determine when arguments are valid or sound. Some of these arguments will be quite simple, but others will be complex. Indeed, in examining what appear to be simple arguments, we will discover that many involve assumptions or missing premises which need to be stated clearly and fully before the argument can be tested.

We shall also be concerned with how arguments and judgments are connected with one another, not just as premises and conclusions, but as a consistent set of beliefs. That is, we will want to see whether the principles or rules we profess are consistent with one another, and also see whether our particular judgments and actions follow from professed principles or rules. We will also be concerned with whether our beliefs are consistent with the beliefs of other persons, and what we can do to reconcile differences.

FINDING THE RULE

In the argument about bombing Libya, we noted that the president appealed to a number of facts. He also seemed to be making inferences from these facts. Thus he seemed to argue:

Either we bomb Libya or terrorism will continue.

Terrorism must not continue.

We (should) bomb Libya.

However, the idea that terrorism is wrong and ought to be prevented is a general truth. It is a claim which applies not only to Libya but to any terrorism whatsoever. Because of this, some of the president's critics wanted to know why he did not advocate bombing Ireland, for instance, or Syria, if he also believed that terrorism was being sponsored by these countries. In other words, by making this premise explicit, the rule could be tested to see whether it was being applied consistently to all cases and, if not, why the cases of Ireland or Syria were supposed to be different.

Once the claim about terrorism is made explicit, the premise about bombing also becomes suspect. Is bombing the only way to stop terrorism? Is it even a way that is likely to succeed? The premise to the argument seems to assume not only that bombing can stop terrorism but also that it is the only way. These claims, whether or not true, are based on general beliefs about what will or will not deter the actions of other nations. It is doubtful that these claims are true, for there are other ways, such as negotiation, and there is good reason to believe that terrorism will continue, and perhaps even increase, after the bombing.

QUALIFYING THE RULE

It is difficult to develop a moral argument without implicitly or explicitly appealing to a rule or principle, and not simply rules about what will happen or is likely to happen if we act in certain ways, but also rules about what would be right or wrong to do under given conditions. Typically, when fully expressed, such rules will tell us that we are either (1) prohibited from performing a specified sort of act, (2) obligated to perform a specified sort of act, or (3) morally permitted or justified in performing a specified sort of act. A moral argument, then, will usually be recast in the form of stating such a rule, indicating that a particular case we are considering is covered by that rule, and hence that the instance under consideration is either wrong, obligatory, or permitted but not obligatory.

Logicians sometimes speak of modalities, and hence of modal propositions. Necessity, impossibility, and possibility, for example, are spoken of as modalities, for a proposition may not only be true, it may be necessarily true, or it may not only be false, but necessarily false. Thus, "Either it is raining or it is not raining" is not only a true proposition but a necessarily true proposition because it is true under any and all conditions. In ethics, we are interested in slightly different but related modalities: obligation, prohibition, and permission.

Not all moral claims have the same force. To say that something is morally obligatory, for instance, is quite different from saying merely that it is morally permitted.

Also note that in the category of permitted acts are acts of heroism and acts of charity. These are sometimes called supererogatory acts, or acts above and beyond the call of duty. Heroes and saints are said to perform such acts. But the logical point we need to understand is that duty is the least that is required of us and that we can often do more than our duty. For this same reason, the word "ought" is ambiguous. It is sometimes used to indicate duty, but it is often used to recommend something that is not a duty. "You ought to take out the garbage" might mean "It is your duty to take out the garbage," or it might mean "It would be a good thing if you took out the garbage" but that you are not obligated to do so.

Thus the rule "Don't lie" might be stated more explicitly as "All lies are morally prohibited." Assuming this rule, and assuming that a given act is an act of lying, we can then conclude that that act is morally prohibited.

The rule about lying, we have assumed, is universal. But upon reflection, we may discover that, as stated, the rule is too strong. That is, we may really believe that lying is not always wrong but only sometimes wrong. We may then amend the rule to read "Lies are sometimes prohibited," or "Some lies are prohibited." Now the argument reads:

Some lies are morally prohibited.

This act is a lie.

This act is morally prohibited.

But this argument is invalid. The previous argument with the unqualified universal premise was valid but, it seems, unsound because the rule appeared false. To make the premise true, we qualified the rule by reducing it from universal to particular. But, by doing this, we made the argument invalid.

The particular statement "Some lies are prohibited" suggests there are reasons why some lies are prohibited and others are not, but it does not tell us what the difference is. However, the rule itself may be modified to express this difference. One may discover that lies are usually considered to be wrong when they harm other people. One might then reformulate the rule to read: "All harmful lies are morally prohibited." This rule is now more specific than the original rule, for it denotes a less extensive class, and it takes into account considerations that the original rule ignored.

Applying a universal rule that is qualified in this way requires more careful attention to the facts of the case or to the interpretation of those facts. When the rule said "All lies are prohibited," all we had to know was that a particular act was an act of lying. In the case of the qualified rule "All harmful lies are prohibited" we would need to know both that the act was a lie and that it was harmful. We would, therefore, need more information. The rule tells us the kinds of facts to look for to determine whether the rule applies.

We do not mean to suggest that the rule about lying is adequate as we have stated it, even in its modified form. The conditions under which lies are considered to be either right or wrong are probably much more complicated than we have so far considered. However, as we shall see, it is important that rules not become too complicated or too highly qualified, for they may then become too difficult to use.

EXERCISES

State whether the conclusions involved in the following arguments involve obligations, permissions, or prohibitions.

1. Sally, a seventeen-year-old high school student is about to buy beer for a Friday party. Her mother reminds her that this is illegal so she shouldn't do it. She answers that such rules are not morally binding. After all, eighteen-year-olds can drink, and she is mature for her age. Some eighteen-year-olds abuse alcohol, and she doesn't. In her opinion, such laws are too arbitrary.

2. Professor Pincher is always telling logic instructors that a more expensive textbook must be evaluated in a more strenuous way than a cheaper text. It is unfair not to give students their dollar's worth.

3. After careful study, the state government determined that it would cost $250,000 to save lives by requiring sophisticated pollution control devices on all electrical generating plants within the state. The governor vetoed the bill calling for such controls and claimed that the price was too high.

4. The committee on Privacy in Social Life placed ads against requiring AIDS tests on all people admitted to hospitals. Such tests would be a violation of individual rights, they claim.

Working Through Arguments

So far we have emphasized the point that moral arguments typically involve universal rules. Rules tell us which kinds of actions are prohibited, obligatory, or permitted. We can then see whether an act is the kind of act covered by a rule and infer from the rule that the act is right or wrong.

In critiquing an argument, however, we must first identify the argument and find the conclusion before we can locate the rule from which the conclusion is supposed to follow. If the person presenting the argument thinks that an act of some kind is prohibited, we should then look for a rule which says that acts of that kind are prohibited. The conclusion tells us the kind of rule to look for as a premise, just as a rule tells us the kinds of facts to look for in drawing a conclusion.

If a rule is not stated but assumed, we may simply ask the person presenting the argument what rule he or she thinks justifies the conclusion. If we cannot obtain this information, we can then supply a rule ourselves by asking ourselves what sort of rule would be needed to make the argument valid. If we find such a rule, we can then ask ourselves whether or not the rule is true or even plausible, for, like the simple rule about lying mentioned above, it may be too simple and hence false. If it is false, then the argument is unsound even if valid. We may then wish to restate the argument by modifying the rule, stating it in a weaker, qualified form. In this form the rule may be true or plausible, but then the argument may be invalid. For example, the president's argument about bombing may be valid if we assume that the United States has an obligation to bomb every country that sponsors terrorism. However, it does not seem sensible to assume that the U.S. really has such an obligation. Many more factors are involved. Thus, once the assumption is modified, the argument may turn out to be invalid.

After we have located a rule, we still need to determine whether the facts of the case fit the rule. Is the act in question really an act of lying? We may need to clarify what we mean by lying. Do we mean by lying simply the saying of something which is not true, or do we mean saying an untruth with the intention to deceive? Or, what do we mean by terrorism? If we cannot answer this latter question, the argument may suffer from hopeless ambiguity. And, as in the case of rules, we also want to know whether the factual claims are true. Even if we know that certain acts were acts of terrorism, we may or may not know for certain that these acts were sponsored by Libya. Independent evidence involving another argument may be needed to support such a claim.

Many moral disagreements depend upon judgments of facts. Arguments about whether the United States should continue the war in Viet Nam, for example, back in the late sixties and early seventies, depended a great deal upon the supposed results of continuing the war or withdrawing. Probably nobody knew for certain what the results would be, so it was difficult to test which factual predictions would be true. We now know what the U.S. did and what did happen as a result, but even now we do not know for certain what would have happened if the U.S. had acted differently.

EXERCISES

Identify or state the rules implicitly or explicitly referred to in the exercises on p. 35.

TYPES OF REASONING

Thus far we have been talking mainly about deductive reasoning. In discussing the validity of syllogisms, we said that an argument is deductively valid if the conclusion is true whenever the premises are true. In deductive reasoning, the conclusion follows necessarily from the premises. In discussing moral rules, we considered moral rules as premises in deductive reasoning, for moral rules are needed to demonstrate that particular actions are right or wrong.

INDUCTIVE REASONING

Deductive reasoning is usually contrasted with inductive reasoning. Deductive arguments are intended to provide conclusive support for conclusions; if the premises are true and the reasoning is valid, then the conclusion is also true. In contrast, inductive arguments do not supply conclusive support for a conclusion; all the premises may be true and the reasoning may be appropriate, yet the conclusion may still be false. Deductive reasoning often proceeds from a consideration of whole classes of things to a consideration of species or members of those classes, on the principle that what is true of all is true of some. In this case, deductive reasoning proceeds from general lawlike statements or rules to instances of those laws or rules, and in keeping with this form of deduction, we have emphasized the importance of rules in moral reasoning.

A common form of induction, called inductive enumeration, proceeds from individual or particular cases to general principles or rules. If, for instance, we see that this duck is white, that duck is white, and all the ducks we have ever seen are white, we might conclude from this that all ducks are white. If so, we would be reasoning inductively from what we find to be true of members of a class to what we then believe is true of the entire class. Because such reasoning can never be conclusive, contemporary logicians usually do not speak of validity in induction but, rather, of probabilities.

However, although in a valid deductive argument a conclusion may follow necessarily from the premises, we still need to know whether the premises are true. If, as previously claimed, it is necessary to have a true universal premise to derive a true conclusion, how can we know that the universal premise is true? One answer is that we can know this only by inductive enumeration, by deriving the universal premise from our knowledge of particulars. But if this is so, then we can never know with certainty that any universal premise is true, and if we cannot know this, we can never know with certainty that any conclusion drawn from it is true!

TESTING HYPOTHESES

What we find, however, is that deduction and induction are complementary types of reasoning. Usually we do not simply draw general conclusions from an enumeration of individual or particular cases. What we do, instead, is (1) form hypotheses about what is true in all cases, based on our limited experiences, (2) deduce from these hypotheses what would be true in other cases if our hypotheses were true, and then (3) see whether our predictions turn out to be true in the other cases. Thus we use deduction in the process of trying to confirm our hypotheses. Confirmation in experience does not prove conclusively that our hypotheses are true, but in the absence of disconfirmation, the weight of the evidence is on our side. We gain more confidence in our general beliefs if they are consistent with our experience.

However, because our moral rules are not merely descriptive but also prescriptive, we cannot test them simply by appealing to our experiences. But we can test moral rules by seeing whether they can be derived from higher principles or rules or by seeing whether they are consistent with other rules we hold. They can also be tested by seeing whether they are consistent with our particular moral judgments. Particular moral judgments are analogous to judgments of particular facts in science. Judgments of particular facts in science can be used to test general hypotheses, but, as in ethics, general hypotheses can also be used to correct particular judgments. The consistency of our beliefs on all levels is the ultimate rational test, not simply the strength of any particular belief. However, the strength of a particular belief may give us reason to question other beliefs to see whether they are consistent with it.

Rules as Hypotheses

In moral reasoning, we can test our general rules by our particular judgments, as well as our particular judgments by our rules. For example, we may reason from the general rule "Killing is wrong" to the conclusion "Killing in an act of robbery is wrong," where killing in an act of robbery is seen as a particular kind of killing that falls under the general rule. If we believe that killing is wrong *in all cases* or that *all* acts of killing are wrong, then, to be consistent, we must also believe that killing in an act of robbery is wrong, that killing for revenge is wrong, and so on. If we believe that only *some* acts of killing are wrong, we cannot logically conclude that killing in an act of robbery is wrong unless we have some additional information that tells us when acts of killing are wrong and when they are not.

Part of the problem with ordinary reasoning is that we often do not make explicit the quantification of our propositions, so when we say "Killing is wrong," the statement is ambiguous with respect to meaning some or all. Thus we need to specify what we mean. But we also need to test whether that is what we really do mean. That is, we may think we believe that all acts of killing are wrong but, upon examination, discover that we also think some acts of killing are morally permitted. That is, we may think that the killing of animals is permitted, or that killing persons in war or in self-defense is permitted. If so, it turns out that we really do not believe that all acts of killing are wrong.

In testing our general beliefs by means of our particular beliefs, we are treating our general beliefs as hypotheses that must be consistent with our particular judgments, just as our particular judgments must be consistent with our general beliefs or hypotheses. Seeing that a general belief is not consistent with a particular judgment is a reason for changing either the

---

R. B. BRANDT
(1910–   )
On Consistency in Ethics

Inconsistency in an ethical statement or principle, or in a group of them, is a fatal defect. If someone uncovers an inconsistency in our ethical views, we feel he has made a mortal thrust; something must then be changed. A person's ethical conviction or convictions, then, must be consistent. Indeed, this is one point on which perhaps everyone in the history of ethical theory has agreed.

From: *Ethical Theory*. R. B. Brandt. Englewood Cliffs: Prentice-Hall, 1959.

---

general belief or the particular judgment, for a person cannot logically believe both. But *which* belief should be changed may depend on a number of factors, one of which is the strength of the belief.

Some people are not pacifists, for example, and hence do not think that killing is always wrong, because they believe strongly that self-defense is sometimes necessary. Of course, they may continue to believe that killing is *usually* wrong, but they now need to distinguish the usual case from the unusual case. It is precisely the making of such distinctions that advances our thinking on moral subjects from simple unqualified claims to more subtle discriminations.

DIALECTICAL REASONING

The testing of some of our general beliefs by seeing whether they are consistent with particular beliefs, or even with other general beliefs, is sometimes called dialectical reasoning, for it is similar to conducting dialogue or conversation, either with oneself or with others. Dialogue, like moral reasoning generally, usually starts with a question we want to answer or a problem we want to solve. It proceeds by suggesting answers and then testing those answers by appealing to other beliefs we hold. In this way we test new beliefs against what William James spoke of as a whole storehouse of beliefs, as well as against the beliefs of others and what we take to be the facts of the case.

WILLIAM JAMES
(1842–1910)
A Storehouse of Beliefs

The individual has a stock of old opinions already, but he meets a new experience that puts them to a strain. Somebody contradicts them; or in a reflective moment he discovers that they contradict each other; or he hears of facts with which they are incompatible; or desires arise in him which they cease to satisfy. The result is an inward trouble to which his mind till then had been a stranger, and from which he seeks to escape by modifying his previous mass of opinions. He saves as much of it as he can, for in this matter of belief we are all extreme conservatives.

From: *Pragmatism*. William James. Cleveland: Meridian Books, World Publishing Co., 1967. First published in 1907.

Such reasoning may also be said to be teleological because it is directed toward goals, ends, or purposes. In moral reasoning, we are trying to find out what is right or wrong, good or bad, and we are also trying to communicate with and, if possible, cooperate with others in an attempt to reach our goals. Thus reasoning, itself a kind of action, may be viewed as a means to these ends, and inconsistent or illogical reasoning as a means of frustrating ourselves in the pursuit of them.

Inconsistent or illogical reasoning is an obstacle to the realization of our goals because, to the extent that we are inconsistent, we really oppose ourselves. That is, an inconsistent person both believes and disbelieves the same thing or asserts and denies the same thing, continually cancelling or taking back what is said. When it comes to action, such beliefs may lead at one moment toward a goal and at another moment away from it, so that no progress is made. Sometimes we say that such people are their own worst enemies because they are constantly contradicting or opposing themselves. But, of course, none of us is always consistent. All of us are likely to profit from examining our beliefs to see whether they cohere.

EXERCISES

In the following examples, determine whether the argument involves deductive, inductive, or dialectical reasoning.

1. Although Tony only recently graduated from law school, he reached the conclusion that many laws are foolish or arbitrary. Some seem even worse; they seem to protect those in power over the victims, especially in regard to things he views as corporate "crimes," such as pollution and unhealthy working conditions. But in the few years he has been working as a criminal lawyer, he has noticed that breaking the law always seems to lead to a moral breakdown, to deception, lies, the dissolution of families, corruption, and so on. He has thus concluded that we all have a *moral* responsibility to obey even foolish or harmful laws.

2. Professor Turgenev, who helped develop explosive devices for nuclear weapons, always valued military strength. He had seen, firsthand, the horror of dictatorship. Now he knows that he has contributed to the development of weapons that increase destructive power by a factor of a billion! He also believes that the world cannot survive long with such power so readily available. Although he still hates dictatorship, he is advising all United States citizens to engage in active noncooperation with organizations that support the development and maintenance of such weapons. He now advocates nonpayment of taxes and refusal to participate in the scientific research relating to weapons.

3. Professor Smith has long advocated religious freedom but knows that such freedoms, even in the U.S.A., are limited in certain unusual cases. He wonders: Suppose we prohibit morally, legally, and absolutely, any government or legal interference with religion. But many religions seem to have practices which run counter to an effective social life. Some religions are intolerant of other religions. Some exercise unacceptable

dominance over their members. Some even seem to practice murder. He decides that even religions must stay within the bounds of acceptable legal practice.

4.   Bob Abdou understands the Marxist claim that moral rules are a way of dominating the working class. He thinks this makes sense. He says we cannot test moral principles by particular judgments because people are dominated by class interests and exploitation. He concludes that we should develop moral principles on the basis of Marx's philosophy. Individual judgments must then conform to these principles. Abdou claims that only in this way will exploitation cease; he believes that exploitation is the most serious problem in national and international life. His ethics instructor, Professor Freeman, claims that Abdou is being inconsistent.

5.   Reverend Giovanni is upset with naturalistic ethics. He insists that morality comes from God in the form of divine commands. It is our job to follow revelation and conform our views of morality to religious teaching.

6.   Dr. Jones, a noted transplant expert, almost daily faces the problem of determining who, on a long list of patients, should receive liver transplants when organs become available. Many of his colleagues feel that certain people should be given priority: younger people over older people, outstanding members of the community over social misfits, wealthy people over poor ones. Dr. Jones believes that such views go beyond his medical expertise; when such criteria are used, endless debates and problems arise. His colleagues disagree over the application of such standards. He has long ago concluded that such criteria are immorally introduced into his professional practice.

SUPPLEMENTARY READINGS

Baier, Kurt. "Good Reasons." *Philosophical Studies*, IV, 1953:1–15.

Copi, Irving. *Introduction to Logic*. 7h ed. Chs. I, II, V, and VI. New York: Macmillan and Co., 1986.

Kahane, Howard. *Logic and Contemporary Rhetoric: The Use of Reason in Everyday Life*. 3d ed. Belmont, Calif.: Wadsworth Publishing Company, 1980.

Rosen, Bernard. *Strategies of Ethics*. Boston: Houghton Mifflin Company, 1978.

Salmon, Wesley C. *Logic*. 3d ed. Englewood Cliffs, N.J.: Prentice-Hall, 1973.

Simco, Nancy and James, Gene. *Elementary Logic*. 2d ed. Belmont, Calif.: Wadsworth Publishing Company, 1983.

Stebbing, Susan. *Thinking to Some Purpose*. Harmondsworth, Middlesex, England: Penguin Books, 1939.

Toulmin, Stephen. *An Examination of the Place of Reason in Ethics*. New York: Cambridge University Press, 1951.

THE LEVELS OF MORAL REASONING

Moral reasoning consists of thinking about what we should do and why we should do it. It involves forming ideas to describe and evaluate actions. Morally significant actions are often referred to by words like "lying," "cheating," "promise keeping," and the like. We use such words to classify actions, and by accepting rules like "Don't lie" or "Don't cheat" or "You ought to keep your promises," we also accept the idea that we should or should not perform such acts.

Thus, moral reasoning often consists of judging a particular action by means of a general rule. An example of such reasoning is illustrated as follows:

All acts of cheating are morally wrong.

This act is an act of cheating.

This act is morally wrong.

THE IDEA OF LEVELS

The idea of levels of moral reasoning follows from the idea that there are more general or more specific ways of referring to actions. Above, we noted that we might refer to a particular act as "this act," an act of which we are immediately aware. We might also refer to some past or future act by describing it in some detail, such as "The lie Joe told me yesterday when he said that he was at home all day." Particular acts are acts that are performed at a particular time and place, and we usually refer to them by specifying the name of the person performing the act and the time and place it was performed, unless, of course, such information can be assumed. But we *understand* such acts and can reason about them only as *instances of kinds* of acts, such as, in this case, an act of lying. The concept of an act of lying is *general*, not particular, because it can be used to classify *many* particular acts.

The idea "morally wrong" is even more general than the idea "lying," for while acts of lying are examples of morally wrong acts, there are many other types of morally wrong acts which are not acts of lying. Because the idea "morally wrong acts" can cover many more kinds of acts, it is more general than "acts of lying." Conversely, the idea "acts of lying" is more specific than "morally wrong acts." Thus, if we were to arrange them in order of specificity or generality, placing the more specific classification lower than the more general classification, we could say that the concept "morally wrong act" is *higher* or more general than the concept "act of lying," or that the latter is *lower* or more specific.

When we reason about the rightness or wrongness of particular acts by reference to a rule, we are reasoning on a *lower level* than if we were reasoning about the acceptability of a rule in view of a higher or more general rule. If we questioned whether all acts of lying were morally wrong, we would be reasoning on a *higher level* than if we questioned whether this or that act was an act of lying.

In this chapter, we distinguish these levels of moral reasoning to illustrate how moral reasoning may focus on one or another level, and to illustrate how in reasoning we move from one level to the next.

EXERCISES

1. Which concept in each of the following sets is the most general?

    a. courage, virtue, temperance
    b. adultery, prostitution, sexual offense
    c. injustice, economic oppression, slavery
    d. killing, murder, harm

2. Knowing the level of terms makes ethical inquiry easier. For example, if we know that all harm is wrong, we also know that all killing is wrong. Make rules out of each of the terms in each set above, showing how these rules are more general or specific. For example, in 4, harm, killing, and murder is the proper order working from greater to lesser generality. Rules based on these terms, in order from more general to less general are:

    a. Do not cause harm.
    b. Do not kill.
    c. Do not murder.

3. In each of these lists of rules, do you think the more general or less general rules are more certain? Which do you think are likely to have more exceptions? Explain your reasons for your opinion.

IMPLICIT AND EXPLICIT RULES

The idea of levels of moral reasoning suggests a certain complexity to moral reasoning that may not be immediately evident to persons engaged in the process of moral deliberation and action. When we are busy acting, we sometimes seem to simply "see" or "feel" what is right or wrong, or at least think we do, without reasoning much at all. In fact, quite often, we simply act out of habit, without even thinking about what we are doing.

Each morning we may get out of bed and brush our teeth and tie our shoes without ever questioning whether we should or should not do these things, and sometimes without even being aware that we are doing them. And yet, when we do, we are following rules, at least implicitly. In fact, at some time or other, we had to learn rules like "Brush your teeth twice a day," and we had to consciously *acquire the habit* of following the rule, so that we would do it automatically and not have to think about it. But even after we have acquired such habits, we often question them when there is reason to think that a particular rule should not be followed at a given time, or when the rule itself may be called into question. Thus, there may be occasions when we are in a hurry and do not have time to brush our teeth, and there may even be occasions when we question whether brushing our teeth twice a day is the best practice to follow.

So people have developed many habits, customs, policies, or practices of which they are not always or even usually conscious, but of which they may become conscious when problems arise. They are usually forced to question a practice when they discover reasons for not following it, or when the practice itself is challenged. They may also have doubts about whether a particular action really is an instance of a general rule, and hence need to clarify the rule or gain a more accurate description of a particular act.

While moral reasoning may seem to be quite simple, because practically everybody does it practically all the time, it can become quite complex. Indeed, it is at least as complex as reasoning in science, say, or in law. But it is also as simple and easy as any reasoning is when we follow established procedures, for there is often no occasion to consciously analyze or criticize our actions. Once we know which roads to take to reach a destination—assuming we have also learned to drive a car—we may simply get in a car and go, without giving much thought to it. But learning to drive a car is quite another matter, and a decision about where to drive may involve questions about distances, alternate routes, road conditions, or even scenery. Likewise, people perform moral acts that are nearly as automatic as driving to work, but that also involve many considerations that, when raised to consciousness and made explicit, can become quite complex.

ACTIONS AS INSTANCES OF RULES

Parents normally try to make certain that someone else is caring for their small children when they are away. However, they may not think much about the morality of providing such care. Similarly, scientific researchers simply assume that statistical data are required for certain types of study without ever wondering whether they are following good scientific practice.

Yet, in either case, these persons are following implicit rules. In the parenting example, the rule might be formulated as follows:

Never leave small children unattended for long periods of time.

We may suppose that whenever parents leave their children, their actions can be judged by this rule: when, for example, they leave for work, or when they go to the movies, or when they go shopping. Each and every time the parents leave the children would be a particular instance covered by the rule. The rule itself, however, is universal, for it covers each and every case in which a parent leaves a child.

Like many rules, this rule is also somewhat imprecise; it does not tell us how small is "small" or how long is "long." These are matters of interpretation, although additional rules could be adopted to make these points clear. The law, for example, sometimes specifies the responsibilities of parents to children of different ages. But even then there may be doubts about the age or maturity of a child that raise questions about whether or how long it should be left alone.

Most moral reasoning goes on at the level of rules. The use of rules governing professional life is an example. For instance, college instructors follow rules in giving examinations and grading students. When a problem arises, as in examining handicapped students, professors usually do not question whether they should follow the rules; instead, they seek clarification of how the rule applies in this particular case. A professor may consult colleagues or the university's affirmative action office to determine how the rule should be applied to handicapped persons. In some cases, it may be appropriate to administer an oral exam instead of a written one, to compensate for the particular handicap.

This sort of moral reasoning may or may not move to a higher level, depending on whether it is necessary to cite a higher rule or principle to justify the rule, or to justify an exception. Suppose the rule about caring for children is generally thought to mean that a mother is obligated in a special way, above and beyond the obligation of a father. This rule may then be questioned as sexist. A higher-level rule prohibiting injustice may invalidate a lower-level rule requiring sexual discrimination. Rules that discriminate between the sexes have been accepted by many, in the past, without question. But as attitudes and moral awareness have changed, these rules have been questioned, not simply to gain clarity but to determine their justification.

EXERCISES

1. Many moral rules are implicit in judgments and behavior. Try to make explicit some of the rules frequently followed by college students or college teachers. Examine these rules to see how they might be defended by appeal to higher-level rules. Again, try to fully express the higher-level rules.

2. Can you think of any rules typically followed by students or instructors that are either vague or morally objectionable? Explain how these rules are vague or why they are objectionable.

JUSTIFYING RULES BY PRINCIPLES

We have noted how people normally follow rules without questioning their justification. Aside from questions of interpretation, there is in fact widespread agreement regarding the rule of parenting mentioned above. Most people would agree that the rule constitutes sound parental practice and that violating it risks harm to children. So, if the rule were questioned, it would seem easy to offer good reasons to show it makes sense. The rule is backed by the knowledge that very young children cannot care for themselves and that parents are primarily responsible for their safety. Indeed, the rule that parents should take care of their children is a more general rule that may be cited in justification for the more specific rule.

(Higher Rule) Parents should take care of their children.

(Lower Rule) Therefore, they should not leave them unattended.

In moral reasoning, therefore, as in science or in law, we sometimes justify particular actions by appealing to rules, and we sometimes justify lower-level, more specific rules by appealing to higher-level, more general rules. However, at some point, it seems, this process must stop. Practically speaking, we cannot go on appealing to higher and still higher rules forever. For reasoning to stop at some point, there must be some "first rule," so to speak, from which all the others are derived.

P. H. NOWELL-SMITH
(1914–   )
On Superior and Subordinate Rules

We may divide the rules actually found in any society into two classes, superior rules and subordinate rules. Subordinate rules are those that nobody would think of calling absolute or ultimate rules of morality or categorical imperatives. The only reason for adopting such rules is that they are connected to some superior rule in one of two ways. Either they are special cases which follow logically from the superior rule in the way that the obligation not to make a false income-tax form follows from the general obligation to tell the truth; or they are supposed to tend to promote some very general object, such as the happiness of others, that we think we ought to try to promote.

From: *Ethics*. P. H. Nowell-Smith. Baltimore: Penguin Books, 1954.

Such "first rules" are usually called *principles,* for the word "principle" is derived from the Latin word for "first." Sometimes principles are also said to be "last" or "ultimate," but confusion can be eliminated by realizing that the appropriateness of terms depends on the direction of reasoning.

That is, when we reason "upward" from particular judgments to rules and from rules to principles, the principles are last or ultimate, but when we reason "downward" from principles to rules to particular judgments, the principles are first.

When we come to principles, therefore, we come to our most general moral beliefs, the moral beliefs from which, presumably, all our other, lower-level moral beliefs are derived. Such principles are often thought to be *absolutely universal*, or true without exception, whereas the rules derived from them are thought to be *generally true*, or true in most cases, but not always true. However, there may be no absolutely universal principles. That is a matter for philosophic and moral investigation.

The point is that first principles will be rules that justify other rules or particular judgments but that themselves are not justified by any higher rules or principles. "Do unto others as you would have them do unto you" seems to be an example of such a principle. Other rules may be derived from it, but there may be no rule or principle from which it can be derived.

JOHN DEWEY
(1859–1952)
On Moral Principles

No fundamental difference exists between systematic moral theory . . . and the reflection an individual engages in when he attempts to find general principles which shall direct and justify his conduct. Moral theory begins, in germ, when any one asks, "Why should I act thus and not otherwise? Why is this right and that wrong? What right has any one to frown upon this way of acting and impose that other way?" Children make at least a start upon the road of theory when they assert that the injunctions of elders are arbitrary, being simply a matter of superior position. Any adult enters the road when, in the presence of moral perplexity, of doubt as to what is right or best to do, he attempts to find his way out through reflection which will lead him to some principle he regards as dependable.

From: *Ethics*. John Dewey and James H. Tufts, rev. ed. New York: Holt, Rinehart and Winston, Inc., 1932.

THEORETICAL ETHICS

Moral reasoning regularly involves justifying particular judgments according to rules, or even justifying more specific rules by reference to more general ones. People sometimes also cite principles, but they usually make no clear distinction between rules and principles, and they rarely attempt to justify their principles. Indeed, many philosophers have argued that there is no way of justifying principles, because principles cannot be derived from any higher or more general moral beliefs. However, in constructing moral theories, philosophers have tried to discover the first principles of moral reasoning, and they have tried to show why they are first. In doing so, they have constructed what are called substantive, or normative, ethical theories, and we will take a closer look at such theories later.

However, we wish to point out here that it is possible to justify first principles, even if first principles, by definition, cannot be derived from higher-level principles. They may be justified, for example, by showing they are consistent with lower-level moral beliefs, just as lower level moral beliefs may be tested by seeing whether they are consistent with first principles. But, for the moment, we merely need to see that reasoning about principles is on a higher level, and it is usually on this level that people begin to express their theoretical beliefs.

NORMATIVE ETHICS AND METAETHICS

In a sense, the level of normative or substantive ethics, the level at which first principles are clarified and justified, is the highest level of moral reasoning. However, it is also possible to question what is going on in moral reasoning generally, as we are in this book, wondering, for example, whether particular judgments can be justified by rules, or rules by principles—or even whether there are first principles. This level is called metaethics. Metaethics is an investigation of the nature of moral reasoning and the meanings of moral terms. One way to distinguish metaethics from substantive or normative ethics is to say that, in normative or substantive ethics, we *use* ethical language and moral reasoning to make moral judgments. In metaethics, however, we *talk about* moral language and moral reasoning in an attempt to understand it.

G. E. MOORE
(1873–1958)
On Substantive Ethics and Metaethics

It is very easy to point out some among our every-day judgments, with the truth of which Ethics is undoubtedly concerned. Whenever we say, 'So and so is a good man,' or 'That fellow is a villain;' whenever we ask, 'What ought I to do?' or 'Is it wrong for me to do like this?' . . . it is undoubtedly that business of Ethics to discuss such questions and . . . to argue what is the true answer. . . .

So much of this is not disputed; but it falls very far short of defining the province of Ethics. That province may indeed be defined as the whole truth about that which is at the same time common to all such judgments and peculiar to them . . . And this is a question to which very different answers have been given by ethical philosophers of acknowledged reputation, and none of them, perhaps, completely satisfactory.

From: *Principia Ethica*. G. E. Moore. London: Cambridge University Press, 1903.

FOUR LEVELS OF JUDGMENT

We have identified four levels of moral judgment. The lowest level is the level of particular judgment, where we make a claim about the rightness or wrongness of a particular act. The second level is the level of moral rules. Moral rules are judgments about the rightness or wrongness of specific kinds or classes of actions. Thus, in moral reasoning, we often appeal to rules to justify particular judgments by placing a particular action within a general class of actions. By appealing to rules, we try to show that particular acts are right or wrong because they have features in common with other particular acts which are also thought to be right or wrong. Lower-level rules may also be justified by appealing to higher-level rules, but because there may be any number of intermediate rules, it is convenient to think of all appeals to rules as being on one level.

The third level of moral reasoning is the level of principles. Principles, we have said, are more general and more abstract than rules, and they are often regarded as being universal, as being applicable to all cases without exception. Mainly, however, moral principles express our highest or most general moral beliefs. We justify rules and particular judgments by reference to them, but we do not justify our principles by reference to higher principles. Ethical theories usually consist of a statement and explanation of such principles and an attempt to show why they are binding upon moral thinking or behavior.

Finally, at the fourth level, we may speculate about the nature of moral reasoning: about whether moral reasoning is possible and about how it works. This is metaethics. In metaethics, philosophers take a position with respect to how we reason in ethics and whether such reasoning can determine whether moral actions are right or wrong. The position of this text is that moral reasoning can determine what is right or wrong, and indeed that there is no other way of making such determination.

THE IMPORTANCE LEVELS

As mentioned above, we usually have no practical reason to question our behavior or even that of others, especially if no one opposes us, or if we do not see any viable alternatives to our action or obstacles in our path. For example, few people would seriously question whether, under ordinary circumstances, parents should care for their children. There may be times when the need for such care is questioned, but these are probably exceptional cases. However, some policies or rules may generate considerable disagreement, or difficulties may arise which cause us to question them. Economic practices, for example, may remain stable for decades, until an economic crisis causes people to doubt their old beliefs.

The belief that the United States government should continue to support shuttle flights was widely accepted until a tragedy occurred. The flights became routine and were thought to be safe and efficient. But after the tragedy, questions of safety, cost, and quality control were given serious consideration. A general practice previously thought to be justified was called into question, and the government could not continue this practice without addressing the faults uncovered in the investigation. The practice of launching shuttles was thought to be justified by the rule that flights should be safe and efficient, and this assumption was found to be false.

Although we could not live in a society unless we agreed upon many types of behavior, we also live in a world in which there is much disagreement about the right thing to do. Some disagreements, in fact, receive widespread public attention and become known as controversial moral or social issues. On such issues, people try to justify their beliefs about particular cases by appealing to general rules, and when these beliefs are questioned they often appeal to more general rules. In so doing, they may be letting other people know where they stand on a given issue, but they usually also want to convince others, because they believe they are right and because they want others to act according to their beliefs. To be convincing, they need to find some common ground on which they can discuss and perhaps resolve their differences. If they disagree about particular cases, they can move to rules, and if they disagree about rules, they can move to principles.

In this process, then, they can (1) make clear to one another their moral beliefs, (2) explain why they hold these beliefs, and (3) try to settle differences of opinion by finding grounds they share. The resolution of moral controversies is not always this simple or straightforward, but the analysis of the levels of moral reasoning provides a model for examining more closely the process of justification.

EXERCISES

In each of the following examples, identify the level(s) of the statements involved (that is, particular judgment, rule, or principle). For each statement below the level of principle, cite a higher-level belief that would support the lower-level belief. In each case, do you think the rule cited is controversial?

1. All vivisection ought to be abolished. It violates the sacredness of life and is devoid of compassion for sentient creatures.

2. Bill, a student, believes that he ought to support his disabled father by working part-time, even though he has two older brothers and an older sister who are working full-time.

3. Dr. Harris decided to lie to his patient, Professor Genovese, by telling him that his tests were negative and that he was well on the path to recovery. Dr. Harris told Mrs. Genovese that her husband had, at most, six months to live.

4. Firefighter Glowery risked her life in an unsuccessful attempt to save a child from a burning building. An observer noted that she acted above and beyond the call of duty. She responded that she was simply doing her job.

5. Howard gets drunk every night after a full day of school and four hours of part-time work. He claims he is not hurting anybody.

6. Sarah joined SADD. She knew how sad it would make her if one of her classmates died in an auto crash after drinking. She felt very bad for the students and families involved when four teenagers in a neighboring town died when their car hit a tree.

7. A major American company admitted to contributing 20 million dollars in gifts to foreign public figures. In its defense a company official claimed that without making the payoffs it could not compete. "A company cannot be concerned about the 'morality' of such payoffs. After all, if a profit is not made, the company will surely go out of business."

A Sample Case: The Abortion Issue

We may be able to see more clearly how we move from one level to another by looking at a highly controversial moral issue. Take the question of abortion. On this issue we find that people often do try to explain their positions, and they also try to convince others by appealing to rules. When these rules are questioned, they often appeal to still more general rules until they arrive at principles. At this highest level, they may still disagree, but they may also find more agreement than they had originally thought. By making their rules and principles explicit, they may be able to find a basis upon which they can eventually reach agreement.

THE U.S. SUPREME COURT
Roe *v* Wade

We forthwith acknowledge our awareness of the sensitive and emotional nature of the abortion controversy, of the vigorous opposing views, even among physicians, and of the deep and seemingly absolute convictions that the subject inspires. One's philosophy, one's experiences, one's exposure to the raw edges of human existence, one's religious training, one's attitudes toward life and family and their values, and the moral standards one establishes and seeks to observe, are all likely to influence and to color one's thinking and conclusions about abortion.

From Roe *v* Wade, 410, U.S. 113.

The Particular Judgments

Suppose there are two people, one contemplating and defending abortion and the other objecting to it. The example would work equally well if one person were debating with herself. Suppose Mary says to her friend, Jane, who is pregnant, that it would be wrong for Jane to have an abortion. Mary states her belief by expressing the particular moral judgment:

"It would be wrong for you [Jane] to have an abortion."

Suppose that Jane thinks she should have an abortion, or at least that, in her case, she thinks an abortion would be morally justified. Thus her belief could be expressed by the particular moral judgment:

"It would be right for me [Jane] to have an abortion."

CITING A RULE

Mary's particular judgment about Jane and Jane's particular judgment about herself are formally contradictory. One of them must be right and the other wrong. Practically speaking, since Jane cannot both have an abortion and not have an abortion, she must choose one or the other of these courses of action. Her action must therefore conform either to Mary's judgment or her own. So suppose that Jane is truly concerned about doing the right thing and wants to discover, by examining Mary's reasons, whether Mary's judgment is correct. Jane asks Mary why she thinks it would be wrong to have an abortion, and Mary replies:

"Well, because abortion is wrong."

When Mary says, "Because abortion is wrong," she is offering a moral rule as a reason to justify her particular judgment that Jane's having an abortion would be wrong. Mary's argument may then be restated as follows:

Abortion is wrong. (Rule)
Therefore, Jane's having an abortion would be wrong. (Particular judgment)

Notice that the rule "Abortion is wrong" is indefinite because it lacks a quantifier. It does not say whether *some* abortions are wrong or *all* abortions are wrong. But the inference would be deductively valid only if the premise "Abortion is wrong" were interpreted as being *universal*, that is to say, as meaning that abortion is *always* wrong, for *all* persons, at *all* times, and under *all* circumstances, and not merely generally or usually so, referring only to some, most, or nearly all abortions. So interpreted, Mary's claim amounts to a denial that any of Jane's personal circumstances are weighty enough to overcome the seriousness of an abortion. Mary's appeal to this rule is then very powerful, for it is meant to rule out any argument in favor of abortion.

So, let us interpret Mary's meaning to be that abortion is always wrong, no matter what, to give her the benefit of a valid argument. The argument would be valid because what is true of all members of a class is true of any particular member. If the statement "Abortion is wrong" did not apply to all cases, then it might not apply to Jane's. Thus, if Jane wishes to attack Mary's argument, she must attack the truth of the rule "Abortion is (always) wrong" by trying to show that it is only sometimes wrong or perhaps never wrong.

CITING A HIGHER RULE

Suppose that Jane then questions Mary's rule. She may be surprised at Mary's claim, she may not fully understand it, or she may want more information to see whether she can attack Mary's grounds for her belief. Jane asks Mary why she thinks abortion is wrong, and Mary answers:

"Well, abortion is wrong, obviously, because killing is wrong."

In making this response, Mary is not simply trying to justify her particular judgment by appealing to the rule "Abortion is wrong"; she is now trying to justify the rule "Abortion is wrong" by appealing to another, more general rule: "Killing is wrong." "Killing is wrong" is a more general rule because it covers not only abortion, which Mary obviously thinks is an act of killing, but other kinds of killing as well.

We should note that this rule can also be interpreted as being absolutely universal or merely typically true, but, to preserve deductive validity, assume that Mary intends it to apply to everyone at all times, in all places, under all circumstances. That may seem a bit extreme, and it may not be a realistic account of how people would defend their opposition to abortion, but this interpretation is adopted to illustrate the levels of moral reasoning.

Mary's argument is now more complex. Her conclusion, "It is morally wrong for Jane to have an abortion," is now supported by the rule "Abortion is wrong" and by a more general rule "Killing is wrong." The conclusion follows from these premises if one assumes that they are universal and if one assumes, as Mary apparently does, that abortion is killing. Mary's argument may then be stated as follows:

Killing is wrong. (Higher-level rule)

Abortion is an act of killing. (Instance of rule)

Therefore, abortion is wrong. (Lower-level rule)

Abortion is wrong. (Lower-level rule)

Therefore, it would be wrong for Jane to have an abortion. (Particular judgment)

CITING A PRINCIPLE

Of course, Jane may agree that killing is wrong but question whether abortion is an act of killing. Or she might question whether abortion is an act of killing in the relevant sense, that is, an act of killing a person. But let us suppose that, instead, Jane persists in asking Mary, "But why do you think that killing is wrong?" Discussions do not always or even usually advance this far, because persons often become impatient with reasoning and sometimes distrust conclusions reached after long deliberations. They often become especially impatient with the reasoning of other people, trusting their own views more, and the answers to such questions may seem obvious to them. Nonetheless, there may be reason to pursue the matter, if indeed there is some doubt or disagreement, and if the parties to the dispute want to clarify the bases of their positions. Indeed, by reasoning, they may hope to reach the truth.

In answer to this last question, then, Mary might reply:

"Because everyone should respect life."

In saying this, Mary indicates that she is "pro-life." She may also be enunciating a principle of natural law theory which claims that life is one of the natural ends of human action. This means that one of the natural purposes of human action is to support human life and protect it from harm. We will examine natural law theory more fully later. The point here is that Mary's argument appears to have moved from the level of rules to the level of principle.

To recapitulate, Mary thinks her particular judgment "It is morally wrong for Jane to have an abortion" is justified by the moral rules "Abortion is wrong" and "Killing is wrong," and these rules in turn are justified by the principle "Everyone should respect life."

Her argument may then be structured to look like this:

Everyone ought to respect life. (Principle)

Therefore killing is wrong. (Rule)

Killing is wrong. (Rule)

Abortion is an act of killing. (Instance of rule)

Therefore abortion is wrong. (Subordinate rule)

Abortion is wrong. (Rule)

Therefore, it is wrong for Jane to have an abortion. (Particular judgment)

THOMAS AQUINAS
(c.1224–1274)
On Natural Law and the Right to Life

For there is in man, first of all, an inclination to good in accordance with the nature which he has in common with all substances, inasmuch, namely, as every substance seeks the preservation of its own being, according to its nature; and by reason of this inclination, whatever is a means of preserving human life . . . belongs to the natural law. Secondly, there is in man an inclination . . . *which nature has taught to all animals,* such as sexual intercourse, the education of offspring and so forth. Thirdly, there is in man an inclination to good according to the nature of his reason, which nature is proper to him. Thus man has a natural inclination to know the truth about God, and to live in society; and . . . to avoid offending those among whom one has to live. . . .

From: *Summa Theologica*. Thomas Aquinas. *Philosophy in the Middle Ages*. Hyman and Walsh, eds. Indianapolis: Hacket, 1973.

EXAMINING THE OTHER SIDE

Now turn to Jane's reasoning in support of her position. Suppose that she is willing to grant that, generally speaking, everyone ought to respect life and killing is wrong, but she is unwilling to grant that killing is wrong without exception. Jane, of course, could pursue other lines of reasoning. For example, Jane could claim the fetus is not a person. But for the sake of example we shall center on the issue of choice, even though in real arguments about abortion people usually present a variety of interlocking views. Suppose that, in reference to her belief that she has a right to an abortion, Jane claims:

"But I have a right to choose."

This statement is somewhat different from the others we have looked at because it can be interpreted as either a general or a particular claim. Jane might mean "I have a right to choose in this particular case," or, more likely, that her right to choose extends to other cases as well. Therefore, "I have a right to choose" may be interpreted as a rule. But this rule is probably an instance of a still more general rule:

"Everyone has a right to choose."

Thus, if asked why she thinks she has a right to choose, Jane might answer, "Because everyone has a right to choose."

Mary, of course, may question this rule, asking Jane why she thinks she has this right, and Jane may answer: "Because I have a right to my own body." In support of this, she might claim that everyone has a right to her (or his) body. If she did this, she might also be interpreted as offering a principle to back up her rules. This principle, or some variation of it, has sometimes been supported by natural rights theories, which are examined in Part II of this text.

Again, for the argument to be valid, the principles and rules must be interpreted as being universal, and for it to be sound, the premises must all be true. Mary, therefore, could question the truth of Jane's premises, just as Jane could question Mary's. Mary could grant, say, that everyone has a right to his or her own body without granting that it entails the right to do with it whatever one wishes, or she might also question whether a fetus really is a part of the pregnant woman's body in the same sense as, say, her heart or her liver is.

But let us suppose that, mainly, they disagree about the principles, or the implications of the principles, of the theories they espouse. Jane doesn't think that respecting life means that we should never kill, and Mary doesn't think that our right to our own bodies entails a right to do what we will with our bodies—or to the life of a fetus one's body contains. It is at this point that the disputants would need to find support for their principles by appealing to ethical theory, as we shall do in Part II.

REGRESSION TO POPULAR METAETHICAL VIEWS

What often happens at this point, however, is that one or both of the parties to the dispute gives up reasoning altogether. She may simply insist she is right, or she may claim that there is no such thing as being right or wrong—or that if there is, nobody can ever know the answer! For example, after failing to convince one another, we often hear people say things like, "I don't care what anyone says," indicating that they will continue to hold their positions dogmatically without considering evidence or reasons. Or they may say, "Who's to say?" or "It's all up to the individual," or "It's all a matter of opinion," or "What's true for you may not be true for me," indicating skepticism over anyone's ability to know moral truth or a belief in the hopeless relativity of such truth.

Such declarations are, of course, conversation stoppers. But we should notice that they conclude the argument in a way that questions the very basis for argumentation. Reasons were given to show that one's opponent's position was mistaken, and that one's own position was correct. The assumption was that we can have good reasons for our beliefs. The conclusion questions that assumption. Obviously something has gone wrong somewhere.

In the next chapter, on obstacles to moral reasoning, we try to find out what has gone wrong.

EXERCISES

1. Select a controversial moral issue and state the reasons offered on each side. For example, what reasons are offered for and against continuing the arms race? Maintaining or eliminating the social welfare system? Testing for AIDS or giving condoms to school children?

2. Which of these reasons are moral rules? Make explicit the rules involved by writing them out.

3. Are these rules ultimate rules, that is, are they moral principles? If not, what are the higher rules or principles from which they are derived?

4. Think about your own opinions on these issues. What reasons do you have for your view? Do you know the principles you would cite to support your position? Try to make a list of your own moral principles. Then review the list, asking yourself whether some of the rules on the list can be derived from other rules.

SUPPLEMENTARY READINGS

Aristotle. *Nichomachean Ethics* (many editions).

Aquinas, Thomas. *Summa Theologica* (many editions).

Bentham, Jeremy. *The Principles of Morals and Legislation* (many editions).

Copi, Irving. *Introduction to Logic.* 7h ed. New York: Macmillan, 1986.

Dewey, John and Tufts, James H. *Ethics.* New York: Holt, Rinehart and Winston, 1932.

Garner, R. T. and Rosen, B. *Moral Philosophy.* New York: Macmillan, 1967.

Moore, G. E. *Principia Ethica.* London: Cambridge University Press, 1903.

Nowell-Smith, Patrick. *Ethics.* Baltimore: Penguin Books, 1954.

Plato. *Republic* (many editions).

Williams, Bernard. *Ethics and the Limits of Philosophy.* Cambridge: Harvard University Press, 1985.

OBSTACLES TO MORAL REASONING

The obstacles to moral reasoning treated in this chapter are related to the levels of moral reasoning discussed in Chapter 3. There, the emphasis was on the importance of distinguishing particular moral judgments from moral rules and moral rules, in turn, from moral principles. On the level of principles, we said that people sometimes develop philosophical theories to defend their claims. Such theories are usually called substantive or normative ethical theories because they are used to justify substantive or normative ethical principles, that is, principles which assert that entire classes of things are good or bad, or that entire classes of actions are right or wrong.

PREJUDICES AGAINST REASONING

METAETHICAL EXTREMES

You also learned about the higher level of reasoning called *metaethics*, in which philosophers (and others) speculate about the nature of moral reasoning and the very possibility of reasoning in ethics. Because it is not unusual for people to express beliefs on this level, this chapter examines how certain popular metaethical opinions present obstacles to moral reasoning. Some metaethical positions are obstacles because they deny the possibility or efficacy of moral reasoning. They assert, in effect, that it would be a mistake to even try to reason in ethics, or to try to settle moral disputes by rational means. They are not metaethical theories that explain how moral reasoning works but theories that claim that it cannot work—or at least that moral reasoning is extremely limited in its scope. Because they deny the very subject matter of this book, they are obstacles we must face even before we begin.

T. H. GREEN
(1836–1882)
On the Subject of Ethics

A writer who seeks to gain general confidence scarcely goes the right way to work when he begins with asking whether there really is such a subject as that of which he proposes to treat; whether it is one to which enquiry can be directed with any prospect of a valuable result. Yet to a writer on Moral Philosophy such a mode of procedure is prescribed, not only by the logical impulse to begin at the beginning, but by observation of the prevalent opinions around him. He can scarcely but be aware that Moral Philosophy is a name of somewhat equivocal repute; that it commands less respect among us than was probably the case a century ago; and that any one who professes to teach or write upon a subject to which this name is in any proper or distinctive sense applicable, is looked upon with some suspicion.

From: *Prolegomena to Ethics*, Apollo Editions. T. H. Green. New York: Tomas Y. Crowell Co., 1969 (first published in 1883).

Basically such beliefs are claims that we cannot justify our actions or resolve our differences by rational means. They amount to claiming that our rational faculties are not adequate to the job of settling practical affairs. They are also self-fulfilling claims, for they prevent us from resolving conflicts through reasoning, from recognizing inconsistencies in our own reasoning processes, or from examining the issues at hand. As we shall see, such beliefs tend to have some basis in truth but, by misplaced emphasis, or by overemphasis, also exaggerate that truth. They may be psychologically satisfying but logically unsound.

Extreme Skepticism

We have discussed some of these metaethical views briefly in Chapter 1, on the nature of morality, for they are views that express very restricted conceptions of the subject. They are treated again here because they also appear to be deep-seated prejudices against moral reasoning that are likely to block our reasoning processes unless we become aware of them as traps.

Extreme moral skepticism is one such position. In this century, it has been expressed by the metaethical theory called emotivism. Emotivism holds that it is not possible to reason about the evaluative aspects of moral judgments because evaluations are simply an expression of feelings or emotions. This theory finds popular expression in the equation of matters of morality with matters of taste. The theory maintains that there are no such things as moral truths because, in its view, ethical statements express subjective feelings and not objective facts. To say "X is good" is to mean "I like x" and nothing more. In popular discussions, people often express this view by saying things like, "Well, that's the way I feel about it and that's all there is to it," or "You're entitled to your feelings and I to mine." The upshot of this position is that moral judgments are neither true nor false. According to emotivism, if one person says "X is wrong," and another says "X is not wrong," they are not contradicting each other.

The clue to the selectivity of this position lies in its use of words like "simply," "merely," or "nothing more," for these are marks of "nothing but" approaches to ethics, that is, of theories which hold that ethics is "nothing but this" or "nothing but that," when, as we saw in Chapter 1, ethics involves many things. Thus, although it seems incontestably true that morality somehow involves feelings or emotions, it also seems patently false that this is all that morality involves. Feelings or emotions may indeed provide a basis for moral reasoning because we must take account of them when reasoning, but ethics is not concerned with feelings alone. Even if it were, we could still reason about what satisfies emotions or desires, and hence about how we should or should not act to produce satisfactions. Indeed, morally speaking, feelings or emotions themselves may be said to be either appropriate or inappropriate, and they may even be corrigible according to moral rules and principles.

The authors recognize that doubts about ethics and ethical reasoning will continue to arise in the minds of readers, but we should not jump to conclusions on the basis of such doubts. The important thing is for us to keep our minds open to the possibility of solving problems by rational means and to see what we can do to improve our reasoning, rather than assume that we are defeated before we start.

Relativism

Individual relativism and cultural relativism are both doctrines which hold that moral reasoning is possible but extremely limited. Both hold that persons can reason about their actions according to personal or cultural codes of conduct but that they cannot use reason to resolve differences between codes. Both are based on the incontestable fact that persons and/or cultures do have codes and that these codes often prescribe different and even contradictory forms of behavior. Thus relativists argue that there can be no answers to moral questions that apply intersubjectively or interculturally. Because reasoning is supposed to stop at the level of personal or social rules, it is supposed to be impossible to apply rational criteria to differences between individuals or groups.

Such reasoning is highly selective, however, for while it takes account of differences, it ignores similarities. The relativist reasons fallaciously that because persons or groups *sometimes* disagree that they therefore *always* disagree, or that if they disagree, there is no rational way of resolving differences between them. But what is true in some cases need not be true of all. Individuals and groups do sometimes disagree, of course, but they also do sometimes agree. Indeed, different individuals and groups have many things in common with one another, and people seem to universally agree on many moral rules and principles. Sometimes what appears to be a difference in principle is really a difference in the application of the principle to different circumstances or differences in factual beliefs. For example, every culture has rules against killing and stealing or concerning promise-keeping and loyalty. Every culture regulates family life and sex, even if they do not always do so in precisely the same way. But even if people disagree, it does not follow that they cannot reach agreement. One of the ways in which people often reach agreement, of course, is by attempting to reconcile differences through reasoning.

Thus individual and cultural relativism exemplify the fallacy of hasty generalization or oversimplification, the fallacy of attempting to draw a universal conclusion from a limited number of particular cases, ignoring that such cases have both similarities and differences. These positions also tend to be guilty of the fallacy of authority, for they appear to assume that moral judgments are true or false because some individual or group says they are, failing to recognize that it is possible for anyone to be wrong.

BERNARD WILLIAMS
On Ethical Skepticism

Ethical skepticism . . . is at the opposite end of a line from skepticism about the external world. It is not . . . like skepticism about psychical research or psychoanalysis, where a real doubt is raised that might come eventually to be accepted, with the result that these activities would meet the same fate as phrenology: we would come to reject them altogether, finding that their claims to knowledge or even reasoned belief were baseless. It is not possible for ethical considerations to meet a collective rejection of that sort. For the individual, however, there does seem to be an alternative to accepting ethical considerations. It lies in a life that is not an ethical life.

From: *Ethics and the Limits of Philosophy.* Bernard Williams. Cambridge: Harvard University Press, 1985.

Relativism, like emotivism, emphasizes subjective factors in moral evaluation but tends to ignore objective conditions that may render moral judgments true or false. Both appear to hold that there are no objectively correct moral answers, that "All is a matter of opinion," so to speak, or that "All depends on the individual" or "All depends on society."

A form of relativism popular today claims that ethical views are determined by economic and political systems. People in capitalistic countries and people in communistic countries are said to have different moral commitments because they have different ideologies or world views. Even people within the same economic structure may have moral views affected by their roles within the system. A manual worker, for example, may have different opinions on moral, social, or political issues than does a business executive because of their different class interests.

Again, we agree that people are influenced by their economic, political, and social circumstances, and that these influences do affect morality. These differences are certainly relevant to moral reasoning, for morality must take all aspects of life into consideration. But we disagree that these differences invalidate moral reasoning. All of us are capable of evaluating our economic, political, and social systems, and such evaluations are sometimes successful in changing our lives. We need only reflect on recent social movements regarding women's rights or civil rights as examples. Ideological or class differences can make moral reasoning more difficult, but they do not necessarily render it invalid or ineffective.

Persons who hold these relativistic doctrines, however, tend to ignore the consequences of their positions, namely that there would be nothing to have an opinion about if there were no objective basis for holding an opinion, or that there would be no point in adhering to one code rather than another if there were no way of critiquing or justifying codes. As a matter of fact, we all do criticize the codes of other persons and societies, and even our own codes and cultures. It would seem, therefore, that this criticism has some basis.

DECISIONALISM

Decisionalism is similar to emotivism and relativism in being subjectivistic, but instead of holding that morality is a matter of emotion or social perspective, it holds that morality is a matter of choice. Most people would not make hard and fast distinctions between emotions, opinions, and choices, but philosophers often do. So what may look like one position to other people may in fact break down into several positions for a philosopher.

In any case, decisionalists do not claim that no reasoning is possible but only that reasoning is never sufficient to reach moral conclusions. No matter what rules or principles we may use, they hold, we must at some point make a decision of our own about what we should do. In its most extreme form, decisionalism maintains that we must ultimately decide which principles or rules we will hold.

As in the cases of emotivism and relativism, there is some justification for holding this position, but in its emphasis upon decision, it excludes other important elements of morality. In the first place, we should distinguish between *determining* what is right or wrong and *deciding* whether or not we will do it. That is, there appears to be good reason for making a distinction between moral judgment and moral choice. A person may judge that an action is wrong, for example, and yet choose to do it. In this way, it seems, we are able to violate our own consciences, and unless we were, it would be difficult to understand how we could be morally culpable for our acts.

Because of this distinction, appeals to choice may be irrelevant to the point at issue. For instance, a person accused of doing something wrong may defend herself by saying, "Well, it was my choice," but the question may not be whose choice it is. In morality, the question is usually whether

---

JEAN-PAUL SARTRE
(1905–1980)
On Freedom and Human Anguish

Who, then, can prove that I am the proper person to impose, by my own choice, my conception of man upon mankind? I shall never find any proof whatever; there will be no sign to convince me of it. . . . It is anguish pure and simple, of the kind well known to all those who have borne responsibilities. When, for instance, a military leader takes upon himself the responsibility for an attack and sends a number of men to their death, he chooses to do it and at bottom he alone chooses. . . . All leaders know that anguish.

From: *Existentialism and Human Emotions*. Jean-Paul Sartre. New York: The Philosophical Library, 1949.

that choice is right or wrong. However, the question of whose choice it is may be relevant when it is a question of who has a right to make a decision. In medicine, for example, medical personnel, families, the patient, and even the government may be involved. There are many issues in which people are deprived of rights they ought to have.

As decisionalists argue, there are also times when reason alone cannot settle an issue. Sometimes, for example, we know that a certain kind of thing ought to be done, but we do not know who should do it. We may know that two or more people should not try to pass through a doorway at the same time, but we may also have no way of knowing who should go first. Thus we could discuss the matter, even argue about it, every time such an occasion arises, but because that seems terribly inefficient, we could also adopt a rule. We could decide that older people will pass through doors first and that younger people will step aside.

Many social rules are exactly of this sort. They enable us to do things gracefully which might otherwise cause a great deal of strife. In many cases there may be no good reason for deciding upon one rule rather than another— for, say, deciding to drive on the left instead of on the right—and people sometimes become resentful of rules for this reason. That is, they see that some rules are arbitrary, that the custom might indeed be different. But the point is that very often, *some* custom must be agreed upon in order to produce the desired effect, even if it does not matter which custom it is.

This consideration alone explains many of the differences between cultures or even different groups within the same culture. These differences are not wholly trivial, for differences in custom can indeed cause conflicts, as when people of different social backgrounds want to get married. However, the solution does not appear to be the rejection or dissolution of all customs whatsoever, as some individualists appear to believe, but some change in the customs themselves, or in the adoption of new customs.

Indeed, rules are frequently determined by choice, as in making up the rules of a game, or in choosing to divide up a task or otherwise cooperate with others in a job of some kind. Rules thus created can be an important element in moral reasoning. Although sometimes necessary, however, decisions alone are not sufficient to account for moral rights and obligations, for if they were, we could decide to make morality into anything we happened to choose. The mistake, then, is to suppose that decision is the only consideration, for we cannot ignore the need to distinguish between rational and irrational alternatives.

Thus, although there is an arbitrary aspect to customs, they are still subject to rational critique. We can reason to determine when social rules are needed, when they need to be altered, and even when or how they should be applied. When it comes to making decisions then, we can reason to determine acceptable or unacceptable ranges of choice.

DOGMATISM

Dogmatists believe they know the answer to ethical questions and, hence, that reasoning is unnecessary. But dogmatists appear to confuse subjective certainty with objective certainty. They appear to think that because they *feel* strongly that their moral judgments are correct that therefore they must be correct. Of course, it is possible to be mistaken even about one's strongest convictions. The dogmatist ignores this possibility of error or refuses to acknowledge it, and hence claims that there is no need to reason.

Unlike the skeptic or subjectivist who holds that reason is not possible on the ground that there are no objectively correct answers to moral questions, the dogmatist holds that reason is not necessary because the answers are known. But dogmatists are very much like skeptics in their refusal to consider reasons for or against beliefs. While skeptics are likely to say things like "Who knows?" or "Who's to say?" dogmatists say "I know" and "I don't care what anyone says." Or, when confronted with an objection to their position, they will say, "That is simply an exception that proves the rule," ignoring the exception.

The dogmatist appears to be guilty of confusing justified conviction with dogmatic assertion. We all have convictions, of course, and we tend to think we are correct in the beliefs we hold. The difference between persons who are not dogmatists and those who are is that the former are willing to consider reasons against their beliefs as well as reasons for them, whereas the latter will consider only reasons that support their positions. The former are open-minded, whereas the latter are close-minded or prejudiced in their beliefs.

Prejudicial Attitudes

Dogmatists and skeptics appear to have this much in common: Both refuse to reason about their beliefs, dogmatists because they think they already know the answers, and skeptics because they think that no one can ever know—or at least that no one can ever prove his or her case.

Both positions cancel any attempt at moral reasoning by assuming, as the major premise to any moral argument, the claim that moral reasoning cannot work. Of course it follows logically from the premise "No instance of moral reasoning will work" that "This or any other instance of moral reasoning will not work." That appears to be a good logical argument for not reasoning at all. But we have tried to show that the premise is false, or at least that it could not be known to be true, without examining particular examples of moral reasoning. The problem is that the dogmatic or skeptical position tries to decide the issue in advance, before actually examining the success or failure of moral arguments. But it is difficult to avoid such prejudices, for they are usually deeply entrenched. They are in fact taught and reinforced by the people around us—even persons in authority. They are also difficult to avoid because, as we have pointed out, they tend to be self-fulfilling prophecies. Those who believe that reasoning will not work usually fail for lack of trying, and hence seem to confirm their theory!

The Danger of Self-Contradiction

One may discover that people who are skeptical in their philosophic ideas about morality are often the very same people who are dogmatic in making moral judgments. That is, they believe that their own moral judgments are correct while at the same time believing that no moral judgments could be correct, or that no one could ever know which moral judgments are correct. It seems they want to have their cake and eat it too, or, in the language of logic, that they are simply contradicting themselves.

Thus we may believe, on a metaethical level, that no moral claims can be justified by reasoning, but we may also believe, with respect to our moral principles, rules, or particular judgments, that our moral claims are rationally justified, and this is a straightforward logical contradiction. We must either give up the idea that moral claims can be justified by reason, or we must give up the claim that no such justification is possible. It is important to face up to such contradictions because, of course, they are logical faults. They also appear to be moral faults. To attempt to eliminate contradictions in one's own thinking is an attempt to achieve integrity as a person. The attempt to resolve conflicts between oneself and others is an attempt to establish an integrated moral community.

ARISTOTLE
(384–322 B.C.)
On Contradiction

For if all opinions and appearances are true, everything must be at once true and false; for many people form judgments which are opposite to those of others, and imagine that those who do not think the same as themselves are wrong; hence the same thing must both be and not be. And if this is so, all opinions must be true; for those who are wrong and those who are right think contrarily to each other. So if reality is of this nature, everyone will be right.

From: *Metaphysics*, Bk. IV, Aristotle. Many editions.

Such contradiction between our philosophical statements and our evaluation of human behavior shows, among other things, that we can be mistaken in our beliefs about ourselves. That is, contrary to popular opinion, we do not always know what is best or true for us. As noted, we can deny on one level of thinking what we assert on another, because, perhaps, we do not notice the contradiction or do not clearly see that it is a contradiction. When, for example, we say things like "What is true for me is true for me and what is true for you is true for you," we may think that we are insulating ourselves from error. We may think that, if all others' beliefs are true for them, then our beliefs are always true for us, and hence that neither we nor anybody else can ever be wrong. But at the same time we also believe that some things *are* morally wrong.

One of the aims of moral reasoning is to help us straighten out this kind of thinking. Otherwise, we can oppose ourselves in our own thinking, denying responsibility for our own opinions and acts and making it virtually impossible to communicate with others in a rational or coherent way. The possibility of such contradiction illustrates as well as anything could the importance of bringing ethical theory in line with moral practice, or conversely, of bringing practice in line with theory, so that our thoughts and actions will cohere.

THE FALSE OPPOSITION OF THEORY AND PRACTICE

We have said that we would try to classify some of the more prominent beliefs which prevent people from reasoning in ethics, and we have said that some of these beliefs are popular metaethical theories. Of course, many people argue that we should not be concerned with theories at all, because they are *only* theories, and hence, presumably not factual, realistic, or practical. Whatever theory we may propose, they will say that the real world is not like that. If we say that people ought to be more rational, they will say that they simply aren't, and that to think they should be is too idealistic. We have often heard people say, "Well, that's just a theory," meaning that we should not pay attention to it.

However, we should not reject theories simply because they *are* theories. Rather, we should reject them if we have evidence for believing they are inadequate. But not all theories need be inadequate. All structured human activity involves theorizing, in the sense of generalizing or hypothesizing, and nearly all theories are practical to the extent that they have at least potential applications.

When people reject theorizing or philosophizing, what they usually mean to reject is *other people's* theorizing or philosophizing, not their own. They have their own theories, but because they think their theories are true, they think of them as facts, not theories. But, of course, a true theory is still a theory, and what we need to find out is *which* theories are true. We cannot find this out simply by finding out *whose* theories they are.

CHARLES S. PEIRCE
(1839–1914)
The Fixation of Belief

Few persons care to study logic, because everybody conceives himself to be proficient enough in the art of reasoning already. But I observe that this satisfaction is limited to one's own ratiocination, and does not extend to that of other men.

From: "The Fixation of Belief." Charles S. Peirce. *Popular Science Monthly*, 12, 1877.

Some theories may be bad because they are false or unsupported, and others may be good because they are true or well founded, but none of them is good or bad simply for being a theory. Practices, likewise, may be either good or bad, but not because they are practices. Ethics concerns itself with what people *ought* to do and not simply with what they do, so we should not conclude that a judgment about human behavior is not relevant because people do not act that way.

The objection has sometimes been made that theorizing is impractical because there is not time to theorize before we act. On a day-to-day basis, we must often respond quickly to situations, acting upon whatever beliefs we have acquired, however good or bad they might be. Yet there are also times when we do have time to question or defend our beliefs, and at such times we can theorize. Whether such theorizing actually influences our behavior depends a great deal on whether it leads us to change our minds and whether we are able to change our habits accordingly. Thus, throughout this book, we try to distinguish various phases of moral reasoning and action, including times when we act upon our beliefs and times when we question or defend them.

THE REAL OPPOSITION BETWEEN THEORY AND PRACTICE

Dogmatism, we suggested, is founded upon a desire to be certain, and skepticism upon the realization that perhaps we can never know anything with certainty, especially in ethics. Thus, both these positions were said to be exaggerations. The truth of the matter seems to be that we can never attain absolute certainty in any field but that we can attain knowledge in the form of warranted beliefs, that is, beliefs that are supported by evidence but that may be mistaken because further evidence may prove them wrong. In modern times we have become accustomed to the idea that scientific knowledge is never absolute or certain, but we find it difficult to become accustomed to the idea that moral knowledge is similar in this respect. Thus we tend to take an all-or-nothing approach to moral truth, thinking that unless a moral theory is absolutely certain, there is no point in holding it. However, it seems more reasonable to distinguish between theories that are well supported and theories that are not.

Once we become accustomed to the idea that our moral theories or our general moral beliefs must be tested, we can then begin to see whether our theories are opposed to our practices or to other beliefs we or others may hold. If our actions do not correspond to our beliefs about how we and others ought to act, then our actions must be wrong, according to our own thinking—or else our thinking is wrong. To be consistent, we must either adjust our action to our thinking or our thinking to our action. If not, we are being dishonest with ourselves and hypocritical towards others, recommending rules that we ourselves do not obey.

EXERCISES

1. Skepticism, relativism, and dogmatism have been characterized as obstacles to moral reasoning. List things that people commonly say which seem to fall into one of these categories, for example, "Who's to say?"

2. After making this list, examine each saying to see how it may be interpreted to mean different things. For example, "Who's to say?" may mean "Who has the right to say?" or it may imply that no one has a right to say anything.

3. Supposing people do express skeptical or relativistic beliefs, do you think they really mean what they say? Or do you think they are not sure, or that they use such sayings as rationalizations?

4. In the case of dogmatism, why do some people think they know what is right without having to demonstrate or justify their belief? That is, why do they *feel* they are right?

5.   Give examples of how decisions are involved in creating moral rules. Explain why such decisions are sometimes necessary. Also explain why it seems that moral rights and obligations cannot be determined by choice alone.

6.   Opposition to theory in favor of practicality is sometimes characterized as anti-intellectualism. What would you say to someone who said that your beliefs were only theories and that his were facts?

7.   What would you say to someone who claimed that it is not important to be consistent?

FALLACIES IN REASONING

We have pointed out that the obstacles to moral reasoning involve logical fallacies such as hasty generalization and appeals to authority. However, we did not explain these fallacies in detail, nor did we point out how such fallacies can present obstacles to moral reasoning on levels other than metaethics. It seems appropriate, then, to list some of the logical fallacies often committed in moral reasoning, to show how they can block progress in reasoning on any level, and to see how they can be avoided.

In Chapter 2, when we distinguished valid arguments from invalid arguments, we usually assumed that the persons engaged in argumentation were interested in discovering truth, that they knew what the issues were, and that the reasons they offered were relevant to their conclusions. In this section, by contrast, we are concerned with cases in which persons are not trying to discover truth or in which they may even be trying to deceive others by confusing or misleading them, as advertisers or politicians may do in trying to win customers or votes. We are also concerned with cases in which people are honestly confused about the issues, because the issues are complex or because it is easy to wander from one point to the next.

For example, if someone says that speeding is always immoral because it is against the law, and another person says that speeding may sometimes be morally permitted because we are not always obligated to obey the law, they both appear to be talking to the same point and to be offering reasons that are relevant to their positions. But if a third party interjects that it doesn't matter because speeding is fun, one may rightly feel that the reason being offered is somehow irrelevant to the issue.

Reasons can be irrelevant and yet seem relevant because there may be a subtle shift in topic. If someone said that running a stop sign is morally permissible in opposition to someone who claimed it illegal, it might appear that they are arguing about the same thing when they really are not. That is, what is morally right or wrong may not coincide with what is legally right or wrong.

Such errors lie in missing the point of the argument or in misinterpreting the point. To make progress in argumentation, it is important to clarify the point at issue and stick to it. Otherwise, one simply shifts topics endlessly.

We are seeking to discover whether the reasons offered to support conclusions establish their truth. But in the fallacies we discuss, the reasons offered are not always relevant. At best they may lend plausibility to a statement, but they do not demonstrate its truth. Nonetheless, such reasoning is often convincing for psychological and not logical reasons because, say, it appeals to things people want to believe or to prejudices they hold.

The Fallacy of Authority

The fallacy of appealing to authority is, roughly, the fallacy of claiming that something is true simply because someone in authority says it is, rather than because it is supported by evidence. Generally speaking, propositions are true or false regardless of who holds them or asserts them, so the question "Who says?" or "Who's to say?" is irrelevant. If this paper is white, it is white regardless of whether you or I or anyone thinks it is. Yet people often claim that something is true because, for instance, the teacher says so, because some famous person says so, or because it is said by some scientist or professional. After all, we learn many things from parents, teachers, and professionals, as well as from our peers, so it seems reasonable to suppose that the evidence we have for our beliefs is the testimony of such people. But anyone can make mistakes. Even if what they say may be useful as a guide, we cannot conclude that something is true only because they say it is.

JOHN SCOTUS ERIUGENA
(c.810–c.877)
On Authority and Reason

Disciple: You urge me to discuss matters reasonably, but I wish you would add something in the way of support from the authority of the holy Fathers to strengthen what you say.

Master: But you are not ignorant I think which is of greater worth. . . .

Disciple: This reason itself teaches us. Authority indeed proceeds from true reason, reason never proceeds from authority. For all authority which true reason does not endorse is seen to be weak. True reason, however, being ratified and rendered immutable by virtue of itself, needs no additional assent from authority to strengthen it.

From: *The Division of Nature*, John Scotus Eriugena, in *Medieval Philosophy*. J. F. Wippel and A. B. Wolter, eds. New York: The Free Press, Macmillan, 1969.

Likewise, nothing is true just because you, I, or society as a whole happens to believe it. So-called "bandwagon" appeals or "everybody's doing it" arguments are examples of appeals to authority where the authority is based on sheer numbers. Citing what is "up to date" or objecting to what is "old fashioned" amount to the same thing. Individual and cultural relativism in ethics, we said, are also forms of authoritarianism in that both maintain that the truth of moral beliefs depends on authorities of one kind or another. Individual relativists claim that something is morally correct "for me" or "for you" because "I say" or "you say," and cultural relativists think that something is right or wrong because "society says." But if this were so, neither I nor you, or variously, neither this society nor that society could be mistaken in its moral beliefs, and the whole idea of being correct or mistaken would appear to lose all sense.

Many people believe, of course, that something is right or wrong because God says so. In ethics, this is called divine command theory. It appears to have greater plausibility than other appeals to authority because, unlike humans, God knows everything. But, of course, not everybody believes in God, and even believers cannot always agree about what God says, so such appeals are not very helpful in practice.

SOCRATES
(c.470–399 B.C.)
On Theistic Ethics

. . . I said to myself: 'Well, and what if Euthyphro does prove to me that all the gods regarded the death of the serf as unjust, how do I know anything more of the nature of piety and impiety? For granting that this action may be hateful to the gods, still piety and impiety are not adequately defined by these distinctions. . . .

The point which I should first wish to understand is whether the pious is beloved by the gods because it is holy, or holy because it is beloved of the gods.

From: *Euthyphro, The Dialogues of Plato.* Plato. B. Jowett, trans. New York: Random House, 1937.

AD HOMINEM ARGUMENTS

To appeal to authorities is, in effect, to have a prejudice in favor of the opinions of some people over others. Similarly, one may have a prejudice against the opinions of some people and argue that their beliefs are wrong because those people are bad or disreputable. These are called *ad hominem* arguments, or arguments against the person.

Just as we sometimes argue, appealing to authority, that some beliefs are good or true because they are the beliefs of Americans, Christians, or Republicans, say, we may also argue against others, claiming that their beliefs are bad or false because they are Communists, pagans, or Democrats. Sometimes name-calling also falls in this category. However, because it is possible for anyone to have either correct or incorrect beliefs, we cannot know which of their beliefs are correct simply by knowing their character or circumstances.

The *ad hominem* argument often takes the form of arguing against someone on the grounds that the person has a special interest in promoting his or her cause. For example, one might argue that you shouldn't believe the teacher's argument that teachers are underpaid, for after all, teachers want more money. Of course, people usually are interested in the causes they support, but they may also be correct in supporting them.

Another example is the "you too" argument. If one is accused of a wrong, he or she may respond by saying, "Look who's talking!" But the accused person may be wrong—even if the accuser is also wrong. The question of my wrongdoing is simply a separate issue from your wrongdoing. On the other hand, in ethics, "you too" arguments may raise questions of equity which are legitimate moral considerations, that is, if you have a right to do something, I may have a right to do it too.

MISPLACED AND PROPERLY PLACED AUTHORITY

Of course, we should not ignore the fact that some people know more than others, at least about some subjects, and that, in the absence of better evidence, it would be foolish to ignore their opinions. Doctors usually know more about medicine, and physicists usually know more about physics than others outside those fields. But, even though we are often justified in following the advice of experts, we should realize that they are not always right. On very important questions, it may be wise to seek more than one opinion or even to investigate matters for ourselves.

We tend to trust experts more when we are confident that they themselves have been faithful to the evidence. In fact, we often inquire about the evidence used by experts and sometimes require that it be checked by others. When we have reason to doubt that experts are guided by evidence because of bias or poor research methods, we tend to be less confident of their opinions. We have a right to be suspicious when persons in authority do not allow us to question their authority, or when they resent our requests for evidence or for a second opinion.

The choice of authorities is itself a matter for practical reasoning, for we need to decide among authorities, and we also need to decide when we will follow their advice. Indeed, we want to make certain they are experts on the subjects in question. A physician may not be the best person to consult on matters of politics, or a politician on matters of medicine. In advertising, famous people often endorse products they never use or about which they may know very little. Yet people are often influenced by these ads. Such appeals are called appeals to *misplaced* authority.

PRACTICAL AND THEORETICAL AUTHORITY

Some people are thought to be authorities because they know more than other people, but others are thought to be authorities because they occupy positions of leadership or power. Thus, a political scientist may know a great deal about politics and yet not have any political power, whereas a government official may have a great deal of political power and not know very much about politics. The former kind of authority is classified as a theoretical authority: an expert on questions of truth. The latter, however, is called a practical or moral authority, for that person has the power to make decisions that are binding on others. For example, the President of the United States has the power to commit the United States armed forces to military action, and Congress has the power to enact laws.

Persons usually have this latter kind of authority, practical authority, within the framework of social institutions. The rules of baseball empower umpires and players to do certain things within that game, and the United States Constitution empowers the president, Congress, and federal courts. These kinds of authorities have been designated, or at least have been accepted, in a division of labor, to do certain kinds of jobs, and others have agreed to accept their decisions as binding within certain limited spheres of action.

Later we shall see how important it is, morally speaking, to have such authorities and to evaluate institutional policies which delimit their powers. But, for now, we should recognize that even though we may be bound by the decisions of practical authorities, they are not necessarily right about factual or theoretical affairs. An umpire, for example, may be as blind as a bat; the president may use poor judgment in commiting troops to action; and the Congress is capable of making bad laws. The laws Congress enacts are indeed laws, but they are not necessarily good laws.

It does not follow that a practical authority is necessarily a good authority, or even that we should have authorities of that kind. These are all questions which, in ethics, are open to investigation. Practical authority always depends on background assumptions, such as the use of force or the acceptance of rules and principles, which are open to question.

THE APPEAL TO FORCE

The above distinctions are related to the fallacy of appealing to force, because people often assume that what is right or wrong in ethics or in politics depends on who has the power to enforce his or her opinions on other people. They reason that children are bound to listen to their parents because children are dependent on their parents, or that citizens must obey their governments because the law enforcement agencies can punish them. This is sometimes called the doctrine of "might makes right" because it supposes that the opinion of the stronger is the correct opinion, or at least that the opinion of the stronger determines what, morally speaking, is correct. This doctrine is also often thought to be the most realistic conception of ethics because it recognizes as its standard not some lofty, unrealistic ideal, but the way the world really works.

THRASYMACHUS
(latter half of fifth century B.C.)
Might Makes Right

. . . What I say is that "just" or "right" means nothing but what is to the interest of the stronger party . . . in every case the laws are made by the ruling party in its own interest; a democracy makes democratic laws, a despot autocratic ones, and so on. By making these laws they define as "right" for their subjects whatever is for their own interest, and they call anyone who breaks them a "wrongdoer" and punish him accordingly.

From: *The Republic of Plato*. Thrasymachus. F. M. Cornford, trans. London: Oxford University Press, 1941.

Yet is does not follow that the opinion or decision of the stronger is necessarily the right decision. As pointed out above, the government may be able to make laws and enforce them, but it does not follow that its laws are good. Nor does it follow that enforcement is always fair. We know in fact that persons and governments often do things which are not right, morally speaking, even if they are legal, and we also know that they often do things that are illegal. So we need to make distinctions between what a person or government has the power to do by sheer exercise of force, and what it has the right to do, either by law or by standards of ethics or morality. The simple point is that something does not become morally correct just because somebody can force us to do it.

However, insofar as consequences may be brought to bear upon the question of rightness or wrongness, the rightness or wrongness of acts can be affected by the sanctions of persons or governments. That is, by enforcement, a government can add bad consequences to an act which the act would not otherwise have, or a parent may add such consequences to the action of a child by punishing the act. Thus the force which others may use in support of their opinions is a factor which should be taken into account in considering the consequences of actions—but it need not always be the deciding factor. That is, we sometimes need to oppose others, just as they may feel the need to oppose us, in order to do what we believe is right. We are obviously not always morally bound to take the easy way out!

Sometimes the appeal to force trades upon a confusion of levels of moral reasoning. Remember, there are four levels of moral reasoning. Often we want to reason at a very general and abstract level about an ideal, say justice. But we know that particular judgments must take into account actual circumstances. Thus a situation which appears to be just in the abstract may also appear to be unwise under actual conditions. For example, we may advocate democracy for a social organization but find that some of the people in it are unwilling to act responsibly. Someone may then argue that democracy is unworkable because some people will take advantage of it. In effect, the ideal is rejected because of a subtle appeal to force, because of the threat that some will refuse to live by it. Initially, this may be an important consideration, but it may be only a temporary obstacle to putting an otherwise sound ideal into practice. A statement of the ideal may be needed to find ways of overcoming obstacles to it. Appeals to force may then confuse the issue by citing obstacles to an ideal as a reason for rejecting the ideal itself.

THE APPEAL TO PITY AND RIDICULE

To appeal to pity is to try to get somebody to feel sorry for you or someone else, and hence to concede an important point in argumentation. It is, one might say, just the opposite of the appeal to force. Instead of saying, "I might hurt you," you might say, "You might hurt me and you wouldn't want to do that!" "Don't fail me in this subject, for then I will not graduate in June!" Such an appeal would be irrelevant if the question were whether the student deserved to pass according to the standards of grading appropriate to the class. However, an appeal to pity might be relevant in an argument about euthanasia, for example, if it could be shown that suffering is a relevant moral consideration—which it certainly seems to be—and if it could also be shown that such a consideration might override prohibitions against killing. Considerations of suffering may also be relevant in cases regarding poverty, sickness, and persecution, or in objections to experimentation on animals.

78

The use of ridicule might be included as a special case of *ad hominem* argument, or as a kind of appeal to force or use of force, but it deserves special mention in any case, because it is so frequently used, because it is so effective, and because, morally speaking, it is so vicious. Quite simply, people often try to defeat their opponents by making fun of them, and the device often works. People who belong to a clique often have great fun ridiculing other people and think that they are reinforcing their own position by doing so. However, as in the case of appealing to authority or in *ad hominem* arguments, it is fairly obvious that no one group has a monopoly on virtue, or for that matter, a monopoly on vice. Persons who ridicule others exhibit both the intellectual fault of bad reasoning and the moral fault of being unkind.

HASTY GENERALIZATION

In inductive reasoning, of course, we always reason from a sample, or from knowledge of part of a class to a conclusion about a whole class, so in this sense, inductive reasoning may seem to be a kind of hasty generalization. However, inductive reasoning need not be hasty. There is such a thing as taking a good sample, governed by scientific procedures or statistical methods. In hasty generalization we are concerned mainly with obviously limited samples, and especially with appeals to unusual cases. We also need to be aware of prejudicial thinking where people recognize evidence which supports their beliefs but ignore evidence which does not. People who are prejudiced against a given group usually mention only the faults of that group but never its virtues. Or, in support of a rule, such as a rule against using drugs, a person may cite only cases where drugs are abused and ignore cases where drugs are properly used.

The fallacy of *accident* is related to hasty generalization. It consists of applying a rule to an exceptional case or to a case for which the rule was not intended. If one opposed the use of drugs for medical reasons on the ground that the use of drugs is wrong, one would seem to be confusing abuses with justified uses. But of course, it is not always easy to determine when a rule does or does not apply, so this is a question examined more carefully in some of the chapters that follow.

BEGGING THE QUESTION

Begging the question, or circular reasoning, is not, strictly speaking, invalid, for in such a case, the conclusion does follow from the premises. Circular reasoning is valid precisely because the reason offered in support of the conclusion is the conclusion itself. It takes the form of arguing that a proposition is true because that same proposition is true. The problem is that the reason being offered is uninformative and provides no independent evidence to support the conclusion. A person who offers such an argument seems to think that he or she can show that the conclusion is true by simply repeating it, or by insisting upon it, or by shouting it. Yet circular arguments are often far more subtle than this, for very often the person who offers them does not recognize their circularity.

JOEL FEINBERG
(1926–   )
On Question-Begging by Definition

The problem of euthanasia in a peculiar way raises difficulties both for the definition of 'murder' as unjust killing and that as killing the innocent. Legal questions aside, am I "morally speaking a murderer" if in response to his earnest request I put an old man suffering from an incurable disease out of his misery? If murder is, by definition, the killing of the innocent, then I am, by definition, a murderer. But notice how unfair this line is to the mercy-killer. It morally condemns him in the most serious way, and at the same time deprives him of any language to defend himself.

From: "On Being 'Morally Speaking' a 'Murderer.'" Joel Feinberg. *Journal of Philosophy*, 61, 1964:158–171.

On the abortion issue, we frequently hear people arguing about whether the fetus is a person. If the fetus is a person, people assume, it has rights. If it is not a person, it does not have rights—or at least not the same rights as a person. However, the word "person" itself is usually used with moral implications to mean something which has certain rights, so the question of whether the fetus is a person may not be a wholly independent issue. That is, those in favor of abortion may simply beg the question by assuming that the fetus is not a person, and those against abortion may beg the question when they assume it is.

Equivocation

One source of confusion in reasoning, obviously, is the fact that words, and sometimes the same words—the same marks or sounds—may have different meanings. Sometimes, of course, different words may have the same meaning. Thus equivocation occurs when a word or expression changes meaning in the course of discussion. In talking about whether somebody or something is religious, for example, persons may not have a clear idea of what they mean by "religious," or they may mean different things by the term, so that, without knowing it, they may not be addressing the same issue at all. One might mean by "religious" the worship of a transcendent God, whereas another might mean by "religious" reverence for anything whatsoever, including nature or even other humans. Obviously something or somebody could be religious in one of these senses but not the other. Likewise, in the abortion controversy, the disputants may disagree about whether the fetus is a person, but they may also have different criteria of personhood in mind.

Such problems frequently arise in ethics because ethical terms are usually general and abstract and hence subject to a variety of interpretations. In Chapter 1 we tried to show that the terms "ethics" and "morality" may be interpreted in different senses. That is why it is important to define one's terms. But it is also important to try to avoid question begging. Philosophers sometimes talk about the "primary" use of these terms, and other people may talk about what they consider to be the "real meaning" of education, of government, or of sports. References to such so-called "real" meanings are often ways of begging the question at issue or of loading the dice in favor of one interpretation or another. It seems better to try to map out the different meanings to see when one or another applies, or to clarify which meaning is under consideration. Sometimes we may have to stipulate what we mean, but we can at least avoid ambiguity and confusion by making our meanings clear.

PSYCHOLOGICAL OBSTACLES

We have pointed out that the obstacles to moral reasoning involve logical fallacies but that they have a very strong psychological appeal. Thus, it is important to recognize not only the logical fallacies involved but also the psychological reasons why we are misled by these fallacies. We cannot, of course, exhaust all psychological considerations, but we may point out a few.

One of the reasons we can make mistakes in reasoning is that we may have acquired bad habits. All of us tend to reason poorly about many things, exhibiting prejudices and expressing ourselves in slogans and clichés. We also tend to hold onto our beliefs because they are accepted by others and thus reinforced. Very often questions of truth do not even arise.

ROGER BACON
(c.1214–1292)
Four Idols

Now there are four chief obstacles in grasping truth, which hinder every man, however learned, and scarcely allow any one to win a clear title to learning, namely, submission to faulty and unworthy authority, influence of custom, popular prejudice, and concealment of our own ignorance accompanied by an ostentatious display of our knowledge . . . But, still worse, men blinded in the fog of these four errors do not perceive their own ignorance, but with every precaution cloak and defend it so as not to find a remedy; and worst of all, although they are in the densest shadows of error, they think they are in the full light of truth.

From: *Opus Maius*, Ch. I. Roger Bacon. R. B. Burke, trans. Philadelphia: University of Pennsylvania Press, 1928.

In moral reasoning there is perhaps an even more serious obstacle. We tend to identify with our moral beliefs, even more than with other kinds, because they express the things we believe are important in life. Questioning our moral convictions may require an alteration in our life-styles, whereas questioning the laws of physics, for example, does not seem to have the same direct implications for our personal lives. Thus, moral reasoning is affected by the same sorts of conservatism we find in other areas, but it faces the added problem of evoking strong personal feelings. That is why, it seems, a serious examination of morality requires both courage and humility: courage, because we may find that others oppose us in our beliefs; and humility, because we may need to recognize our mistakes. Courage and humility are moral virtues involved in any serious inquiry after truth.

CONCLUSION

In this chapter we have argued that the reasons given to block moral inquiry do not establish their intended conclusions. This is not to say, of course, that moral reasoning is always successful. The success of reasoning depends to a great extent on the quality of the reasoning and the willingness of the participants to become engaged in an honest quest for truth. That is why we have tried to show how various prejudicial beliefs about moral reasoning can block that quest, and how, in turn, these obstacles can be overcome.

The coming chapters examine various principles of moral reasoning which have been advocated and defended by ethical theory. We will see how these principles can be applied to practical issues. This will be the real test of moral reasoning, to see whether its promise can be realized, and to what extent. However, in this process we shall also discover that there is nothing magical about moral reasoning, any more than there is anything magical about reasoning in other fields. That is, in ethics, as elsewhere, it is possible to fail in reasoning, by failing to reach agreement, say, or by failing to find a solution to a particular problem. But we have also tried to show in this chapter that a temporary failure need not be interpreted as an insuperable obstacle. Even where differences of opinion exist, we can attempt to clarify the differences, locate the problems, and try to discover viable alternatives for finding solutions. Moral reasoning is not the whole of the moral life, of course, but it is a very important part of that life. We need to reason, and we need to reason as well as we can, but we also need to act upon that reasoning in an attempt to lead more effective and satisfying lives.

EXERCISES

What fallacies do you think are committed in the following arguments? In addition to naming the fallacy, try to explain how the argument goes wrong.

1. "First, we shall call a statement an 'ethical' one if it contains one of the following phrases: . . . 'is a desirable thing that;' 'is morally obligatory;' 'is one's moral duty.' . . . Of course, a statement is an ethical statement if it *denies* that something is desirable, morally obligatory, and so on." (From R. B. Brandt. *Ethical Theory*. Englewood Cliffs: Prentice-Hall, 1959.)

2. Look who's calling the frying pan black! You've done those things as much as I have.

3. Don't pay attention to Reverend Videotube. He's a fundamentalist minister who's simply out to make as much money as he can.

4. No one can know what is right or wrong. Science is value neutral. If you don't believe me, most of the scientists and philosophers of science in this century have said the same thing.

5. Of course euthanasia is morally wrong. The law simply cannot sanction killing, because judges and juries cannot know what goes on in the hearts or minds of men.

6. Because science is morally justified, the acts of scientists are also justified. Therefore, in the name of science, it is morally permissible for scientists to experiment on humans or animals, or to develop highly explosive devices capable of destroying the world.

7. Because athletics is not politics, athletics should be free from political considerations. It is therefore wrong for nations to boycott the Olympics.

8. It's a myth to think that gas heated homes are cheaper to heat than electrically heated homes. Electrically heated homes often have lower heat bills than gas heated homes. We have a study which says so.

9. All Croatians are mad bombers. I read about some Croatians in the newspaper who hijacked an airplane and threatened to blow it up. They are certainly terrorists who advocate violent means to free their homeland. The Contras, on the other hand, are freedom fighters.

10. Egoism is the doctrine that everyone always acts in his or her own self-interest. I know it is true because no example can prove it wrong. If you give me a case of altruism, I can always reinterpret it to fit my theory.

11. Teams should not be allowed to have designated hitters. That's not really baseball. That's not the way the game is played.

SUPPLEMENTARY READINGS

Bacon, Roger. *Opus Maius* (many editions).

Copi, Irving. *Introduction to Logic.* 7h ed. New York: Macmillan, 1986.

Engel, Morris. *With Good Reason: An Introduction to Informal Fallacies.* 2d ed. New York: St. Martin's Press, 1982.

Gauthier, David P., ed. *Morality and Rational Self-Interest.* Englewood Cliffs, N.J.: Prentice-Hall, Inc., 1970.

Hare, R. M. *The Language of Morals.* London: Oxford University Press, 1957.

Kahane, Howard. *Logic and Contemporary Rhetoric: The Use of Reason in Everyday Life.* 3d ed. Belmont, Calif.: Wadsworth, 1980.

Olson, Robert. *The Morality of Self-Interest.* New York: Harcourt, Brace & World, Inc., 1965.

Peirce, C. S. "The Fixation of Belief." *Popular Science Monthly,* 12, Nov. 1877:1–15.

Rand, Ayn. *The Virtue of Selfishness.* New York: New American Library, 1964.

Sartre, Jean-Paul. *Existentialism and Human Emotions* (many editions).

Sellars, W. and Hospers, John, eds. *Readings in Ethical Theory.* New York: Appleton-Century-Crofts, 1970.

Stevenson, C. L. *Ethics and Language.* New Haven: Yale University Press, 1944.

Urmson, J. D. *The Emotive Theory.* London: Hutchinson University Library, 1968.

Wall, George B. *Introduction to Ethics.* Columbus, Oh.: Charles Merrill Publishing Co., 1974.

Warnock, G. J. *Contemporary Moral Philosophy.* New York: St. Martin's Press, 1967.

Williams, Bernard. *Ethics and the Limits of Philosophy.* Cambridge: Harvard University Press, 1985.

PART TWO

ETHICAL
THEORIES

V

KANTIANISM AND UTILITARIANISM

Kantianism and utilitarianism have influenced twentieth-century moral philosophy in English speaking countries probably more than any other ethical theories. Immanual Kant, an eighteenth-century German philosopher, is regarded by many ethical theorists today as one of the most important figures in the history of moral philosophy, and utilitarianism, which was developed by the nineteenth-century British philosophers Jeremy Bentham and John Stuart Mill, seems to be debated by Anglo-American philosophers more than any other theory.

The prominence of a theory in academic, philosophic circles, of course, does not always reflect its popularity in other fields, or in ordinary life. Indeed, in ordinary moral reasoning, people do not usually think much about theory at all. They usually draw upon elements of several different theories without consciously advocating any of them. But, as we shall see, there are both Kantian and utilitarian elements contained in ordinary views about morality, and these theories have had an impact on reasoning in other fields as well. The Golden Rule, which says that we should do unto others as we would have them do unto us, expresses a principle of morality very similar to Kant's first principle of practical reasoning, and utilitarianism emphasizes the importance of considering the consequences of actions, as we often do. Utilitarian theory has also been applied in the fields of psychology and economics, in determining the values of consequences according to the principles of pleasure and pain, or according to individual preferences.

Each of these theories captures important elements of moral reasoning, but not the same elements. They are therefore incomplete, because neither of them takes into account all aspects of morality, and hence oversimplifies and overstates its claims. In the chapters that follow, we will explain moral theories that point up other important features which must be taken into consideration in developing our overall moral view. At this point, however, we wish to emphasize the importance of Kantian and utilitarian elements.

KANTIAN ETHICS

Kant is important in the history of ethics because he stressed two widely accepted principles of morality: (1) that moral judgments must be founded on universal rules, or upon rules which are applicable to all persons in the same way, and (2) that persons must always be treated with respect, as ends in themselves, and not be used as means only. He also emphasized the idea that moral principles and rules are superior to nonmoral considerations, and hence are not reducible to principles or rules of other kinds.

THE PRINCIPLE OF UNIVERSALIZABILITY

Kant placed great stress on the role of reason in determining what is morally right or wrong, on the importance of consistency in moral reasoning. Thus the main emphasis in his moral philosophy is on justice, on treating everyone the same according to moral rules, or on applying rules consistently to all cases.

Kant thought that a principle of justice is presupposed in moral reasoning. He felt that we use such a principle in making moral judgments, even though we may not be aware of it. We appeal to such a principle, for example, whenever we complain of being treated unfairly, thinking that others have been granted privileges denied to us, or that we are not judged by the same rules as they. By the same token, Kant felt that others should be judged by the same standards as we, or that the same rules should be applied to all.

IMMANUEL KANT
(1724–1804)
On Universalizability

I am never to act otherwise than so *that I could also will that my maxim should become a universal law*. Here now, it is the simple conformity to law in general, without assuming any particular law applicable to certain actions, that serves the will as its principle, and must so serve it, if duty is not to be a vain delusion and chimerical notion. The common reason of men in its practical judgments perfectly coincides with this, and always has in view the principle here suggested.

From: *Fundamental Principles of the Metaphysics of Morals*. Immanuel Kant. T. K. Abbot, trans. London: Longmans, Green, and Co., 1907.

Kant claimed that such a principle of justice is the first principle of moral reasoning. It has since been referred to as the principle of universalizability, or the principle of generalization, because it requires us to test moral rules by seeing if we can apply them universally, in the same way to all persons.

Expressing this principle, Kant said that we should obey those maxims which we can will to be universal laws. He believed that there is a moral law, analogous to the idea of natural law, and that laws are by definition universal. If there is a moral law, he reasoned, then it must be universal. To find out if a maxim or rule is a moral law, therefore, Kant concluded that we must test it for universality.

A simple example may help us to understand Kant's claim. Suppose that at lunchtime the university cafeteria line is quite long. I may think it is a good idea to sneak in front of the line because I am in a rush and hungry. Let's say then that I do it and get away with it. The next day I am in the line again, waiting my turn, and find that another person crashes the line ahead of me. I am annoyed and condemn that person for not waiting her turn. Somebody says that she is probably in a hurry, but I will not accept that excuse. Thus I am applying a rule to another person in a way that I do not apply it to myself. In this sense, I am inconsistent in holding that persons should not crash the line, even if they are in a hurry, and in also holding that it is permissible for me to crash the line when I am in a hurry. Kant believes that I should hold myself to the same rules I apply to others—or that, if I am willing to make an exception of myself, I should be willing to make an exception of others under the same circumstances.

Now one might think that the reason for having such a rule would be to avoid chaos, that is, that the consequences of having and obeying such a rule would be better than acting independently of it. That may be true, but that is a utilitarian consideration. Kant claims that consequences are irrelevant to determining our duty. He holds that our duties are not *hypothetical*, or dependent on consequences, but *categorical*, or independent of consequences. Thus, he says, "the moral worth of an action does not lie in the effect expected from it, nor in any principle of action which requires to borrow its motive from this expected effect."

Take the example of a person who considers breaking a promise because it is inconvenient to keep it. To justify the action, that person would need to accept the maxim that persons are justified in breaking promises when it is inconvenient to keep them. But could that person will this maxim to be a universal moral law? According to Kant, this maxim could not be willed to be a universal law, for such a law would defeat the purpose of promising. To promise is to assure that one will do what one says, even if it turns out to be inconvenient. To believe that one is justified in not keeping a promise, just because it is inconvenient, contradicts that claim. The action is wrong, therefore, not because failing to keep a promise may have bad effects, but because the maxim needed to justify it cannot be consistently maintained.

CATEGORICAL IMPERATIVES

If the moral law is universal in the sense that it applies to everyone, then everyone is also bound by the moral law and there are no exceptions to it. In maintaining that moral laws are "categorical," Kant meant that they are not subject to conditions or qualifications. Add to this consideration the idea that moral laws, unlike physical laws, are not descriptive but prescriptive, and one arrives at Kant's full blown notion of moral laws as "categorical imperatives."

IMMANUEL KANT
(1724–1804)
On Categorical Imperatives

But we can conceive an imperative where the end is governed by a condition which commands not subjectively but objectively. Moral imperatives are such. That, for example, 'Thou shalt not lie.' This is no problematic imperative, for in that case it would mean, 'If it harm thee to lie, then do not lie.' But the imperative commands simply and categorically: 'Thou shalt not lie;' and it does so unconditionally, or under an objective and necessary condition. It is characteristic of the moral imperative that it does not determine an end, but flows from the free will and has no regard to ends.

From: *Lectures on Ethics*. Immanuel Kant. Louis Infield, trans. New York: Harper Torchbooks, 1963.

Such commands, it seems, must be made by someone. But who gives these commands? According to Kant, everyone is sovereign in this respect, for everyone dictates the moral law to himself or herself. Kant spoke of this aspect of his doctrine as the "autonomy of the will," but he might also have called it the authority of conscience. In a sense, he thought that everybody should follow the dictates of his or her own conscience, but he also thought that everyone's conscience should be rationally formed. That is, Kant was not an individualist who thought that each person had a right to hold different moral opinions. Rather, he thought that, if consistent, each person would arrive at the same conclusions, namely the moral law itself.

In other words, Kant believes that, as rational agents, people are authors of moral rules. But, because he assumes that reason is the same for all people, they will all discover the same rules. Thus, for example, when anyone asks whether cheating on a test is permitted by the moral law, he or she will discover that it is not permitted. That is, everyone is capable of seeing that cheating on tests defeats the very purpose of testing, and hence that it cannot be willed to be a moral law.

FORMAL AND MATERIAL CONSIDERATIONS

When discussing his principle of universalizability, Kant said that he was interested in uncovering a formal principle of practical reasoning, not a material principle. The word "formal" is derived from the word "form," which roughly means the shape or structure of a thing, as opposed to the material out of which that thing is made. The word "formula" has the same derivation. Thus different things may be made of different materials but have the same shape or structure, or different things may be arranged according to the same formula. A formal principle, then, is meant to express a shape or form which can be applied to many different things under many different circumstances. It is like a pattern which may be used to block out pieces of dough for baking, or different fabrics in making clothes. Just as a contractor needs forms to give shape to poured concrete, Kant felt that we need (and have) a form for determining the moral law, namely his principle of universalizability. It applies to all laws or rules, regardless of the material or content of our reasoning, whether we are reasoning about keeping in line at the cafeteria, keeping our promises, or telling lies.

Kant thought that only a formal principle could provide the kind of universality or necessity that belongs to the moral law. Material considerations, including matters of empirical psychology, he felt, could produce only contingent or hypothetical conclusions. However, Kant also allowed that there are material considerations in moral reasoning. His second and material principle of practical reasoning is that we should always treat persons as ends in themselves and never as means only.

We have already pointed out, according to Kant's philosophy, that persons are the makers of the moral law, for persons are rational beings. As such, Kant reasoned, they must be treated with respect. In other words, on his view, the moral law is not only made by persons but also for persons, and all persons count equally under the law. This means that persons should never be regarded as mere property, or that they should never be used simply as instruments. We must always recognize and respect the humanity in others. While we may in a sense use and benefit from the actions of others, we must not violate their dignity as persons. We may rely on waiters and waitresses, but if we mistreat them, disregarding the fact that they are rational beings possessed of rights and dignity, we violate the principle, even if we give them a large tip. Kant even claimed that a murderer, about to be hung for a crime, deserves respect, and that the death sentence itself may be a respectful act because, in justice, the criminal deserves to be punished!

MORALITY AND MOTIVATION

In effect, Kant held that our motive or reason for doing what is right should be because it is right, because it is the morally right thing to do, and not because it will make us happy or bring us profit or success. On his view, we should obey the moral law because it is the moral law. To obey the moral law for any other reason would be a wrong reason. A person

---

IMMANUEL KANT
(1924–1804)
On Duty for Duty's Sake

On the other hand, it is a duty to maintain one's life; and, in addition, everyone has also a direct inclination to do so. But on this account the often anxious care which most men take for it has no intrinsic worth, and their maxim has no moral import. They preserve their life *as duty requires*, no doubt, but not *because duty requires*. On the other hand, if adversity and hopeless sorrow have completely taken away the relish for life; if the unfortunate one, strong in mind, indignant at his fate rather than desponding or dejected, wishes for death, and yet preserves his life without loving it— not from inclination or fear, but from duty—then his maxim has moral worth.

From: *Fundamental Principles of the Metaphysics of Morals*. Immanuel Kant. T. K. Abbot, trans. London: Longmans, Green, and Co., 1907.

might do what the law says to make a profit—for economic reasons—but, according to Kant, such a person would not have a right motive for acting, morally speaking, and such action would have no moral worth.

Imagine a lifeguard who saves the life of a drowning person. The lifeguard may do so for a variety of reasons: because, for example, he or she expects to be treated as a hero, or because he or she feels sorry for the drowning person. However, on Kant's view, these are not moral reasons. The only morally good reason or motive, Kant says, is *because* the moral law requires it. Thus, if the lifeguard not only does his or her duty, but also does it *because* it is his or her duty, the action then has moral worth.

In this sense, Kant held a very strict view of morality. He recognized, as most of us do, that persons may do good things for bad reasons, or at least for reasons that are not morally admirable, such as personal gain; but he also thought that doing one's duty from natural inclination, because it feels good, is lacking in moral worth. He did not want to rule out the possibility that a person may feel good for doing what is right, but he did not think that should be a person's reason for doing it. That is, feeling good may be a *consequence* of doing what is right, but, on Kant's view, it should not be the *motive*.

Kant also seemed to have in mind the idea that every science or discipline has its own principles and rules, and that answers within that science or discipline are determined only by those principles and rules—not by external considerations. Thus answers in mathematics, say, would be determined by mathematical principles and not principles of psychology. An answer to mathematics is not correct because, say, it makes someone feel good. Likewise, an answer in morality is correct because it is determined by moral principles and rules. It is not correct because it conforms to external or ulterior consider- ations. In this sense, one might say that morality, as any other discipline, is independent and self-contained. One conforms to the correct answers in any field because they are the correct answers in that field. Any other reason would be irrelevant or superfluous. Once one has the answer, there is nothing more to say.

Kant's idea that we should be motivated by a desire to obey the law, just because it is the law, has been the subject of much criticism. But certainly Kant was right in distinguishing good motives from bad motives. We know that persons can do good things from bad motives, or the right things for the wrong reasons. The main issue is whether a morally good person must always be motivated by a desire to uphold the moral law—or whether, indeed, such motivation is ever necessary. Kant's reasoning is that a morally good person is one who wants to do what is morally right. Therefore, such a person, having found what is right, does it because it is right.

Resolving Conflicts of Rules

Furthermore, because there are many moral laws, it would seem that they must sometimes conflict. That is, in order to obey one rule, the critics say, we must sometimes disobey another, in which case we simply cannot obey all the rules. The duty to preserve life, for example, may be in conflict with the duty to tell the truth. A doctor may lie to a patient in order to preserve the patient's life, because the doctor may have good reason to believe that the truth would be too much of a shock for the patient to bear. But if it is always wrong to lie, a doctor should never lie to a patient, even when lying is in the patient's best interest.

Kant stated explicitly that we should never lie, although he was not untroubled by this position. In view of apparent exceptions, how could he maintain this stance? Well, one way of avoiding conflict would be to maintain that all moral laws are negative. If all moral laws were in the form of "Don't lie" or "Don't cheat," then it would always be possible to obey all of them by never doing any of the prohibited acts. The doctor in our example would not be choosing to kill the patient by telling the truth, or by refusing to lie, although the patient may in fact die. Kant thought that we are responsible only for our acts, or what we choose to do, and that we are not responsible for unintended consequences. So a doctor who refuses to lie does not thereby choose to bring about a patient's death, although death may be a predictable result.

Another way of resolving conflicts of rules would be to hold that some rules take priority over others. Indeed, Kant could argue that such rules as "Don't lie" or "Don't kill" are fundamental moral laws which apply to all persons and cannot be overridden by less general, derivative, job-oriented rules, such as the ethics of physicians which bid them to save lives. Indeed, this second consideration may be combined with the first, for the fundamental laws may be negative and without exception, whereas derivative rules may be affirmative and have exceptions. A person may always refrain from lying or killing, but a person cannot always be telling the truth or saving lives.

A third possibility would be to include the exceptions in the rules, universalizing the exceptions, and thus making them part of the law. Instead of arguing that persons should never kill, say, one might argue that persons should never kill except in cases of self-defense, applying this exception to all cases and making it part of the law. That is, following Kant's principle, no one should be considered an exception unless anyone would be considered an exception for the same reason.

CONSEQUENCES AND ENDS

On Kant's view, consequences or subjective aims do not determine the law. Yet, when Kant gives examples, we find that he often refers to purposes or ends. He argues that fundamental human purposes would be defeated if moral laws were disobeyed. It would be wrong for persons to lie, cheat, break promises, or destroy property, he says, for such actions would defeat the purposes of communication, of making promises, or of owning property. It would be inconsistent, he felt, to allow someone to break a promise, or to refuse to pay a debt, on grounds of inconvenience or hardship, for such allowances, if universalized, would defeat the purpose of making promises, or of making contracts in which debts are incurred. In citing these purposes, he seems to give ground to the very kinds of teleological theories he claims to oppose.

IMMANUEL KANT
(1724–1804)
The Duty to Repay One's Debts

Suppose . . . the maxim of his action would be expressed thus: when I think myself in want of money, I will borrow money and promise to repay it, although I know that I can never do so. Now this principle of self-love or of one's own advantage may perhaps be consistent with my whole future welfare; but the question now is, is it right? . . . How would it be if my maxim were a universal law? Then I see at once that it could never hold as a universal law of nature, but would necessarily contradict itself. For supposing, to be a universal law . . . , the promise itself would become impossible, as well as the end that one might have in view in it, since no one would consider that anything was promised to him, but would ridicule all such statements as vain pretenses.

From: *Fundamental Principles of the Metaphysics of Morals*. Immauel Kant. T. T. Abbot, trans. London: Longmans, Green, and Co., 1907.

We also said that Kant's principle of universalizability is a formal principle, without content, which must be applied to material considerations. Kant spoke of material considerations in speaking of the dignity of persons, and he realized that his principle must be applied to maxims or rules of action. But utilitarians have argued that such maxims could arise only by considering consequences. Indeed, one might try to reconcile Kant's position with utilitarianism by holding that consequences must be taken into account in determining moral laws, but that once moral laws have been determined, the laws apply categorically, as Kant had maintained.

However, aside from the fact that moral reasoning, as any other kind of reasoning, must be applied to some subject matter, it is important to recognize that, as a bare minimum, rationality is determined by the consistency of beliefs. Whatever else Kant may have maintained, he insisted upon rationality, and hence upon consistency in moral thinking. He thought that simple justice requires treating all cases alike, or in judging all persons, including ourselves, by the same set of rules. This is a matter that certainly deserves emphasis, because so much injustice consists in maintaining double standards, in applying rules inconsistently, or in changing rules arbitrarily.

The principle of universalizability calls attention to the need to justify differential treatment. We are sometimes justified in treating different cases differently, but differences in treatment need to be justified by differences in the cases themselves. That is, as a matter of consistency, we should treat relevantly similar cases similarly and relevantly different cases differently. The problem of moral reasoning is then the problem of trying to determine when cases are relevantly similar or different. Following Kant's view, what counts as a reason for or against an act in one case must also count as a reason for or against an act in other cases as well.

For example, it seems proper in some circumstances to make exceptions for physically handicapped people. In many parking lots today there are special spaces for physically handicapped persons to park their cars. It seems reasonable to take physical difficulties into consideration where differences in physical ability are involved. However, it would be both demeaning and

unfair to have a different set of academic standards for the physically handicapped, for differences in physical ability need not affect academic performance. Such differences may require special aids in learning, but they would
not normally dictate different measures of achievement.

EXERCISES

1. Identify which view in each of the following pairs is more in accord
   with Kant's ethics. Explain why it seems more Kantian.

   a. Whenever a promotion is considered, Bob, a supervisor in a bank,
      always tries to figure out which employee needs the raise more.
      Alice, also a supervisor at a bank, claims that a supervisor should
      base promotions, not on need, but solely on job performance.
   b. Sally thinks that women's sports should be funded at a lower
      level than men's sports, even at large state supported universities.
      She argues that women's sports are less popular. Harry disagrees,
      saying this would be just another form of discrimination in a
      world that already discriminates against women too much.
   c. Ken believes that the United States should be engaged in a program
      of assassination against terrorists. Sam rejects this idea saying
      that such action would be against the law.
   d. Barbara believes that it is wrong, indeed barbaric, to execute
      children, that is, anyone under 18, for murder. Jane disagrees
      saying that, as long as they understand the crime they commit,
      they should be appropriately punished, even if that means
      execution.
   e. Jim believes that the workers in his plant should work faster
      because this would lead to greater profits. Todd, his partner,
      remarks that workers are not machines; moreover, a faster pace
      is likely to cause more accidents.

2. Critique each of the following on the basis of Kant's categorical
   imperative and/or his respect for persons principle.

   a. Felicia pads her expense account. She reasons that everyone does
      it; besides, she thinks she is not paid enough.
   b. Rich is not going to teach today. He says he needs a break and
      calls in sick.
   c. Pete promised to help his friend, Bob, fix his roof. But in the
      meantime, he was offered free tickets to see the Browns play
      Miami. Pete is trying to figure out how to break his promise
      without losing Bob's friendship.
   d. The local public housing authority evicts a ninety-two-year-old
      woman. She has broken several minor rules and is always late
      with her payment. They evict her, even though she is confused
      and doesn't know where to go. After the local newspaper runs
      a story on the issue, a spokesperson for the housing authority
      says that they treat all people equally.
   e. Dr. Burk sometimes lies to his patients, telling them they will
      be fine even though he knows that their diseases are terminal.
      He argues that although lying is usually wrong, it is proper to
      tell a lie to somebody who cannot handle the truth.

3. Explain what you think Kant means by his principle of universalizability. Give examples of actions you think cannot be justified by this principle and of actions that you think can.

4. Try to find examples of cases in which rules seem to conflict. Do you think Kant's principle can be used to resolve such conflicts, or do you think it is incapable of resolving them? Explain.

5. Try to find examples of cases in which people actually appeal to Kant's principle, or something like it, in justifying or criticizing acts.

6. How important do you think motives are in determining the morality of acts? Would you say that a person who had good motives, but failed in his or her attempts to do good, was a bad person? Would you say that a person who succeeds in doing good but has bad intentions is a good person? Do you think we can separate the rightness or wrongness of an act from the intention or motive of its agent?

7. Kant makes a distinction between formal and material considerations. Give examples to illustrate this distinction between form and matter. In reviewing these examples, do you think this distinction is an absolute distinction or a relative distinction? That is, do you think that form and matter are relative to context, such that what is form in one context may be matter in another? Are there then any *purely* formal considerations?

8. We have indicated briefly that utilitarians think Kant's principle needs to be supplemented by a consideration of consequences. Do you think Kant's principle can determine what is right or wrong without considering consequences, or do you think a consideration of consequences is necessary? Give examples to support your position. Consider, for instance, the question of whether doctors should tell the truth to their patients or whether doctors, or anybody, should ever lie.

9. Kant says we should respect persons as ends and never treat them as means only. Again, consider examples of such treatment and ask yourself how his principle applies to questions of human rights: the rights of women, for instance. Do you think such respect can be given without considering the consequences of our acts, without considering how persons will be helped or harmed by what we do?

10. Kant says we should always do our duty, once determined, without considering consequences. Could we not then consider consequences in determining what our duty is? Discuss.

11. Do you think that the moral law is self-contained? That is, do you think it is possible to determine moral duty without taking psychological considerations into account, or economic, or even physical considerations? Could the moral law be determined separately from what goes on in the rest of life?

Utilitarian Ethics

Utilitarianism claims that it is our duty to produce good consequences and to avoid evil consequences, insofar as this is possible. According to standard interpretations, we ought to produce "the greatest happiness for the greatest number of people." Thus, the utilitarian principle is sometimes referred to as "the greatest happiness principle."

Kant maintained that moral duties cannot be determined by considering the consequences of actions; by contrast, utilitarians have held that consequences and consequences alone determine what is morally right or wrong. The utilitarians have not rejected Kant's principle of universalizability altogether, however, for they too insist upon consistency in moral reasoning. Utilitarians have usually held that universalizability holds only for the first principle of ethics and not for subordinate rules, that is, that the principle of utility applies to everyone without exception, but that subordinate moral rules like "Don't lie" or "Don't steal" can have exceptions. Subordinate moral rules can have exceptions, they argue, because obedience to such rules does not always produce the best consequences.

Likewise, everyone counts in utilitarian calculations. As John Stuart Mill put it, everyone counts as one and no one counts as more than one. This means that, in calculating the consequences of actions, everyone affected by an action must be considered. In this way, utilitarians also agree with Kant in thinking that persons ought to be regarded as ends of action and not as means only.

There are then two important considerations in utilitarian theory: (1) determining the rightness or wrongness of actions according to the values of consequences, and (2) determining the values of consequences according to effects on people. Actions are judged to be right or wrong as means of achieving good or avoiding evil. But what sorts of consequences are good or evil?

In the classical, traditional forms of utilitarianism, as advocated by the nineteenth-century philosophers Bentham and Mill, utilitarianism was a hedonistic theory which maintained that consequences should be evaluated according to the principles of pleasure and pain. That is, they believed that consequences were good only if pleasurable, or bad only if painful, since they thought of pleasures and pains as components of happiness or unhappiness. But we should keep in mind that the utilitarians had a very broad conception of pleasure, for they included in its meaning all forms of satisfaction, whether intellectual, emotional, or physical.

Utilitarians believe that, no matter what we are doing, we must consider the happiness of everyone affected by our action. Suppose a student, Fay, plans to cut class. According to utilitarianism, Fay must consider the pleasures and pains this action will cause, not only now, but into the future. She must weigh the effects of her action for herself, her friends, relatives, and teachers. The pleasure she gets from cutting class must be balanced against the worry it causes her concerned parents, or the inconvenience it causes her classmates or teacher. Cutting class now may also make it more difficult for her to pass a test next week. On the utilitarian view, she is justified in cutting class only if doing so would produce a greater balance of pleasure over pain, for all persons concerned, than would any other alternative. In other words, if there is an alternative with better consequences, cutting class would be morally wrong.

J. S. MILL
(1806–1873)
On Pleasure and Utility

Those who know anything about the matter are aware that every writer, from Epicurus to Bentham, who maintained the theory of utility, meant by it, not something to be contra-distinguished from pleasure, but pleasure itself, together with an exemption from pain; and instead of opposing the useful to the agreeable or the ornamental, have always declared that the useful means these, among other things. Yet the common herd, including the herd of writers, not only in newspapers, and periodicals, but in books of weight and pretension, are perpetually falling into this shallow mistake.

From: *Utilitarianism*. J. S. Mill (many editions).

EGOISM AND ALTRUISM

Hedonistic utilitarianism, as advocated by Bentham and Mill, is usually distinguished from egoistic hedonism, as advocated by the ancient philosophers Democritus and Epicurus. Utilitarianism is a doctrine which emphasizes altruism or benevolence, whereas egoism is concerned only with a person's own self-interest. In advocating the good of all, or the good of society, utilitarianism obviously expresses a concern for persons other than one's self. However, it does not teach us to ignore ourselves either. To say that everyone counts as one means that we do not count more than other people, but it also means that we do not count less. According to utilitarianism, the view that morality is concerned only with the effects of actions on others is wrong, as is the view that we should be concerned only with ourselves.

Utilitarianism's appeal lies in advocating that we try to help people and not harm them, no matter who they are. It implies that we may be required to sacrifice our good for the good of others, if indeed that is necessary to promote the common good. Thus utilitarianism recognizes what Kant called the constraining aspect of morals, that morality sometimes requires us to do things we do not like to do, or things which require sacrifices from us. But it also recognizes that we have duties to ourselves, and hence should not neglect or harm ourselves unnecessarily.

Utilitarians have had some trouble trying to show that we have this sort of obligation, however, for their arguments in favor of the pleasure principle also seem to favor an egoistic interpretation. The reason behind the utilitarian view, in contrast to egoism, seems to be Kantian, that principles by their very nature apply to all cases, and hence to all persons the same way. If pleasure is the principle, then pleasure determines what is good, regardless of whose pleasure it is. That is, it would seem inconsistent to argue that my pleasure counts as a reason but that your pleasure does not. However, my pleasure may be a reason for my doing something in a way that your pleasure cannot be, for it may be the case that I can be motivated only by my pleasure and not yours. That is at least the kind of argument that has been presented by egoistic hedonists. In rebuttal, altruists have argued that we can indeed be motivated by altruistic concerns.

JOSEPH BUTLER
(1692–1752)
On Benevolence and Self-love

First, there is a natural principle of *benevolence* in man; which is in some degree to *society*, what *self-love* is to the individual. And if there be in mankind any disposition to friendship; if there by any such thing as compassion, for compassion is momentary love; if there be any such thing as the paternal or filial affections; if there be any affection in human nature, the object and end of which is the good of another, this is itself benevolence, or the love of another.

From: *Fifteen Sermons Preached at the Rolls Chapel*. Joseph Butler (many editions).

Psychological and Ethical Hedonism

There is some ambiguity in hedonistic theories, including utilitarianism, regarding the exact nature of the claims being made. Hedonists sometimes seem to argue that people always do in fact seek pleasure and avoid pain, and sometimes that they ought to do so. The former position is called psychological hedonism—a supposedly descriptive view—and the latter, ethical hedonism—a prescriptive view. Only the latter, it has been argued, is an ethical position, but it seems that empirical evidence can establish only the former view. The question then is: how can ethical hedonism be derived from psychological hedonism? How can we get a prescription from a description, or an "ought" from an "is?"

Upon investigation, the answer seems to be that many hedonists held neither of these positions. What Bentham and Mill seem to have held is

---

JEREMY BENTHAM
(1748–1832)
On Two Sovereign Masters

Nature has placed mankind under the governance of two sovereign masters *pain* and *pleasure*. It is for them alone to point out what we ought to do, as well as to determine what we shall do. On the one hand the standard of right and wrong, on the other the chain of causes and effects, are fastened to their throne. They govern us in all we do, in all we say, in all we think; every effort we can make to throw off our subjection, will serve but to demonstrate and confirm it . . . . The *principle of utility* recognizes this subjection, and assumes it for the foundation of that system, the object of which is to tear the fabric of felicity by the hands of reason and law. Systems which attempt to question it, deal in sounds instead of sense, in caprice instead of reason, in darkness instead of light.

From: *An Introduction to the Principles of Morals and Legislation*. Jeremy Bentham (many editions).

---

that "pleasure" *defines* "good," a view that the twentieth-century philosopher G. E. Moore attacks. This interpretation is called analytic hedonism. On this view, it follows that, whenever anyone says that a thing is good, they mean that it is pleasurable. It then follows from this that, if one wants to produce good, then one should aim at producing pleasure. It may not be true that everyone always does so; furthermore, it probably makes no sense to say they should. Because, by definition, goodness determines what people should or should not do, there is no need to prescribe doing what is good. That would be redundant. Of course, hedonists may be wrong in thinking that pleasure defines good, but it would be difficult to deny that the word "good" is sometimes used this way.

However, not all utilitarians have been hedonists. G. E. Moore, a twentieth-century utilitarian, argued against what he considered to be the classical utilitarian view: namely the view that "pleasure" defines "good." In doing so, he maintained that things other than pleasure could be good, and hence that things are not good because they are pleasureable. He maintained, for example, that beauty is good in and of itself, or intrinsically good. Thus Moore seemed to think there are several ultimate goods which persons should try to produce by their actions. But he was also a utilitarian in believing that actions are right or wrong according to their consequences, or according to the balance of good and evil produced.

Contemporary Utilitarianism

Most writings in contemporary utilitarianism seem to ignore the question of hedonistic versus nonhedonistic theories of value. The usual practice is to speak of units of good and evil produced by actions without specifying how good and evil are determined. Frequently, however, utilitarians speak of wants, desires, or preferences as the bases of evaluation, as if anticipated pleasures, enjoyments, or satisfactions determine ultimate value. There is no longer any one and only one utilitarian theory of ultimate value. We certainly cannot assume that all utilitarians are hedonists. But they do seem to share the idea that the rightness or wrongness of actions is determined by consequences. Debates among them tend to focus on how the utilitarian principle should be interpreted, or on how consequences should be weighed.

One reason why utilitarians today speak of desires or preferences, rather than pleasures, is that they seem to be easier to calculate. It is very difficult to know how much pleasure a person receives from a particular act. If Jim gives a gift to his brother, Fred, Jim may never really know how much happiness or pleasure Fred receives from the gift. Some people act very excited when they receive a gift, even if it gives them a small amount of pleasure, while others may show little emotion, even when they are quite pleased. It is not only difficult to know how much pleasure each person receives; it is even more difficult to compare the pleasures of one person with those of another. But we can tell whether a person prefers one thing to another, say, a watch over a portable T.V. If the cost is the same, and if Fred buys the watch instead of the T.V., we have reason to conclude that Fred prefers the watch. Thus for many philosophers (and economists who use utilitarian calculations) talk of preferences seems to be a way of avoiding many of the difficulties which arise in trying to calculate quantities of pleasure.

J. J. C. SMART
(1920–   )
On Classifying Utilitarians

An act utilitarian judges the rightness or wrongness of actions by the goodness and badness of their consequences. But is he to judge the goodness and badness of the consequences of an action solely by their pleasantness and unpleasantness? Bentham, who thought that quantity of pleasure being equal, the experience of playing pushpin was as good as that of reading poetry, could be classified as a hedonistic act utilitarian. Moore, who believed that some states of mind, such as those of acquiring knowledge, had intrinsic value quite independent of their pleasantness, can be called an ideal utilitarian. Mill seemed to occupy an intermediate position. He held that there are higher and lower pleasures. This seems to imply that pleasure is a necessary condition for goodness but that goodness depends on other quantities of experience than pleasantness and unpleasantness. I propose to call Mill a quasi-ideal utilitarian.

From: *An Outline of a System of Utilitarian Ethics.* J. J. C. Smart. Victoria, Australia: Melbourne University Press, 1961.

THE GREATEST GOOD

A great deal of controversy among utilitarians has been focused on the question of what is meant by "the greatest good for the greatest number." Aside from the question of how goodness itself may be determined, there is a question of whether the idea of the greatest good should be understood collectively or distributively. If the principle is interpreted collectively, then persons should try to produce the greatest good for society as a whole, but not necessarily for each and every individual. For example, a rise in unemployment may combat inflation, and this may help more people than it hurts; collectively speaking, this would be good for society as a whole, but the gain for the majority would be harmful for the minority. If the principle is understood distributively, the welfare of each individual should be maximized; but it may be impossible to do this.

There are also different ways in which the greatest good can be calculated, given various ratios of good and evil, and some philosophers have questioned whether the idea of a greatest good even makes sense. Considering the ratios of good and evil, would an act producing twenty units of good and ten units of evil be a better act than an act which produced five units of good and no units of evil? The former would produce the greater balance of good over evil, but the latter causes no harm at all. Utilitarians have usually opted for the interpretation which favors the greatest balance of good over evil, and hence would declare the first act the better of the two acts. However, this interpretation is by no means intuitively obvious.

Most contemporary utilitarians also seem to believe that the theory requires everyone to always perform the best possible act open to them at any given time. People are supposed to do the best possible thing. But critics of this doctrine have pointed out that it violates the traditional and ordinary moral distinction between acts that are duties and acts that are above and beyond the call of duty. That is, they think that utilitarianism, as usually interpreted, requires far too much. Normally we think of duties as minimal requirements, not maximal ones, such that, by doing our duty, we can "get by," so to speak. But heroes and saints do more than merely "get by," for they do much more than they are required to do. As a consequence, we give them medals or erect statues in their honor.

JEREMY BENTHAM
(1748–1832)
On the Principle of Utility

An action may then be said to be conformable to the principle of utility, or, for shortness' sake, to utility . . . when the tendency it has to augment the happiness of the community is greater than any it has to diminish it.

From: *An Introduction to the Principles of Morals and Legislation.* Jeremy Bentham (many editions).

However, it is possible to give utilitarianism a less stringent interpretation. Bentham, for example, in some passages of his work, says it is our duty to do more good than evil and not to do the greatest possible good. Hence, on this interpretation of the principle, there may at any time be several acts which are right or permitted, if each would produce more good than evil. Our utilitarian duty would be to do one or another of these acts, but no particular one, and we could always do more than our duty by doing our duty plus something more.

QUANTITIES OF GOODNESS

Jeremy Bentham is famous for his hedonistic calculus, the idea that we can actually calculate the quantities of good and evil produced by our actions. Mill apparently disagreed with Bentham, thinking that pleasures can be distinguished by quality as well as quantity. For example, Mill thought that intellectual pleasures are intrinsically better than physical pleasures. But the idea of qualitative distinctions has generally been rejected by utilitarians as being both unworkable and nonutilitarian. The idea that some things are qualitatively better than others seems to be a carryover in Mill's philosophy from traditional self-realization theory and its concept of a hierarchy of values, as we shall see. In any case, how can quantities of pleasure be measured?

Well, one of the criticisms of utilitarianism is that they cannot. There appears to be no way of determining units of pleasure and pain, or units of value generally. And if the quantification of the values of consequences cannot be accomplished, it seems that the utilitarian theory is unworkable, not only in practice, but in principle as well. It also appears that goods are incommensurable, for they are not all of the same kind and could not be measured against one another, even if there were units of each kind of good.

Some utilitarians have responded by arguing that we do in fact estimate, in a commonsensical and perhaps rough way, the relative values of the consequences of acts. If we do it, then it can be done. But how? Well, others have argued that, while we cannot determine units of value, we can rank the values of things ordinally in scales of preferences. Thus, for any given individual, it is possible to know that that individual prefers, likes, or enjoys some things more than others, and hence that, for that individual, some things have more value than others. But, even if so, there is a problem with intersubjective orderings. We may know who prefers what, but we may still not know how much weight to attach to these preferences, or whose preferences should be given greater weight.

General Criticisms of Utilitarianism

The above-mentioned issues have been debated by utilitarians, but they have also been raised by philosophers of other schools as criticisms of the utilitarian position. In addition to the matter of quantifying values, critics have pointed out that the consequences of actions go on forever, or at least that there is no way of knowing when or where they stop. So there simply is no way of knowing what the consequences of any action will be, even if we could predict the future, which, as the critics point out, we are not very good at doing. In answer to this, G. E. Moore and J. J. C. Smart, for instance, have argued that consequences are like "ripples in the pond." The consequences close at hand count most, for consequences tend to die out over time and distance. Although this is often true, it is not always true, for some acts seem to have great consequences for long periods of time, and even for great numbers of people. The writing of Mill's *Utilitarianism*, for instance, still has great influence today, and it is highly doubtful that anyone could have known that a century ago.

The main criticism brought against utilitarianism, however, is that it is an immoral philosophy, on the ground that, if one did what the theory says we should do, one would commit immoral acts. Readers have perhaps heard people criticized for being utilitarians, or for taking a utilitarian approach to life. This normally means that a person uses "the ends to justify the means," or that a person tries to justify immoral acts by an intended good outcome. In utilitarianism, of course, acts are judged to be morally right or wrong by their outcomes, but judging acts in this way seems to violate ordinary moral intuitions.

For example, critics have pointed out that utilitarianism can justify the punishment of an innocent person, or that it can justify the violation of a trust. If punishing an innocent person, by torture or execution, say, would produce more good than any alternative act, it would seem to be our utilitarian duty to punish that person. Or, if we could do more good by giving money to the poor, instead of repaying a debt, we ought not to repay the debt. But critics argue that it is simply wrong to punish an innocent person, or to refuse to pay a debt if one is able to pay. They argue that it is not consequences, or at least not consequences alone, which determine what is right or wrong.

103

ACT AND RULE UTILITARIANISM

In recent decades, a new type of utilitarianism has been developed which is supposed to meet these objections. This new type of utilitarianism is called "rule utilitarianism." We will not try to explain this theory in great detail in this chapter, because the considerations it raises will be treated again in subsequent chapters on moral rules. However, rule utilitarians have argued, in effect, that rules are necessary to supplement the principle of utility. These "middle rules," so to speak, which are less general than the principle, but more general than particular judgments, are supposed to be needed to apply the principle to particular cases. Thus, according to the rule-utilitarian view, the principle should be used to determine rules, and the rules in turn should be used to judge particular acts.

Thus rule utilitarianism is a two-staged or two-phased theory. It considers the process of justifying rules to be separate from the process of justifying particular acts. It thus seems to be able to meet the criticisms of opponents who claim that utilitarianism can justify punishing innocent persons, breaking promises, or refusing to repay debts. On the rule view, as J. S. Mill said, utilitarianism can justify moral rules as well as any other theory, and such rules are needed in making moral judgments. So utilitarianism can try to justify rules which prohibit the punishment of innocents or the breaking of promises on the ground that such rules will produce more good, or are likely to produce more good in the long run, than any other alternative.

Rule utilitarianism is thus distinguished from act utilitarianism. According to act utilitarianism, each and every individual act is supposed to be judged on its own merits: that is, according to its consequences, as compared with other alternative acts. According to rule utilitarianism, by contrast, individual acts are supposed to be judged, not by their consequences, but by moral rules. However, rule utilitarianism is a type of utilitarianism and should not be confused with Kantianism, for the rules of rule utilitarianism are supposed to be justified by consequences, whereas the rules of Kantianism are not. A rule utilitarian would justify a rule against stealing, for example, because having such a rule, or obeying it, would produce better consequences than not having such a rule, or not acting upon it. A Kantian, on the other hand, would justify a rule against stealing by arguing that it is consistent with, and even required by, the very concept of property or ownership: to say that stealing is permitted is self-contradictory, regardless of any consequences stealing may have.

When confronted with the alternative of stealing, therefore, an act utilitarian would need to consider the consequences in each case. What would happen if I stole this watch? What would happen if he took that money? Notice that acts of stealing, or of any other kind, are not held to be right or wrong because they are acts of that kind. An act of stealing may be right in one case but wrong in another, depending on its consequences, as compared with the consequences of alternative acts. But, for a rule utilitarian, acts are judged to be wrong because of their kinds, for example, because they are acts of stealing or lying. That is what it means to say that an act falls under a rule, for a moral rule tells us that some kind of act is right or wrong, and an individual act is judged to be right or wrong because it is an instance of that rule. But, presumably, rules also need to be justified, and rule utilitarians argue that moral rules must be justified by the principle of utility, by showing that better consequences will be produced by acting on a rule than would be produced by acting without it.

J. J. C. SMART
(1920–   )
On Hedonistic Act Utilitarianism

I shall take the paradigm of utilitarianism to be hedonistic act utilitarianism, a theory that has come down to us through Jeremy Bentham and Henry Sidgwick . . . According to this paradigm, what it is right to do on any occasion is to maximize the total happiness (now and at all future time) of all sentient creatures, whether humans, other animals, or extraterrestrials (should we ever have to do with these last). The theory has an obvious appeal. What could be better than to maximize happiness? Any theory that was not equivalent to hedonistic act utilitarianism would imply that on occasion one should make the world less happy than it would otherwise be.

From: "Utilitarianism and Its Implications." J. J. C. Smart. *New Directions in Ethics.* J. P. DeMarco and R. M. Fox, eds. Boston: Routledge & Kegan Paul, 1986.

Act utilitarians like J. J. C. Smart have accused the rule utilitarians of "rule worship." Act utilitarians believe that the principle should be applied directly to each act. They argue that an act is right only if that act produces more good than any other alternative and not because it conforms to a rule. Rules, Smart argues, are at best superfluous, for if they enjoin us to perform the act with the best consequences, they do not produce a result different from act utilitarianism, and they are at worst nonutilitarian, for if they enjoin us to act in a way that does not produce utility, they violate the principle.

A third view, called cooperative utilitarianism, argues against the act view in maintaining that utility cannot be maximized by looking at acts in isolation from one another but only by looking at the consequences of acts performed in a mutually supportive way. It holds that the best consequences cannot be produced unless people cooperate in bringing them about. This view is in some ways similar to the rule view, for the rule view also considers the conjunction of acts in determining consequences, but cooperative utilitarianism does not require rules. What it does require is that individuals be open to cooperation with others in trying to produce the greatest amount of good.

CONCLUSION

Hedonistic utilitarianism is appealing because it focuses on a class of goods, namely pleasures, which everyone seems to want. But there is some reason to think that not all goods are pleasures, or at least that pleasurableness does not always make things good, as ideal utilitarians have maintained. The appeal to consequences also seems reasonable, even commonsensical, until one reflects on the difficulties involved in calculating the consequences of actions. We have pointed out, for instance, that it is difficult to quantify and predict consequences, and it is also difficult to know at what point a consideration of consequences should stop. And when it comes to pleasures or happiness, it is doubly difficult to predict what will make people happy.

A consideration of consequences seems more appropriate in cases where the effects of actions are relatively easy to calculate and where the preferences of the persons affected are well known. It also seems appropriate *after* the basic rights or duties of persons have been taken into consideration, or when it can be shown that two or more alternative courses of action are morally permitted. It may also be relevant when it becomes difficult to make a moral determination on other grounds.

Act utilitarianism is much simpler and perhaps theoretically more satisfying than rule utilitarianism, but, for reasons given, it also seems more difficult to apply. Rule utilitarianism modifies utilitarianism in a way that makes it more complicated, but that also brings it closer to ordinary patterns of moral reasoning. The rules of rule utilitarianism are the kinds of rules regularly cited by people when they seek to justify or criticize acts. Nonetheless, a principle is needed to justify rules, to determine when rules apply or have exceptions, and to determine what should be done in cases where there are no rules. Thus, while rule utilitarianism recognizes the importance of subordinate rules, it also recognizes the importance of principle in providing a decision-procedure in ethics.

EXERCISES

1. Return to Exercise 1 on Kant. In looking at each pair of opinions, determine whether utilitarian standards are being applied. Can act-utilitarian opinions be distinguished from rule utilitarian views?

2. Return to Exercise 2 on Kant, and critique each case according to the utilitarian principle. Do you think that, in any of these cases, either an act utilitarian or rule utilitarian would reach the same conclusion as a Kantian?

3. Try to determine whether the following acts (or judgments) are justified or prohibited by the utilitarian principle. Do you think a rule utilitarian might reach a different answer than an act utilitarian would? Discuss.

   a. Harry argues that high unemployment should be tolerated because it keeps down the cost of labor and makes American goods cheaper. This makes American products competitive with Japanese goods, he says.
   b. Linda believes that books criticizing religion should be banned from local libraries. She says that people are very sensitive about their religious convictions and that conflict between religions, which such books cause, produces great strife.
   c. The police catch a person who claims to have planted a bomb in an abortion center in another city. The person tells them that the bomb will go off at 11:00 A.M., the busiest time for the center, but he refuses to tell them where the bomb is. One of the officers decides to torture the person in order to find out where the bomb has been placed. He thinks he can do this without anyone knowing.

If the prisoner reports his action, he figures he can simply deny
it.

d. Matt and Lena give more attention to one of their daughters than
    to another. They argue that their older daughter has much more
    potential than the younger, that she will benefit more from the
    attention, and, therefore, that she will be able to do more good.

e. When returning home each night, Alan always walks across his
    neighbor's lawn. He has little reason to fear being caught, and
    he figures it doesn't matter anyway, because there is already a
    path worn in the lawn. He knows that the owner of the house
    hates the fact that people take short cuts across his lawn, but when
    the owner complains, Alan commiserates with him, saying that
    people should have more respect for property.

4. Try to answer the following questions in view of the material covered
    in this chapter.

    a. Utilitarianism is said to be a consequentialist ethical theory because
        it judges actions according to the values of consequences. But
        how does it evaluate consequences; i.e. how does it determine
        which consequences are good or bad?

    b. Supposing one knows which consequences are good or bad; how
        does utilitarianism propose that we determine how we should
        act; i.e. how, according to this theory, are we supposed to
        determine what is right or wrong?

    c. What similarities are there between utilitarianism and Kantianism?
        What are the differences between these theories? Do you think
        that utilitarian considerations are opposed to Kant's philosophy,
        or do you think they are consistent with it?

    d. What problems arise in trying to judge actions on the basis of
        consequences? Do you think that these problems pose a strong
        objection to either the truth of utilitarian theory or to its practicality?

    e. What is the difference between act and rule utilitarianism? How
        does rule utilitarianism seem to combine Kantian and utilitarian
        considerations?

    f. What objections can an act utilitarian bring against rule
        utilitarianism? What objections can a rule utilitarian bring against
        act utilitarianism?

    g. G. E. Moore is famous for his objections against hedonistic
        utilitarianism. What was G. E. Moore's position?

    h. How does hedonistic utilitarianism differ from ancient egoistic
        hedonism or Epicurianism? What arguments are there for thinking
        that human acts are not exclusively self-interested?

    i. What is the difference between psychological hedonism and ethical
        hedonism? Is there a third alternative to these views?

    j. How does J. S. Mill's conception of hedonism seem to differ from
        Bentham's? Do you think Mill has any justification for his position?

    k. Try to think up cases in which utilitarian considerations are
        decisive. Explain each of these examples as fully as you can,
        pointing up how the arguments turn on utilitarian grounds.

    l. Can you think of any examples in which utilitarian considerations
        are not decisive or cases in which you think they may be irrelevant
        or even immoral?

    m. Do you think that moral rules can be justified on utilitarian
        grounds? Examine several moral rules and ask yourself whether

we should obey them because of the consequences of obeying or not obeying? Once we have such rules, do you think we should simply obey the rules, or do you think we should once again consider consequences in determining whether we should obey? In other words, do you think that exceptions to moral rules can be justified on the basis of consequences? Give examples.

SUPPLEMENTARY READINGS

Bayles, Michael, ed. *Contemporary Utilitarianism.* New York: Doubleday and Co., 1968.

Bentham, Jeremy. *An Introduction to the Principles of Morals and Legislation.* Chs. 1–4 (many editions).

Broad, C. D. *Five Types of Ethical Theory.* Ch. 5. London: Routledge & Kegan Paul Ltd., 1930.

Kant, Immanuel. *Fundamental Principles of the Metaphysics of Morals* (many editions).

Korner, Stephen. *Kant.* Baltimore: Penguin Books, 1955.

Lyons, David. *Forms and Limits of Utilitarianism.* Oxford: Oxford University Press, 1965.

Mill, John Stuart. *Utilitarianism* (many editions).

Moore, G. E. *Principia Ethica.* London: Cambridge University Press, 1903.

Paton, H. J. *The Categorical Imperative.* New York: Harper & Row, Publishers, 1965.

Regan, Donald. *Utilitarianism and Co-operation.* Oxford: Oxford University Press, 1980.

Ross, Sir William David. *Kant's Ethical Theory.* New York: Oxford University Press, 1954.

Sidgewick, Henry. *The Methods of Ethics.* New York: Macmillan, 1874.

Singer, Marcus George. *Generalization in Ethics.* New York: Random House, 1961.

Smart, J. J. C. and Williams, Bernard. *Utilitarianism: For and Against.* London: Cambridge University Press, 1973.

CHAPTER

VI

SELF-REALIZATION AND NATURAL LAW

The theories studied in this chapter are not taught or studied as much in academic circles today as are Kantianism and utilitarianism, but they have had considerable influence upon western civilization. Moreover, by considering these theories, we will be able to expand our conception of moral reasoning and moral life.

These theories—self-realization and natural law—should strike us as familiar, once we become acquainted with their basic ideas. Self-realization theories, for example, claim that all of us have an obligation to improve ourselves as individuals and as social beings. They enjoin us to "realize" or "actualize" our potentialities.

Natural law theories, in turn, are founded upon conceptions of "human nature," or upon God's law. They are usually also self-realization theories which hold that we should express our talents according to our nature as human beings, or become what God has created us to be.

We should notice similarities between these theories and Kantianism or utilitarianism, but there are also important differences. Mainly, the theories studied in this chapter will call attention to the importance of personal development and of understanding one's place in the natural world.

SELF-REALIZATION THEORY

Self-realization theory is one of the oldest types of ethical theory, and it continues to have a strong hold on moral thinking even today. It dates back at least as far as the ancient philosophers, Plato and Aristotle. Throughout history it has provided a theoretical basis for the ethics of several of the world's major religions, and, in this century, for the psychology of several so-called "humanistic" schools. The main idea of the theory is expressed in popular slogans which tell us to be all that we can be, that we should "grow" as persons, or that we should actualize our potentiality. Whether we know it or not, when we criticize people for failing to use their talents, we are probably criticizing them on the basis of self-realization philosophy. Or when we praise people for their achievements, we are praising them on similar grounds.

However, it doesn't make much sense to say that people should do whatever they have the ability to do, for some of the things they can do are rather silly, rude, and even morally wrong. A moral theory which did not prohibit anything would not be much of a theory. That is probably why many people today are opposed to the recent form of self-realization theory characterized by the saying "Do your own thing," for one's "own thing" may be morally wrong. Traditional self-realization theories, however, do not hold that people are permitted to do anything they wish.

Types of Self-Realization Theory

Self-realization theories can be classified in a number of ways. Some, for example, are egoistic in focusing on individual achievement and others altruistic—or at least social—in holding that persons have responsibilities to people other than themselves. The nineteenth-century German anarchist, Max Stirner, brought individualist thinking to its extreme. He viewed society solely as a means to his own benefit. He only recognized one moral law, the development of his own power. Other individualists, such as the economist and social critic, F. A. Hayek, view self-centered individual achievement, especially in the economic realm, as the best path toward social advancement. Plato and Aristotle, on the other hand, often spoke of individual development based on self-interest, but they also felt that individuals had responsibilities to the state, and that persons could develop best within a well ordered society. Likewise, the nineteenth-century philosopher, Hegel, spoke of individuals as parts of society, pointing out that society as a whole develops throughout history, actualizing *its* potentiality.

Thus, in self-realization theory, the relationship between the individual and society has often been regarded as a relationship between part and whole, as arms and legs, for example, are parts of the body. In such theories, society was not thought of as simply a collection of individuals. Morality was founded on the idea that people are, or ought to be, team players, rather than upon the idea that they are, or ought to be, in competition with one another. That is, instead of thinking they should improve themselves in order to win over others, persons were supposed to use their talents to cooperate with others, in order to improve society as a whole. They were also supposed to measure their success, not by comparison with the accomplishments of others, but according to whether they were doing their best.

For example, Philip, a music student, practices music faithfully every day, but he does so in order to become a better musician than anyone else in his family, all of whom are musically inclined. He is motivated, in other words, by competition. Suppose his brother, John, also practices faithfully, but he does so in order to become as good a musician as he can be. He is motivated by the desire to develop his own talent, and doesn't worry about whether he is doing better or worse than Philip. Now suppose further that Philip and John have a sister, Jenny, who not only practices her music regularly but also tries to cooperate with others in musical practices and performances. Let's say she even works to support the local orchestra by selling tickets and soliciting contributions. Indeed, she is also engaged in political action to improve opportunities for others, for she realizes that individual achievement is dependent on social opportunity, just as the good of society depends on individual achievement. Philip, John, and Jenny are all interested in self-realization, but Philip is mainly interested in winning, John appears to think that he is responsible only to himself, and Jenny believes that she needs to coordinate her efforts with those of others, in order to benefit society as a whole.

Self-realization theories can also be distinguished by the number of goods, or the specific kinds of goods, that they feel ought to be realized. A self-realization theory might be monistic, holding that there is ultimately only one kind of good, or pluralistic, in holding that there are many ultimate goods. The nineteenth-century philosopher, Frederick Nietzsche, for example, seemed to think that individual creativity was more important than any other value, and hence that even pleasure or happiness ought to be sacrificed in its name. In some ways his philosophy represented nineteenth-century romantic idealism: the celebration of individual achievement, a dedication to artistic goals, and hence an acceptance of the idea that persons should suffer to achieve their ends. His idea of "the will to power" can be interpreted as a desire for self-expression, a desire to actualize individual potentialities by discovering and following personal standards of excellence, as, presumably, a creative artist does.

FRIEDRICH NIETZSCHE
(1844–1900)
The Will to Power

The noble type of man regards *himself* as a determiner of values; he does not require to be approved of; he passes the judgment . . . he knows that it is he himself only who confers honour on things; he is a *creator of values*. He honours whatever he recognizes in himself: such morality is self-glorification. In the foreground there is the feeling of plenitude, of power, which seeks to overflow. . . . The noble man honours in himself the powerful one, him also who has power over himself . . . who takes pleasure in subjecting himself to severity and hardness, and has reverence for all that is severe and hard.

From: "The Transvaluation of Values." Friedrich Nietzsche. *Great Traditions in Ethics*, 2d ed. Albert, Denise, and Peterfreund, eds. New York: American Book Company, 1969.

Self-realization theories are often deceptive in this respect, for many of them seem to be both monistic and pluralistic. Plato, for example, says that the ultimate goal is "goodness itself," and Aristotle says it is "happiness."

These sorts of statements make these theories seem monistic. But when one looks at them more closely, one discovers that the ultimate good cannot be achieved, or even be understood, except by reference to a number of other more specific goods.

Thus Plato claims that we cannot define goodness itself, but he does think we can understand specific kinds of goods which, he says, "participate" in it. And, as soon as Aristotle says that happiness is the end of human action, he calls it a truism and immediately tries to find out what kinds of things people actually want or need. So theories that appear to be monistic in holding that there is only one ultimate end often turn out to be pluralistic in holding that there are many parts or aspects of this end, or different means of achieving it.

In any case, because one may suppose that there are many goods appropriate to human life—or many ways in which people can actualize their potentialities—self-realization theories often face the problem of having to order the goods, determining an order of importance. In a system which holds that there are many ultimate goods, the problem of conflicting goods must be faced.

THE HIERARCHY OF GOODS

Philosophers who have argued in favor of self-realization theory have usually supposed that some ends are higher or more noble than others. The popular idea that there are higher and lower goods is in keeping with this kind of philosophy; intellectual things, for example, or artistic things, are usually thought to be higher than nonintellectual or nonartistic things. This philosophy is also in keeping with the popular belief that some species of things are more important than other species, that people, for instance, are more important than animals or plants. When people argue about whether or not a fetus is a person, they obviously attach importance to something's being a person, as opposed to its being a mere organism, say, or an inanimate object. In traditional religious ethics, God and angels were thought to be higher than people.

SAINT AUGUSTINE
(354–430)
On Evil

What is called evil in the universe is but the absence of good. In the bodies of animals, disease and wounds mean nothing but the absence of health . . . All things that exist, therefore, seeing that the Creator of them all is supremely good, are themselves good. But because they are not, like their Creator, supremely and unchangeably good, their good may be diminished or increased. But for good to be diminished is an evil, although, however much it may be diminished, it is necessary, if the being is to continue, that some good should remain to constitute the being.

From: *Enchiridion*. Saint Augustine. J. F. Shaw, trans. *The Works of Aurelius Augustine*, Rev. Marcus Dods, ed. Edinburgh: T. & T. Clark, 1892.

In arguing that people ought to be all that they are capable of being, therefore, self-realization theorists usually held that it is better to be some kinds of things than others, and that, even within species, the realization of some kinds of goods is better than others. They thought that the highest capacity of humans was rationality. People ought to be rational, they argue, because it is better to be rational than irrational, but also because, by nature, people are rational animals. They are the only animals capable of rationality, and by being rational, they more fully realize the potentiality of their species than they would if they were not rational.

According to the same line of thinking, evil is thought to be the privation of good, or the lack of goodness which something could possess. If, for example, rationality is a good which persons can possess, then it would be a fault to lack rationality. That is, irrationality, relative to humans, is evil. It is the lack or privation of a good they are capable of possessing.

On the other hand, in holding a pluralistic view, some self-realization theorists have argued that it would be morally wrong to dedicate oneself to one and only one limited good—even if that good were reason itself. Aristotle, for example, who defined people as "rational animals," recognized that people require animal goods, as well as goods that are specifically appropriate to them as people. Even though he thought of rationality as the highest of human goods, he also thought that a life of reasoning alone, or a life of intellectual contemplation, was suitable only for gods. Thus, on his view, an artist who sacrificed all else in the name of art, or a scientist who sacrificed people in the name of science, would be guilty of moral fault, for she or he would be mistaking one human good, or one part of human life, for the whole.

The Harmony of Goods

The ancient Greeks particularly were much impressed by the ideas of harmony and moderation, as opposed to the ideas of chaos and excess. Harmony and moderation—the measured or ordered life—seemed to them to be on the side of the good, and they thought that reason provided this harmony or order. Thus Plato argued that justice is "the harmony of the soul according to reason," and Aristotle claimed that virtue consists of finding "the mean between extremes." On both views, reason orders actions to prevent conflict, to produce greater cooperation among individuals, and to coordinate acts. Without such harmony, the realization of some potentialities would be blocked.

For example, a person who is addicted to eating may find it very difficult to study, for eating, or the desire to eat, may repeatedly break the concentration of study. A person who is a workaholic may be successful on the job, but that same person may neglect family responsibilities, or even his or her own personal health. Likewise, a person who spends most of his or her time sleeping or watching T.V. is likely to have little time to pursue a career. In other words, an exclusive dedication to any one kind of good prevents them from realizing other goods which they are also capable of achieving.

Thus Plato spoke of the good soul as a harmonious soul, a soul which is not in conflict with itself. Aristotle spoke of ethics as a mode of reflection according to which we can plan our actions over a long period of time, arranging our activities so they do not conflict with one another or with the activities of other persons. On both these views, at least part of the function of reason consists in allotting different times to different activities, such as eating at mealtime and sleeping at bedtime. It also consists in ordering the actions of different people, so that each person is doing his or her allotted task, contributing to the greater good of society as a whole. The just state, according to Plato, is the well ordered state. The chief fault of individuals, or even of classes of people, he thought, is insubordination.

PLATO
(c.427–347 B.C.)
On Insubordination

Must not injustice be a strife which arises among the three principles—a meddlesomeness, and interference, and rising up of a part of the soul against the whole, an assertion of unlawful authority, which is made by a rebellious subject against a true prince, of whom he is the natural vassal—what is all this confusion and delusion but injustice, and intemperance and cowardice and ignorance, and every form of vice?

From: *Republic*, Bk. IV. Plato. *The Dialogues of Plato*. B. Jowett, trans. New York: Oxford University Press, 1892.

The idea of insubordination today has an authoritarian connotation, carrying with it the idea of disobedience to some authority. Strictly speaking, however, it means not making something subordinate which should be subordinate, or not keeping things in their appropriate order. But it is true that Plato and Aristotle were Greek aristocrats who, as the name "aristocrat" implies, thought that society should be ruled by the "best" people. The best people, or those most fitted to rule, on Plato's view, were "philosopher kings." Hence Plato's philosophy is often criticized today for being authoritarian, and more recent, twentieth-century versions of self-realization theory have tended to be more democratic. The American philosopher, John Dewey, for example, who was much like Aristotle in being a pluralist, was also more individualistic and more democratic in his conception of political life.

SELF-REALIZATION VERSUS UTILITY

Self-realization theorists have not been opposed to the idea of pleasure or happiness, but they have not thought of pleasure as the specific end of human action, or as the one quality which makes right acts right. Aristotle, for instance, thought that the direct pursuit of pleasure was not appropriate to human beings. People, he felt, are capable of higher pursuits, such as intellectual activities, although he also thought that such activities would be pleasant or satisfying. Thus he thought that people should aim at achieving specifically human goals and that pleasure or satisfaction would be a byproduct of such activities.

ARISTOTLE
(384–322 B.C.)
On Happiness and the Function of Man

Presumably, however, to say that happiness is the chief good seems a platitude, and a clearer account of what it is is still desired. This might perhaps be given, if we could first ascertain the function of man. For just as for the fluteplayer, a sculptor, or any artist, and, in general, for all things that have a function or activity, the good and the 'well' is thought to reside in the function, so would it seem to be for man, if he has a function.

From: *Nichomachean Ethics.* Aristotle. *The Works of Aristotle.* W. D. Ross, ed. Oxford: The Clarendon Press, 1925.

Self-realization theories are like utilitarianism in being teleological. However, traditional self-realization theories were founded upon a conception of definite end-states which people are supposed to achieve by their actions, whereas utilitarianism is open-ended in sanctioning whatever produces the greatest amount of happiness. The utilitarian, John Stuart Mill, apparently tried to combine both of these ideas in claiming that some kinds of pleasure are "higher" or better than others, but he did not make it clear how qualitative differences between pleasures offset quantitative considerations.

Speaking as if he were a self-realization theorist, Mill said that intellectual pleasures are higher than bodily pleasures, but he did not claim that such higher pleasures are necessarily more pleasing than lower pleasures. By contrast, traditional self-realization theorists usually viewed "lower" bodily goods or needs as a necessary precondition or means to higher mental or spiritual goods. They did not need to weigh quantities of the one kind against quantities of the other. Because, for example, we need to eat and sleep in order to pursue intellectual activities, then eating and sleeping are means to those ends. There appears to be no need to measure quantities of eating and sleeping against quantities of intellectual activity, nor does it seem possible to do so, as these appear to be incommensurable goods.

TELEOLOGY AND CONSEQUENTIALISM

Traditional self-realization theories were usually much more clearly teleological than utilitarianism in being concerned with the goals persons intend to achieve by their actions and not with consequences as such. Ends and consequences are not identical, for, although ends may be looked upon as intended consequences, consequences need not be intended. It is also true that persons do not always succeed in producing the consequences they intend. So there seems to be a real difference in judging actions according to ends or intentions, on the one hand, and in judging them according to consequences, on the other.

Many of the consequences of actions are accidental or unintended. Parents may take their children to a movie, thinking that they themselves will not enjoy it, but they may find the movie more entertaining than they had imagined it would be. Their intention is to please their children, not themselves, but their action has the consequence of being pleasing to themselves as well. Sometimes, however, when we intend to help others, we harm them instead, or we may inadvertantly harm ourselves, even when we think we are doing ourselves some good. Thus the difference between a teleologist and a utilitarian is that the teleologist focuses on the intention as the factor that determines the morality of the act, and the utilitarian focuses on the consequences. Intentions also tend to be determinate or specific, whereas consequences are indeterminate. Persons usually know what they intend to accomplish by their actions, but they cannot always know what the consequences of their actions will be.

However, goals and consequences are related in a number of ways. Goals, we said, may be spoken of as intended consequences. We also judge the success or failure of an intention by looking to see what is actually done. But sometimes we distinguish the goodness or badness of an act, based upon a consideration of its consequences, from the goodness or badness of the agent who performs that act, based upon his or her intentions. That is, we may say that someone is a good person, for intending to do well, even though that person does bad things—by failing to do what is intended.

Intentions and consequences may also be combined in judging acts, as we shall see soon, when we discuss the Thomistic doctrine of "double effect." According to this doctrine, an agent may be held culpable for performing an act with bad consequences, even if those consequences were not intended, if the unintended consequences were known or predictable, and if, say, they were also severe. A person who drives recklessly may not intend to do harm, but he or she may know, or be able to predict, that harm is a likely consequence of reckless driving. Thus, the law often holds people responsible for reckless acts, or for negligence, even though they intend no harm.

THE LESSONS OF SELF-REALIZATION THEORY

Self-realization theory may be criticized because of the demands it makes upon individuals, because its standard is excellence. We hear much talk today about the need to avoid stress and how we can make ourselves feel good by lowering our expectations or reducing our goals. We are sometimes told to be nonjudgmental, to be forgiving of our faults, and even to meditate, exercise, or diet as an easy way to a better life. Although such advice may help us avoid excess, it tends to miss the point, so central to self-realization theory, that there can be deep satisfaction in achievement. There is satisfaction to be found in the struggle to achieve a goal, as well as in the accomplishment of it—as a student, a parent, or in a profession or even a hobby.

Self-realization theory also tells us that, aside from making us feel good, achievement is a realization of our powers as human beings. Furthermore, developing our talents enables us to help others. Many positions of responsibility require appropriate training. For this reason, self-realization theory calls attention to the fact that people need opportunities to grow and develop. Societies can be criticized if they fail to provide such opportunities, or if they deny them to certain classes of people. Thus, many self-realization theorists have emphasized the need for giving social support to individual development. As a society provides a better support system, in education, jobs, and recreation, individuals are likely to gain satisfaction from using their talents.

In resolving moral problems, self-realization theorists ask which course of action best contributes to the realization of human potentiality. In so doing, they judge actions teleologically, as means to ends. Ends or goals may be viewed as individual or social, depending upon the theory, although individual and social goals are often viewed as being interdependent. Some theories hold that there is one ultimate or supreme goal of moral action; however, because people are capable of doing many different kinds of things, the good life has also been thought to consist of a harmony or balance among many goods. On this view, acts are not judged in isolation from other acts, but as they fit into a plan of action, or as they may be coordinated with other acts. And because some goals seem more appropriate to humans than others, acts which contribute to these goals are judged to be better acts. Acts that frustrate specifically human ends are judged to be morally wrong. Given a choice between challenging intellectual or artistic pursuits, say, and a life of leisurely inactivity, the self-realization theorist would choose the former over the latter. Anti-intellectual or antisocial acts would be judged to be wrong. However, because lower level goods are needed to support higher level activities, and because they are also good in themselves, lower level goods cannot be excluded from a life of rational activity.

EXERCISES

1. Critique each of the following from the standpoint of self-realization theory. Ask yourself whether any of the actions or opinions under consideration can be justified by self-realization theory, or whether such action or opinion would be judged to be wrong. Also consider the difference between theories which emphasize individual development and those which have an important social dimension.

    a. Jean believes that life is too short to become uptight about anything. She wants to enjoy herself as much as possible. However, her husband, Tom, has a career as a stockbroker, and he puts in sixty hours a week on his job. Jean claims that all Tom can do is talk about stocks. Even when they go out to dinner, he carries a beeper and frequently has phone conversations with clients. When she complains of this, he says she is lazy and that she should try to make something of herself.

    b. Bart, a teenager, really hates to practice the piano, but he likes to perform, and his music teacher tells him that he has talent. When Bart wants to go out and have fun, his father tells him he should practice more. "How else," his father says, "can you become a great pianist?" But Bart's sister often defends him, arguing that it is more important for Bart to have fun than it is for him to become a great pianist. Besides, she adds, what if he sacrifices his life to the piano and still turns out to be only a mediocre player?

    c. Lorenzo likes to travel, and tells his father that he wants to study abroad where he will meet new people and have new experiences. His father is concerned about this, however, for Lorenzo does not seem to have any career goals. The father thinks that Lorenzo

117

should begin planning for a career by entering a pre-med program or a business school so that he can get ahead in the world and make a good living. But Lorenzo thinks his father is stuck in a rut, that all his father can think about is work and money, and that he has no appreciation of the higher things in life.

d. Mike, who is twenty-nine years old, considers himself a poet, although he has never published anything. He does not have a job and lives with his mother. His mother supports him, but she works as a cook in a local hospital where the pay is not high. She thinks she should support her son in developing his talent, but Mike's friend, Diane, who is also a poet, thinks that he should leave home and find a job. She tells him it is simply wrong to continue living off his mother, especially as his mother must sacrifice so much.

e. A local state politician, Senator Fisher, believes in open admission to college. He argues that open admission gives everyone an equal opportunity. However, his colleague across the aisle, Senator Hayes, claims that colleges should admit only the best students. Hayes argues that open admission lowers standards in education. He also believes that the less talented students will not profit from it, and hence will waste time, effort, and money they could use for other pursuits.

2. Try to answer the following questions on the basis of the material contained in this chapter.

a. Explain your understanding of self-realization theory. How does it differ from utilitarianism? Give examples of both kinds of reasoning.

b. What is the difference between a monistic self-realization theory and a pluralistic theory? In what ways can monistic theories also be pluralistic?

c. What is meant by a hierarchy of goods? Do you think there really is such a hierarchy, that is, that some goods are higher than others? If not, how would you explain the general belief that people are more important than other animals?

d. What does it mean to say that evil is the privation of good? Do you think this is true? Is pain the privation of pleasure?

e. According to the theories of Plato and Aristotle, how does reason "harmonize" the goods?

f. Explain the distinction between consequences and ends. Illustrate how different conclusions may be drawn on the basis of these different considerations.

g. In what ways are ends and consequences related? Give examples of cases where you think you would judge an act on the basis of *both* intentions and consequences. In such cases, would you make a distinction between the rightness or wrongness of the act and the culpability of the agent?

NATURAL LAW THEORY

Self-realization theory is the basis of some forms of so-called "natural law" theory, but, historically, natural law theory has taken many forms. In a sense, any theory which holds that there are universal moral principles, which are somehow founded in "human nature," can be labelled a natural law theory. Any set of universal moral principles can be considered a set of natural moral laws. However, not all philosophers analyze human nature in exactly the same way, nor have they always arrived at exactly the same principles.

We have seen that, in traditional self-realization theory, morality was supposed to have a foundation in nature, because the potentialities of things are determined by species, and species, in turn, are divisions of nature. On this view, therefore, the moral law may be said to be determined by nature. But much the same thing may be said of almost any theory. The hedonistic theory of value is founded on the fact that people are sentient beings and the belief that sentient beings seek pleasure and avoid pain. Thus one might include hedonism among the forms of natural law theory, for hedonism maintains that some actions are naturally right and others naturally wrong, according to the principles of pleasure and pain.

Theories as various as those of the Stoics and Thomas Aquinas, on the one hand, and Thomas Hobbes and Immanual Kant, on the other, have referred to moral principles as "natural laws." But, in his conception of human nature, Hobbes, for example, thought that people are basically egoistic, whereas Aquinas believed people can be motivated by love. Nonetheless, all such theories hold that morality is founded upon characteristics which humans share, and that moral rights and obligations are determined by possibilities and limitations inherent in nature itself.

STOICISM

Like Plato and Aristotle, the ancient Stoics emphasized knowing one's place in nature and living in harmony with nature. Indeed, they sometimes seemed to think that one could know one's duty simply by knowing that place. For example, the Stoic Epictetus said that, if one wanted to know one's duties toward one's father, one should consider the fact that he is one's father. Duties were supposed to follow from one's station in life, as, indeed, they often do. The Stoics also stressed the importance of peace of mind, and they thought that peace of mind could be achieved, not by the pursuit of pleasure, but by submitting passions to rational control.

EPICTETUS
(336–264 B.C.)
On Things Within Our Power

There are things which are within our power, and there are things which are beyond our power. Within our power are opinion, aim, desire, aversion, and, in one word, whatever affairs are our own. Beyond our power are body, property, reputation, office, and, in a word, whatever are not properly our own affairs.

From: *The Discourses of Epictetus with the Encheiridion and Fragments.* Epictetus. George Long, trans. London: George Bell and Sons, 1877.

Their first principle, as enunciated by Epictetus, was that we should be concerned only with things which lie within our power or that we should not be troubled by things beyond our control. They were saying, in effect, that we must recognize natural limitations. Stoicism influenced a number of philosophers throughout history, including Spinoza, for example, who emphasized the importance of knowing one's place in nature and accepting one's lot in life.

It may seem strange to many people today to be told that they should accept the circumstances in which they find themselves, that a slave, for example, should accept the condition of slavery. But Stoics have argued that it is irrational for us to become upset over conditions we cannot change. Because we cannot change the circumstances of our birth or heritage, for example, or the fact that we will die, the Stoics felt that we should not worry about such things. Such worries destroy one's peace of mind. Thus people who are always upset "because the grass is greener on the other side of the fence" cannot be content, for no matter what they have, they seem to want something more. They fail to recognize that every life has limitations, and that, in order to attain peace of mind, a person must learn to accept suffering as an inevitable part of life. Thus the acceptance of one's place in nature, or in society, was one of the fundamental tenets of Stoic philosophy.

The Stoics so stressed the idea that people are governed by nature that they sometimes seemed to confuse moral laws with the laws of nature. We should note, however, it is one thing to say that we are bound by the law of gravity, say, a law of nature, and quite another thing to say that we are bound by a moral law, say, that we ought to keep our promises. To say that we are bound by the law of gravity means that we *cannot* violate it; but to say that we are bound by a moral law, such as a duty to keep our promises, means that we *should not* violate it. If we could not violate moral laws, there would be no point in exhorting one another to obey them.

THOMISTIC ETHICS

The best known form of natural law theory, still very influential today, was developed by Thomas Aquinas in the thirteenth century. Thomas Aquinas was a teleologist and self-realization theorist who followed the teachings of Plato and Aristotle. He was also influenced by Stoicism. He was, in fact, a Christian who tried to reconcile these ancient philosophies with the teachings of Christianity. So one of the major differences between his views and theirs lies in his emphasis upon such religious virtues as faith, hope, and charity. But Aquinas believed that reason and faith could be distinguished and that the domain of natural morality, determined by reason, is not dependent upon faith.

At the foundation of moral reasoning are several basic goods appropriate to the nature of persons. These goods are ends toward which persons are naturally inclined. They include, for example, life and health, knowledge and truth, friendship and society. Aquinas believed that everyone should always be open to the realization of these goods and hence never oppose them. While he did not think that persons could always consciously seek

120

each and every good, he did think that persons should be positively oriented towards them, and that they should promote them as they can. He also seemed to believe that they should never do anything deliberately to prevent the realization of these goods, by causing death, for example, by lying, or by being antisocial.

THOMAS AQUINAS
(c.1224–1274)
On Natural Law

Hence this is the first precept of law, that *good is to be done and promoted, and evil is to be avoided*. All other precepts of the natural law are based upon this; so that all the things which the practical reason naturally apprehends as man's good belong to the precepts of the natural law under the form of things to be done or avoided.

Since, however, good has the nature of an end, and evil, the nature of the contrary, hence it is that all those things to which man has a natural inclination are naturally apprehended by reason as good, and consequently as objects of pursuit, and their contraries as evil, and objects of avoidance. Therefore, the order of the precepts of the natural law is according to the order of natural inclinations.

From: *Summa Theologica*. Thomas Aquinas. *Philosophy in the Middle Ages*. A. Hyman and J. Walsh, eds. Indianapolis: Hacket, 1973.

Thus, on Thomas' view, there appear to be some very definite moral evils, actions which are definitely wrong. It is always wrong to intentionally kill, it seems, to intentionally deceive, or even to block the acquisition of knowledge. Yet he allowed that persons may be justified in killing in self-defense, say, or in war. His reasoning on this subject was that we have a right to promote our own goods and to protect ourselves from those who would attempt to kill us. Thus, he thought that, without contradiction, an act of self-defense may be viewed as an attempt to preserve life, not an attempt to destroy it, even if the death of another is caused in the process.

DOUBLE EFFECT

Such an interpretation is possible if one classifies and judges acts according to the intentions of an agent, or what the agent actually chooses to do, and not simply by the consequences of such choice. Thus an act of killing could be considered a murder, or a morally significant act, only if the agent intended to kill, and not if the killing were accidental. Killing in self-defense could be justified, therefore, if the agent did not intend to kill but merely intended to protect his or her own life. The killing would then be an unintended effect. However, if a person chooses to kill, as a means to an end, the killing would be morally wrong.

The principle of "double effect," mentioned only briefly by Aquinas, has received much attention by Aquinas scholars, and there appears to be little agreement about how it should be interpreted, or on how extensively it should be applied. Some interpret the principle very conservatively, as above, and others give it a more liberal interpretation, thinking that the unintended effects of actions may outweigh the intended effects. For instance, scientific researchers may intend to advance knowledge through human or animal research, but the effect of doing so may cause death or suffering. Depending on how one interprets the doctrine of double effect, such action may be viewed as either morally right or morally wrong. Indeed, if one accepts the more liberal interpretation, then one seems to move away from a consideration of intentions alone to a consequentialist or utilitarian view.

THOMAS AQUINAS
(c.1224–1274)
On Intentions and Consequences

The consequences of an action are either foreseen or not. If they are foreseen, it is evident that they increase the goodness or malice. For when a man foresees that many evils may follow from his action, and yet does not therefore desist therefrom, this shows his will to be all the more inordinate.

From: *Summa Theologica*. Thomas Aquinas. *Philosophy in the Middle Ages*. A. Hyman and J. Walsh, eds. Indianapolis: Hacket, 1973.

COMMISSION AND OMISSION

In the abortion controversy, some Thomists have argued that the intentional killing of a fetus is always wrong, although they have allowed that the life of a fetus may be risked in trying to save the mother's life—or that the mother's life may be risked in trying to save the fetus. In keeping with Aquinas' doctrine, they believe we should try to save both, even if we do not succeed. Others, however, are apt to argue that certain consequences, such as the severe defect or suffering of a deformed child, can tip the balance in favor of killing, or at least in favor of allowing a fetus to die.

The distinction between intentional killing and allowing someone to die holds for theories based on intentions. If, however, one is interested only in consequences, the result, namely death, is the same in either case. On the Thomistic view, killing is an example of an act of commission, whereas allowing to die is an example of an act of omission. If one thinks about it, we all allow other persons to die all the time, because we do nothing to prevent it. Normally we do not think this is morally wrong unless we think there is a special obligation to care for someone, when a doctor is treating a patient, for example, or when a parent is caring for a child. Even then, natural law theorists have argued that we do not have an obligation to use extraordinary means to save a life. On the side of commission, practically everyone agrees that, except for very unusual cases, it is morally wrong to intentionally take a human life.

According to any theory, it seems, we will want to make a distinction between natural evils and moral evils, evils for which humans are not responsible and evils for which they are. As mentioned above, persons cannot be held responsible for every death, both because they do not cause every death and because they could not prevent every death. Thus moral responsibility or culpability is usually associated with human agency, with human causality and freedom of choice. Thomists believe that persons can be morally responsible only for freely chosen acts; they do not think that persons are responsible for effects not chosen. But the word "responsible" is ambiguous, for we may mean by it either that an act was chosen by a person or that it was caused but not chosen.

THOMAS AQUINAS
(c.1224–1274)
On Practical Reason

The practical reason, on the other hand, is concerned with contingent matters, which is the domain of human actions; and, consequently, although there is necessity in the common principles, the more we descend towards the particular, the more frequently we encounter defects. . . . truth or practical rectitude is not the same for all as to what is particular, but only as to the common principles; and where there is the same rectitude in relation to particulars, it is not equally known to all.

From: *Summa Theologica*. Thomas Aquinas. *Philosophy in the Middle Ages*. A. Hyman and J. Walsh, eds. Indianapolis: Hacket, 1973.

Aquinas also recognizes that people cannot always know what is morally right or wrong. Thus he holds them responsible only to the dictates of their consciences, or to their own subjective views of right or wrong—even if such views are mistaken. He further points out that people can have certain knowledge only of first principles; regarding particular matters, he holds, there is more room for error, for differences of opinion, and even exceptions.

CRITICISMS OF THESE VIEWS

As one might expect, criticisms of natural law theory are likely to focus on its use of the word "natural," or on the interpretation of that term. The standard criticism, already anticipated, is that anything people do is natural. Therefore, it seems, the term "natural" cannot really serve to distinguish good things from bad things, or right from wrong. It is just as natural to lie, a critic may point out, as it is to tell the truth.

The same may be said of human intentions or inclinations. The things people are naturally inclined to do, or the things they ultimately intend to do, may be good or evil. Therefore it seems impossible to establish a distinction between moral goodness and moral evil on the basis of human intentions or inclinations. People seem to be as naturally inclined to be selfish, say, or to seek revenge, as they are inclined to be good.

Moreover, how can we distinguish between natural and unnatural acts? How do we know that it is "natural" to let rain fall on our heads, say, and "unnatural" to use an umbrella? Or if it is "natural" to use an umbrella, then why isn't it "natural" to use contraceptives? Why is it "natural" to use medication to prevent disease but "unnatural" to withhold medication? If, as some people claim, the one kind of act interferes with God's plan— i.e., the natural order—then how do we know that the other does not?

Finally, why is it better for actions to be natural than unnatural? If it is smarter or wiser to be unnatural, then why not be unnatural? If it is unnatural to perform an operation to save a person's life, then it seems that, in such a case, we should do the unnatural thing. If people who want babies can have them by artificial insemination—an unnatural means—then it seems they should use the artificial or unnatural method.

ANALYZING THESE CRITICISMS

The answers a natural law theorist would give to these criticisms are contained in the account we have given of natural law theory. In the first place, the distinction between good and evil is not made by claiming that some ends are good and others evil. The traditional view is that all ends are good; evil is supposed to be a privation of good. Thus, ultimately, all intentions or inclinations are supposed to aim at what is good—or at least what is *thought* to be good. Evil arises in the choice of means, or in a misconception of ends or goals.

However, insofar as the distinction between the natural and unnatural is supposed to carry weight as a distinction between good and evil, we must allow that it is difficult to establish any conclusion on this basis alone. Sometimes people argue for moral conclusions on evolutionary grounds, claiming that some characteristics are suited for survival and some are not. But such "survival of the fittest" theories, which appear to appeal to facts alone, or to "natural" selection, are simply theories that disguise value claims. That is, they hold that survival is more important than any other value, and hence that anything which promotes survival is good or "natural."

One might argue that it is natural to try to survive, but this is probably not true of every person all of the time. Even if it were true, it would not follow that every person should try to survive—unless survival could be shown to be the only end of human action, or the only end which people *ought* to seek. That is, natural law theories must be careful to avoid the fallacy of trying to derive an "ought" from an "is," or values from facts. As we have pointed out, the mere fact that people do things, or desire to do them, does not by itself prove they should.

The idea of self-realization also seems too narrow to account for the whole of morality. The emphasis on self seems too narrow, for, obviously, we have obligations to others as well. But others are also "selves," and most self-realization theories are not, or at least do not intend to be, egoistic. In emphasizing a respect for selves, they usually mean a respect for persons, and this is a point on which practically all moral theories agree.

Whatever their limitations, we should recognize that self-realization theories and natural law theories are correct in emphasizing the importance of looking at the facts, at the possibilities and limitations of human actions and, hence, at causal connections and probabilities. To ignore such considerations is to ignore reality. Such theories also point out that moral goodness is human goodness, something humans are capable of doing, and something which is good for them. They call attention to common wants and needs—features which humans share—and hence grounds for agreement and cooperation.

EXERCISES

1. How do you think a Stoic or a Thomist would respond to the following cases? Do you think that either Stoicism or Thomism provides a satisfactory basis for resolving these issues?

   a. Frank is married and has two small children. However, he can't get over the fact that he is no longer free to lead a single life. He often flirts with women other than his wife and is sometimes unfaithful. When his wife says she will no longer tolerate his behavior, he says she just doesn't understand men, for all men are that way by nature.

   b. Sam frequently lies to cover up the fact that he tends to ignore his responsibilities. For example, he sometimes fails to keep appointments and fails to complete assignments on time. When asked about this, he says that he does not have enough time, that he has been ill, or that he is the kind of person who can't perform under pressure.

   c. Mildred is a member of Sane Motherhood. She argues in favor of abortion as a means of family planning, and she also thinks it helps prevent overpopulation. When confronted with the criticism that abortion is killing, she responds by pointing out that people die by the thousands every day and that "pro-lifers" do nothing to prevent it.

   d. Mary Ann believes that it is wrong to kill animals for food and clothing. Animals, she reasons, have feelings and a strong desire to live. Therefore it is wrong to kill them, for the same reason it is wrong to kill people.

   e. Mr. Williams is upset because, he claims, the doctors killed his wife. She was seriously ill for years and, when she was dying, they failed to use all means possible to save her life. They even "hinted" that perhaps he would want her dead because she was suffering and making his life difficult. The doctors, however, defend themselves by saying that they did not kill her; they simply withheld treatment that may have prolonged her life.

2. Try to answer the following questions on the basis of the material discussed in this chapter.

   a. What are some of the "basic goods" of Thomistic ethics? Do you think that these goods are really more fundamental than other human goods? Consider possible counterexamples.

   b. What is the principle of "double effect"? How can it be used to justify self-defense? Do you think that self-defense could be justified in some other way?

   c. Extend the principle of double effect to other types of cases. Could it be used to justify euthanasia, for example, or war? Could it apply to abortion?

   d. In Question c, you may want to make a distinction between acts of omission and acts of commission, for example, between killing and allowing to die. Is such a distinction open to a utilitarian? Could it make any difference in utilitarian calculations?

e. Examine your own ideas about ethics and ask yourself whether you are a Kantian, a utilitarian, a self-realization, or a natural-law moralist. That is, examine the kinds of judgments you make on particular issues and ask yourself whether these judgments can be justified by one or another of these theories. For example, if you are opposed to abortion, could your position be justified on utilitarian grounds? If you are pro-choice, could your position be justified by Thomistic ethics? Explain.

SUPPLEMENTARY READINGS

Aquinas, Thomas. *Summa Theologica* and *Summa Contra Gentiles* (many editions).

Aristotle. *Nichomachean Ethics* (many editions).

Brumbaugh, Robert S. *The Philosophers of Greece*. Albany: SUNY Press, 1981.

Copleston, Frederick. *A History of Philosophy*. New York: Image Books, 1950.

Epictetus. *The Discourses of Epictetus with the Encheiridion and Fragments*. George Long, trans. London: George Bell and Sons, 1977.

Guthrie, W. K. C. *The Greek Philosophers*. New York: Harper & Row, 1950.

Jordan, James N. *Western Philosophy, From Antiquity to the Middle Ages*. New York: Macmillan, 1987.

Kaufman, Walter A. *Nietzsche*. Princeton: Princeton University Press, 1950.

Kohlberg, Lawrence. "The Development of Children's Orientation toward a Moral Order: 1. Sequence in the Development of Moral Thought." *Vita Humana,* Vol. 6, 1963: 11–13.

Mill, J. S. *Nature and Utility of Religion*. New York: Liberal Arts Press, 1958.

Oates, W. J., ed. *The Stoic and Epicurean Philosophers*. New York: Random House, 1940.

Owens, Joseph. *A History of Ancient Western Philosophy*. New York: Appleton-Century-Crofts, 1959.

Wippel, John F. and Wolter, Alan B. *Medieval Philosophy*. New York: The Free Press, Macmillan, 1969.

VII

SOCIAL CONTRACT THEORY

Social contract theories—sometimes also referred to as "contractarian" or "contractualist"—maintain that many, if not all, moral obligations stem from promises, agreements, or contracts. They all assert that people create at least some of their duties by choosing to accept them, although some social contract theories have a natural law foundation, believing that some duties are not mere conventions.

Social contract theory supports the belief that moral rules are created by people, of their own free choice. It is not wholly unlike Kantian ethics, for Kant spoke of the autonomy of the will, the idea that persons are authors of the moral law. Social contract theory is also like Kantianism in emphasizing the importance of rules in moral reasoning and the need to apply rules consistently to all cases. Thus social contract theory focuses on justice, as did Kant.

But Kant did not think that a contract was required in order to establish the moral law. He did not think that the moral law was dependent on promises or agreements. Social contract theorists introduce a social basis for morality, based on consent, and this is a potentially dynamic element in their theory, for it seems to allow for the possibility that moral rules may be changed over time. Hegel, who in many respects was a follower of Kant, criticized Kant's philosophy for just these reasons, because Kant seemed to think that each individual could somehow invent the moral law alone, and that the moral law is always completely formed everywhere at once.

TYPES OF CONTRACTARIANISM

Social contract theory, like other forms of moral philosophy, has a long history. It has been a theory of government, if not also a theory of ethics, at least as long as democracy has existed, since the time of the ancient Greeks. Indeed, even natural law philosophers have recognized that there is human law, or conventional or "man-made" law, in addition to the natural law or divine law.

Sometimes, of course, philosophers have supported the divine right of kings and not the right of the people to create their own laws or governments. Social contract theorists differ from other philosophers in holding that the rules of government, or the rules of society, should be determined by the consent of the governed, but they also differ among themselves on the form such government or society should take. Thomas Hobbes, for example, defended the monarchy, while John Locke argued in favor of a limited, representative form of government. John Rawls, a contemporary contractarian, has developed a theory that attempts to reconcile the value of human freedom with a fair distribution of opportunity for all.

Aside from the kinds of society advocated, these theories also differ in being either pure or mixed forms of contractarianism. A pure social contract theory is one which holds, positively, that all moral principles and rules are created by the social contract, or, negatively, that there are no moral rules or principles which exist prior to the formation of a contract, determining how it should be formed. A mixed social contract theory is one which holds that many moral rules are created by contract but that there are principles, not dependent on the contract, that determine how it should be formed.

Thomas Hobbes' theory seems to be a pure social contract theory, for he claims that there are no moral constraints on people prior to entering a contract, whereas Locke offers us a mixed theory, for he holds that there are universal moral principles that condition the kinds of contracts that can be formed. Thus, following Locke, Thomas Jefferson wrote that there are certain God-given rights which cannot, or should not, be taken away by governments or men. Locke's theory is "mixed," therefore, for he is a natural rights theorist with respect to basic principles and a social contract theorist with respect to the establishment of government and laws.

THE CONDITIONS OF FREE CONSENT

Although social contract theories differ from one another in these ways, they all attach importance to the rationality, universality, and freedom of consent required in forming a contract. Not just any agreement between persons is supposed to form a contract, but only a rational agreement, and an agreement that is freely entered by the contracting parties. Even Hobbes, who supported monarchy, argued that it was rational to enter a social contract, and that, in order to do so, persons must choose to surrender certain freedoms to the state.

Typically, contractarians are quite scrupulous about the requirement of free choice. They not only disapprove of coercion in entering a contract; they also disallow a consent to rules based on social conditioning or propaganda. Because, however, the beliefs of most people are conditioned by membership in some particular, historical community, contractarians try to avoid such influences by positing a hypothetical "state of nature," or an

---

THOMAS HOBBES
(1588–1679)
On Free Consent

Whensoever a man transferreth his right, or renounceth it; it is either in consideration of some right reciprocally transferred to himself; or for some other good he hopeth for thereby. For it is a voluntary act: and of the voluntary acts of every man, the object is some *good* to himself.

From: *Leviathan*. Thomas Hobbes. 1651 (many editions).

"original position." That is, they try to imagine what it would be like to exist under conditions where persons are free from social rules and obligations, or from any kind of institutional constraint. Such a state or condition may be thought to exist prior to the creation of society, and the persons in it may be supposed to be free to create social rules. The question they face then is: what kinds of rules should we create?

The device of positing a state of nature, or an original position, may be thought of as a kind of intellectual game—although a very serious game, for the results are supposed to be applied to real life. In this game, the inhabitants of a state of nature, or an original position, are asked if they need any ethical rules, and, if so, what kinds of rules they require. But they cannot create any rules which would grant special privileges or rights to themselves, as individuals, or as members of a group. The rules for playing this game are supposed to eliminate the advantages of special interests by requiring universal agreement among the players, and the injurious effects of prejudices are avoided by denying individuals any prior claim to special treatment under the rules.

Persons may never have existed in a state of nature, prior to any type of social organization, or if they did, we may never know what that was like. But that is not the point. According to contractarianism, the important question is: if we could make up the rules—or change them—what kinds of rules would we want? Or more precisely, from a moral point of view, what kinds of rules would be fair or just?

To even answer this question, however, we need to have some information. We need to know something about human nature, or about what it means to be fair or just. We need, in other words, rules for playing this morality game, and that is what the theories provide. Some do so by providing an account of human nature, what people are supposed to be like in a state of nature, prior to entering a social contract, as does Hobbes. Some theories provide an account of what it would mean to select social rules in a fair, free, and disinterested way, as does Rawls.

Thus we may look upon a social contract theory as a decision procedure for selecting moral rules. The description of the state of nature, or of the original position, sets up the conditions for selecting the rules, or the manner in which they may be selected. It determines what kinds of reasons may be offered in support of the rules, or what kinds of tests any given rule must meet.

Such a decision procedure can be quite simple. We may wonder, for example, whether the way Jones divided a cake is fair. Suppose the person who cut the cake was forced to take the last piece of cake. Would such a person cut the cake the way Jones did? This simple procedure may help us determine whether the given division of the cake is fair. In the social contract tradition, the decision procedure embodied in the state of nature or the original position is much more complex; but it always abstracts from the way we do things now and tries to determine how things should be done from an independent vantage point. In the cake cutting example, the consideration of selecting last provides a vantage point for making a decision about the fairness of the way pieces are cut.

EXERCISES

1. How does social contract theory differ from self-realization theory or natural law theory?

2. What is the difference between a "pure" social contract theory and a "mixed" theory?

3. Discuss examples of persons isolated from the main stream of society: street gangs, say, or fictional people isolated on an island, or people isolated by the devastation of war. What are the effects of a breakdown of social institutions and rules? Are such effects inevitable, and do they show that there is an underlying "human nature"?

4. Do you think there is any way of determining what people would be like without society?

5. Under conditions where social rules have not yet been developed or agreed upon, what can people do to determine which rules should be accepted, and what can they do to win acceptance? Variously, what obstacles might persons face in trying to win acceptance for social rules?

HOBBES' POSITION

Thomas Hobbes, a seventeenth-century philosopher, hypothesized that, prior to entering a social contract, people live in a state of nature. In this state of nature, he supposed, all persons are free to do whatever they wish, without restraint of any kind, except for opposition from others. Because there is no government or social organization, there are no rules; and where there are no rules, he inferred, nothing is either right or wrong.

Hobbes is perhaps most famous for his seemingly dim view of human nature. He thought that people are essentially egoistic or self-interested. In seeking goods for themselves, they are in constant competition and conflict with one another. As a result, they have no peace or security and live in constant fear of suffering and death. It is just this deplorable condition, contrasted with the blessings of civilized life, which Hobbes offers as a reason for leaving the state of nature and entering a social contract.

THOMAS HOBBES
(1588–1679)
On the State of Nature

So that in the nature of man, we find three principal causes of quarrel. First, competition; second, diffidence; thirdly, glory.

The first, maketh men invade for gain; the second, for safety; and the third, for reputation . . .

Hereby it is manifest, that during the time men live without a common power to keep them all in awe, they are in that condition which is called war; and such a war, as is of every man, against every man . . .

From: *Leviathan*. Thomas Hobbes. 1651 (many editions).

In the state of nature, no one can benefit from the protection of laws. No one can benefit from the many goods produced by social organization and cooperation. Thus Hobbes concludes that the only rational thing to do would be to enter into a covenant establishing a government which can make and enforce laws. The only rational alternative to living in a state of war of every person against every other person would be to choose a state of peace in which extreme individualism and freedom are restricted.

The price of entering such a covenant, Hobbes recognized, is the surrender of individual freedom, for morality, or law, is always a constraint on freedom. Hobbes was not a libertarian who held that liberty is always more important than everything else, for he believed that at least some liberties should be sacrificed in order to achieve a greater good. This greater good he summed up by the word "peace," but he also meant civilized living: greater sociability, greater productivity, and greater security. Ultimately, then, Hobbes thought that it would be in each individual's self-interest to enter into a social contract— or that it is in everyone's self-interest to be morally good.

Although one might think that Hobbes would be in favor of a democratic, republican, or parliamentary form of government, he actually favored the monarchy. He claimed that, in transferring their freedom to the government, the people should transfer it to an individual who would act in their place, a monarch who would make and enforce the laws. Indeed, strict enforcement of the law was supposed to be an incentive for obeying the law. One could have faith in the contract, Hobbes felt, and believe that one's own interests would be served by it, only if the laws were enforced. On Hobbes' view, strict enforcement ensures that it will always be in everyone's interest to uphold the law.

CRITICISMS OF HOBBES' THEORY

As one might expect, Hobbes' theory has been criticized for his seemingly pessimistic view of human nature. Assuming people are egoistic, he describes life in the state of nature as being "solitary, poor, nasty, brutish, and short." But there is probably as much reason to suppose that people would be loving and kind. Indeed, it is difficult to know what people would be like without society. Anthropological evidence suggests that primitive people are at least

131

as good as modern industrialized people—and as bad—toward friends and enemies respectively. The philosopher Jean Jacques Rousseau seemed to believe the very opposite of Hobbes, that people are fundamentally good but are corrupted by society. The truth probably lies somewhere between these two extremes, that people are "naturally" good in some respects and bad in others, and that society sometimes improves them and sometimes corrupts them, depending on many factors.

Hobbes has also been criticized for holding that there could not be any morality before entering a social contract; that the state of nature is an amoral world. However, people would need to recognize values of some sort in order to have reasons for creating a society. But Hobbes does not regard such values as moral values. He maintains that the reasons for entering a social contract are purely prudential, not moral. He believes that there are no moral obligations—no moral rights or duties—prior to the enactment of laws, but he does seem to recognize values, in the form of human goods, even in the state of nature. This raises the question of whether the values of the social contract are themselves merely prudential.

Hobbes might also claim that his argument applies only retrospectively, that we can know the advantages of belonging to a society only after we have experienced those benefits. We can now thank our lucky stars that we no longer live in a state of nature. We now know what it is like to live in a civilized world, and hence know what would be lost by returning to a barbaric existence. But, in knowing this, we also know that we have a price to pay; we must restrain liberty in order to maintain civilization.

THOMAS HOBBES
(1588–1679)
On Keeping Promises

Again, one of the contractors, may deliver the thing contracted for on his part, and leave the other to perform his part at some determinate time after, and in the mean time be trusted; and then the contract on his part, is called PACT, or COVENANT: or both parts may contract now, to perform hereafter: in which cases, he that is to perform in the time to come, being trusted, his performance is called *keeping of promise,* or faith, and the failing of performance, if it be voluntary, *violation of faith* . . .

From: *Leviathan.* Thomas Hobbes. 1651 (many editions).

There are other related problems. Hobbes often talks as if we ought to obey the laws because it is in our own self-interest to do so, but he also says that we are bound to do so, as a matter of practical consistency, because, by entering the contract, we have promised to uphold the law. These appear to be entirely different reasons. The latter, it seems, could not be binding unless there were a prior obligation to keep promises not dependent on contract. If all obligations or duties are determined by the contract, then contracts cannot be founded on a prior duty to keep promises.

On the other hand, if individual duties to the state are founded on self-interest, it would seem that people should not support the state when their interests are not being served. The interests of the state, or of society, and the interests of individuals do not always coincide. In times of war, for example, people are drafted into the military and are sometimes killed. It is difficult to see how such service is in their individual interest. Why then should they serve? The only answer, it seems, according to Hobbes, is fear of punishment. But, in some cases, the punishment, or the likelihood of punishment, poses less of a risk than service to the state. It would seem that some social motive is required—perhaps even a sense of justice.

One of the lessons we can draw from Hobbes' theory is that, without social rules and institutions, life would be worse than it is. Indeed, according to the Hobbesian game, the consequences of being asocial, or antisocial, are very harsh. A life without moral rules would be a life of fear and trembling. Hobbes' account may be exaggerated in this respect, but there is some truth in what he says. He certainly seems to be right in holding that many of the benefits of civilized living would not be possible without government, without law, or without social rules.

JOHN LOCKE: NATURAL RIGHTS

The positive side of Hobbes' position, relative to the other views we have studied, is that it emphasizes the importance of social organization, of government, and of community. Even if there are universal moral principles that are not dependent on convention or contract, there is also a host of rules that are so dependent. Such rules seem to be needed to supplement more fundamental moral principles. Thus some contractarians, such as John Locke, have argued in favor of a social contract, while at the same time believing that there are more fundamental principles.

John Locke spoke of these more fundamental principles as natural rights. He held that persons have certain rights—certain God-given rights—which other persons or governments do not have a right to take away. Among these are the rights to life, liberty, and property. In this respect, Locke's philosophy, unlike Hobbes', is very similar to natural law theory. It is like natural law theory in holding that it is wrong to take another's life, or to steal, except in very extreme circumstances, when, for example, basic rights are threatened. It is unlike Hobbes' theory, for Locke felt that the rules of government, or the social contract, must conform to the laws of God.

JOHN LOCKE
(1632–1704)
On Natural Rights

To understand political power aright, and derive it from its original, we must consider what estate all men are naturally in, and that is, a state of perfect freedom to order their actions, and dispose of their possessions and persons as they think fit, within the bounds of the law of Nature, without asking leave or depending upon the will of any other man.

From: *Two Treatises on Government.* John Locke. 1690 (many editions).

Locke's description of the state of nature is mainly a catalogue of these rights, and of correlative obligations. Even in the state of nature, people are expected to respect the rights of their neighbors. But Locke also recognized that government was needed to make judgments and settle disputes, even among well intentioned people. He also thought that government was needed to punish crimes and deter aggression. He held, therefore, that the basic function of government was to enforce the natural laws, or to protect natural rights.

Yet, in contrast to Hobbes' conception of government, Locke attributes to government a very limited role. Because, in the state of nature, people are born free, it is the job of government to maintain and protect their freedom. People, he thought, are best off when they are allowed to go their own way and tend to their own business.

EVALUATING LOCKE'S POSITION

If we play the Lockean game, we assume that people have a pre-ordained right to life, liberty, and property. Social morality and law have the limited function of protecting people from aggression. Government is founded to protect basic rights. Other contracts may be made between free, consenting parties, for their own mutual benefit, but there is no obligation to help the poor or disadvantaged, to distribute the wealth, or to improve production by means of cooperation and social organization. Indeed, in so emphasizing the constraints of natural law, or natural rights, Locke is reluctant to allow the government very much to do.

Locke does focus on important human values, such as freedom. However, he also seems to assume that people are generally better off when left alone by the government, or by other social institutions. He seemed to think that individuals are, by and large, independent of one another, and that they can freely enter contracts for the things they need. But this view of individual independence was probably exaggerated even in Locke's day; today it seems clearly false. Today's world is one of multiple, complex interdependencies. Production is highly organized and institutionalized. Specialization reigns in the professions. The rules of social life govern almost everything we do. Even the value of money is closely regulated by government agencies. Some may argue, in sympathy with Locke, that we are worse off because of this, but it seems clear that modern life would be impossible without it.

JOHN LOCKE
(1632–1704)
On Popular Government

Men being, as has been said, by nature all free, equal, and independent, no one can be put out of this estate and subjected to the political power of another without his own consent, which is done by agreeing with other men, to join and unite into a community for their comfortable, safe, and peaceable living, one amongst another, in a secure enjoyment of their properties, and a greater security against any that are not of it.

From: *Two Treatises on Government*. John Locke. 1690 (many editions).

If one looks closely, one can see that both Locke's position and Hobbes' position have utilitarian elements, in emphasizing the ultimate pleasure or well-being of individuals. The main difference between them, in this respect, is that Hobbes has such a dim view of human nature that any form of social change would appear to be an improvement. Locke, by contrast, sees people as basically responsible and reasonable, and hence in little need of improvement. Hobbes argues for strong government to restrain individualism, and Locke argues for weak government to allow individualism greater expression.

In any case, we should perhaps thank Locke for so emphasizing the need to restrict the powers of government, and for insisting upon the importance of equality, freedom, and popular consent. The requirements of the natural law, as Locke conceived it, and the results of majority rule, may not always coincide, but Locke thought that people would try to protect their natural God-given rights, and hence not consent to a government that did not respect those rights.

Rawls' Theory of Justice

John Rawls, a contemporary social contract theorist, believes that the major fault of traditional social contract theories is their reliance on theories of human nature. His theory of justice sets forth conditions that must be met in order to reach an agreement that would be fair to all. Proceeding from what he calls the "original position," he outlines a procedure designed to produce universalizable rules.

Rawls defines his original position as a hypothetical state in which people are guaranteed freedom and equality in the selection of moral principles. Thus, he imagines that they choose the rules of their society under a "veil of ignorance," not knowing things about themselves that would make them prejudiced, and not knowing the place they will occupy in the society they choose to form. Hence, in his original position, Rawls abstracts from considerations of race, creed, sex, ethnic origin, intelligence, strength, and class. Each person knows only that he or she wants certain basic goods, such as wealth, income, freedom, and respect.

JOHN RAWLS
(1921–   )
The Original Position

Thus we are to imagine that those who engage in social cooperation choose together, in one joint act, the principles which are to assign basic rights and duties and to determine the division of social benefits. Men are to decide in advance how they are to regulate their claims against one another and what is to be the foundation charter of their society. Just as each person must decide by rational reflection what constitutes his good . . . so a group of persons must decide once and for all what is to count among them as just and unjust. The choice which rational men would make in this hypothetical situation of equal liberty . . . determines the principles of justice.

From: *A Theory of Justice*. John Rawls. Cambridge: The Belknap Press of Harvard University Press, 1971.

These hypothetical people understand the need for social cooperation. They understand, for their own well-being, that some people will have more or less of the social goods than others. These people are not supposed to be envious, but they do want what is good for themselves. Thus they are supposed to be interested in themselves and impartial toward others.

The Rawlsian game, then, is to determine what such people would select as principles of justice. Because they want what is good for themselves, are not envious, and are not willing to take chances with important goods, they try to ensure that they will have as much as possible. For these reasons, Rawls says, they will accept two principles of justice: (1) that each person should have as much freedom as possible that is compatible with a like freedom for others and (2) that all other basic goods should be equally distributed, unless an unequal distribution is to the greatest advantage of the least well off.

Rawls believes that, if we were not prejudiced, we would always take the welfare of the least well-off to be the test of our moral rules. Rawls also believes that freedom is uniquely important, and hence should be equally enjoyed by all. In speaking of freedom, he has in mind freedom of religion, for example, and freedom of speech and assembly. Thus Rawls' theory contains libertarian political elements, such as Locke's emphasis on the importance of individual freedom, but it also stresses the distribution of goods to persons who are disadvantaged. Indeed, it is Rawls' blending of these views that makes his theory appealing as a synthesis of contemporary political positions.

Rawls' view is more abstract than the traditional social contract theories. Hobbes and Locke wrote about the state of nature as if it were a real place. Rawls' original position is purely hypothetical. It is designed to help us make decisions about principles of justice from a vantage point he believes is completely fair. For example, we may wonder whether certain people deserve more income than others. For Rawls, the way to avoid a prejudiced answer to this question is to ask what people in the original position would think. Because they all want more rather than fewer goods, Rawls believes they would be unwilling to let others have greater income unless they also benefitted from it. No one knows whether they will be the people with greater income. But they do know that it is not in their interest to deny others a greater income, if that income also benefits them. For instance, by giving managers more, companies may run more efficiently, and thereby allow labor greater income. However, many Japanese business people believe that, in relationship to labor, managers in the U.S. make too much. They argue that less inequality increases efficiency. If this is true, then according to Rawls' second principle, large inequalities between management and labor would be unjust.

EXAMINING RAWLS' THEORY

Rawls seems to have been successful in establishing a test to determine whether or not moral rules are tainted by undue self-interest. Indeed, when it comes to making decisions about the large scale distribution of goods that have been produced in a cooperative way, his method seems especially strong. However, not all moral questions arise on this level, and for this reason Rawls' theory seems incomplete.

His method, like Kant's, also seems to ignore historical conditions; in fact, it *requires* us to ignore them. But we cannot simply wipe the slate clean and redesign society. In real life situations, decisions are affected by existing institutions and practices, and by the expectations of other people. We cannot simply ignore those expectations, nor can we change social institutions overnight. Even if we could, it is not clear that it would be desirable to do so, for the costs may be too high.

THE WASHINGTON STATE CATHOLIC CONFERENCE
On Weighing the Constraints of Prejudice

Another problem arises in cases where a Catholic community is rent by deep-seated prejudices against lesbians and gays. In such circumstances it may be impossible to hire homosexuals, even those who do not act out, without having Catholic institutions wrecked or severely hampered in their operation by prejudiced individuals. In such cases those in authority have to balance the harm to the community caused by the destructive activities of these prejudiced persons against the injustice resulting from being pressured not to hire homosexuals or to terminate those already hired. In certain circumstances, those in authority may judge prudentially that they will have to give in to the pressure. In other circumstances they will prudentially judge that the common good is better fostered by taking a firm stand and braving the wrath of persons blinded by prejudice . . . No matter what decision is taken, solid efforts must be made to root out such prejudicial attitudes and activities from the community.

From: *Catholic Northwest Progress.* Washington State Catholic Conference, 1983.

Because, as Rawls recognizes, the rightness or wrongness of one person's behavior is dependent upon what others will do, or what they may be expected to do, the effectiveness of Rawls' theory depends on universal acceptance. As we noted in commenting upon Hobbes' theory, it would not be just (or advantageous) for one person, or even a few persons, to follow his theory if others did not do so as well. In this sense, Rawls' theory may be looked upon as proposing an ideal we should try to achieve, but which, at present, is not necessarily binding in fact.

Rawls' theory seems opposed to natural rights and natural law traditions, for there seem to be no principles that govern the behavior of people in the original position prior to their choice of principles, or prior to the social contract. The contract is supposed to bring these principles into existence. Yet Rawls offers us rules for playing his social contract game; game rules govern the behavior of the participants prior to the choice of principles. Thus one may argue that Rawls really does have antecedent principles, disguised as procedural principles, but functioning as substantive moral principles.

Indeed, if we are asked to strip away some of the characteristics of people and not others—such as their prejudices but not their self-interest—doesn't this amount to saying that some characteristics are more fundamental than others, or that some are morally relevant or appropriate? The sorting out of prejudices from the original position already assumes, it seems, prior to the creation of society, a principle of justice as a condition for the creation of principles of justice. In any case, it is not clear that the idea of principles which all people may be expected to rationally choose is any different from traditional ideas of natural rights or natural laws.

Thus, it appears that the same arguments raised against natural law theory may also be brought against Rawls; why are some of the characteristics of people considered "natural," or, in this case, characteristics of people in the original position, and others "nonnatural" or socially created? Moreover, can Rawls' method really eliminate prejudice, because the people in his original position are, after all, only hypothetical people, and we—real people—must do their thinking for them? Rawls defines his inhabitants of the original position as self-interested, but this may be a bias he introduces. It seems difficult, if not impossible, to invent a decision-making process that will ensure justice without already making assumptions about what is or is not just, or about which of the many characteristics of people are relevant to determining what is morally right or wrong. In other words, it seems difficult to avoid loading the dice, or begging the question, in favor of the conclusion one wishes to reach.

THE VALUE OF SOCIAL CONTRACT THEORY

Social contract theory makes an important contribution to our understanding of morality by calling attention to the need for social rules. Indeed, Locke's theory seems to fail because he attached too little importance to social rules and placed too much emphasis on natural law. Even Rawls' theory barely makes a start, by proposing principles of justice, but failing to pay much attention to the hundreds and thousands of rules and practices which give substance to daily life. Natural law theorists call attention to the need for social institutions and practices, but they still tend to look at them *eternally*, as if unaffected by temporal conditions, and hence out of the context of historical affairs. In this sense, contractarians are not much different from traditional natural law theorists or utilitarians.

The philosophers we will study in the next chapter will call some of these assumptions into question. Pragmatists, for example, "take time seriously," as they say, and hence see ethics in its historical context. Existentialists take choice seriously, and hence see that choice is not always determined by reason, or by prior rational constraints. Rule-deontologists, in turn, question the idea that there is only one principle that governs morality—such as a principle of justice, or a principle of utility. Like the pragmatists, they will introduce a pluralistic conception into morality; a pluralistic conception already anticipated by Aristotle, for example, and by Aquinas, in holding that there is a number of ultimate goods.

EXERCISES

1. Consider whether any of the following arguments is supported by the views of Hobbes, Locke, or Rawls.

   a. Harriet, Jack, and Joe are discussing international relations. Harriet is in favor of a very powerful central world government. She argues that, with nuclear weapons in the hands of so many governments, the chance of complete destruction is real. She believes that a weak body, like the United Nations, cannot possibly keep the world safe from such wholesale destruction. Jack and Joe claim that nuclear weapons have not been used for years. That is because nations do act in responsible ways, they say, at least to a degree. Jack thinks that, on the international scene, things are just fine. Joe believes that the United Nations needs to be made stronger and should be given the authority to address, in a serious and effective way, the problem of world poverty and starvation.

b.   Kai believes that socialism is a better system because capitalism makes the rich richer and the poor poorer. Judy argues that there is already too much socialism. It makes people irresponsible and dependent, she feels. In her view, we need more capitalism.

c.   Jim deplores the fact that there is so much drug-related crime. He thinks that only with a stronger government, even a near dictatorship, can such crime be controlled. He wants the army to patrol city streets. The way things are, he says, some neighborhoods are not safe. However, John thinks that such patrols will cause more harm than good, and that they will not address underlying problems. He calls for job education, drug rehabilitation, and increased welfare support.

d.   Elena claims that women face great inequality. She points to the fact that, on the average, women make less than 70 percent of the income of men. She believes that rejection of the equal rights amendment is a sign of injustice. Margaret argues that the income of men and women should be determined by the market.

e.   Julian believes that anyone who can get away with cheating on his or her income tax would be a fool not to do so. Pete thinks that the income tax is fair because it supports people in need and is graduated, so that richer people pay a greater percentage. He argues that it is our responsibility to pay.

2.   Based on your reading of the text, try to answer the following questions.

a.   How does Hobbes describe the state of nature. Do you think that, without social rules, people would behave as Hobbes maintains?

b.   What, according to Hobbes, are the main reasons for entering a social contract? Do you think that his reasons for accepting and obeying moral rules are adequate? Discuss.

c.   How does Locke's theory differ from Hobbes'? What different assumptions do they make? What differences are there in their conceptions of the functions of government?

d.   What does Rawls mean by his "original position" and by "a veil of ignorance"? How are these conditions related to his conception of justice?

e.   Compare the moral and political views of people today with those of Hobbes, Locke, and Rawls. Can you identify any group of people, large or small, that tends to think of life in Hobbes' terms, or Locke's, or Rawls'? Do you find that your own thinking is similar to the theories of any of these philosophers? In what ways?

SUPPLEMENTARY READINGS

Buchanan, James. *The Limits of Liberty: Between Anarchy and Leviathan.* Chicago: University of Chicago Press, 1975.

Gauthier, David. *Morals by Agreement.* Oxford: Oxford University Press, 1986.

Gough, J. W. *The Social Contract.* 2d ed. Oxford: The Clarendon Press, 1957.

Hobbes, Thomas. *Leviathan* (many editions).

Locke, John. *Two Treatises on Government* (many editions).

Nozick, Robert. *Anarchy, State, and Utopia.* New York: Basic Books, 1974.

Rawls, John. *A Theory of Justice.* Cambridge, Mass.: The Belknap Press of Harvard University Press, 1971.

Rousseau, Jean-Jacques. *The Social Contract* (many editions).

VIII

CONTEMPORARY ETHICAL THEORIES

In a sense, all of the theories we have been discussing are "contemporary." They are all theories that are studied and applied today, even if they came into existence in ancient, medieval, or early modern history. However, the theories discussed in this chapter are relatively new in inception and express characteristics of present-day thinking more than some of the traditional theories do. By "recent" or "contemporary," we mean the early or middle part of the twentieth century, and even the late nineteenth century, as these periods are said to be "recent" or "contemporary" when considered from a historical point of view.

JOHN DEWEY
(1859–1952)
On Monistic Theories

Ethical theory . . . has been singularly hypnotized by the notion that its business is to discover some final end or good or some ultimate and supreme law. . . . But they have differed from one another because there was one point in which they were agreed: a single and final source of law. Others have asserted that it is impossible to locate morality in conformity to law-giving power, and that it must be sought in ends that are goods. And some have sought the good in self-realization, some in the greatest possible aggre-gate of pleasures. And yet these schools have agreed in the assumption that there is a single, fixed and final good. They have been able to dispute with one another only because of their common premise.

From: *Reconstruction in Philosophy*. John Dewey. New York: Henry Holt and Co., 1920.

141

There are various features of these theories that seem to express relatively modern points of view. One of these features is the denial of absolutes and an emphasis on relativity. Another is an emphasis on plurality or multiplicity, and hence particularity or individuality, as opposed to unity and universality. That is, some of the following theories hold that moral rightness or wrongness is relative to individuals, or to contexts, and some hold that there is no one and only one moral principle that applies to all cases.

Indeed, all of the following theories focus on the importance of lower-level rules and judgments, or decisions, below the level of principles, as such lower-level rules and judgments, or decisions, are supposed to be needed to supplement principles, to test principles, or even to replace them. Thus the theories considered in this chapter call attention to problems that arise in attempting to apply the kinds of principles defended by traditional theories, and hence move us closer to actual applications.

ACT AND RULE DEONTOLOGY

Deontology is a philosophical position which holds that certain kinds of moral actions are right or wrong in and of themselves, regardless of consequences. Deontology is contrasted with teleology, which maintains that the rightness or wrongness of acts is dependent solely on ends or consequences. Kant's ethical theory is said to be deonotological because Kant denied that consequences are relevant to making moral determinations. Kant thought that rules could be determined by his principle of universalizability and that the rightness or wrongness of particular acts is determined by rules.

There is, however, another class of philosophers called rule deontologists who, like Kant, hold that the rightness or wrongness of moral acts is determined by moral rules, but who differ from Kant in denying that moral rules can be deduced from a higher principle. Indeed, they hold that there is no moral principle higher than the moral rules themselves. Because, according to their theory, moral rules cannot be derived from any higher principle, moral rules must be known directly by intuition. Sir David Ross, the chief exponent of this view, maintained that we are morally bound to obey moral rules, not because they can be deduced from some higher principle, but because we intuit them to be *the* rules of morality. Thus, on his view, there is no higher court of appeal.

W. D. ROSS
(1877–1971)
On Self-Evident Principles

I am assuming the correctness of some of our main convictions as to *prima facie* duties, or more strictly, am claiming that we *know* them to be true. To me it seems as self-evident as anything could be, that to make a promise, for instance, is to create a moral claim on us in someone else. Many readers will perhaps say that they do *not* know this to be true. If so, I certainly cannot prove it to them: I can only ask them to reflect again, in the hope that they will ultimately agree that they know it.

From: *The Right and the Good.* W. D. Ross. Oxford: Clarendon Press, 1930.

When rule deontologists speak of moral rules, they have in mind such rules as "Don't lie," or "Don't steal," or "You ought to keep your promises." They think that, when we make moral judgment about a particular act of lying, by saying, for example, "It was wrong for Jack to lie to Jane," we can justify our particular judgment by appealing to the moral rule "Don't lie." If, however, someone asks us, "Why do you think it is wrong to lie?" the rule deontologist thinks that there is no way to justify the rule. On the rule deontological view, all we can say is that it is morally wrong to lie and that, if one doesn't see *that*, then one is morally blind!

To say, as Ross does, that moral rules are ultimate or underived is tantamount to saying that the moral rules are themselves the first principles of moral reasoning. However, instead of holding that there is one first principle, he holds that there are several. But, if there are several first principles, then the problem of conflicts of principle, and hence of exceptions to principles, seems to arise once again. For this reason, Ross held that moral rules apply in what he called a "prima facie" sense. They apply "all things being equal," or under normal circumstances, but not necessarily under unusual circumstances, or "all things considered."

Ross wanted to allow for the possibility of exceptions, so he did not want to maintain, as Kant did, that moral rules are categorical imperatives. However, in denying that they apply universally, or without exception, Ross did not want to say simply that they sometimes apply and sometimes not. Such a position, on his view, would be far too weak. Rather, he held that we must always consider all of the rules, and that it is necessary to obey all of them, except when the rules conflict, or under very exceptional circumstances. So, on his view, the rules hold, unless there is good reason to believe that an exception should be allowed.

The Appeal of Rule Deontology

Rule deontology, like several other theories we have considered, has a certain intuitive appeal, and hence seems to be justified by common sense. We do in fact appeal to moral rules to justify our actions, as we have pointed out earlier. However, we have also raised the question of justifying rules, and rule deontology responds by claiming that, at a certain fairly high level of generalization, moral rules can no longer be justified by appealing to higher principles or rules. That claim also appears to make sense, for it seems that our reasoning must stop somewhere—so why not at the level of moral rules? Why, indeed, should we suppose that rules can be, or must be, justified by one and only one higher principle?

Well, the claim of rule deonotologists is that moral rules cannot be justified by a single principle. One good reason for holding such a position is that the principles of all the other theories seem to hold, and that the principles of one theory cannot be derived from the principles of another. As defended by their adherents, the other theories are exclusive. But why not simply combine them, by holding all the principles, and hence denying that they exclude one another? To do so would be to espouse many principles, or many high-level rules, which, like the original principles of traditional theories, are supposed to be underived from higher principles. The only difference would be that no one principle would be supreme. Under appropriate circum-

143

stances, then, any principle or rule might have exceptions, for it might give way to some other principle or rule.

Thus one could have a system of rules that would respect the traditional values of natural law theory and Kantianism, say, and also the principle of utilitarianism which bids us to promote happiness and avoid pain. Such rules would bind us to treat life as a very important value, except, say, in the case of extreme suffering, when we may be morally permitted, even required, to withhold life support. The duty to respect life, or not to kill, would be nearly absolute, except in very extreme circumstances, as in self-defense, say, or in cases of extreme and irreversible suffering.

Such exceptions might be included in the rules, but the rules might then become overly complicated and difficult to teach or learn. Indeed, it may be impossible to include every exception in the rules, for it may be impossible to imagine every circumstance in which an exception would be justified. It may be necessary to consider exceptional cases as they arise, or to include, in teaching the rules, only relatively common exceptions.

ACT DEONTOLOGY

In rule deontology, we see philosophers moving away from a rather simple system, which justifies all moral rules and particular acts by one principle, to a more complex or pluralistic system in which there are many ultimate rules or principles. Rule deontologists deny that all moral rules are derived from one principle, but they appear to believe that all morally right acts can be justified by a limited set of rules.

However, by parity of reasoning, one might also deny that any limited set of rules can justify all morally right acts or determine which particular acts are wrong. If the rules can have exceptions, and if all possible exceptions cannot be included in the rules, then the rules are simply inadequate for determining what is right or wrong in all cases. We not only cannot derive the rules from one principle, we cannot derive the rightness or wrongness of any particular act from any rule or set of rules. Therefore each particular case must be judged on its own merits, or, more accurately, we must simply intuit in each and every particular case whether a particular act is right or wrong.

H. A. PRICHARD
(1871–1947)
The Mistake of Moral Theory

The sense of obligation to do, or of the rightness of, an action of a particular kind is absolutely underivative or immediate . . .

The negative side of all this is, of course, that we do not come to appreciate an obligation by an *argument* . . .

From: "Does Moral Philosophy Rest on a Mistake?" H. A. Prichard. *Mind*, 21, 1912: 21–37.

This is, in essence, the position called act deontology. It holds that acts really are right or wrong in and of themselves, but it also holds that the only way we can know whether any act is right or wrong is by direct intuition, not by reasoning. H. A. Prichard, the best known advocate of this position, held that every particular act is different from every other particular act, and that it is impossible to find any one feature or combination of features that makes all right acts right. Thus he held that there is no way of deducing the rightness or wrongness of acts from principles or rules.

The rule deontologist may hold that, in general, lying is wrong, but his position is weakened by allowing that this rule, or any rule, may have exceptions. If a rule can have exceptions, then a particular moral judgment cannot be justified by considering that rule alone. Other factors must be taken into consideration. But this is tantamount to saying that particular moral judgments cannot be justified by rules alone, or, variously, that acts are not right or wrong simply because they obey or disobey rules. But every particular act is either right or wrong. If we cannot know this by appealing to principles or rules, then the only way we can know it is by considering the act itself, in all of its details, under the particular set of circumstances in which the act is performed.

Prichard did not hold that reasoning has no place in morality, but he did hold that reasoning is never sufficient to determine which acts are right or wrong. After looking at all the aspects of an act, he thought, including consequences, and past promises or commitments, we still need to make a judgment about the act that does not follow from those considerations alone.

Universality, Generalization, and Particularity

It is a virtue of rule deontology and act deontology that both call attention to the difficulty of (1) establishing first principles in ethics and, perhaps as importantly, (2) showing how principles can be applied to particular cases. Rule deontology maintains that it is impossible to generalize to the point of establishing any one principle as the only principle from which all moral judgments are derived. Act deontology adds to this the claim that particular acts, because they are so different from one another, cannot be covered by general rules, no matter how many, or how detailed, such rules may be. Act deontology especially calls attention to the richness and diversity of particular concrete conditions, in contrast to abstract, universal principles or rules. There is a great distance between the two, which may be mediated by intermediate rules, but which can never be closed entirely, if the act deontologists are correct.

In calling attention to these three levels of moral reasoning, namely principles, rules, and particular judgments, act and rule deontologists also remind us that the confidence we have in moral rules or particular judgments may sometimes be higher than the confidence we have in moral principles. We noted earlier that people usually know what they believe in particular cases, and they often know what rules to cite to justify particular judgments, but they do not often know what principles to cite in order to justify their rules. Thus they may be more skeptical about moral principles than they are about moral rules or particular judgments. Because this is so, they may not be inclined to test their rules or particular judgments by appealing to principles but, on the contrary, would be inclined toward testing principles by appealing to their lower-level beliefs.

They might then seem to be reasoning backwards, so to speak, from lower-level beliefs to higher-level beliefs, rather than from the general to the particular. And this is precisely what an act deontologist like Prichard maintains. He maintains that we can reason *inductively* from our lower-level, particular judgments to our higher-level generalizations or rules, but we cannot reason *deductively* from higher to lower. On his view, we do not really use our higher-level beliefs as principles, or as criteria, to support our lower judgments, such that our judgments are derived from those principles, but simply as *summaries* or generalizations of what otherwise we intuitively believe.

Thus there appears to be a basis for claiming that these positions are true. But we should not ignore the characteristics of moral judgment and moral reasoning discussed at the beginning of this book. That is, we should not forget that moral judgment is not merely descriptive or fact-stating but prescriptive or normative. In moral reasoning, we do not simply compare our ideas with independent facts or states of affairs. Rather, we judge facts, states of affairs, or actions to be good, bad, right, or wrong, according to rational criteria. We do not and could not judge particular acts independently of principles or rules, or independently of the *kinds* of acts they are. That is why we normally speak of particular acts as "cases," for "cases" are instances of kinds. Without general classifications we could not know how to characterize a particular act or evaluate it from a moral point of view.

The particularism of act deontology might make sense if the act deontologist were talking about descriptions; but, because deontology necessarily concerns prescriptions, its thesis appears to lose all sense. Indeed, insofar as it tells us nothing about how to determine what is right or wrong in particular cases, and could not do so without generalizing, it ceases to be a theory about how we should act. At least it is not a theory about how to reason in ethics, for its principal aim is to deny the efficacy of reasoning.

We do not, however, want to lose sight of the fact that people often make particular judgments without consciously or explicitly knowing which rule or principle is involved, and hence that it may be necessary to analyze particular judgments to discover principles or rules. We need to test our particular judgments by seeing if they can be derived from principles or rules, but we also need to see if our principles and rules are consistent with our particular judgments. Our confidence in our particular judgments is not a sufficient reason for denying the need for principles or rules, but we can use our particular judgments to test principles and rules. In this way, we will be able to hold onto the idea that particular judgments are important in moral reasoning without surrendering the idea that ultimate justification depends on the coherence of all our beliefs.

Coherence means that our beliefs "hold together." In the strongest sense of coherence, our beliefs support one another, each giving us reason to believe the others are true. In the weakest sense, beliefs are coherent if they are consistent or do not contradict one another. In a complex set of beliefs, some may mutually support one another, others may be merely consistent, and still others may be contradictory. In aiming at coherence, we should attempt to maximize mutual support and minimize conflict. This needs to be done on all levels of moral reasoning and between levels. We should expect principles to cohere with other principles, rules with rules, particular judgments with particular judgments, and principles with rules and particular judgments. This means that, following Kant, we must continue to ask why we think particular acts are right or wrong, and whether we are willing to apply the same reasons consistently to all cases.

ACT AND RULE UTILITARIANISM

Act utilitarianism is the view that each and every particular act must be judged directly by the utilitarian principle, according to the consequences of that act. Rule utilitarianism, by contrast, urges the following of rules which, if followed, would maximize utility. That is, the act utilitarian advocates reasoning directly from the principle to the particular act, and the rule utilitarian advocates reasoning from the principle to rules, and then from the rules to particular acts.

Act and rule utilitarianism are similar to act and rule deontology, except that act and rule utilitarians accept a single, ultimate principle of morality, namely the utilitarian principle, and act and rule deontologists deny that there is any such principle. Act utilitarians, like act deontologists, believe that each and every particular act must be judged on its own merits, or that moral rules alone do not determine the rightness or wrongness of particular acts. But act utilitarians think that each particular act must be judged by the utilitarian principle, whereas act deontologists think that the rightness or wrongness of particular acts can be known only by direct intuition.

Act utilitarians and act deontologists both agree that any kind of act may be either right or wrong, depending on particular circumstances, and hence that the question of rightness or wrongness cannot be settled by citing moral rules. The classification of acts into right kinds and wrong kinds does not determine which acts are right. However, on the rule utilitarian view, like the rule deontological view, rules are supposed to be necessary for making moral determinations. The difference is that rule utilitarians believe rules are derived from the principle of utility, and rule deontologists believe that rules are not derived from any principle.

Thus, in considering whether a lie is morally right or wrong, both act and rule utilitarians would consider the consequences. However, while an

---

J. J. C. SMART
(1920–   )
On Rule Utilitarianism

In general the rightness of an action is *not* to be tested by evaluating its consequences but only by considering whether or not it falls under a certain rule. Whether the rule is to be considered an acceptable moral rule, is, however, to be decided by considering the consequences of adopting the rule. Broadly, then, actions are to be tested by rules and rules by consequences . . .

From: "Extreme and Restricted Utilitarianism." J. J. C. Smart. *Philosophical Quarterly*, 6, 1956: 344–54.

---

act utilitarian examines the consequences of each lie separately, the rule utilitarian looks at all lies as a class. The act utilitarian asks whether this lie or that lie will increase utility, but the rule utilitarian asks whether it would be better or worse to have a rule that covers lies generally. Neither believes that we can simply intuit that acts are morally right or wrong, or which rules we should follow, as do act and rule deontologists.

From the utilitarian point of view, both act and rule deontology are theoretically inelegant because neither provides a way of ultimately justifying moral claims, and *that*, according to utilitarians, is precisely what a moral theory should do. Rule deontologists do offer rules as reasons, but, without a supreme principle, there is no way of justifying rules, and there is no way of resolving conflicts of rules, except, perhaps, by appealing to intuition. But appeals to intuition, from the standpoint of utilitarians, is simply a way of being dogmatic, or of admitting that one has no reasons to justify lower-level beliefs.

The Rule Utilitarian View

The distinction between act and rule utilitarianism, however, is rather recent, and it appears to have been influenced by the rise of rule deontology. As an explicit doctrine, rule utilitarianism came into existence after World War II, partly as a response to criticisms of utilitarianism by deontologists, and partly as a reinterpretation of classical utilitarian positions. What is now called act utilitarianism was previously the standard interpretation of utilitarianism, namely, that the utilitarian principle applies directly to each and every particular act, without any need of intermediate rules.

As pointed out earlier, judging particular acts by their consequences, according to the utilitarian principle, has been criticized by deontologists. Such utilitarian judgments were said to violate ordinary moral intuitions or commonsense moral beliefs. That is, if one reasons as an act utilitarian, one might violate moral rules that prohibit lying or stealing, say, on the ground that such violations produce good results—using ends to justify means. However, if the utilitarian principle were used to justify moral rules, and such rules were then used to justify particular judgments, utilitarianism would seem to have a way of meeting this criticism.

Indeed, by adopting rules, rule utilitarianism seems to combine the best features of utilitarianism and rule deontology, supplementing the former with rules and the later with a principle to justify the rules. Rules would be justified by showing that they are the best rules to have in order to maximize utility, and acts would be justified by showing that they conform to the rules.

The justification of particular judgments by rules, and the justification of rules by principles, of course, is just the pattern of reasoning we have been illustrating throughout this book. Act utilitarianism and act or rule deontology seem to fail because they omit one or another of these levels of reasoning. Rule utilitarianism seems adequate because it includes them all. Act utilitarians, however, believe that they have a correct account of moral reasoning, and hence that intermediate rules are not necessary to justify particular acts. They think that the commonsense appeal to rules is mistaken and that rule utilitarians have misinterpreted the function of rules. Therefore, we will want to take a closer look at the function of rules in moral reasoning, to see that there are different kinds of rules, and why one or another of these kinds may be necessary, or at least useful, for determining which particular acts are right or wrong.

Two Kinds of Rules

In a famous article, John Rawls distinguished two kinds of rules: practice rules and summary rules. Practice rules, he said, actually define a practice, and hence determine what kinds of acts conform to that practice. We cannot determine whether or not an act conforms to a practice without considering such rules. Thus practice rules are necessary when a question of practice is at issue, and it seems to be just these kinds of rules that, according to Rawls, the rule utilitarians have in mind.

For example, it is a rule of baseball that a batter who makes three strikes is out. This is a practice rule, for it defines what counts as striking out. There would be no way of determining what counts as a strikeout without the rule. Many rules in the "game of life" are like this, for there are rules that determine what perjury means, what adultry means, or what it means to break a promise. Rawls supposes that acts are right or wrong because they conform or fail to conform to such rules.

JOHN RAWLS
(1921–   )
On Summary Rules

The point of having rules derives from the fact that similar cases tend to recur and that one can decide cases more quickly if one records past decisions in the form of rules. If similar cases didn't recur, one would be required to apply the utilitarian principle directly, case by case, and rules reporting past decisions would be of no use.

From: "Two Concepts of Rules." John Rawls. *Philosophical Review*, 64, 1955: 3–32.

Summary rules, however, are not of this kind. Summary rules are merely summaries of particular judgments that have been made in the past. They note that certain kinds of acts were judged to be right or wrong in the past and hence may be used as "rules of thumb" to predict what kinds of acts are likely to be right or wrong in the future. However, acts are not right *because* they conform to summary rules. On Rawls' interpretation, practice rules are normative, but summary rules are not. Practice rules actually determine which acts within a practice are correct, but summary rules are merely inductive generalizations about the rightness or wrongness of acts independently determined. Thus it seems that act utilitarians can admit summary rules and still maintain that the utilitarian principle alone determines what is right. In other words, act utilitarians think that summary rules are sometimes useful, but they do not think that summary rules are necessary for making moral judgments. On their view, summary rules can always be disregarded by appealing directly to the utilitarian principle itself.

But what of practices? Presumably, act utilitarians cannot allow that practices ever determine what is right or wrong in particular cases, for that would amount to saying that acts can be right or wrong independently of consequences. Society may have its practices, but, presumably, a good act utilitarian would not obey such practices unless obedience produced more good than any alternative act. Thus, on the act view, practice rules appear to be either superfluous or nonutilitarian. But an act utilitarian may find summary rules useful, for summary rules may serve as a way of making predictions about the rightness or wrongness of future acts.

A Critique of These Views

For these reasons, act utilitarians have accused rule utilitarians of being "rule worshippers." That is, act utilitarians see no reason for following rules when such actions violate the utilitarian principle. Act utilitarians also fail to see how the *definition* of a practice can make that practice either right or wrong. We can define what promising means, for instance, or what it means to keep or break a promise, but it does not follow that it is always wrong to break a promise, for there may be good reasons to do so. If such rules hold, they seem to hold only in a prima facie sense, that is, unless there are good reasons to break them.

Another difficulty with the rule-utilitarian view lies in trying to determine precisely why any rules at all would be required in order to apply the utilitarian principle. Well, one answer seems to lie in the need for practices, a need that has been emphasized by social contract theorists and even cultural relativists. For, even if it were possible to determine that some particular acts are right or wrong by appealing directly to the utilitarian principle, it does not seem possible to make all determinations in this way. Certain practices or institutions are needed to produce certain kinds of desirable results. It is therefore necessary to follow the rules of those practices or institutions in order to achieve those results.

If so, what reasons are there to suppose that act utilitarians can do without rules? The act utilitarian can argue that we should follow the rules of society only when doing so produces greater utility than any other alternative, but he fails to notice that the maximization of utility is often not possible without rules. If we can do more good only by creating and following social rules, then the rules of society are necessary to produce the best consequences. Rules may not always be necessary, and it may not always be necessary to follow them, but it would be necessary to follow them when doing so produces more good. This means that it is at least sometimes necessary to adopt rules and to act according to them, even according to the act-utilitarian view. These practice rules would not by themselves determine what is right or wrong independently of the principle, but the principle would also not determine what is right without the rules. Thus practice rules would be necessary to supplement the principle of utility, but unlike the rules of rule deontology, utilitarian rules would not function independently of the principle.

Moreover, utilitarianism also appears to require summary rules. That

150

is, summary rules do not seem to be merely convenient, but they also seem necessary for the application of the utilitarian principle. If, as mentioned above, in criticism of act deontology, it is not possible to judge particular acts except as instances of kinds, and if it is not possible to make predictions about acts except as instances of classes of acts, then it is simply not possible to judge particular acts according to the principle of utility without making inductive generalizations, or without inductive rules. That is, if we cannot predict future consequences without using inductive generalizations, then we cannot judge particular acts except as instances of certain kinds of acts, or as instances of inductive rules. And if so, summary rules would be normative and not simply convenient guides, for it would be irrational to act without them.

The rules of morality that are usually thought to be natural, or not dependent on the conventions of society, such as the basic rules of natural law theory, or of rule deontology, are probably summary rules, when looked at from a utilitarian point of view. That is, rules about lying or killing, say, are rules which tell us that, all things being equal, lying and killing are acts that normally have bad consequences. These are rules which hold, not absolutely, but in a prima facie sense, because they may have exceptions in special cases.

Practice rules—the rules enacted by society—would also hold in a prima facie sense, but they would be brought into existence in order to achieve certain goals. They would not be derived simply from the application of the principle in past experience. Thus, in accepting practice rules, it would seem that utilitarianism would need to allow for a creative element in moral reasoning, that is, for the creation of moral rules that cannot be deduced from the principle alone.

EXERCISES

1. Examine the following cases and ask yourself how you would resolve them if you were (1) a rule deontologist, (2) an act deontologist, (3) a rule utilitarian, and (4) an act utilitarian. In each case, ask yourself whether the theory provides a clear procedure for resolving the issue and, if not, why not.

   a. Avery considers cheating on his income taxes. He has suffered severe financial reverses since the beginning of the year. Among other things, he lost his job because his company went out of business. Because he is falling behind on his house payments, he is also afraid that his family will have to move and his teenage children will need to change schools. But, by exaggerating his expenses, he believes he will receive a refund of about $1,800. This, he thinks, will be enough to cover expenses until he can find a new job. The government, he thinks, will not miss this small amount of money and would probably waste it in any case.

   b. Ashley is unhappily married, but she does not believe in divorce. However, she is attracted to a male friend that her husband does not know about, and she is tempted to have an intimate relationship with him. She is afraid that, if her husband found out, he might divorce her, and yet she also thinks it would be wrong to deceive him. Her friend, Laura, urges her to continue the relationship in secret, pointing out that her husband is not likely to find out. In that way, everyone will be happier, she says, for ignorance is bliss.

c.   Bob is suffering from AIDS and wants to commit suicide, but he is afraid to do it by himself. He has asked his friend, Harry, to help him, but Harry is uncertain about what he should do. Harry knows that Bob is suffering and that he will probably die within the year anyway, but he also knows that Bob's mother is opposed to suicide and would want her son to live as long as possible. She thinks the pain can be kept under control, but Harry feels certain that this is not true.

d.   Hilary and Perry know that their next-door neighbors physically abuse their own children. They have reason to believe that the abuse is severe, but they are not sure what they should do about it. They consider reporting the case to the authorities, but they are afraid that this will do little good, for the children might then be separated from their parents and be without a home. They also do not want the neighbors to think they are busybodies who pry into other people's affairs.

2.   Try to answer the following questions.

a.   What is the difference between act and rule deontology? What are the strengths and weaknesses of each?

b.   Consider a particular case: say, whether you should repay on time a debt that you had promised to repay or use the money to help someone in need. Do you think you could resolve this issue by appealing to moral rules? If not, do you think that you should rely on your moral intuitions instead?

c.   What is the difference between act and rule utilitarianism? What are the strengths and weaknesses of each of these positions?

d.   How does rule utilitarianism differ from rule deontology? Why do rule utilitarians think their theory has advantages which rule deontology lacks?

e.   Explain the difference between practice rules and summary rules? Which of these two types of rules is emphasized in rule utilitarianism? Can either type of rule be allowed by act utilitarians? Discuss.

THE PRAGMATIST CRITIQUE

Pragmatism is a philosophy that originated in the United States at the end of the nineteenth century. It is like utilitarianism in many respects, in its emphasis upon practicality, for instance, which, according to both theories, is measured by the consequences of actions. Both philosophies continued to be influential in the twentieth century, for both were critical of more traditional, speculative philosophies, and tended to emphasize empirical methods. But pragmatism is less static and absolutistic than utilitarianism. It places a great deal of emphasis on creativity, and on pluralism and relativity.

Like utilitarianism and natural law theory, pragmatism is teleological. But, like rule deontology, it does not hold that any one end or principle is absolute; and it maintains that moral rules and institutions may be modified by history.

Like nearly all of the theories we have considered, pragmatism emphasizes the importance of reasoning in ethics. But it also holds that reasoning must adapt itself to changing conditions. For this reason, it is also contextualistic, maintaining that solutions are relative to situations, goals, and available means.

DEWEY'S RELATIVISM AND CONTEXTUALISM

John Dewey, one of the chief exponents of pragmatic philosophy, is famous for several contributions to moral theory. One of these is his idea of how intelligent thinking is directed to the solution of a problematic situation. Following William James and Charles S. Peirce, other American pragmatists, Dewey viewed thinking as a problem-solving activity, or as Peirce put it, a way of resolving doubt. Typically, a problem arises when we want to do something but do not know how to achieve our goal. Our way may be blocked and we may not know how to overcome or remove the obstacle.

In such a situation, Dewey held, we need to formulate a hypothesis—perhaps several hypotheses—about how to solve our problem, and we also need to test our hypotheses by acting upon them, to see if they will work. Thus hypotheses—or ideas or beliefs—are tested in action, by the consequences of acting upon them, and our hypotheses need to be changed or modified if they do not work. This is the scientific method, according to Dewey, the method of testing our beliefs by experience.

JOHN DEWEY
(1859–1952)
The Experimental Method in Ethics

A third significant change that would issue from carrying over experimental method from physics to man concerns the import of standards, principles, rules. With the transfer, these, and all tenets and creeds about good and goods, would be recognized to be hypotheses. Instead of being rigidly fixed, they would be treated as intellectual instruments to be tested and confirmed—and altered—through consequences effected by acting upon them. They would lose all pretense of finality—the ulterior source of dogmatism . . .

From: *The Quest for Certainty.* Ch. X. John Dewey. New York: Minton, Balch and Co., 1929.

But, of course, we not only test our beliefs by experience—by acting on them—we also guide our experience by our beliefs. Thus reasoning is a two-directional and phased activity in which we (1) use our general ideas to guide our actions and (2) use our actions to test our general ideas. Reasoning is not simply deduction from principles, as the utilitarians or Kantians seem to think, nor is it simply induction from particular cases, as the act deontologists appear to hold. On Dewey's view, general principles or rules are not absolute but relative to particular judgments, and particular judgments are not absolute, for they are relative to principles or rules. Thus moral reasoning, like scientific reasoning, is an ongoing process in which we test our particular judgments by our general beliefs and our general beliefs by our particular judgments.

If one adds to this the Jamesian idea of a "storehouse of beliefs"—the idea that every new belief needs to be fitted into our entire stock of beliefs—we may then see that, according to pragmatism, general ideas are not only tested by particular ideas and vice versa, but that our general ideas are also tested for coherence with other general ideas. That is, each of our beliefs is part of a whole system of beliefs and hence can be tested ultimately only by seeing if it coheres with that system. Sometimes, however, the system itself, or part of a system, must be modified to accommodate a new belief, or a new set of beliefs. Thus, morality may be supposed to change as our old system of moral beliefs is changed to accommodate new ideas about slavery, or women's rights, say, or by a respect for individual freedom or privacy.

In these respects, pragmatism is different from both traditional rationalism and traditional empiricism. Rationalist philosophers have held that certain general ideas are absolute and that particular judgments must be deduced from them. Empiricists have held that particular judgments are absolute and that general ideas must be derived from the particular. But pragmatism holds that general and particular beliefs are relative to one another, so the ultimate test of truth is the coherence of all beliefs with one another.

Dewey in particular extended this idea to include other people. On his view, it is not just the coherence of our own beliefs that serves as a test of truth, but the agreement of our beliefs with those of other investigators. As in Kant's philosophy, beliefs are tested by their universality, but not simply by what each person can will to be universal. They are tested ultimately by what people in general will accept after they have applied appropriate rational tests. Thus, there is an element of social contract theory, and of democracy, in Dewey's view of ethics as a way of testing the truth of ideas.

THE ENDS MEANS CONTINUUM

We have said that pragmatism, like natural law theory, is teleological, and also that it has elements of utilitarianism. The utilitarian J. S. Mill held that actions originally conceived as means to ends can also become ends in themselves, and Dewey seemed to echo this idea in holding that the distinction between ends and means is not absolute but relative.

On Dewey's view, almost any action may be either an end or a means, depending upon how it is viewed by an agent. People eat in order to be able to work, for example, and they work in order to eat. People follow social rules to produce other goods, but they also feel it is important to follow the rules in order to have a civilized, rule-governed society. So, according to Dewey, what is an end in one context may be a means in another. Ends and means are linked in a continuum, in the ongoing process of life. On Dewey's view, there are no ultimate ends for the sake of which all else is done. Everything we are concerned about counts, but nothing counts absolutely.

JOHN DEWEY
(1859–1952)
On the Neglect of Means

It is impossible to form a just estimate of the paralysis of effort that has been produced by indifference to means. Logically, it is truistic that lack of consideration for means signifies that so-called ends are not taken seriously. It is as if one professed devotion to painting pictures conjoined with contempt for canvas, brush and paints; or a love of music on condition that no instruments, whether the voice or something external, be used to make sounds. The good workman in the arts is known by his respect for his tools and by his interest in perfecting his technique.

From: *The Quest for Certainty*. John Dewey. New York: Minton, Balch and Co., 1929.

Within the ends means continuum, ends are used to judge the rightness or wrongness of actions viewed as means. But Dewey also held that ends can be evaluated according to available means. That is, an action may be judged to be right or good because it is productive of an end, but an end may also be judged to be good, or at least suitable as an object of realistic action, if it is attainable by available means or resources. Thus it may be a good thing to fly, and anything that enables us to fly may be a good thing to use as a means to that end. However, under given conditions, it may not be possible for us to fly, in which case that would not be a good thing to aim at doing, for it would not be a realistic goal. As Kant has said, "ought" implies "can," and Dewey, following Hegel, pointed out that there is a real difference between mere aspirations, or romantic ideals, and realistic or practical goals.

If we add to the notion of evaluating ends by means the idea that ends are means to still other ends, then ends may be evaluated in two different ways: (1) by available means, or by attainability, and (2) as means to other ends. By combining these, one obtains a third test: namely, the coherence or compossibility of the whole network of ends and means, given our knowledge of existing states of affairs and our ability to predict the future.

We may know, for example, that we have a certain amount of excess income that will enable us to purchase a long-desired luxury item. In this case our end is attainable by our means. But we may also know that, if we purchased the item, we would not have enough time to use it, given the other demands of life. We would then have reason to modify our goal, even though attainable, because it does not fit in with other goals, or because it would interfere with the means of achieving other things we desire.

These considerations are very similar to those emphasized by traditional self-realization philosophers who thought of morality as a harmonious or balanced life. As in Plato's philosophy, or Aristotle's, rules serve to order our lives, to avoid conflicts, to make it possible to realize many different goals, and to cooperate with others. By way of analogy, Dewey viewed moral reasoning in biological terms, as a kind of Darwinian adjustment of the organism to its environment; a way of seeing how we can adapt ourselves and our societies to the changing demands of life.

APPLYING THE THEORY

For the pragmatist, there are some issues about which we have little doubt. We have enough experience to know that, in general, harming others, telling lies, or breaking promises is morally wrong. Acting according to such rules normally fits in well with our whole system of beliefs. Indeed, we probably act according to these rules as a matter of habit. However, situations may arise which we find perplexing. We sometimes face genuine doubts about which course of action we should follow. In such cases, pragmatists would have us consider the alternatives and ask ourselves about the consequences of acting one way or another. We might try to find out what others did in similar circumstances and what the results of their actions happened to be. If possible, we might even experiment to find out for ourselves what would happen if we chose one or another alternative. If one course of action seemed not to work, we might then try another, until we have found what appears to be a solution to our problem.

Suppose a person finds that her marriage is not working very well. Among other things, her husband no longer seems to respect her wishes and is mean to the children. She would like to continue the marriage, but it is becoming intolerable. One alternative would be to seek a divorce. Considering this alternative pragmatically, she would ask herself what the consequences would be, for herself, for her children, and even for her husband. How would she support herself? How would she take care of the children? How would the children respond? Divorce is possible, but she might conclude that the cost is very high. Her life-style and that of other members of her family would change drastically. To avoid these unfavorable consequences, she might then explore other alternatives. She has tried to reason with her husband, but that didn't work. She has tried to convince him to join her in seeing a marriage counselor, but he refused. Perhaps he would agree to a trial separation? In that way, everyone might find out whether that would be the best alternative, or whether indeed they should all try harder to make the marriage work.

In this case, the woman finds that her old habits and beliefs are not adequate for solving the problem. She needs to respond in new ways, and hence needs to imagine what would happen if she adopted one or another new course of action. She also wants to preserve as much of her old way of life as possible; at least she wants to disturb herself and others as little as necessary. Thus, in reviewing the alternatives, she reasons that divorce would be very costly. Because negotiation has been unsuccessful in the past, she infers that it will be unsuccessful in the future. So she finally decides to experiment by suggesting or even forcing a trial separation. In this way she and others can experience the consequences of being separated without becoming fully committed to divorce or to a continuance of the marriage. Staying married or becoming divorced are not final solutions to her problems or those of her family, but either may be an end she decides to seek, and either may serve as a means of attaining other goals that she and other members of her family would like to attain.

What of Moral Absolutism?

Many people are opposed to pragmatism because of its rejection of absolutes. Are there no correct answers? Is it not the case that actions are either right or wrong and not just right or wrong when viewed in a certain way? Is it not the case that the natural law theorists, the Kantians, and the utilitarians have a point in holding that what is right or wrong is not simply a matter of opinion or perspective?

In fairness to the pragmatists, we should point out that moral truths are bound to be relative in some sense or other, even if they are not relative in all senses. That is, if as Aristotle and even Aquinas and the utilitarians have maintained, moral goodness is what is good for human beings (and perhaps even other sentient creatures), then moral goodness is relative even on their accounts. Even if some things were absolutely good for persons, the goodness of those things would still be relative to persons.

We should also notice that, in its relativism, pragmatism is not indifferent to factual considerations, such as facts about persons, their psychological states, or their desires or wants. Indeed, pragmatism insists that we take account of such facts in determining what is right or wrong. It insists that we be realistic in setting our goals and in selecting means of achieving ends. So pragmatism does not recommend that we do things arbitrarily, on a whim, or without due consideration.

However, we probably should make a distinction, not always clear in pragmatic writers, between the relativity of knowledge and the relativity of what is known. It may be true that we need to be constantly willing to modify our beliefs in order to maintain an open mind and to learn; but the answers we obtain may be true or false independently of our means of knowing. That is, certain things may be true of the world whether we know them or not, and certain kinds of acts may be good or right even though we believe they are bad or wrong. So the means we use to arrive at the truth may be distinguished from conditions that make our beliefs true. The process of arriving at truth may involve relativities that truth itself does not. Even so, from the standpoint of human knowledge, truth is an ideal, for we have no way of knowing truth except by trial and error. We still need to examine, reason, and test our ideas to find out if they are true.

But perhaps pragmatism is wrong in holding that there are no absolutes known to us, or that there are no absolute ends of human action or of moral reasoning. Consistency in reasoning, which is espoused as a goal even by pragmatists, seems to be one such end, even if it cannot always be achieved. That is, we may need to tolerate inconsistencies in our systems of belief until we find ways to eliminate them, but we can hardly surrender consistency as an ideal without surrendering the ideal of reason itself. It also seems to be the case that life and truth, for instance, are very basic goods, as Aquinas and Kant have maintained. These goods seem to be presupposed in any value system, for there can be no other values without life, and there can be no honest inquiry into value without a respect for truth. If these are not moral absolutes, they must be very close to being such, and they certainly must be ranked above other less fundamental goods.

However, even if life and truth, or reason itself, are among the most fundamental human goods, we have seen that there is reason to believe in exceptions to rules founded upon these goods. Life, for instance, is a very fundamental good *when it is good,* but life is not always good. Thus, even if we have reason to presume that, generally speaking, life is good because it makes possible all other goods, there are times when the things it makes possible are bad. That is, life is a condition of evil as well as good. So, whatever we hold to be important as end values, we still need to consider *why* we regard such things as valuable, or under what conditions. This is tantamount to saying that even they are relative goods. We need not be hedonists or utilitarians who hold that life is valuable only when it produces more pleasure than pain, but we may want to hold, nonetheless, that an extremely painful life is not good.

EXERCISES

1. In each of the following cases, explain what you think would be a pragmatic approach to the problem. Then explain in what respects you think this approach would be pragmatic.

   a. You discover that there is inadequate housing for the poor. Many people are living on the streets, and some of them are hungry and cold. What can you do about it? What *should* you do?

   b. Penny and Curtis have very unruly children, ages nine and twelve. They are constantly in trouble at home, in school, and even with the law. The children are not afraid of being caught disobeying rules, for they are never punished very severely. What should their parents do?

   c. Edmund believes that medical experimentation on animals is morally wrong. It causes them great suffering and usually leads to death. But Derek thinks that such experiments are necessary in order to find cures for human disease. He thinks that Edmund is wrong in trying to have such experiments stopped. Is there any way of resolving the issue between persons who want to protect animals on the one hand, and persons who want scientific progress, on the other?

   d. Clare pokes fun at her friend's husband, Bob, who does all the cooking for his family. Clare thinks that cooking is women's work and that Bob is not manly. Clare's daughter would like to tell her mother that she is old-fashioned and even mean, but she does not know how to do it without hurting her. What alternatives are open to Clare's daughter?

   e. Freeman is a college instructor who uses the honor system when giving tests. But when he leaves the room during examinations, several students regularly cheat. Ted, a student in the class, is angry about what is going on. He works hard studying and feels that the teacher should take precautions to prevent cheating.

However, he is afraid that if he mentions this to the teacher, the other students may find out and turn against him. Perhaps even the teacher would resent his criticism. What should he do?

2. Try to answer the following questions based on your reading of the text.

a. What are some of the features of pragmatism? In what ways does it differ from other theories discussed in this chapter? In what ways is it similar to them?

b. Explain some of the ways in which Dewey's theory is relativistic. What does he mean by his "ends means continuum"?

c. How do pragmatists think we can test our moral beliefs? Can we test any of our values independently of other values we hold? Discuss.

d. What objections would a pragmatist raise against utilitarianism? Against Kantianism? Against act or rule deontology?

e. What is the role of tradition in pragmatism? Does tradition have any bearing on what is right or wrong? Are traditions subject to any kind of criticism? Explain.

f. Does tradition play any role in any of the other theories we considered? If so, how?

EXISTENTIALISM

Existentialism is not explicitly a moral philosophy in exactly the same sense as many of the other theories we considered. It does not offer us a principle or principles, or a system of rules. It is more like act deontology in holding that moral judgments cannot be deduced from principles or rules. However, unlike act deontology, it does not hold that certain kinds of acts are right and others wrong. Rather, it is more like emotivism in holding that there is no objective distinction between right and wrong, good and bad. But, instead of holding that the value of actions is determined by emotion, existentialists have tended to hold that value is determined by choice. In this sense, existentialism is more of a metaethical theory than a normative ethical theory, for it tells us that because choice is necessary, we cannot determine what is right or wrong by reasoning alone.

The French existentialist Jean Paul Sartre thought that we make things valuable by choosing them. Sartre seemed to hold that we can choose to live whatever kind of life we wish, and it is therefore up to each of us to choose the kind of life we want for ourselves. On his view, each person is totally responsible for his or her choices and for what happens as a result of choice. He also held that there are no excuses, for there is no one to blame for our actions but ourselves.

AUTHENTIC AND INAUTHENTIC CHOICE

However, in describing alternatives for choice, several existentialists have made a distinction between authentic and inauthentic choice, although some

159

of them use different names for this distinction. Heidegger uses the words "authentic" and "inauthentic," but Sartre, for example, makes a distinction between what he calls good and bad faith. Kierkegaard talks about choosing between the ethical and aesthetic modes of human existence. They all seem to have in mind the idea that we can reason honestly or dishonestly in an attempt to justify our behavior; we can either lie to ourselves and others or we can tell the truth. Although they often claim to be merely describing these different modes of behavior, it seems fairly clear that they consider the authentic mode to be morally desirable and superior to being inauthentic.

On Sartre's view, the inauthentic person is a pretender, a person who is always trying to please others, or at least trying to present a good image of himself to them. Such a person is basically a liar, according to Sartre, for, in order to make himself look good in the eyes of others, he pretends to be something he is not. In American idiom, he is a phoney, or a person who is always play acting. In the words of Kierkegaard, such a person is simply a member of the crowd, not a true individual, who is always motivated by what "they" think or what "they" say, and has no ideas of his own. To Nietzsche, such people have slave mentalities, for they are subservient to the opinions of others. In popular discussions today, these ideas are often expressed in debates about conformity and nonconformity, or by the insistence of some people that their choice is indeed their choice and not the business of anyone else.

SIMONE DE BEAUVOIR
(1908–1986)
On Human Responsibility

But if man is free to define for himself the conditions of a life which is valid in his own eyes, can he not choose whatever he likes and act however he likes? Dostoievsky asserted, "If God does not exist, everything is permitted." Today's believers use this formula for their own advantage. To re-establish man at the heart of his destiny is, they claim, to repudiate all ethics. However, far from God's absence authorizing all license, the contrary is the case . . . he bears the responsibility for a world which is not the work of a strange power, but of himself, where his defeats are inscribed, and his victories as well.

From: *The Ethics of Ambiguity*. Simone de Beauvoir. New York: Philosophical Library, 1948.

In a sense, existentialism reflects the Kantian idea of individual autonomy and the belief that we should do things because we believe they are right, and not because of some other motive. Kant said that each person determines the moral law for himself or herself—which is tantamount to saying that each and every person should act according to his or her own conscience, and not simply to please others, or to make a profit. The difference is that Kant thought that there is one moral law for everyone, whereas some existentialists seem to think that each person may make up different rules. Thus the notion of being an individual in existentialism tends to mean having one's own personal style. Nietzsche compares the individual to an artist who makes his or her own life into a work of art.

The Intrinsic Value of Actions

Existentialism also tends to follow Kantianism in holding that actions are not right or wrong because of their consequences. The emphasis in existentialism is more upon the attitudes one has in acting, on *how* one acts more than upon *what* one does, and hence upon one's involvement in or commitment to his or her project. Actions are supposed to have value, according to Kierkegaard and Sartre, for example, because of our subjective involvement in them, and not because of consequences. The consequences, after all, may be quite different from what we expect, as they often are. There is no point wasting one's life doing things that are boring, just because other people say we should. Existentialists are fond of reminding us that in the end we will all die, and, indeed, that we may die at any time. We should therefore do things that have value in and of themselves, things we make valuable by becoming involved in them, and hence find exciting.

This particular aspect of existentialism has been mentioned by other philosophers—by Aristotle, for example, and by Dewey—that the value of living is living, and not something else produced by us. We—our lives—are the end product of the moral life. Morality is not dedicated to some other kind of good. So it is the quality of our lives that is at issue, and we should not waste our lives on false values, or on actions that are not rewarding to us or to others. Like the American philosophers Emerson and Thoreau, existentialists bid us to live and not waste our lives merely preparing to live.

Of course, all philosophers are concerned with the distinction between illusion and reality, and, in ethics, between true value and the mere appearance of value. Indeed, the point of reasoning in ethics is to make this distinction, so we do not purchase a bill of goods, so to speak, just because "they" say we should. However, existentialists do not believe that something is wrong for us just because it is advocated by others, or that something is right for us just because we believe it is. Indeed, we often believe things have value and later come to realize in experience, in action, that our beliefs were false. In this respect, existentialism is like pragmatism, for it holds that the value of our beliefs must be tested in action.

Reason and Choice

Existentialism is often criticized for being too subjectivistic in its account of morality and for defending arbitrariness. The idea that anything goes, or that anything whatsoever can be justified, certainly seems to follow from the idea that values are created by choice. However, in other respects, existentialism is a very strict moral philosophy, in holding that persons are wholly responsible for their lives or in maintaining that they can never blame others, or fate, for what happens to them. However, in order to make a point, it seems that existentialism also exaggerates that point. But this should not obscure the fact that it does have a point to make.

Sartre, for example, argues that rules or principles are not always sufficient to determine what is morally right or wrong. Although he appears to be correct in this, it does not follow that rules or principles are not necessary, or even that they are never sufficient. Rules and principles may always be necessary to moral judgment, even if not sufficient, and they may sometimes be sufficient, even if not always so.

Sartre gives us examples of controversial issues, when rules conflict, or when the rules seem to be too general and vague to give adequate information about a particular case. The principle "Do good and avoid evil," for example, can be ridiculed because it does not tell us what is good or what is evil, and it does not therefore tell us what to do in any particular case. But, nonetheless, it seems that such a principle is presupposed in any judgment we make.

JEAN-PAUL SARTRE
(1905–1980)
On Indeterminacy and Choice

What could help him choose? Could the Christian doctrine? No. Christian doctrine says: Act with charity, love your neighbor, deny yourself for others, choose the way which is hardest, and so forth. But which is the harder road? To whom does one owe the more brotherly love, the patriot or the mother? Which is the more useful aim, the general one of fighting in and for the whole community, or the precise aim of helping one particular person to live? Who can give an answer to that *a priori*? No one.

From: *Existentialism and Humanism*. Jean-Paul Sartre. Philip Mairet, trans. London: Methuen, 1942.

Sartre gives an example of a young man who, during the war, cannot determine whether he should stay at home with his mother or join the resistance. The rule "Do good and avoid evil" does not help him much. The rules "Honor thy parents" and "Be patriotic" do not help much either, for, in this case, those rules seem to conflict. So Sartre says the young man must simply decide.

But we should notice that the young man is not faced with a decision and no information whatsoever. The rules in fact determine his alternatives for choice, even if they do not make his choice for him. Indeed, if he were not interested in doing good and avoiding evil, he would not have a moral problem at all. Sartre's point therefore is not that rules and principles are irrelevant or unnecessary, but only that, in this kind of case, they are not sufficient. That is, in addition to using rules, we may need to make choices, not only about whether we should do what we judge to be right, but in order to determine what is right.

We have already considered philosophies which take the indeterminacy of rules and the necessity of choice into account. Social contract theory, for example, recognizes that rules can be brought into existence by choice or agreement, and that such rules are necessary to society. When such rules are inadequate, we can change the rules, modify them, or make up new rules, as we often do. We also make up rules individually to govern our personal lives and hence create our own styles of living. But our personal rules need not conflict with basic moral rules, or with the rules of society, even though they can.

The Individual and Society

We have said that our own beliefs are not correct or incorrect because they agree or disagree with the beliefs of society—because we conform or do not conform to others. But there is often a conflict between individual beliefs and those of other people. Indeed, as children, we often think that the beliefs of others are being imposed on us, that we are not doing what *we* want but what *they* want us to do. We learn to accept and internalize many of the things we are taught, making them our own; but on some issues, we may also continue to oppose other people.

The ideal, it would seem, would be to create a society in which people agree with one another in their fundamental beliefs, but a society in which they are also free to pursue their own individual interests as long as the pursuit of those interests does not infringe on the basic rights of others. Indeed, any reference to basic rights supposes that there are common ideas, or ideas which, upon reflection, we would all come to recognize, if we were rational.

These are points upon which theories other than existentialism have placed a great deal of emphasis. If everyone has different conceptions of what is right, then it would seem that no one really has any rights which others have a duty to respect. To carry the idea of each person's doing his or her own thing to its logical conclusion would mean anarchy. But we also want to allow for individual differences, and we want individual satisfactions to serve as a test of social rules. The rules themselves need to be justified by the good they do.

We also want to allow, and even insist, as the existentialists seem to do, that persons are bound by their own consciences, and hence that it would be inauthentic or dishonest of them to follow ideas they do not believe. Indeed it would be strange to advise people to do what they believe they should not do. Rather, if we disagree with them, we should try to convince them to change their minds. Failing that, we may need to oppose them, in order to be faithful to our own beliefs. But it does not follow from this that we can never agree, or that we do not have common ideas upon which we may be able to reach an agreement. In fact, one of the reasons we seek agreement is that both we and our opponents want agreement, or peace and friendship, and not opposition or war.

To share the beliefs of others, to have the same interests and appreciations, is to be of one mind with them—to be kindred spirits, so to speak, or to belong to the same family or community. Such a state is certainly desirable if it does not ignore other basic human drives or needs, and this is why we must take account of all human goods, not simply social ones. Existentialism reminds us that we can sacrifice our own individuality because of our herd instinct—because of our need for acceptance and approval—but also that we should not allow the rules of society to override individual goods.

CONCLUSION

According to the theories discussed in this chapter, we have learned that particular moral judgments cannot be derived from one and only one first principle, that moral rules are necessary, and that, even then, there may be decisions to make in the choice of rules, or in applying rules to particular acts. Thus, if these theories are correct, moral reasoning is not simply a deductive process in which particular moral judgments are derived from first principles. There are intermediate steps. Indeed, our judgments on lower levels—sometimes characterized as "moral intuitions"—may be used to test our rules and principles.

In the concluding sections of this book, we will want to use these insights in applying theories to actual cases, just as we will want to use the insights of the other theories we have considered. In the process, however, we will need to amend all of the theories, to make them compatible with one another. Mainly, we will need to remove from each its exclusive claim to truth, recognizing that each has an important point to make, but that each applies only to a given level, stage, or phase of moral reasoning.

EXERCISES

1. Return to the previous sets of exercises included in this chapter. What might an existentialist say in response to each of the cases under consideration?

2. What do existentialists mean by authentic and inauthentic choice?

3. What reasons are there for thinking that moral issues cannot be settled by rules or principles, and hence that choice is required?

4. Do you think that our choices can create moral obligations? Consider the making of promises. It seems that, in making a promise we can choose to take on an obligation. Do we therefore have an obligation?

5. If choices can create obligations, do you think that obligations can be created by choice alone? What else may be required?

6. If obligations are determined by choice, are there any obligations that are not so determined? Give examples.

7. What criticisms would existentialism bring against other moral philosophies? Do you think that any of these criticisms are sound?

SUPPLEMENTARY READINGS

Barnes, Hazel. *An Existentialist Ethics.* New York: Random House, 1967.

Barret, William. *Irrational Man.* New York: Doubleday Anchor Books, 1958.

Bayles, Michael D. *Contemporary Utilitarianism.* New York: Doubleday Anchor Books, 1968.

Dewey, John. *Theory of Valuation*. Chicago: University of Chicago Press, 1939.

Fisch, Max. *Classic American Philosophers*. New York: Appleton-Century-Crofts, 1951.

Geiger, George. *John Dewey in Perspective*. Chs. 3 and 6. London: Oxford University Press, 1958.

Greene, Marjorie. *Introduction to Existentialism*. Chicago: University of Chicago Press, 1948.

Guignon, Charles. "Existentialist Ethics," in J. DeMarco & R. Fox, eds. *New Directions in Ethics*. London: Routledge and Kegan Paul, 1986.

Hare, R. M. *Freedom and Reason*. Oxford: The Clarendon Press, 1963.

Lyons, David. *Form and Limits of Utilitarianism*. Oxford: The Clarendon Press, 1965.

McDermott, John, ed. *The Philosophy of John Dewey*. Vols. I & II. Chicago: University of Chicago Press, 1981.

Olafson, Frederick A. *Principles and Persons: An Ethical Interpretation of Existentialism*. Baltimore: Johns Hopkins, 1967.

Prichard, H. A. "Does Moral Philosophy Rest on a Mistake." *Mind*, Vol. 21, 1912: 21–37.

Rawls, John. "Two Concepts of Rules." *Philosophical Review*, Vol. 64, 1955: 3–32.

Ross, W. D. *The Right and the Good*. Oxford: The Clarendon Press, 1930.

Sartre, Jean-Paul. *Existentialism and Humanism*. Philip Mairet, trans., London: Methuen and Co. Ltd., 1942.

Smart, J. J. C. "Extreme and Restricted Utilitarianism." *Philosophical Quarterly*, Vol. 6, 1956: 344–54.

Toulmin, Stephen. *An Examination of the Place of Reason in Ethics*. New York: Cambridge University Press, 1951.

_____. *The Philosophy of William James*. Chicago: University of Chicago Press, 1977.

PART THREE

DEVELOPING AND APPLYING A CODE

DEVELOPING A SET OF PRINCIPLES

We have argued that moral principles are needed to justify moral rules and particular moral judgments. However, we have seen that ethical theories disagree about what the ultimate principles are, or even whether, indeed, there is only one principle. However, each of the theories identifies an important aspect of moral reasoning, even if, as our criticisms indicate, it is incomplete in oversimplifying and overstating its claims. A more adequate theory, it seems, would necessarily be more complex, for it would need to take account of several principles and various stages and phases of moral reasoning.

In this chapter, therefore, we will try to show how an effective set of moral principles can be developed by drawing upon the insights of the several theories. Part of our argument for the principles we develop will be that they do have theoretical support, even though not all of the principles are supported by all of the theories. We will also try to support our principles by arguing that they are widely accepted and frequently used. Because of their widespread acceptance, the principles carry a great deal of force in moral argumentation and can be effectively used to resolve moral disputes.

CHARACTERISTICS OF PRINCIPLES

THEORETICAL SUPPORT

Although there is widespread agreement about moral principles, there is not much agreement about which moral theory is correct. Thus, in citing theoretical support, one may be citing a reason for a principle which is less convincing than the principle itself. A person may believe that it is reasonable to consider the benefit or harm of following a particular course of action, for example, without endorsing either utilitarianism or hedonism. That is, one may seriously question whether utilitarianism correctly explains how we should weigh the consequences of actions or whether hedonism offers a correct account of benefits and harms. Likewise, one may feel that justice requires treating similar cases similarly, as Kant had maintained, without accepting Kant's conclusion that there are no exceptions to moral rules. So a person may feel that a theory has an important point to make without accepting the manner in which it makes that point, or even the reasons it offers to support its position.

Nonetheless, we have seen that moral theorists do not advocate principles for no reason at all. They do offer evidence to show that the principles they defend play an important part in moral reasoning, even if sometimes they seem to overstate their case. The fact that a major moral theory supports a principle is itself a prima facie reason for giving serious consideration to that principle. The theoretical support of a principle suggests that there are good reasons for taking that principle into account, and it invites us to examine the reasons a theory offers to support its claims. In examining the theoretical support for a principle, we are likely to gain a greater appreciation of why we ourselves should accept that principle.

Because, in theorizing, there is a strong impetus toward unity and simplicity, there is also a strong tendency to believe that, ultimately, there must be only one principle. A belief in many ultimate principles seems theoretically inelegant, for it creates a problem of indeterminacy in application. That is, if we have more than one principle, it seems possible for our principles to conflict in a given case, for one principle may require an action that is forbidden by another principle. Regardless, some philosophers have argued that there is no one and only one principle of morality, that there are several ultimate values or rules according to which people should live.

One reason for adopting a pluralistic view is that theories which have only one stated principle tend to find that their principle is too general, too abstract, or too vague to be useful in making moral determinations, and hence that it needs to be supplemented by subordinate principles. Indeed, in this way, theories frequently overlap, because the first principles of one theory may be accepted as subordinate principles or rules in another theory. For example, rule utilitarianism accepts the rules of rule deontology as subordinate principles, while rule deontology includes utilitarian considerations among its rules. Likewise, egoists have allowed that persons may be required to do good for others when it serves their own self-interest, and altruists have allowed that, although people are not always justified in acting according to their own self-interest, they sometimes are. Such considerations suggest a need for several principles, even if it seems theoretically desirable to have only one.

The Prima Facie Restriction

If we accept several moral principles, the problem of conflict must be faced head on. If it is possible for the principles to conflict, the principles cannot apply absolutely without exception. Another way of saying this is that, if there is more than one principle, the principles apply in a prima facie sense, or "other things being equal." This means that any given principle may be qualified or overridden in a particular case by a consideration of highly unusual circumstances, or by a conflict with other principles. Thus, in developing a set of principles, it seems that we will need to add this prima facie restriction.

KURT BAIER
(1926–   )
On the Meaning of "Other Things Equal"

The first point to note is that usually when we claim that something is a good reason for doing a certain thing, we mean that it is so, *other things being equal*. When I smoke my fiftieth cigarette, my reason for doing so—if I have a reason at all—may be that it will satisfy a craving which interferes with my work.

Other things being equal, 'it will satisfy a craving' is a good reason for doing that which will have this effect. But in this case, other things are of course not equal. There are very many good reasons against my smoking my fiftieth cigarette. Smoking is very expensive. It is bad for my health . . . And so on.

From: "Good Reasons." Kurt Baier. *Philosophical Studies*, 4, 1953: 1–15.

Prima facie principles may seem weaker than absolute principles, but they also possess a number of strengths. In a sense, they are even stronger than absolute principles, for absolute principles may give the illusion of strength when they have little or no strength at all. For example, if we hold a principle absolutely, there seems to be nothing we can do when apparently exceptional cases arise, or when there seems to be good reason for violating the principle. The acceptance of one and only one absolute principle can prevent us from considering the complexities and subtleties of moral reasoning, making us insensitive to issues. If we hold our principles absolutely, it may also be more difficult to reach agreement with others, when their principles conflict with ours. In being more flexible, prima facie principles enable us to avoid these difficulties.

Indeed, we may be deceived in claiming that our principles are absolute or without exception. For instance, we may hold that the principle "Never harm people without good reason" is an absolute principle, but we may fail to recognize that it is absolute only because the phrase "without good reason" is included in it. But the addition of the phrase "without good reason" is practically equivalent to saying that the rule holds in a prima facie sense, that is, that it holds unless there is some good reason for thinking that it does not hold. Likewise, the rule "Never murder" may be taken to be absolute, but it is also deceptive, for the word "murder" means unjustified killing, and we still need to determine when acts of killing are justified and when they are not. As soon as we ask ourselves, "Is killing always wrong?" we realize that there may be times when it is not wrong, as in cases of self-defense.

The Burden of Proof

To say that principles hold in a prima facie sense is not to say simply that they sometimes hold and sometimes do not hold. It means that they hold unless there are very good, weighty reasons for allowing exceptions to them. That is, the "burden of proof" or *onus probandi* lies in justifying the exceptional case. When judging a case, we should assume that all of the principles apply to it, and hence that the type of action under consideration will be justified or forbidden by the principles. An exception should be allowed only when principles conflict, or when there is a very strong conviction to the contrary. Even when we have a strong conviction that would entail an exception to a principle, we should look for another principle to justify that conviction, a principle that would justify an exception in other cases as well.

For example, we all believe that it is good to promote life and wrong to intentionally cause death, but we are faced with problems about what we should do in cases of extremely painful, irreversible illness. Even natural law theorists, who argue that we should never kill, allow that we are not obligated to use unusual or heroic means to keep people alive. We may also question the justice of expending medical resources on a relatively few terminally ill individuals when we could do much more good by allocating such resources to the many more people who presently receive little or no medical care.

A good set of principles will reflect such conflicts in reasoning, and hence include a principle that requires us to respect life, as well as a principle that requires us to prevent suffering. Of course, a single principle might be stated in such a way as to include both considerations, but such a principle or set of principles should be specific enough to reflect the possibility of conflict. A set of principles that does not reflect reasonable grounds for conflict in such cases would not be a complete set. Thus, the burden of proof requirement, which is meant to underscore the force of prima facie principles, also points to the need for having more than one principle, or for trying to develop a complete set.

Intersubjective Agreement

Moral principles are implicit in the judgments we make. They are the ultimate reasons that support our moral claims. Their usefulness resides in their power to provide reasons for criticizing or justifying actions, for resolving doubtful cases, and for settling disputes. In order to serve these purposes, our principles must be made explicit. They must also be shared. They must be common or universal principles to which all of us can appeal in moral argumentation. To support our principles, therefore, we need to show that they are universal, or at least that they are widely shared.

One way of showing that principles are widely accepted, of course, is to show that they are actually cited by people in many different societies or cultures and in a variety of cases. Such principles may also be supported by the world's major religions; they may be incorporated in the laws of nations; and they may be expressed in the universal condemnation of certain acts such as so-called "crimes against humanity." They are also likely to express a respect for basic human needs, wants, and desires, and hence be grounded in our knowledge of human nature. Even if not openly asserted by all people, they may be shown to be implicit in the judgments they make. As evidence for such principles, we can survey the kinds of actions people approve or disapprove, including the reasons they offer to support their claims.

The widespread acceptance of principles, or intersubjective agreement, strengthens our ability to settle disputes between individuals, groups, and even cultures. However, in citing such agreement in principle, we do not want to maintain that agreement alone is an adequate test. We have suggested that moral principles should be grounded in human nature, in our knowledge of our own needs, wants, and aspirations, and in our knowledge of the needs and expectations of others. We have also said that moral principles need to pass various tests of reasonableness or rationality.

The test of rationality is a test of whether our judgments form a coherent set. Thus, we have said that we can test our higher-level beliefs by seeing if they support our lower-level convictions, just as we can see if our lower-level judgments are consistent with our higher-level beliefs. We can also see if our higher-level beliefs, our rules and principles, are consistent with one another. In order to assure coherence, we have argued that it is necessary to qualify our principles by holding that they apply in a prima facie sense.

The test of reasonableness, in turn, is a test of our willingness to take the reasons of others into account, taking seriously the things they regard as important, even when we disagree with them. In this way, we not only respect the opinions of others, we also allow ourselves to learn from them by taking their perspective into consideration. Reasonableness then becomes a test of rationality, for it is a way of seeing whether our beliefs are consistent with the beliefs of others, and of seeing how we can reconcile our differences. In attempting to justify our beliefs, we naturally try to convince others, for our ability to do so vindicates the intersubjectivity of our claims.

SCOPE OR GENERALITY

As we shall see, there are different ways of stating principles. They may be stated in ways that are more general, covering more cases, but, as a consequence, they tend to become rather vague and less informative. When they are more specific, they cover fewer cases but give us more information. If we opt for the first alternative, we are likely to have a very short list of principles; if we opt for the second alternative, a very long list.

There is, then, no correct number of principles. As a practical matter, we do not want a very large number, for they would then be too difficult to remember, to teach, or to apply. On the other hand, as we have said, if they are too few, they are not likely to give us adequate information, and hence will need to be qualified or supplemented by subordinate rules.

The criterion of simplicity, mentioned earlier, is related to scope or generality, for it has to do with the number of principles we use. We said that theorists generally believe that the fewer principles the better. This guideline appears to be based partly on aesthetic considerations, for a simpler theory seems more elegant than a complicated one. However, simplicity also bears on practicality, for simplicity affects efficiency. As we have pointed out, deliberation and judgment are easier if there are fewer principles to apply. Simplicity also affects the power of principles, for when there are fewer principles, more cases can be decided by each principle, making each principle a more powerful tool. If there are too many principles, it becomes difficult to know which principle to use, or whether any given action conforms to all the principles.

AFFIRMATIVE AND NEGATIVE PRINCIPLES

People sometimes observe that morality is taught to them in a negative way, as a list of "don'ts" instead of "do's," or as a set of prohibitions or restrictions rather than a list of prescriptions of positive things to do. They may also point out, rightly, that such teaching tends to emphasize negative reinforcement, or punishment, rather than positive reinforcement, or reward. However, there are several reasons why fundamental principles are likely to be expressed in negative form.

One reason is that negative principles tend to be determinate in a way that positive principles are not. That is, implicitly, negative principles seem to cover all cases, and hence apply to everybody all of the time, whereas positive principles are often not clear about when they apply, or to whom. "Don't lie" carries the implication "never, under any circumstances," but "Tell the truth" leaves open the question of when or under what circumstances. It is possible to satisfy negative principles by never doing what they prohibit, but it is not possible to satisfy universal positive principles, just because a person cannot always be doing what they say we should. One cannot always be telling the truth, for example, for, among other things, one does not always know the truth. Even if one did, one could not always be telling each and every truth.

Basic principles are also supposed to tell us what is morally necessary, as opposed to what is morally desirable. "Morally necessary" is what is usually meant by the words "duty" or "obligation." We use these words to indicate things people are morally *bound* to do, or are bound not to do, from a moral point of view. Such things are the very minimum that is expected of us, morally speaking. But such minimum requirements are usually expressed in a negative way, as evils we should avoid, rather than as positive goods we should try to achieve. We are minimally expected not to go around killing people, but we are not required to help each and every person stay alive. This does not mean that we have no positive obligations, but only that it is difficult to discover positive obligations that apply to everyone in the same way. Positive obligations are usually role-specific in that they apply only to persons in special circumstances. That is, parents have certain positive duties to their children, and teachers have certain positive duties to their students, but these duties do not apply to people who are not parents or teachers.

Of course, we do not usually consider persons morally good if they merely refrain from doing harm to others and never do any positively good acts. But there are many positively good things that people can do, and, except for special circumstances, it seems desirable to allow them a wide range of freedom in choosing among such goods. Later we will discuss more

---

J. S. MILL
(1806–1873)
On Perfect and Imperfect Duties

Now it is known that ethical writers divide moral duties into two classes denoted by the ill-chosen expressions, duties of perfect and imperfect obligation: the latter being those in which, though the act is obligatory, the particular occasions of performing it are left to our choice—as in the case of charity or beneficance which we are indeed bound to practice, but not towards any definite person, nor at any prescribed time. In the more precise language of philosophic jurists, duties of perfect obligation are those duties in virtue of which a correlative *right* resides in some person or persons; duties of imperfect obligation are those moral obligations which do not give birth to any right. I think it will be found that this distinction exactly coincides with that which exists between justice and the other obligations of morality.

From: *Utilitarianism.* Ch. V. 1863 (many editions).

---

fully positive duties that are related to social roles and the choice of vocation or career.

Finally, in speaking of the general requirements of principles, we want to mention that the characteristic of negativity is tied to the other requirements we have discussed. For instance, negative principles tend to be general, even universal, rather than specific, and hence are wider in scope than positive duties. For this reason, they are more powerful, for they apply to more cases. They are also more likely to win widespread agreement or support, for people are more likely to agree on evils that should be avoided than on positive courses of action. Our basic list of principles, therefore, will be stated as a list of negative obligations. At the same time, these principles are based on the recognition of a number of positive goods that ought to be promoted, such as life and truth, and that a morally good person will be positively oriented toward these goods.

EXERCISES

1. What are some of the advantages and disadvantages of monist and pluralist ethical theories, that is, of theories having one principle as opposed to theories having more than one principle?

2. What does it mean to say that principles apply in a *prima facie* sense?

3. What reasons are there for placing a "burden of proof" on exceptions?

4. What kinds of support are offered in defense of principles? That is, where do the principles come from and how can they be tested?

5. In what ways may principles be too broad or too narrow?

6. Explain the difference between affirmative and negative principles. Why are negative principles said to be more determinate than positive principles? Do you think the whole of morality can be covered by negative principles alone?

7.   Think of your own moral education. Was morality taught to you in essentially negative terms, as a list of "Don'ts" or did you receive instruction to do positively good things? What sorts of things have you been taught that you should do? Do you feel a moral obligation to do positively good things, or do you only feel an obligation to avoid doing things that are wrong? Give examples.

THE FIRST PRINCIPLE: DO NO HARM

We are now in a position to begin developing a set of principles. We are interested in uncovering a set of principles that will address basic human concerns and that are, therefore, capable of winning widespread support. One such principle would be a prohibition against doing harm. Given the Kantian requirement that principles apply to everyone in the same way, the principle "Do no harm" means that we should not harm others, but also that we should not harm ourselves. In its most obvious sense, perhaps, it means that we should not harm anyone physically, but, as we shall see, it can be taken to mean other forms of harm as well.

This principle seems almost self-evident. As one might expect, the dominant ethical theories tend to support it. Most people would readily agree to it. In one form or another, it is included in legal systems, and it is supported by the world's leading religious traditions. The principle appears to be implicit in many of our moral judgments, and it is often made explicit. When a child on the playground says, "Stop it, you're hurting him," that child justifies a particular judgment by pointing out that an action causes harm. We ourselves, of course, do not want to be harmed, and we often complain when others harm us, or at least when they do so intentionally or are careless. It is implicit in such complaints that no one should do such things.

Such a principle seems to be part of moral codes generally, and it has been expressed in various ways by moral theories. In holding the principle "Avoid evil," Thomas Aquinas specifies killing as a kind of evil that should be avoided. The natural rights theorist, John Locke, claims that persons have a right to life and property, maintaining that it is wrong to harm people by taking their lives or property from them. The utilitarian principle bids us to avoid evil or, according to hedonistic accounts, to avoid causing pain. The law protects our persons and property against others, and governments have been instituted to protect nations against, among other things, invasion from foreign lands.

The principle "Do no harm" is general and somewhat vague, but it is not wholly uninformative. Although it does not tell us what to count as harm, we do in fact know what counts as harm, at least in many cases, even if in some borderline cases we may not be quite sure. Indeed, this principle looks very much like the principle "Avoid evil," for the words "evil" and "harm" are often thought to be synonymous. We have seen that acts of omission, or failures to do good, may also be counted as evils, as in traditional self-realization theory. However, omission of good is not included in what we mean by harm. By "harm" we mean the actual destruction, removal, reduction, or prevention of some positive good, and not simply

G. J. WARNOCK
(1923–   )
Abstaining from Maleficence

The propensity *not* to act injuriously towards others whenever one has, or might have, some "natural" inclination to do so, while perhaps not specially creditable in ordinary circumstances, is still very clearly of fundamental importance; for it is obvious what a gangster's world we should find ourselves in without it—and indeed do find ourselves in, when and so far as this disposition is absent.

From: *The Object of Moralty*. G. J. Warnock. London: Methuen & Co., 1971.

the failure to do good. Thus, as harms, we are not thinking of failures or even refusals to help people. We are thinking of doing things to them which diminish their well-being in some way.

In many cases, we know what counts as bodily harm, such as killing or physically maiming someone. But if we said "Do no bodily harm," the principle would seem unnecessarily narrow. We also want to include psychological harm, which, in some cases, can be even worse than bodily harm. Psychological harm is often more difficult to detect, and there may be less agreement about the sorts of actions that are psychologically harmful. However, we do learn from our own experience and that of others, as well as from the teachings of psychology, what is likely to be psychologically harmful. We know, for example, that constant criticism can have a negative affect on motivation and learning, and that it can damage personality, just as we know that certain frightening experiences can be traumatic.

The stealing of property is normally considered a harm, although the extent of harm may be affected by how much is stolen or how much wealth the victim has. As Locke argued, people's possessions are in a sense extensions of themselves. Taking away possessions can cause serious physical harm by depriving people of food or shelter, for example, or a means of earning a living. It can also cause psychological harm because people can become emotionally upset by the loss of goods. People may suffer considerably from the loss of prized possessions, even if those possessions have little monetary value, or are not necessary for life. Moreover, poverty, or financial insecurity, is one of the most serious threats to a person's sense of well-being.

Also included in the idea of harming persons is the idea of interfering with their advancement or development, including the pursuit of their own well-being or that of others. To prevent people from learning, for example, is to prevent them from developing as persons, and to prevent them from helping somebody else to learn is to prevent others from developing. We may prevent people from developing as persons by damaging their health or by stealing their property, but also by denying them opportunities. Denying a person the time, space, or peace of mind to pursue his or her own interests falls within this category, although it may manifest itself as a form of psychological or physical harm as well. Again, this is not the same as failing to help. Harm requires positive action, whereas failure to help requires no action at all.

Our first principle is "Do no harm." By further specification, it may be said to include the subordinate principles or rules:

1. Do not harm anyone physically.

2. Do not harm anyone psychologically.

3. Do not hinder anyone's development.

These principles are very powerful, for they cover a large number of cases. They can always be cited as reasons against actions perceived as harms. As prima facie principles, they place the burden of proof on exceptions. If someone is causing obvious harm, the burden of proof is on that person to show that his or her act is justified as an exception. Of course, a person accused of causing a harm may wish to plea that the act is not really harmful. There is often room for dispute about what sorts of actions cause harm, as in medicine, for example, where there may be disagreement over the negative side-effects of medication. There may also be a question about the extent of harm.

In this connection, we should distinguish ends and means. What is harmful in itself may sometimes be justified as a means to something else. Or it may at least be tolerated as an undesirable but necessary side-effect. Thus surgery, for instance, which would normally be considered harmful in itself, as a violent act against a person's body, is often considered good, or at least a necessary evil, as a means to a greater good. We should note that it is the intention of the surgeon and others involved in the decision, and their estimate of probable results, which determines whether or not the act in question is justified. That is, the justification of the act depends on the value of the result they hope to achieve and the probability of their achieving it. Such an act would not be justified if the harm of surgery were likely to outweigh the good accomplished by it, or if, say, the person performing the surgery were known to be incompetent. The justification of such acts usually also presupposes an intention, even a commitment, to perform still other acts in the future, such as closing the wound or providing medication, and the probability that this intention will be fulfilled. Thus the justification of an immediate harm usually involves factors that extend beyond the act in question, such as future states of affairs, interpersonal commitments, and even institutional support.

Athletic contests are another example. Persons are often thought to be justified in inflicting harm upon one another within the context of playing a game or participating in a sport, because, even though the harm is probable, it is not intended, and the risk is freely taken. The risk of harm is thought to be a necessary means of attaining whatever good games provide, such as the development of athletic prowess. But, even in sports, we usually attempt to reduce risks by providing protective equipment and enacting rules that will prevent injuries. Some so-called sports, such as bullfighting or cockfighting, have been ruled illegal. In these cases, it seems that the harm is not merely probable but certain; it is in fact intended. That these sports are not entered into freely by the animals may be another consideration. In any case, many feel that these sports have no redeeming value.

Indeed, we often sacrifice to achieve a goal, and when we do, we do harm, or at least allow harm, in order to achieve what we take to be a greater good. The good we achieve, or intend to achieve, is therefore supposed to redeem the harm by giving it value. But there is considerable room for disagreement about how much good, or specifically which sorts of good, will justify given sorts of harm. Many people do not feel that the joys of football or boxing, say, justify the injuries incurred by participants, and there appears to be no way of knowing exactly how much harm, or how much risk, is justified.

What we do seem to know is that a harm can be justified by a greater good, or that it can be justified by the avoidance of a greater evil. In the latter case we need simply appeal to the principle in order to justify what appears to be an exception to the principle, by showing, in effect, that we are avoiding more harm than we cause. In many cases, as in the professional activities of doctors or dentists, we assume that they will not intervene unless they think a greater harm can be prevented. A momentary pain now may prevent a great deal of pain in the future; or, variously, interventions which cause temporary inability may improve long-term performance.

EXERCISES

Determine whether or not the following actions are prohibited by the first principle: Do No Harm. In each case, explain whether or how the principle is violated.

1. Harry routinely gets drunk on Saturday nights and gets into a fight with his wife, Sally. The fights usually remain verbal, with Harry denigrating his wife and children.

2. Lucy drives in a wild manner. She says she's never hurt anyone, so she can't see anything wrong with her driving.

3. While on patrol, Officer John was attacked by a gang of teenagers. Although badly beaten, he was able to draw his gun and shoot one of them. The youth lost the use of both of his legs.

4. Four Corners, Texas, is a small town. Everyone knows everyone else's business. Chuck has been involved in a quarrel with Jim and has threatened Jim's life. Sarah, owner of a local hardware store, sells Chuck a pistol, which he uses on Jim. Sarah later says she thought Chuck intended to use the pistol, but that was not her business.

5. Lucy, a bartender, knew Leslie was getting drunk, but gave her more to drink anyway. Leslie then hit and killed a child while driving home from the bar.

6. Alice and Joe believe that studying textbooks is bad because it promotes Godless humanism. They refuse to let their two children, Alicia and Erica, study at home and only reluctantly allow them to attend school.

7. Sam voted against the school tax issue. He says the schools are wasting too much money already.

8. Maude is always critical of people she meets for the first time. Her husband, Pete, says this is harming him because she feels the same way about him. Many of the people she criticizes work in Pete's

company and are, in many ways, much like him. Therefore he thinks Maude is almost always criticizing him.

9. Jim loves to ski. His roommate, Joe, says that skiing is too dangerous. Jim says he is allowed to hurt himself if he wants to.

10. Raoul lives in a depressed country. He believes that the dictator of that country is stealing foreign aid money and goods. He has decided to assassinate the dictator, believing that a certain high ranking general will take command, and, in all probability, rule in a way that is somewhat fairer. The result of all of this, he believes, will be that some lives will be saved by using the aid more effectively.

11. Jane Silver, M.D., a member of Physicians Against Nuclear Weapons, argued against the maintenance of nuclear weapons on the basis of the probable harm involved. Senator Stone thinks she is naive; he believes that the Soviets, with strong non-nuclear forces, would be engaged in one adventure after another, perhaps against the United States, if we disarmed.

Some of the above problems suggest that probable harm is nearly as objectionable as actual harm. Thus the principle may be extended to say "Do not harm or perform actions leading to highly probable harm." What special burden does this extension place on applying the principle? Hint: What counts as highly probable?

The Second Principle: Do Not Be Unfair

We not only expect others to respect our physical and psychological well being, we expect to be treated fairly. Thus, the principle "Do not be unfair" is well supported in ordinary, commonsense morality. It is also supported by Kantian ethics and social contract theories that feature a principle of justice. Justice, or fairness, is not a principle of utilitarianism, and utilitarianism has been criticized for not taking this principle into account. However, even John Stuart Mill thought that a just world would be a happier world, and hence that a rule of justice could be derived from utilitarianism. Of course, a Kantian or contractarian would give the concept of justice or fairness a central place, whereas, in utilitarianism, it occupies a derivative position. Presumably, a utilitarian would sacrifice the claims of justice in order to maximize utility, if that should turn out to be necessary, whereas a contractarian does not think that a rational individual would sacrifice fairness to individuals merely to increase the sum total of happiness.

The Meaning of Fairness

There appear to be at least two different meanings of fairness, the latter of which is dependent on the first. In what appears to be the more fundamental sense, we mean being judged or dealt with in the same way, by the same rules or standards used in judging or treating others—in the same or in relevantly similar circumstances. In this sense, if an instructor uses different

JOHN RAWLS
(1921–   )
The Priority of Justice Over Utility

Since each desires to protect his interests . . . no one has a reason to acquiesce in an enduring loss for himself in order to bring about a greater net balance of satisfaction. In the absence of strong and lasting benevolent impulses, a rational man would not accept a basic structure merely because it maximized the algebraic sum of advantages irrespective of its permanent effects on his own basic rights and interests. Thus it seems that the principle of utility is incompatible with the conception of social cooperation among equals for mutual advantage.

From: *A Theory of Justice*. John Rawls. Cambridge: Harvard University Press, 1971.

standards to assign grades to different students in the same class, his grading practices are unfair, unless there is a morally relevant difference to be taken into consideration. Some of the students in the class may be undergraduates and others graduates, so the instructor may feel, rightly, that graduate students should be judged by higher standards than undergraduates. However, civil rights movements are based on the argument that racial or sexual differences are not morally relevant, and hence that different races or sexes should be judged in the same way.

There is another meaning of fairness according to which goods are supposed to be distributed among persons so that everyone receives his or her "fair share." The idea here is that when goods are divided, they should be divided evenly, unless there is a good, morally relevant reason for not doing so. Hence, if two people share a pie, each should receive half of the pie, unless there is some other morally relevant reason for giving one person more than the other. When it comes to eating, one person may be hungrier than another, or larger, and these may be relevant considerations. But, according to this meaning of fair, it is not enough to be treated in the same way as another, according to the same rule, for it is possible to have rules that ignore fair distribution.

In adopting the principle "Do not be unfair," we have in mind the simpler, more fundamental idea of judging everyone by the same standards in the same way, because we are trying to uncover principles that everyone can accept, or on which there is widespread agreement, and there is not as much agreement about the second, distributive sense of justice or fairness as there is about the first. The idea of judging all people by the same standards is a much more fundamental and universal principle than the idea of giving all people an equal share of goods, or even a basic minimum number of goods, as in the idea, say, of a minimum standard of living. Some would argue, for example, that merit should be taken into account, and hence that the nonmeritorious do not deserve to be compensated or rewarded. But these sorts of questions, we feel, however important they may be, are subordinate issues that can be settled only by applying our more fundamental principles. They are questions, it seems, that can be settled only by adopting much more specific subordinate rules, for the justification of such rules is likely to depend on existing conditions.

For example, under conditions of extreme scarcity, it may be impossible to distribute goods equally, for then everyone would die; or in times of prosperity, there may be excess goods only for some people, in which case some would necessarily have more than others. In such cases, merit might be used to justify unequal distributions, but under given conditions, other factors may be of even greater importance.

To appeal to the principle of justice or fairness then, as we understand it, is much like appealing to Kant's principle of universalizability, or to the need for consistency in the application of rules or standards. Indeed, the idea of consistent application seems to be implied by the very idea of having a rule or standard. It would be odd to claim that something is one's standard of measurement and then not use it in making measurements! But some standards are meant only for limited classes of people. They are meant only for persons in certain categories, such as doctors or teachers, for example, or husbands and wives. The determination of which classes of people should be included in or excluded from a rule may be controversial, but, all things being equal, a rule should be consistently applied to everyone it covers.

The "all things being equal" qualification merely emphasizes again the prima facie nature of principles, for there may be overriding considerations. There would be little point in insisting upon one's turn to serve, according to the rules of volleyball, say, when it is suddenly discovered that the gymnasium is on fire. The threat of serious harm can override considerations of justice; but even then, as a matter of consistency, one should be able to generalize exceptions. We assume that the rules of a game hold as long as it is reasonable to continue playing the game. But baseball games, for instance, are cancelled because of rain. In baseball, the provisions for cancelling games are themselves included in the rules; but, of course, they need not be.

THE DISTINCTNESS OF THE PRINCIPLE

The principle "Do not be unfair" is different from the principle "Do no harm," even though unfairness may be construed as a kind of harm. Being unfair to people may cause them harm, for it may cause them physical loss or psychological stress. But it may not. It seems that a person could rightfully object to a procedure on grounds of unfairness, even if that person were not harmed by it—or even if nobody were. That is, one might object that, according to a standard, a wrong judgment was made, regardless of the consequences. This is what a number of deontologists like Kant have wanted to claim, that a reason for objecting to an action is that it is wrong in itself, according to a standard, regardless of consequences. If one makes a mistake in adding a column of numbers, then, according to the rules of simple arithmetic, one is wrong, regardless of how people may be affected by the results. Likewise, if it is wrong to assign an "A" instead of a "C," according to standards of grading, the instructor should not assign an "A," even if the student benefits from it.

But, again, we must add "all things being equal," for the rules of arithmetic, or even the rules of a game, are not strictly analogous to the rules of morality. These other types of rules apply to a restricted domain. They may even serve to define that domain. But the rules of morality do not define morality. They must give way to the all inclusive nature of morality itself, as indicated by the expression "all things considered." In the first place, our desire for justice or fairness is only one of the goals of human action: it is not the sole concern. Thus, the principle of fairness applies unless overridden by still other considerations, or, quite simply, unless there is a justified exception. In the second place, the rules that are supposed to be applied to everyone in the same way are supposed to be justified rules. If there is some reason for thinking that a rule is not justified, that in itself may be a good reason for not applying it, or for not applying it in a particular case. Because not all standards are good standards, some of them may need to be abolished or changed.

However, once a rule has been announced, people usually expect it to be applied, and human expectation is itself a factor to be weighed when all things are considered. Indeed, it is difficult to observe considerations of justice unless the rules are well defined and known by the persons affected. Changes in the rules, or exceptions to them, should be publicized, if fairness is to be observed. The purpose of having standards is to use them, and standards that are not known or understood cannot be effectively used.

The principle of justice is, therefore, a formal principle that applies to other subordinate rules or principles. It does not determine what, substantively, those other rules will be, but it does specify that, once determined, they should be consistently applied. If one doesn't like the rules, one can try to change them, or one can try to initiate political action to have them changed. However, if one tried to change the rules, one would be directing his attention to a higher level of moral reasoning than if one complained of injustice according to an existing rule.

EXERCISES

Which of the following violate the fairness rule? Explain whether it is a serious or a minor violation. Can the burden of proof be met? Do any of these examples also violate the harm principle?

1. Sally decided to invite only half of the basketball team to her birthday party. She invited only those in the eleventh and twelfth grades because she knows them better.

2. Consider the same situation as in Question 1, except in this case Sally invites only black players.

3. Mr. and Mrs. Jones send one child to an excellent private school known for individualized attention. The other child is sent to an overcrowded public school and is not given much guidance or attention after school hours.

4. Harvey always takes two hours for lunch, even though his contract allows only one hour. He claims he works harder during the other six hours.

5. The president knew it was illegal to send military aid to the rebels in a small South American country, but did it surreptitiously. When this was discovered she claimed that without such aid Communism would be on the rise in the Americas.

6. When Jimmy doesn't know the material well enough, he always finds a way to cheat. He says that all he really needs is to graduate. He thinks that much of school is a waste of time, but he always learns the material he believes he will need to know after graduation.

7. Professor Smith hates to say unkind things about his former students. Therefore, he always praises his students in letters of recommendation.

8. Harvey (from Question 4) cheats on his income tax. He claims more deductions for charity than he should. He says nearly everyone cheats in some way or other and the tax codes are written with that in mind. He refuses to pay some rich person's tax, especially when many millionaires pay no tax at all.

9. The government allows eastern European political refugees to enter the country but not Central American refugees. The government denies this, but officials say privately that the cold war demands such discrimination.

10. The military denies help to any movie company doing a war story that is not complimentary to them. They claim they deny help only to those companies that fail to portray the military in an accurate way. After all, they say, respect for the military is essential to the security of the country.

11. Popi sells antiques. She knows that most people cannot tell cut glass from pressed glass, so she claims that many pressed glass pieces are cut glass. She does not sell them at a higher price than the antique books cite, but sells them more readily as cut glass, and the buyer always seems happier to find such a bargain.

THE THIRD PRINCIPLE: DO NOT VIOLATE ANOTHER'S FREEDOM

Just mentioning the word "freedom" is enough to stir strong feelings. Individual opposition to authority, class struggles, and even national liberation movements have been waged in its name. The Declaration of Independence, for instance, claims that persons have certain God-given rights and that among these are the rights to life, liberty, and the pursuit of happiness. Indeed, even John Stuart Mill, who, as a utilitarian, places a premium on happiness, argues forcefully for individual liberty as a necessary condition for happiness.

CLARIFYING THE PRINCIPLE

Often when we think of freedom, we think of being free *from* something; prisoners want to be freed from jail, or children from parental authority. We want to be free from restrictions or limitations which hinder or prevent

184

J. S. MILL
(1806–1873)
On Liberty

The principle is that the sole end for which mankind are warranted, individually or collectively, in interfering with the liberty of action of any of their number is self-protection. That the only purpose for which power can be rightfully exercised over any member of a civilized community, against his will, is to prevent harm to others. His own good, either physical or moral, is not sufficient warrant. He cannot rightfully be compelled to do or forebear because it will be better for him to do so, because it will make him happier, because, in the opinions of others, to do so would be wise or even right.

From: *On Liberty*. J. S. Mill. 1859 (many editions).

---

our choice. However, we might also want to be free *for* doing certain kinds of things, or, in other words, to have the opportunity to do them. In discussing this third principle, we are concerned primarily with negative freedom, or with not blocking another's freedom of action; we are not specifically concerned with positive freedom, or with providing opportunities. In other words, a person is free to do something, in the sense of the word "freedom" we have in mind, if nobody will prevent that person from doing it. It does not mean that the person has the ability to do it, or that anyone has the responsibility for providing him or her with the means to do it. The principle states only that nobody should interfere.

If I have freedom of speech, for example, no one should prevent me from speaking; but it may turn out that I have nothing to say, or even that I am unable to speak. If I have freedom of religion, no one should prevent me from worshiping; but I may not have a religion or wish to worship in any way. If I have freedom to choose a job, no one can force me to take a job; but, on the other hand, no one has a responsibility to give me a job either—at least not according to this principle as we interpret it. One could mean these other things, but here, at the beginning, we are looking for very general, minimal requirements, which can be widely accepted, and it is easier to accept a principle that prohibits interference than one that enjoins positive support.

This principle may look very much like our first principle "Do no harm," especially as we included under the first principle the rule "Do not hinder the development of others." Indeed, one and the same action may violate both these principles. If we prevent another person from choosing an education, we block that person's development and freedom. Indeed, we block that person's freedom to develop. However, persons may be provided with the means of development without being allowed the freedom to choose how they will use them. A parent, for example, may provide children with every possible advantage and yet dictate what they will do.

We not only want to do things that will be good for us and others, we also want to be able to choose which of these things we will do. We want to develop as persons, but we do not want others to dictate how we develop. It is quite possible that the plans they have for us would be even better than the plans we have for ourselves, but we nonetheless want to be able to choose our own course, according to our own judgment. The fact that the course we have chosen is *our* course, *our* way, somehow makes it more important to us. It gives us the feeling that we are unique or autonomous beings, not simply slaves. The idea that we must answer to ourselves is also in keeping with the idea that a moral judgment is a matter of conscience and that a person can perform a free, morally relevant act only according to his or her own reasons and choice, not by force. In other words, to respect the freedom of others is to respect the fact that they are persons or that they are responsible moral agents. We say "of others," in this case, because it seems, with respect to oneself, one has no alternative but to follow one's own reasons, unless forced not to do so.

THE PRIMA FACIE PROVISO

But, again, we must recognize that this principle is not absolute. One of the restrictions on human freedom, quite obviously, is morality itself. If something is morally wrong, it is something that a person should not do, something that that person should not freely choose. If there were no limits on freedom, there would be no morality, or at least no moral obligations.

Likewise, if one person thinks that what another person is doing is morally wrong, the first person may have a right to try to prevent the second person from doing it—thus interfering with his or her freedom. If I believe it is wrong to kill, then it seems that I would be justified in trying to prevent others from killing. Just what precisely I may be justified in doing may be subject to dispute, but it seems that I cannot be required to respect another person's right to kill, because, generally speaking, persons do not have this right. Thus, when parents deny freedom to children, they usually do so because they want to prevent their children from doing wrong, from harming themselves, for example, or from interfering with their own development. Likewise, when the state restricts the freedom of its citizens, it usually does so in the interest of the state, thinking that it would be wrong for people to attack or to erode beneficial social institutions.

Although freedom, like justice, is itself a good, it is only one kind of good. Its goodness also seems dependent on other kinds of goods. To be free is to be free *for* something or other or to be free *from* something or other; thus, without a specification of what this something or other is, freedom seems to have little or no value in itself. That is, freedom to do or not do things is relative to those things. A freedom to do nothing at all would seem to be no freedom at all. Moreover, moral freedom appears to be freedom to do good, not freedom to do evil. We cannot condone morally bad acts on the ground that they are freely chosen; *that*, if anything, seems to make them worse. What we can do, however, is to tolerate error in the name of freedom. We can allow people to make mistakes on the ground that they need to act and think for themselves because, as moral agents, they need to discover for themselves what is bad or good. As stated above, we can also allow them a wide range of choice in determining which good acts they will perform, even if we try to deter them from performing acts that are morally wrong. Basically, we have said, the moral principles tell us what we cannot do, but they leave open the possibility of choosing among many positive goods.

Before moving ahead in developing a set of moral principles, we want to mention that, in emphasizing the negative principle that bids us not to interfere with the freedom of others, we do not mean to assert that positive freedom is unimportant or that we should not try to provide opportunities for people. We simply feel that the negative principle of noninterference is more fundamental and less controversial than a positive principle that would require us to provide opportunities. It is a less stringent requirement, for it is much easier to satisfy. It therefore satisfies our notion of a basic, minimal requirement of morality, which each of our principles is supposed to be.

EXERCISES

Which of the following violate the freedom principle? Explain whether it is a serious or a minor violation. Can the burden of proof be met? Do any of these also violate the harm or the fairness principle?

1. The government of South Africa has a rigid set of rules restricting the movement of blacks.

2. The township decided to stop all cars and test for drunk drivers. Two people were killed in each of the last two years, and all the accidents involved drunk drivers.

3. The township refuses to allow liquor stores in residential areas.

4. A suburb believes that too many cars from the city are using its streets. To stop this practice, it sets up barriers.

5. The dean refuses to allow the student newspaper to print any articles or letters critical of the school administration.

6. The State Department refused to grant a passport to two people who had spoken in favor of disarmament.

7. The city imposed a 10 P.M. curfew on children under the age of sixteen.

8. A private religious school expelled a student who worked as a model for a large downtown department store. She modeled evening clothes.

9. Blacks believe that they will be physically threatened if they enter a nearby neighborhood. Whites in that neighborhood deny that blacks are unwelcome, but they believe that they walk into the black neighborhood at their own risk.

10. A high school teacher always recommends a teaching career to girls doing above average but not excellent work. In similar circumstances, boys are advised to choose from a variety of careers, ranging from science and sales to education.

SUBORDINATE PRINCIPLES

We have seen that moral principles can reinforce one another, even though, in some cases, they can also conflict and have exceptions. Usually, if one obeys one principle, one will obey the others as well. If one tries to avoid harming others, one is also likely to respect their freedom or to be fair toward them. Indeed, in drawing out the implications of these combined principles, one discovers that they support other subordinate principles. These subordinate principles, in turn, serve to amplify the basic principles already discussed.

The Legality Principle: Do Not Break the Law

In the case of the principle "Do no harm," we specified subordinate principles or rules such as "Do no bodily harm" and "Do no psychological harm." The principles of fairness and liberty can also be given further specification. In emphasizing the importance of justice, for example, prima facie obedience to the law seems required. Laws are generally regarded as the backbone of social life. They are usually respected and supported by the vast majority of people. They are also enforced. Because they tend to remain in force over relatively long periods of time, they become dependable; our expectations about how others will act are partly determined by them, and for this reason alone, their violation typically disrupts social life.

The idea of fairness, that laws or rules should be applied to everyone in the same way, suggests the idea that everyone should obey the law. The implications of the fairness rule can also be further specified by saying: "Keep contracts" or "Keep promises," for the rules we are expected to apply are often the result of expressed or implied contracts or promises. Such rules are created, in effect, by people who expressly agree to govern themselves by them, as in elections, or who implicitly agree to be governed by them, as in the acceptance of customs. There is a practical inconsistency in making a contract or promise and then failing to keep it, for it is generally understood that contracts or promises are binding under normal conditions, or unless there is a good reason to break them.

The legality principle is supported by the principle "Do no harm," as well as by the principle of fairness, for once expectations are created, such as the expectation that a rule will be enforced, people can be seriously harmed by failure to enforce it. Because they may come to depend upon the enforcement of a law for their well-being, as they often do, failure of enforcement can deprive them of material or psychological goods. People can be psychologically harmed by the betrayal of a trust, by feelings of insecurity, or by a loss of personal esteem. They can be harmed physically, of course, because the protection of material goods and the effectiveness of business transactions depends by and large on law, custom, and contract. When laws are broken or disregarded by large numbers of people, the laws cease to be effective and society itself begins to disintegrate.

Of course, not all laws or customs are good. Some are not good because, say, it would be harmful to follow them or because they are unfair. Thus, our principles can be brought to bear upon the law itself, as a basis for criticizing or defending it. It is also the case that, no matter how good a law may be in its intent, it is not likely to be effective unless enforced and obeyed. Ironically, lack of enforcement or disobedience may be a good reason

---

ARISTOTLE
(384–322 B.C.)
On Lawful Acts

Since the lawless man was seen to be unjust and the law-abiding man just, evidently all lawful acts are in a sense just acts; for the acts laid down by the legislative art are lawful, and each of these, we say, is just. Now the laws in their enactments on all subjects aim at the common advantage . . . so that in one sense we call those acts just that tend to produce and preserve happiness and its components for the political society.

From: *Nicomachean Ethics*, Bk. V. Aristotle. *The Basic Works of Aristotle.* McKeon, ed. New York: Random House, 1941.

---

for disobedience, for there may be little point in obeying an ineffective law, unless one hopes to set an example by showing respect for the law.

Thus, the extent to which laws establish moral obligations depends on a number of factors: on whether they are justified by moral principles, on whether they are generally enforced by law enforcement agencies, and on whether they are generally obeyed. Tax laws that are unfair to the poor, for example, may be harmful if enforced, or obeyed. On the other hand, laws pertaining to the leashing of dogs may be ineffective if unenforced or disobeyed. There would not be much point in my leashing my dog if nobody else leashed theirs and if no one in authority seemed to care—although one might worry about selective enforcement or a lawsuit. The *moral* weight of such a law, as a law, depends on its being fairly enforced *as a law*, even though there may be an independent reason for doing what the law says— if, for example, one has a vicious dog!

We want to maintain a distinction between what is legally right and what is morally right, but at the same time hold that we are, generally speaking, morally bound by the laws and customs of society. The mere fact that a law or custom is not the best way of doing things may not be a sufficient reason to justify disobedience. If it is the way things are done, and hence the way in which most people will be willing to act, it may be better to follow the law or custom than to disobey it. It may be better to follow the fire department's rules for leaving a burning building even if one knows a better way out, if it turns out that the building is on fire and there is little chance of convincing others of the better plan. Changes in laws or customs often require time and timing, for it takes time for something to become a new law or custom, and there are appropriate times for trying to introduce changes, for example, when one is likely to succeed. In the meantime, it may actually be better to obey an old law or custom until it can be changed.

The legality principle carries only prima facie force. Some laws and some violations of law are, of course, more serious than others. A law prohibiting murder, say, is obviously more serious than a law prohibiting spitting on the sidewalk. But even serious laws—even good laws—may have exceptions. Even though a law applies in almost all cases, there may still be exceptions. It may be wrong to kill except in self defense. Indeed, the law's interpretation of justifiable self-defense may be narrower than that of morality. Children who kill their parents to avoid torture may not be justified in the eyes of the law because private citizens are not authorized executioners, and the parents are supposed to receive a fair trial. However, private citizens often cannot wait for the police, cannot contact them, or cannot be persuasive against the testimony of others. In such cases they may be justified in "taking the law in their own hands," morally speaking, even if they are not legally allowed to do so.

THE OPPORTUNITY PRINCIPLE: DO NOT DISCRIMINATE

The legality principle is supported by practically all people and by practically all ethical theories, for it is difficult to imagine a good society in which laws and customs are not taken seriously. Increasingly we have come to believe that prejudice and discrimination are morally wrong and extremely harmful to society and individuals. We now generally believe that it is wrong to discriminate against people on the basis of race, creed, sex, national origin, or political belief. The opportunity principle tells us that it is morally wrong to discriminate against people for those reasons, and, as in the cases of other prima facie principles, it places the burden of proof on those who claim exceptions.

One might argue that women should not be employed in certain jobs because they are too weak or too temperamental, but such arguments are based on the false claim that strength and temperament are sexually determined. Empirical evidence shows that this is false. If it is reasonable to limit jobs to persons who are physically strong, then it follows that the test for employment should be strength, not sex. Of course, in some cases, sex may be a relevant consideration. In some circumstances, such as rape, a person of the same sex may be a more sympathetic counselor, and the victim may be more comfortable with a person of the same sex. That is, the opportunity principle does not prohibit discrimination based on job-relevant considerations, but it does prohibit discrimination on the basis of factors that are not job-relevant.

The opportunity principle is an extension of the principle "Do no harm," as specified by the subordinate principle "Do not hinder another person's development." However, it also presupposes the principle of fairness, for it tells us that we should not deny opportunities to one person that we allow for another unless there is some morally relevant difference between the persons or their cases. It is a further specification of the legality principle in telling us that we should not deny anyone the opportunities or rights provided by law, but it is also a principle for critiquing the law when the law is unfair. Finally, it expresses a deep respect for individual liberty, for individual freedom is practically useless without meaningful opportunities for choice. Thus, the opportunity principle is supported by all of the other principles we have discussed, but it deserves special emphasis, for it is easily overlooked or ignored.

Aside from the fact that people sometimes consciously discriminate against others, they often are not aware of their own prejudices. To call attention to the opportunity principle is to call attention to the ever present possibility of prejudice and the need for justifying the exclusion of any group of people from the benefits of a rule or institution. The principle also calls attention to the need to create opportunities; people are simply not born with equal advantages, and it is usually wrong to exploit the weaknesses of others. It is especially difficult to eliminate prejudices that are deeply ingrained in habits, customs, and laws.

To argue against prejudice, however, is not to say that we have a duty to create equal opportunities; that, certainly, is not always possible. Nor must we always treat everyone the same. This duty, like the others, is essentially negative. Even then, as we have said, there may be good reason for treating some people differently from others or for not allowing them exactly the same opportunities. In a division of labor, as on a football team, some people are allowed to catch passes and others are not. The rules discriminate, but apparently for good reason. People have different jobs to do, and because they do, they must be allowed different options or rights. In almost any organization, some people will function as leaders and their rights and duties will be different from others. But, normally, such differences should apply only to a given job or organization and not otherwise, and they should be looked upon as temporary assignments of position, not permanent rights.

Practices and Ideals

The opportunity principle receives more support from some ethical theories than from others, but we have seen that any theory that emphasizes individual fairness and social justice would tend to give it support. The principle also has wide support in ordinary views of morality, although it may seem to lack the same universal support as other principles we have considered. The reason for this is that many people are quite prejudiced and hence seem not to accept the principle. But even people who are prejudiced usually do not admit to being prejudiced. They do not usually admit that they discriminate against others because of religion, sex, or race. Rather, they claim that there are factual differences that support differential treatment.

They may say, for example, that women should not be employed in a certain field because the work is too strenuous, but not because they are against women. Thus, they do not oppose the principle; instead, they try to show that their claim is a relevant and justified exception to the principle. But, of course, in this case, the claim may be false or it may be irrelevant. More often than not, what is said against certain groups of people is true enough, but it is also true of other groups as well, and hence does not constitute an exception. No one group seems to have cornered the market on ignorance, for example, or on laziness, or even irrationality. So, in saying such things, the principle itself is not usually opposed. Those who reject the principle outright are thought to be morally insensitive.

To say that a principle is accepted, however, is not to say that it is obeyed. The opportunity principle is a good example. While most people seem to believe in it, they often find that in practice they disobey. Of course, an act that violates a principle is wrong, unless the act in question is a justifiable exception. But we are not concerned with whether people do what they think is right. Of course they should. What we are concerned about is *discovering* what is right, what principles we can use in making such determinations, and how we can ground those principles.

We also wish to point out that while principles of the type we have uncovered are necessary to settle disputes over subordinate rules or particular judgments, they cannot by themselves settle every case. For this reason, the principles need to be supplemented by subordinate rules. Indeed, we have claimed that there is a general obligation not to break social rules, in the form of laws, customs, or practices, and there could not be such an obligation unless there were subordinate rules. We will consider subordinate social rules in the chapters that follow to see how they function in moral reasoning. We will also critique such rules in the light of our principles to see how old rules may need to be changed or abolished or how new rules may need to be brought into existence. In these respects, we should come to appreciate our roles as creators of rules, as well as rule followers.

EXERCISES

What principle or principles were violated in the following cases? Explain. Do you think the case is a justified exception? What other information do you think would be relevant?

1. You meet a friend at a restaurant. The friend arrived early. When you arrive, the friend says, "I ordered your favorite lunch for you; I knew you would love it."

2. A parent keeps a child indoors all day long, refusing to let the child ride a bicycle, go swimming, or do anything that risks physical injury.

3. A student cheats on an exam but argues to his roommate that everyone else is doing it. As a matter of fact, cheating is common in this class and the teacher does nothing to stop it.

4. At Centerview High, the school pays for the uniforms, trips, and meals of the football team but not of the cheerleaders or band. School officials argue that football earns money for the school and that, as a matter of policy, only sports are subsidized.

5. A man cheats on his wife by having an affair. When she learns about it he says, "I didn't hurt anybody. I was just having a little fun."

6. A defensive end hits the quarterback after a pass is thrown, intending to injure him. His team is penalized, but he argues, "It was worth the penalty, for I put him out of the game. After all, football is a rough game."

7. A "friend" calls on the phone and says, "Are you doing anything tonight?" You say, "No." He says, "Good, then you can drive me to the airport. I have a plane to catch."

8. A company executive continues to order the dumping of toxic wastes near drinking water because, he says, "No one has the right to interfere with free enterprise; environmental protection laws are a Communist plot!"

9. Most people in government and throughout society seem to think that the recreational use of drugs like cocaine should be prohibited because they are addictive and a possible harm to the health of the users. Some such drugs are hallucinogenic and impair functioning. But many of these same people are uncritical of the use of tobacco or alcohol. Regarding the latter, some people argue that individuals should be free to choose; in any case, drinking and smoking are socially approved.

10. Your cousins bury the body of your dead aunt, their mother, without inviting anybody to the funeral. You and other relatives who loved the aunt are deeply hurt, but your cousins argue: "Funerals are dumb. Why spend a lot of time and money on a dead person who cannot appreciate it anyway?"

SUPPLEMENTARY READINGS

Aristotle, *Nichomachean Ethics* (many editions).

Baier, Kurt. "Good Reasons." *Philosophical Studies,* Vol. 4, 1953: 1–15

Beauchamp, Tom and Childress, James. *Principles of Biomedical Ethics.* Oxford: Oxford University Press, 1979.

Hare, R. M. *Freedom and Reason.* Oxford: Oxford University Press, 1963.

Harrison, Jonathan. "When Is a Principle a Moral Principle?" *Proceeding of the Aristotelian Society,* Sup. Vol. 29, 1954: 111–34.

Mill, John Stuart. *Utilitarianism* and *On Liberty* (many editions).

Rawls, John. "Outline of a Decision Procedure for Ethics." *Philosophical Review,* Vol. 60, 1951: 177–97.

Raz, Joseph. *The Authority of Law: Essays on Law and Morality.* Oxford: The Clarendon Press, 1979.

Richards, David. *A Theory of Reasons for Action.* Oxford: The Clarendon Press, 1971.

Ross, Sir David. *The Right and the Good.* Oxford: The Clarendon Press, 1930.

Scheffler, Israel. "Justification and Commitment." *Journal of Philosophy,* Vol. 51, 1954: 180–90.

Singer, Marcus. *Generalization in Ethics.* New York: Random House, 1961.

Taylor, Richard. *Good and Evil.* Buffalo, N.Y.: Prometheus Books, 1986.

Thiroux, Jacques. *Ethics: Theory and Practice.* 3d ed. Ch. 6. New York: Macmillan, 1986.

Toulmin, Stephen E. *An Examination of The Place of Reason in Ethics.* Cambridge: Cambridge University Press, 1958.

APPLYING MORAL PRINCIPLES

In Chapter 9, we developed a set of moral principles that has theoretical backing, that has widespread acceptance, that is embedded in the practices of important social institutions such as law and religion, and that expresses universal human wants and needs. Our purpose in explicitly stating such principles is to use them in moral reasoning as a justification for subordinate rules and particular acts. We are now in a position to apply these principles in a critique of social institutions and practices and in our attempts to resolve controversial moral issues.

DIRECT AND INDIRECT APPLICATIONS

The process of applying moral principles may be either direct or indirect. That is, we may argue for or against an action in a particular case by appealing directly to principles, or we may try to justify or criticize an action indirectly by appealing to social rules or practices that, in turn, are supposed to be justified by the principles. But, in this chapter, we shall be concerned primarily with direct appeals to principles; in the following chapters we will consider how subordinate social rules can be justified or how such rules can be used to supplement principles in judging particular acts.

Because, as we shall try to show, our set of basic principles is not by itself sufficient to determine what is right or wrong in every case, subordinate rules will be necessary to make some determinations. One reason for this is that our basic principles are very general, negative prescriptions (or prohibitions) on which everyone, or nearly everyone, may be expected to agree;

the list does not indicate specific, positive, and socially relative duties that are more complex and variable than basic principles. Such specific, positive duties, we have said, are often stated as rules of social institutions that govern individual roles, offices, or functions, or are simply "expected" according to social customs or practices.

P. H. NOWELL-SMITH
(1914–   )
On the Need for Rules

Moral rules are necessary for two main reasons. In the first place every man has a great variety of aims which cannot all be fully achieved because they conflict with each other. If a man wants to be prime minister or a great pianist, for example, there are many other things that he also wants to do but cannot do if he is to achieve this particular aim.

But the achievement of co-ordination between a man's own aims is clearly an unimportant reason for having moral rules when compared with the need for co-ordinating the aims of different people. Indeed, until we mention this, we hardly seem to have touched on *moral* rules at all; for, although we do sometimes talk about duties to ourselves, most of our duties are duties to others.

From: *Ethics*. P. H. Nowell-Smith. Baltimore: Penguin Books, 1954.

Nonetheless, basic principles are necessary to justify subordinate rules and particular acts. Indeed, as we shall try to show in this chapter, many acts can be justified by appealing directly to the principles. The principles may also be used to show that many acts are unjustified, even without appealing to subordinate rules. Thus, in moral reasoning, we can often reason directly from moral principles to judgments about the rightness or wrongness of particular acts. Indeed, attempts to adopt, reject, or modify rules are themselves special cases of applying principles to particular acts, namely the acts of attempting to adopt, reject, or amend rules.

The main point we wish to make here is that our basic principles can be used to resolve a large number of moral issues, even though, by themselves, they cannot settle every case. The resolution of some conflicts, we have said, will require the addition of subordinate rules in the form of laws or social practices. Of the cases that can be resolved by using principles alone, some will be quite simple and others complex. In demonstrating the use of these principles, we will proceed by considering some of the simpler cases first, and then cases that are more complex.

THE STEPS OF APPLICATION

It may be helpful at this point to restate the principles uncovered in the last chapter. The basic principles are:

1. Do no harm.

2. Do not be unfair.

3. Do not violate another's freedom.

As a result of considering the implications of these principles, the list was expanded to include other subordinate principles. Under "Do no harm," for example, we included:

Do not harm anyone physically.

Do not harm anyone psychologically.

Do not hinder anyone's development.

And, considering the implications of the other two principles, we added:

Do not break the law.

Do not discriminate.

Generally speaking, any act is morally right, or morally permitted, if it does not violate any of the principles, and any act is morally wrong, or prohibited, if it violates one or more of them. The first step in applying the principles, therefore, will be to ask: are any of the principles violated?

As we move along, however, we will want to take account of important qualifications, such as our prima facie restriction which allows that there may be exceptions in unusual cases. We shall also want to take into account the ought-implies-can restriction, or the simple point that people cannot be obligated to do the impossible. Thus, when it is not possible to obey all the principles, the violation of a principle may be allowed as a necessary or unavoidable evil. We will also want to consider the degree or seriousness of violations, for some violations of principle may be minor, even insignificant, whereas others are quite serious. Finally, where questions of probability arise, we will want to consider the likelihood of violation, as in cases of probable harm. These considerations introduce a considerable amount of complexity into the question of whether or not a given act conforms to or violates the principles.

Step One: Are Any Principles Violated?

In the simplest sort of cases, we may find that an act under consideration is in clear violation of one or more of the principles and is, therefore, morally wrong. Or, we may find that a given act conforms to all the principles and is, therefore, right or morally permitted. A particular act of killing or violence, for example, may be judged to be morally wrong because it is a case of serious harm to another human being. A particular act of withholding material goods or money from some individual or group may turn out to be a case of serious injustice to that individual or group.

Such cases may be clear violations of principle, if, indeed, there is no good reason for allowing an exception. We may allow that a person who is starving is justified in stealing a small amount of food if that person has no legitimate way of earning a living, but we cannot allow that a professional

---

> ### DOROTHY L. SAYERS
> ### (1893–1957)
> #### *A Simple Case of Justice*
>
> I am not complaining that brewing and baking were taken over by men. If they can brew and bake as well as women or better, then by all means let them do it. But they cannot have it both ways. If they are going to adopt the very sound principle that the job should be done by the person who does it best, then that rule must be applied universally.
>
> From: *Are Women Human?* Dorothy L. Sayers. Grand Rapids: William B. Eerdmans Publishing Company, 1980.

criminal is justified in stealing large amounts of money, especially if other options are open to him or her. The burden of proof placed on exceptions may be met in the first case, but it is obviously not met in the second.

But, of course, such simple cases are rather uninteresting because there is little doubt about them. In such cases, a person may find it difficult to do what is right, or to avoid doing what is wrong, but there should be no difficulty in *knowing* what is right or wrong. That is, a person may be tempted to harm another, or to be unjust, to gain financial advantage, say, or simply to gain revenge, but that person should also know full well that such acts are morally wrong.

Professional criminals habitually break the law, perhaps without conscience, just as persons who are morally depraved habitually violate moral principles. But, usually, ordinary civilized people do not even consider performing acts that are clearly wrong. That is, they do not have to rule out the option of killing or stealing, for they do not consider such acts to be options at all. At least they would not entertain such acts as real, live alternatives, except under very unusual circumstances. They might consider harming another person in self-defense, but only because they think that self-defense is a justified exception to the principle that prohibits harm. Or, as we have said, they may sometimes be tempted to violate a principle in order to gain an advantage for themselves, or a special privilege for someone they like, but they would at least know that, morally speaking, they should not do such things.

The more interesting cases, not of struggling to do what is right, but of trying to determine what is right, are of course more complex. They are cases of doubt, or of controversy, about the right thing to do because there are reasons—even good reasons—on both sides.

STEP TWO: IS THE CASE AN EXCEPTION?

Cases can become complex when there are reasons both for and against performing a particular act. Doubts about the right thing to do may arise, for example, when a parent worries about whether to punish or restrict the behavior of a child. The parent may know that, in punishing the child, some harm will be done, and hence that one of our principles will be violated; yet, the parent may feel that such limited harm may benefit the child in the long run by helping to make the child a more disciplined person. Or, the parent may try to prevent harm to a child by requiring that child to be

198

home at an early hour, and yet worry about unduly restricting that child's freedom.

In such cases, there appears to be a conflict of principle, for by observing one principle, another principle seems to be violated. On a strict reading of our principles, cases of conflict are likely to be rare because the principles are stated in negative form. It is often possible to avoid doing, or to choose not to do, the kinds of things prohibited by the principles. But we also said that a morally good person does not simply refrain from performing prohibited acts. A morally good person actually tries to prevent harm or injustice, for example, and in so doing may find that she cannot do both. Thus, indirectly at least, the failure to discipline a child may actually produce harm.

JANE ENGLISH
Is Abortion Justified Killing?

The abortion debate rages on. Yet the two most popular positions seem to be clearly mistaken. Conservatives maintain that human life begins at conception and that therefore abortion must be wrong because it is murder. But not all killings of humans are murders. Most notably, self defense may justify even the killing of an innocent person.

Liberals, on the other hand, are just as mistaken in their argument that since a fetus does not become a person until birth, a woman may do whatever she wishes in and to her own body. First, you cannot do as you please with your own body if it affects other people adversely. Second, if a fetus is not a person, that does not imply that you can do to it anything you wish. Animals, for example, are not persons, yet to kill or torture them for no reason at all is wrong.

From: "Abortion and the Concept of a Person." Jane English. *Canadian Journal of Philosophy*, 5, 1975: 233–43.

Therefore, conflicts may arise because the choice of a positive course of action according to one principle violates another principle. In the above example, the parent's desire to foster the child's development, by punishing or restricting it, is in apparent conflict with the principle which says that we should not cause harm and the principle which says that we should not violate another's freedom. In fact, we may suppose the parent has a special obligation, prescribed by a subordinate social rule or practice, to positively foster the child's development. Hence, it is not only the parent's desire, but also the parent's duty as a parent, that seems to conflict with the principles. Nonetheless, punishing children by inflicting harm, and restricting them by limiting their freedom, are violations of principles that need to be justified as exceptions.

STEP THREE: HAS THE BURDEN OF PROOF BEEN MET?

In the above examples, the parent may indeed be justified in restricting the child or in punishing it if the restriction or punishment is not extreme and if, therefore, the restriction or punishment does not cause the child serious or lasting harm. Thus, a temporary and limited harm, or a minor infraction of principle, may be tolerated as a means of promoting the child's own interest, that is, as a means of respecting the child's development and freedom, and hence as a means of conforming to the spirit of the principles involved.

In these cases, therefore, we may not only find that an act is an exception to one or more of the principles, but we may also find that the burden of proof placed on exceptions is satisfied. Such exceptions will normally be justified by appealing to reasons that are themselves consonant with one or more of the principles, as a limited amount of discipline is consistent with the idea of respecting a person's development, for it actually promotes such development. However, a parent who seriously harms a child in disciplining it, showing little or no concern for the child's welfare, does not act in a manner that is consistent with the spirit of the principles.

When we look for a reason to justify an exception, therefore, we should look for a reason that can be supported by a principle, or by reference to one or more of the kinds of goods the principles are meant to protect. We should also try to see if we can generalize the exception to include not only this case but other similar cases as well.

In the parenting example, we should ask if we would allow any parent to use discipline or punishment of the type in question in relevantly similar circumstances. Comparison of comparable circumstances may include, for instance, consideration of the age of the child or the type of offense. It may even include a consideration of the times in which we live, for the amount of psychological harm inflicted on a child by punishment may depend on current customs and expectations. In general, we should be concerned with whether the action is likely to cause the child more harm than good.

Even when we have special knowledge of a case, which makes it different from most other cases, we may still include that special knowledge in our generalization. For example, we may know that a particular child is sickly or retarded, and hence exempt that child from certain forms of discipline, but our reason for such exemption is based upon the idea that any such child should be excused. The exception would still apply to all cases of the same kind; this simply turns out to be a more highly specialized case.

Two Moderately Difficult Cases

With these steps in mind, let us consider two moderately difficult cases that are similar in some relevant respects but different in others.

Case 1: As a member of the university's promotion committee, I am asked to evaluate my cousin's request for promotion. It is not generally known that we are related, because we serve in different departments and have different last names. Even though I do not believe my cousin is fully qualified, I consider voting for her. And, although I am not especially close to my cousin, my aunt would be very disappointed if my cousin were not promoted, as would my father. "After all," I say to myself, "blood is thicker than water."

Case 2: I own a small construction business and need a helper for the summer. My niece, a college student, needs a summer job. She is a very good worker, but I know that the student I hired last

> year is somewhat better. I think that the difference between them
> is not great enough to override my interest in helping family
> members. I conclude, therefore, that I should hire my niece instead.

We may begin by asking, according to Step 1: are any of the principles violated? Well, considering the first principle, it seems that in neither case would I be causing anyone direct or serious harm. I certainly would not be causing anyone physical harm. Indeed, in the first case, I am trying to avoid psychological harm to my relatives. In the second case, I might also be trying to avoid disappointment to my niece.

I might be said to be hindering the development of those who were excluded from promotion or excluded from employment because of my choice, but it is not clear in the first case that my cousin's promotion would exclude the promotion of other qualified people. In the second case, someone is definitely denied a job, but that would be true no matter who is chosen. Because only one person can be hired, someone is necessarily excluded. When a selection is made among people, the exclusion of some people follows as a necessary evil. In any case, the first principle does not require us to provide opportunities for people; it prohibits us from hindering their development.

However, both cases seem to be violations of the second principle "Do not be unfair." If, in the first case, I voted for the promotion of my cousin, I would be applying criteria for promotion in her case that I would not apply to others. In fact, I would be applying less stringent criteria, and, in doing so, I would also be violating the duties of my office. Thus my decision in favor of my cousin would also violate the subordinate principle "Do not break the law," for the criteria of promotion may be said to be the laws, policies, or practices that define the duties of my office. Likewise, anyone who applies for promotion may be expected to be judged by these criteria. If one has any other expectation, one is either ignorant of the rules or expects to be treated with favoritism, and hence unjustly, as a special case. The perhaps minor and uncertain disappointment of relatives does not seem to offset the erosion of institutional trust and the personal injustice caused by breaking the rules.

DIFFERENCES IN THE CASES

In the second case, the social practices and expectations are quite different. People who run small businesses or hire people to work in their homes are often expected to hire members of their own families—sometimes for even less money than they would pay others, and sometimes even without compensation. Mere expectation may not by itself justify a violation of fairness, but the exception in this case may be universalizable, meeting the burden of proof. That is, we may all be willing to tolerate, even require, a certain amount of partiality towards family and friends, as a condition necessary to strengthen family ties or friendships, at least within certain spheres. Just where we draw the line between justified familial loyalties and the seemingly more impersonal requirements of public justice may differ according to customs, but it seems that the line must somehow be drawn. Because this is a question of justifying social rules, however, we will address it more fully in the chapters that follow.

The point we wish to make here is that, although our two cases look quite similar, there seems to be an important difference between them. That is, partiality in the first case seems to be unjustified because we are dealing with a public institution, a public office, and rules or practices that require people to act according to accepted standards. In the second case, the standards, if any, are neither rigid nor clear; it is in fact accepted practice to allow people wide discretion in hiring relatives, and in some cases the hiring of people who are not relatives would seem odd. We often expect children to work for their parents or relatives, with or without remuneration, as a form of help to the family, and as a way of training them for future work. Thus, laws requiring fair hiring practices usually apply only to agencies of a certain type or size.

SOCRATES
(c.470–399 B.C.)
Does One Prosecute One's Father?

Socrates: I suppose that the man whom your father murdered was one of your relatives—clearly he was; for if he had been a stranger you would never have thought of prosecuting him.

Euthyphro: I am amused, Socrates, at your making a distinction between one who is a relation and one who is not a relation; for surely the pollution is the same in either case, if you knowingly associate with the murderer when you ought to clear yourself and him by proceeding against him . . . even if the murderer lives under the same roof with you and eats at the same table, proceed against him.

From: *Euthyphro, The Dialogues of Plato.* Plato. B. Jowett, trans. New York: Random House, 1937.

We do not mean to suggest here that there is no room for differences of opinion; but, given the principles, such differences may be resolved by appealing to societal facts, in the form of rules or practices, and the circumstances of the persons involved. Indeed, there may be special considerations that would alter one's determination. If, for example, in the second case mentioned above, I have promised the person I had hired last year that she would be hired again this year, I would have a special obligation to hire her, all things being equal. Even if such a promise were made, however, I might be relieved of the responsibility to fulfill it, if, say, that person did not want the job or could not take it. That is, when we say our answer "depends on circumstances," we should look at the circumstances to see how our answer depends on them, or how the circumstances affect the application of the principles.

A MORE DIFFICULT CASE

Case 3:   Mr. Smith is terminally ill. His life has deteriorated both mentally and physically. He seems to be suffering a great deal but cannot communicate. He once told his family that he would prefer to be dead rather than be in the state he is in now. Therefore, his wife, Joan, wants to kill him, but her children are against it. They argue that it is wrong to kill and that she would probably go to jail, causing herself and her family great suffering.

Problems of euthanasia are difficult for various reasons, not the least of which, of course, is the apparent conflict of principle. Our first principle bids us to do no harm, but both killing and the prolongation of suffering are harms. If we try to avoid death by using lifesaving techniques, we may prolong suffering unnecessarily; but if we try to end the suffering, we either cause death or allow the person to die.

Because our principles are negative, it is appropriate to distinguish causing death from allowing to die. In this case, Joan would not be violating our principle if she allowed her husband to die, but she would violate it, it seems, if she did anything to cause his death. In this way, we can distinguish withholding medication, say, or some other form of treatment, from shooting him, say, or giving him poison. But we may also suppose that family members have a special duty to care for one another in a positive way, and hence that Mrs. Smith ought to try to keep her husband alive. If she did not have this special obligation, it would seem that she could simply let him die. Thousands of people die every day and, justifiably, most of us do nothing to prevent it because we have no special obligation to do so—and probably could not do so if we tried.

But the problem here, as we have phrased it, is not one of allowing to die, but one of actual, premeditated killing. In any case, the option of allowing her husband to die naturally, without artificial life support, might mean that he would still continue to suffer for quite a while. So her question is whether she should kill him now. However, to do so seems to be a violation of our first principle, which prohibits killing, and our subordinate principle, which requires people to obey the law. Because these principles apply in a prima facie sense, the question here is whether this is a justified exception.

The answer, it seems, depends on a number of factors. One of our suppositions is that Mr. Smith is terminally ill. But there may be a question of the certainty or probability of his death, or the amount of time it will take him to die, with or without medical care. There is also a question about the degree of suffering, and this may be difficult to answer because he cannot communicate. There is also a question about what his own choice would be, even though he once expressed the wish to die under these circumstances. People do sometimes change their minds, of course. Given these doubts, and given that the law prohibits such action, one might justifiably conclude that it would be wrong to violate the law and the moral principle on which it is based.

MORALITY VERSUS LEGALITY

But suppose one is convinced that Mr. Smith's suffering is extreme, that it will continue for a long time, and yet that there is no prospect of recovery. Let us also suppose that pain-relieving drugs are not effective or are not available in his case. One might very well reason that, in such a case, there would be no point in keeping him alive, that the reason for keeping people alive is because they have a life to live. But *ex hypothesi*, Mr. Smith no longer has a life to live. He could continue to exist, but only in a biological sense, as an organism, and even then, only in a very undesirable way. That is, the prohibition against causing harm by causing death is based on the premise that life has value; but, if we have good reason to believe that life no longer has value in a particular case, that premise no longer holds.

What this means is that in this case as in others, what is morally right or wrong is not necessarily the same as what is legally right or wrong. Euthanasia, for example, may sometimes be justified, morally speaking, even if it is legally wrong. The law may not be able to distinguish clearly between cases when euthanasia is justified and when it is not, for the law is concerned with intentions and motives in cases of killing, and it is not always easy to determine what a person intends. People who kill others in the name of mercy may really be trying to make life easier for themselves, and they may even be trying to profit from another person's death, even though they *say* they were trying to relieve the other person's suffering. But, on the other hand, a person who kills another out of mercy can know his or her own intentions. So the law may have to draw lines that are more restrictive than morality in order to prevent abuses. Although there may be evidence of motive or intention, judges and juries cannot read other people's minds.

In the case we are considering, Mrs. Smith might have moral justification even if her act would be considered legally wrong. She has a prima facie obligation to obey the law, but other considerations may outweigh the legal prohibition. But, even if so, she must still take the legal consequences into account. That is, she must still consider the possibility that she will be arrested and convicted for murder. In that case, she may indeed cause a great deal of suffering for herself and her family.

BERTRAM AND ELSIE BANDMAN
On the Right to Live or Die

But even for a person, the right to die is not as high a priority right as the right to live, because a consequence of the right to die is the final elimination of a person's freedom. A person who chooses to die cannot take back his decision after it has been acted on. So safeguards are needed to assure that the desire to die is the firm conviction of the patient.

There may even be extenuating circumstances in which the prolonged suffering of a person may have beneficial consequences that enhance other persons' possibilities of living. The right to live outweighs the right to die. So, in a pinch where the lives of others depend on overruling a person's right to die, his right to die justly gives way to their prior right to live.

From: "Rights, Justice, and Euthanasia." Bertram and Elsie Bandman. *Beneficent Euthanasia.* Marvin Kohl, ed. Buffalo: Prometheus Books, 1985.

At this point we are likely to find ourselves weighing consequences, or psychological benefits and harms, in a way that makes it even more difficult to reach a determination. There is no way of measuring the amount of suffering that Mrs. Smith will endure by being in jail against the suffering Mr. Smith will endure by being kept alive. Mrs. Smith might avoid arrest and prosecution if she killed Mr. Smith in an undetectable way, or in a way that is difficult to prove, but even then success is uncertain, and she and her family might still suffer from feelings of guilt.

Mrs. Smith and her family might also try to change the law, of course, but that is likely to take time and hence would not resolve their present dilemma. In some states there are provisions for "living wills." Persons can give their written consent for the withholding of care while they are still conscious and free from the pressures of being in pain. But, even then, doctors or relatives are not usually allowed to kill. Usually they are only allowed to withhold treatment.

Nonetheless, an act which is wrong, given existing laws, may be right, morally speaking, after the laws have been changed. In this way, laws really can supplement the principles, by giving them greater precision in special cases, and hence affecting the ways the principles apply.

A Recapitulation

We are trying to illustrate both the power of our principles and their limitations. We have shown that some cases can be settled fairly easily by appealing directly to the principles, and that others can be settled by appealing to the principles and existing laws or social rules. Thus, we have illustrated that the application of principles can be facilitated by the use of social rules and that sometimes the principles cannot yield a determination without them. Hence our principles, by themselves, do not enable us to settle disputes in every case. Sometimes we need social rules, and sometimes we need more information.

The steps to follow in applying the principles are as follows. We should ask ourselves:

1. *Are any principles violated?* If any principle is violated by a particular act, then that act is wrong (unless it turns out to be a justified exception). If no principle is violated, then the act is right; that is, it is morally permitted.

2. *Is the case an exception?* When an act violates a principle, there may be reasons for thinking it is a justified exception. Exceptions are needed when there are conflicts between principles, or conflicts in the application of a single principle. Strictly speaking, conflicts arise when a positive course of action, in keeping with the spirit of the principles, violates one or more of the principles.

3. *Has the burden of proof been met?* The burden of proof on exceptions may be met, we said, in the following ways:

    a. by showing that it is in keeping with one or more of the principles.
    b. by showing that the exception can be generalized to cover other, similar cases (and may in fact conform to social or institutional rules).

     c.   by showing that the exception would be a less serious violation
         of principle than other alternatives.
     d.   by showing that the violation is indirect.
     e.   by showing that the violation is highly improbable or at least uncer-
         tain.

In attempting to meet the burden of proof in a particular case, one might argue that causing a minor harm would prevent a greater harm. In such a case, one would be arguing for an exception to the first principle: "Do no harm," by appealing to that same principle, and hence meeting Condition a. In so doing, however, one would also be meeting Condition c, arguing that the violation is less serious than its alternative(s). If the harm caused by the violation were uncertain, Condition e, that would strengthen the case for the exception, and if it were also indirect, Condition d, the case would be stronger still.

Consider, for example, medication given to cure an infection. The medicine has minor side-effects; say, it makes a person extremely drowsy for a short time and might possibly cause organ damage if taken over long periods of time. Taking or administering the medicine is an apparent violation of our first principle, "Do no harm," for it reduces a person's ability to function properly, even if only for a short time, and it may indirectly cause organ damage. But the harm done directly is minor compared to the harm avoided. The more serious side effect is highly improbable and indirect. Therefore, the use of medication in this case meets the burden of proof.

Variously, on a battlefield, a surgeon may give special consideration to wounded soldiers who seem most likely to benefit from treatment. Those who are badly wounded and not treated may complain that they are victims of injustice, thinking that the surgeon violates our second principle, "Do not be unfair." But the surgeon might argue, however, that the very serious cases would probably die no matter what he did, and that the least serious cases can wait for help. In doing so, he would be arguing for an exception to the justice principle on the basis of the harm principle, holding that, in this way, he could do more good or avoid more harm. He might also cite standard practice, arguing that this is the way surgeons are "supposed" to act, or are "expected" to act, under these conditions. He certainly would be basing his judgment on probabilities as well, for he is not in a position to be absolutely certain about the consequences of either treating or failing to treat each and every patient he meets.

MARK COPPENGER
On the Right to Treatment

If we must select some for treatment, and so, in effect, some for death, how shall we do it? If there isn't enough serum or equipment or there's a shortage of transplant organs, who will get what's available? Shall we proceed on a first come, first serve basis? Or shall we hold a lottery? Perhaps we should determine who can best serve society, or whose loss would be most tragic. Such questions were once appropriate to kidney dialysis. And with each new cure, there is the possibility of similar conflict.

From: *Bioethics: A Casebook*. Mark Coppenger, ed. Englewood Cliffs: Prentice-Hall, 1985.

However, it is fairly obvious that if the side-effects of medication were more harmful than the illness it is designed to cure, one would not be justified in taking the medication. Generally speaking, higher risks may be taken to avoid otherwise certain or highly probable harms, especially if those harms would be serious. A person standing in a window of a burning building, with flames leaping at her back, may be justified in trying to jump a great distance to safety, even though success is highly improbable. But that same person might be morally wrong in taking that same risk under normal conditions.

We can allow people to take chances if the probability of harm is not high, or if the probable harm is not great. Sports are a good example, for, in many sports at least, the probability of harm is not high, or if it is, the probable harms are relatively minor. We tend to tolerate such harms if they are indirect or unintended, thinking that direct or intentional harm is morally wrong. Boxing and hockey are often criticized because the participants actually try to harm one another. In sports where the likelihood of harm is great, we also expect players to wear protective equipment.

In any case, we do not expect anyone to cause more harm than is necessary to produce a desirable goal. If we have a choice between medicines that are likely to produce the same effect, we should choose the medicine that has the least serious side effects. If one needs to play rough in order to have fun, then one should at least develop rules, or wear equipment, that will reduce injury. If one needs to harm another in order to prevent harm to herself or others, then one should cause as little harm as may be needed to accomplish this aim. Thus, if one can scare off a robber with a shot in the air, or at least stop him with a shot to his body, there is no need, and hence no justification, for shooting him six times, say, after he is down.

EXERCISES

1. Using the principles and procedures discussed in this chapter, try to determine whether the following decisions are justified. In each case, explain how the decision either conforms to or violates one or more of the principles. If a case is an exception, also explain why you think that the burden of proof can or cannot be met.

   a. Alice and Bob have two children, both of whom have disabilities. One of their children, Cybil, has a physical disorder that hinders her reading ability, but she is otherwise quite normal. The other child, Bobby, is severely retarded. Alice and Bob know they cannot afford special care for both children, so they decide to provide special schooling only for Bobby. They feel that, with such care, Bobby will at least be able to learn simple tasks such as feeding himself. Cybil, they conclude, will have to get along in the public school system, even though it is somewhat inferior to private programs.

   b. In 1968, during the war in Vietnam, Jim received notice that he was inducted into the Army. He knew the likelihood was high that he would be sent to fight in the war. He also believed that the war was wrong, that the U.S. should not be involved in it. Therefore, he decided to flee to Canada to avoid the draft.

c. Ray is seventy-five years old and has lung cancer. His doctors expect him to die within six months, but they do not tell him or his family. Instead, they tell him that his recent x-rays show that his tumor has been almost completely destroyed by radiation, which is true. What they do not tell him is that the tumor is likely to grow back. They reason: why make him and his family unhappy? By thinking he is cured, they can all enjoy his remaining life.

d. Diane believes that her college is guilty of racism in its hiring practices. In fact, she has access to evidence that shows this is true. However, when asked by a local reporter if the college discriminates against blacks, she lies. She says that she does not know of any evidence to support that claim. At home she tells her husband that if the truth were known, the college would be denied federal funds. She is also afraid of losing her job.

e. The U.S. government decides to retaliate against terrorism by bombing several military installations in Libya. Predictably, more than a hundred civilians are killed, as are many Libyan soldiers and three American flyers. Over the next few months terrorist incidents diminish slightly but then resume.

f. Bob, who is thirty-eight years old, is becoming increasingly unhappy with his job. His income is good, but he finds his job boring. He has always been interested in law and would like to attend law school. But his wife and children object. They say he should have gone to law school years ago but, by his attending now, their standard of living will drop. The costs of going to school may even entail selling the house and renting a smaller place for the next few years.

g. Two businesswomen apply to join the local chapter of a national men's club. They argue that women should have the opportunity to join, for the club provides business contacts, and the exclusion of women is unfair. The local officers of the club deny their application, however, because the club's charter excludes women. They admit that perhaps the club's rules should be changed, but they say they are bound by the rules.

h. Some students have been carrying weapons to high school. During the last two months, two students were seriously wounded by gunshots. The principal of the school decided to initiate random, unannounced searches of the students in order to check for guns. Some members of the community argued that the searches violated the students' constitutional rights by depriving them of privacy and liberty. Furthermore, they argue, the searches will not necessarily prevent violence. The principal replied that, in this case, there is clear danger to students and teachers alike, and the severity of the problem justifies this minor infraction of student rights.

i. Sam, a well-known thief, was caught shoplifting. Three policemen immediately arrived at the scene, and when they tried to arrest Sam, he became violent, swinging his arms and kicking his legs. In order to stop him, one of the policemen hit Sam with a nightstick, knocking him to the ground. The policemen then put handcuffs on Sam and took him to jail. Sam later complained of police violence, but they said he had it coming to him.

j. Harry grew tired of hoodlums breaking into his store, so he bought a gun and kept it near him at all times. Late one night, when he was asleep in his apartment above the store, he heard someone at the window in the next room. He picked up his gun, went into the room, and turned on the light. When he saw two large teenagers climbing in through the window, he shot both of them several times.

2.   Do you think any of the above cases cannot be resolved with the principles and procedures discussed in this chapter? In such cases, do you think that additional information would make a difference? What difference would it make?

ORDERING THE PRINCIPLES

We have allowed that our fundamental set of principles is limited in a variety of ways. While the principles exclude entire classes of actions, they do so only in a prima facie sense, because there may be exceptions. We also said that, in some cases, the principles may need to be supplemented by subordinate moral rules.

We have tried to solve the problem of conflicts between principles by (1) adopting a set of negative principles and (2) stipulating that they apply in a prima facie sense. A third way of trying to resolve problems created by conflicts between principles is to order the principles. That is, one might hold that some one or more of the principles is prior, higher, or more important than the other principles, and hence overrides them in cases of conflict.

THOMAS SCANLON
(1940–   )
On the Conflict between Freedom and Law

An autonomous man may, if he believes the appropriate arguments, believe that the state has a distinctive right to command him. . . . How strong this reason is—what, if anything, could override it—will depend on his view of the arguments for obedience to law. What is essential to the person's remaining autonomous is that in any given case his mere recognition that a certain action is required by law does not settle the question of whether he will do it. That question is settled only by his own decision, which may take into account his current assessment of the general case for obedience and the exceptions it admits.

From: "A Theory of Freedom of Expression." Thomas Scanlon. *Philosophy and Public Affairs*, 1, 1972.

If, for example, one believed that freedom is more important than protection from harm, then one might argue that we should risk harm in order to achieve freedom, when, of course, it is impossible to have both at once. For example, one might argue that seat-belt laws, meant to protect us from harm, are a violation of freedom, that people can always choose such protection if they wish. Or, if one prized security more than freedom, one might argue that we should surrender our freedom, if, by doing so, we could make life more secure.

Some people will order their ultimate values in one way, and others another, although they may not always do so in the same way, under all circumstances. Indeed, there is often good reason for ranking the principles in one way, given one sort of problem, and in another way, given a problem of another kind. Variously, there may be good reason for ordering the principles in one way under one set of circumstances and in another way under different conditions. That is why we did not rank our principles in an *a priori* way, that is, prior to considering the contexts or circumstances of application.

THEORETICAL ORDERINGS

On one extreme, some moral theorists have argued that there is no rational way of ordering principles to solve problems of conflict or of resolving ideological differences. They have claimed that such orderings are simply matters of arbitrary choice, emotional preference, or cultural conditioning. Decisionalists, for example, argue that one simply has to choose the kind of life, or the kind of system, one would ultimately like to have, and Marxists have argued that people are historically determined to accept one or another value system.

On the other extreme, some theorists have argued that such matters can be settled by logical analysis, and hence that some principle or other can be *proved* to be the one and only principle, or the highest principle, for all places and times. Classical utilitarians, for instance, seem to have believed that one would be irrational if one did not accept the principles of pleasure and pain as ultimate values, or the greatest happiness principles as the ultimate principles of obligation. Kant thought one would be irrational if one did not apply his principle of universalizability.

Thus, according to the one extreme, it has been held that no principle can ever be shown to be prior to the rest, and according to the other extreme, some principle or other is supposed to always and necessarily occupy the highest position. It is our position that principles can be ordered according to objective, rational considerations, but that such ordering will not always be the same. We also allow that individual preferences and cultural factors may be important considerations, and that sometimes persons may simply have to choose.

NATURAL CONSIDERATIONS

We have not ordered our principles. We have not claimed that any one of them is superior to the others or takes precedence over them in all cases. We have included Kantian, utilitarian, libertarian, and even natural law considerations within our set of basic principles, without holding that any one of these theories is wholly correct.

But this is not to say that there can be no reason for ordering principles one way or another. Indeed, there does seem to be a natural order of principles based on more or less fundamental human wants or needs. That is, life itself seems more fundamental than any other human good, for, without life, no other goods are possible. Thus, other goods necessary for life are hardly less fundamental: food and drink, say, without which life cannot long be sustained.

Sex, however, is not necessary for life—at least not for the lives of people who engage in sexual activities—although it may be necessary for procreation. The need for clothing and shelter, or protection from the elements, depends a great deal on climate, and the need for protection from other people depends on whether one is in fact threatened by them. So these do not seem to be quite so fundamental, or at least not invariable needs.

Freedom and knowledge are not absolutely necessary for life, but they do seem necessary to a distinctively human existence, so we might say that they are nearly as fundamental as life itself, for they are needed for human expression and development. Thus, when we come down to cases, we are apt to find that considerations of life, health, and security take precedence over considerations of justice, freedom, or opportunity, just because the latter are not possible without the former. But, when we have provided for basic needs, their satisfaction is no longer an immediate or pressing concern. Our attention naturally shifts to other considerations, such as those of freedom and opportunity. When we are healthy, we want to do things, so we look for things to do and opportunities to do them.

RALPH W. CLARK
(1944–   )
On Serving the Greatest Need

We ought to help those people the most who are the most in need of help. That is, concern for others is to be understood in terms of a variable scale, where the greatest concern is to be addressed to those who have the greatest needs. For example, if a person is born crippled, he or she should be given the extra help needed to be happy by those of us who are best able to give help. Another example is the "Robin Hood" principle that is part of the justification for a graduated income tax. The idea is that money from the rich should be given to the poor in order to make people more nearly equal in how well off they are.

From: *Introduction to Moral Reasoning*. Ralph W. Clark. St. Paul: West Publishing Co., 1986.

Indeed, when we have opportunities, we face a different sort of problem, the problem of determining which of the opportunities we should choose. Having chosen to take advantage of one or another opportunity, we then become concerned with how we can not only do what we have chosen but how we can do it well. So our problems keep changing according to conditions as our more fundamental needs and desires are met.

CONTEXTUAL CONSIDERATIONS

The contexts in which moral problems arise are determined by such considerations. They are determined by what, under a given set of circumstances, people need to do in order to continue their lives and advance toward their goals. Most of the people today who live in highly industrialized countries do not face the problem of trying to satisfy basic needs. At least they do not usually face such problems unless they lose their health or their jobs. But there is a minority that frequently, even continually, confronts such problems, and a large percentage of the people of the world are under-nourished and without adequate shelter or security.

Thus, the problems we face, and the conditions under which we face them, will determine by and large which principle or value takes precedence over which other principle or value. We pointed out in the last chapter that extremely sick persons are often justified in surrendering a large portion of their freedom, at least for a limited period of time, by putting themselves under medical care, accepting the role of being a patient and institutional restrictions on their behavior. On the other hand, healthy individuals are often justified in risking minor injury to themselves and others, in playing games, say, or in trying to achieve worthy goals. They may even risk serious harm, even death, if the probabilities are low. After all, we face some risk no matter what we do. We can never guarantee that we or others will not be harmed, although we can certainly try not to harm anyone.

On a social or political level, we have also pointed out that conditions can affect policy decisions. In a society of extreme scarcity, feeding starving people is likely to be a more important consideration than freedom or justice, unless, perchance, in a tyrranical regime, the threats to freedom or justice are more life-threatening than the scarcity of food. In times of crises, civil liberties are often restricted. But, in normal times, or in times of prosperity, questions of freedom and opportunity are of primary concern.

However, in the case of a given individual, there may be little or no chance of survival, or little time left to live. Or in the case of some segment or percentage of a society or a group, there may be little or nothing anyone can do to save everyone from hunger or death. In such cases, as regrettable as it may be, energy and resources may need to be diverted where they can do the most good, as we pointed out in our example of the battlefield physician. The same problem arises in a family where not every child can receive the same care, and hence some children receive more attention than others.

The Relatedness of Issues

In order to settle the issues, therefore, we need to look at them very carefully, to determine where exactly the problem lies. We also need to look at them, not as isolated issues, but "all things considered," or as they bear upon one another. Thus, for example, it does not seem wise to try to distribute all goods or money among all people equally, just because there are people in need, or because there are people who have little or no money. If there were no concentrations of wealth in organizations that produce and distribute goods, there would be fewer goods to go around and probably little or no means of distributing them. On the other hand, not all concentrations of wealth can be justified for this reason, for some organizations may be too big to be efficient, or too profitable, given the needs of others.

Questions such as these are often addressed in a random, *ad hoc* fashion by private forms of charity, but they usually need to be solved by large-

> ## THOMAS DONALDSON
> ### (1945–   )
> ### *On Justifying Corporations*
>
> To say that an organization produces wealth for society is not sufficient to justify it from a moral perspective, since morality encompasses the entire range of human welfare. To say something produces wealth is to say something morally good about it . . . but it fails to tell us what else the thing does, or how its process of creation affects society. Consider the example of a nuclear power reactor. To say that a nuclear reactor generates electricity is to say something good about it, but it fails to consider the reactor in the context of the possibility of meltdowns, the storage of nuclear waste, the costs of alternative production, and so forth.
>
> From: *Corporations and Morality*. Thomas Donaldson. Englewood Cliffs: Prentice-Hall, 1982.

scale social organization. That is why we need institutions in the form of governments, business organizations, and schools, for example, and rules governing the actions of these agencies. Although we will address these matters more directly in the next chapter, we want to point out here that individual actions will be either supported or constrained by the forms of existing institutions. Solutions to problems will be affected by the ways in which a given society or culture has ordered its priorities. Thus, ideology and cultural norms may indeed influence what should be done under given conditions, for they will determine, to a large extent, what is possible.

When problems arise concerning medical care, for example, one of the factors involved is the extent and quality of available medical services. Another factor is the structure of the institutions that deliver medical care. These things can be changed, and they are in fact changing, but we must take into account the limitations and possibilities of existing institutions. We may believe that, morally speaking, medical care should be readily available to all people, but that may not be possible under present conditions. We have to try to do with what we have and, at the same time, try to change our institutions and practices to advance closer to our goals.

Our questioning usually begins where the problem is immediately felt, but it may then proceed to a consideration of other problems related to it. Thus, what may seem to be a simple problem of justice within an institution may shift to a problem about the justice of that type of institution, or to a question of its efficiency. Thus people may begin by thinking that everyone should be treated alike, or that they should have the same rights and duties, until they see the need for a division of labor. The question then may be, not whether people should have different jobs, but which job they should have and according to what criteria.

ULTIMATE INDETERMINACIES

After all is said and done, however, reasonable people may still disagree about the justification of a given course of action because they have different estimates of the facts, or different estimates of the possibilities. They will usually not disagree about the desirability of satisfying all of our principles, when that is possible, but they may continue to disagree when principles conflict. Very often such disagreements could be settled if persons really could know in advance the actual outcomes of alternative courses of action. We may know what has happened in the past but we must try to predict, as best we can, what will happen in the future.

Concerning desired outcomes, or supposed ideal states of affairs, there may be disagreements according to cultural conditioning or individual preferences. However, given our principles, the range of morally justified choice is limited, and many differences of opinion can be resolved. The fact that there is some room for choice in the ordering of principles, in the selection of subordinate rules, and in individual actions, is not necessarily a theoretical fault. It seems that any theory should allow for a wide range of justifiable choice in order to give to human freedom and creativity their proper due. Although the application of principles can narrow the range of morally acceptable choice, there is still room within morality for cultural variation and individual taste.

A TEST CASE

A good example of a conflict in principle arises in the case of capital punishment. So called "retributivists" argue that *in justice* those who have committed a crime *deserve* to be punished, sometimes even by being put to death. They say that the law needs to be enforced so those who disobey it do not gain an unfair advantage over those who obey. This, one might say, is a Kantian sort of argument, emphasizing the importance of justice over utility.

Utilitarians, by contrast, have argued that the only reason for punishment is to produce some future good, or to avoid some future evil. Thus, they emphasize the rehabilitation of criminals and the prevention of crime. There would be no point in punishing someone just for the sake of punishment, they argue. In some cases, punishment may have no utility at all. In the case of capital punishment, the person being punished is certainly not rehabilitated, and the punishment may not really deter others. It prevents *that* person from committing another crime, but there may be other more humane ways of accomplishing the same result.

In this case, we have what appears to be a conflict between our justice principle and the principle which bids us to do no harm. Punishing wrongdoers appears to be just, but it also causes them harm. Such harm may be viewed as a deterrent, or a form of self-defense, but we have previously argued that, under normal circumstances, it would be wrong to kill unless there were no other, viable alternative. In the case of capital punishment, there do seem to be other alternatives—although one might argue that they are less effective in preventing criminals from committing crimes.

Thus, if one were a Kantian, one might give justice priority over utilitarian or consequentialist considerations; or, if one were a utilitarian, one might give consequentialist considerations more importance than considerations of justice. But, when we come down to cases, other factors seem relevant to making a rational determination. For example, the cruelty of the punishment is a relevant consideration. For, even if death were supposed to be necessary, some methods of execution are less painful than others. Today, many states that retain capital punishment have rejected the electric chair, or hanging, in favor of lethal injection, on the ground that the latter is more humane. When it comes to deterrence, empirical evidence is relevant to making a determination. We need to examine whether punishment of any sort really does deter crime, and, if so, what sorts of punishment.

Arguments on this issue also take place in a historical context and must take into account actual conditions. That is, we must consider, for example, the nature of existing institutions the effectiveness of prisons and the justice of our court system. Under primitive conditions, as on the battlefield, it is often impossible to have trials or to take prisoners, despite the rules of war. Given the present overcrowding of prisons, it is probably also unrealistic to expect rehabilitation, and, given racial discrimination, we cannot always expect justice from our courts. So, while we might apply our principles one way under what we consider to be ideal conditions, we may need to apply them in another way under existing conditions. However, at the same time, we may also try to move toward what appears to be an ideal state, by improving our penal institutions, for example, or our courts.

There is also room for a reasonable difference of opinion on this issue. One reason for such difference is that it is difficult to make accurate predictions about the results of alternative courses of action. We can argue that existing forms of punishment, including the death penalty, are not very effective deterrents to crime, but, because detection and punishment are so uncertain, it may be the inefficiency of the police, or the leniency of the courts, that is at fault.

In any case, the indeterminacy that results from a conflict of principles allows for different morally justified solutions. Even if the death penalty were a necessary means of preventing crime, or of ensuring justice, there would still be alternatives for carrying it out. Some of these, of course, may be ruled out as inhumane. If, on the other hand, crime can be prevented, or justice served, without severe forms of punishment, there may still be different forms of justified punishment. So there is room for cultural variation on this issue, even individual differences. One parent may be justified in wanting to send a child to its room, and another may be justified in wanting to deny it a privilege of some kind. Neither would be wrong, but some decision still needs to be made about which course of action will be followed.

EXERCISES

1.   In the previous set of problems, indicate where you think there is a conflict of principles. Then indicate how you think this conflict can be resolved.

2.   Consider ordering the principles, and how this may change under various circumstances. In determining your answer, ask yourself whether your ordering of principles is determined by an examination of the conditions or contexts in which the problem arises, or by cultural, individual, or theoretical predisposition.

3. Do you think your position can be generalized so that all reasonable people would be expected to agree with you? All people of a given culture?

4. Do you think that your judgment on each of these issues is the same as judgments you would make in other, similar cases? If not, why not? Where do you think the difference lies?

SUPPLEMENTARY READINGS

Aristotle. *Nichomachean Ethics* (many editions).

Aquinas, Thomas. *Summa Theologica,* Hyman and Walsh, eds. *Philosophy in the Middle Ages.* Indianapolis: Hacket, 1973.

Bayles, Michael D., ed. *Contemporary Utilitarianism.* New York: Doubleday, 1968.

Bierman, A. K. *Life and Morals.* Ch. I. New York: Harcourt, Brace, Jovanovich, 1980.

Brandt, Richard B. *Ethical Theory.* Englewood Cliffs: Prentice-Hall, 1959.

Garrer, R. T. and Rosen, Bernard. *Moral Philosophy.* New York: Macmillan, 1967.

Hare, R. M. *Freedom & Reason.* Oxford: Oxford University Press, 1965.

Kant, Immanuel. *Foundations of the Metaphysics of Morals* (many editions).

Plato. *Republic* (many editions).

Ross, W. D. *The Right and the Good.* Oxford: The Clarendon Press, 1930.

Toulmin, Stephen. *An Examination of the Place of Reason in Ethics.* New York: Cambridge University Press, 1951.

SUBORDINATE MORAL RULES

We have pointed out that our principles are limited in a number of ways. Problems of application can arise when there is a conflict of principles. Also, because the principles are negative, they do not prescribe positive courses of action. Because of these limitations, we said, our basic principles need to be supplemented by subordinate moral rules. Subordinate rules, in the form of social practices and institutions, can help us solve conflicts of principles and determine positive moral obligations.

Indeed, as we have seen, the justice principle, which requires us to apply standards consistently to all cases, presupposes subordinate rules. The legality principle, which requires us to obey the law, presupposes that we have laws. So we have not assumed that our principles apply in a "state of nature," so to speak, prior to the existence of society, but in a society that already has rules, practices, institutions, and laws. That is why, in the last chapter, we recognized that the application of principles is affected by the kinds of rules or laws in force. However, we did not then consider how or why existing rules or institutions should be changed, or how or why new rules or institutions should be brought into existence.

Our basic system of principles does not tell us directly *how* to improve existing social forms, although it can show *that* change is required. We can always criticize an existing rule or institution in the light of our principles, but the principles do not tell us how to go about creating better rules and institutions, or a better society. For that, creativity and initiative may be required. The legality principle, for example, does not tell us what kinds of laws we should have, and the justice principle does not tell us how to create

---

THOMAS AQUINAS
(1224–1274)
On Natural and Human Law

But it must be noted that something may be derived from the natural law in two ways: first, as a conclusion from principles; secondly, by way of a determination of certain common notions. The first way is like to that by which, in the sciences, demonstrated conclusions are drawn from the principles; while the second is likened to that whereby, in the arts, common forms are determined to some particular . . . : e.g. that *one must not kill* may be derived as a conclusion from the principle that *one should do harm to no man* . . . the law of nature has it that the evil-doer should be punished, but that he be punished in this or that way is a determination . . .

From: *Summa Theologica*. Thomas Aquinas. *Basic Writings of Saint Thomas Aquinas*. A. Pegis, ed. New York: Random House, 1948.

---

just practices. In like manner, the principle that bids us to do no harm does not tell us how to avoid harm. Such indeterminacy leaves room for variations in the application of the principles, and, hence, for cultural and individual differences.

CORRELATIVE POSITIVE DUTIES

For these reasons, our system of basic principles does not cover the whole of morality. It specifies several minimal, negative obligations, or prohibitions, and it rather conservatively requires us to apply existing standards consistently and to obey the law. But we have also said that our negative principles are founded on a recognition of and respect for positive values, namely the values of life and health, for example, and of justice and freedom. Why then should we not adopt a set of corresponding positive principles that would tell us to promote such goods?

Well, of course, we should. In so doing, however, we should remember why we adopted a set of negative principles in the first place. Our basic principles were intended to express minimal requirements which would be determinate, easy to obey, and capable of winning consent. Negative principles, in the form of prohibitions, are determinate because they prohibit entire classes of actions. They are relatively easy to obey because they really do not require us to do anything, but merely ask us to refrain. For these reasons, people are also more likely to agree upon them. That is, people are more likely to agree on a principle that prohibits harm, for example, than on a principle that requires them to help one another, partly because it requires less of them, and partly because it is clear about what it requires. A principle that tells us to help others cannot tell us how, when, or whom we should help, without losing its generality and force as a principle. That is why specific positive duties need to be stated by less general, subordinate rules.

If, then, as a correlative to "Do no harm," we adopted the principle

"Avoid doing harm," or even "Help others," several questions would remain unanswered. We would, of course, have to add the "ought-implies-can" restriction (there is no obligation to do the impossible), because it is not always possible to help others, just as it is not always possible to avoid doing harm. Less obviously, moreover, it may not always be good to help others, for they may not need our help or want it. Even when they do need help, they themselves, or someone else, may be in a better position to help. Certainly people can interfere with one another in trying to help. That is why we said earlier that they need to coordinate their actions in trying to do good. There are also many different ways in which we can be of help, and it is not always easy to determine which way to choose. Helping a person in one way often precludes helping that same person in another way, just as helping one person may preclude helping another.

J. O. URMSON
(1915–   )
On Saints and Heroes

We may imagine a squad of soldiers to be practising the throwing of live hand grenades; a grenade slips from the hand of one of them and rolls on the ground near the squad; one of them sacrifices his life by throwing himself on the grenade and protecting his comrades with his own body. It is quite unreasonable to suppose that such a man must be impelled by the sort of emotion that he might be impelled by if his best friend were in the squad; he might only just have joined the squad; it is clearly an action having moral status. But if the soldier had not thrown himself on the grenade would he have failed in his duty?

From: "Saints and Heroes." J. O. Urmson. *Essays in Moral Philosophy*. A. I. Melden, ed. Seattle: University of Washington Press, 1958.

So the principle "Avoid doing harm" or "Help others" is likely to be indefinite in a way that "Do no harm" is not. Presumably we should try to help some people sometime, somehow, but we cannot always be helping everybody at all times and in all possible ways. Even if we could, it is not clear we should; and even when it would be good, it is not always a duty. That is, as we have mentioned before, some actions are above and beyond the call of duty. It is possible to do more than duty requires by performing acts that are saintly or heroic. Again, these are reasons why our fundamental principles do not tell us the most we can do, but the least that is required of us, morally speaking.

Nonetheless, we should recognize that there are positive correlates to our negative principles, which point to the goods that our negative principles are meant to protect. Such positive principles have received various names in the history of ethics. Thomas Aquinas, for instance, referred to them as "counsels of perfection," and John Stuart Mill called them "duties of charity." We might also refer to them as the "duals" of the principles we have already adopted, as long as we recognize that these positive principles do not have the same force as our original set of negative principles.

Positive principles indicate that it would be good for us to promote such things as life, health, human development, justice, and freedom, even if we are not obligated to do so in all cases, all of the time. They point to the kinds of things we can do to make ourselves better persons and our society a better place in which to live, even if they do not tell us how to do it. For this purpose, we have said, more specific rules are required.

Positive principles are made specific by subordinate rules, practices, or customs, which govern social institutions and roles. Such rules identify specific duties, telling us who is supposed to do what, and under what conditions. However, they also provide reasons, at a higher level, for obeying social rules, or for fulfilling the duties of our stations in life. Indeed, positive principles provide a basis for critiquing social practices or customs, for such practices or customs may be ineffective or counterproductive. The positive principles may also be cited as reasons for allowing exceptions. They are similar to our negative principles, therefore, in providing reasons for justifying, rejecting, or modifying lower-level rules.

THE DUAL OF "DO NO HARM"

The dual of a negative principle will prescribe a positive course of action. Thus, the dual of the principle "Do no harm" may be stated as "Avoid doing harm" or as "Help others." "Avoid doing harm" is weaker than "Help others" in that it requires less of us than "Help others," but it requires more than "Do no harm." It does not require that we come to the assistance of those in need, but it does require that we try to prevent harming anyone.

Consider, for instance, the principle "Avoid doing harm" in relation to driving an automobile. One might suppose that driving an automobile recklessly does not, or at least need not, actually harm anybody, and hence that it need not violate the principle "Do no harm." Even if harm were done by reckless driving, it is not usually done intentionally. But if we suppose that people should try to avoid doing harm, then it seems that they should also avoid driving recklessly, at least when such driving is likely to cause harm. Thus, an action that is not directly forbidden by a strict interpretation of the principle "Do no harm" could be forbidden by the correlate or dual of the principle, that is, "Avoid doing harm."

The principle "Help others" is even more demanding. If someone were in an accident, say, it might require us to help that person. But it could do so, of course, only under appropriate conditions. In the first place, one would have to be in a position to help. But it might also be the case that others are in a better position to help and even that our action might interfere with theirs. So we are not likely to be bound by the principle "Help others" as often as we are by the principle "Avoid doing harm." In either case, these principles are highly indeterminate, until and unless we have knowledge of existing conditions. Even then, subordinate rules may be needed to determine particular obligations, and there may be considerable room for choice.

Consider again the question of reducing harm in driving automobiles. The driving of automobiles causes a large number of injuries and deaths. But what should we do to avoid these harms? Some people propose driving at a lower speed—at 55 m.p.h. on open highways, say, instead of 65 or 70.

Of course, we could reduce automobile accidents to zero by not driving at all, but we think of the use of automobiles as a positive good. Therefore we need to weigh the advantages of driving automobiles against the risks.

Agreement on such issues is often difficult to reach because there are so many different ways of trying to solve the problem. People also have special interests in one or another of the possible solutions. Because there are so many ways of trying to avoid harm, or of trying to help others, some decision needs to be made about which courses of action will be followed and who should follow them. There are also decisions that need to be made about how tasks will be performed and how much time, energy, and resources will be devoted to them. That is, we still need subordinate rules.

EXERCISES

State the dual or correlative positive principle for each of our negative principles. In each case, is there a mean between extremes, as "Avoid harm" is a mean between "Do no harm" and "Help others"? Is there any case in which there is no dual, or in which the positive principle says exactly the same thing as the negative? For example, Does "Be just" say the same thing as "Do not be unjust"? Discuss.

CONVENTIONAL RULES

We are all bound by conventions, by social institutions and practices, by laws and authorities, at home, at work, and in the community. Table manners, traffic regulations, business transactions, and even international affairs are all governed by conventional rules, as well as by moral principles. Some such rules are explicitly stated, even written down and enforced by governments; others are simply assumed or "expected," and are enforced by social approval or criticism. In either case, the force of conventional rules can be quite real; agents may be punished or rewarded for obedience or disobedience. Obedience or disobedience of conventional rules may also cause a great deal of harm or good.

Social rules and conventions not only govern behavior, they also define institutions and social roles, and hence give them meaning. A judge in the courts has certain defined powers that set limits to his socially or legally acceptable behavior and, at the same time, enable us to understand the significance of his actions. This is true of other social roles as well, including those of teachers and students, for example, or employers and employees. We understand social roles by understanding what people do in them, or more precisely, what they are allowed to do, or are not allowed to do, according to socially accepted rules or practices. The violation of such rules is usually thought to be a moral fault, and much of our day-to-day moral reasoning is devoted to defending, interpreting, or amending such rules.

J. L. MACKIE
(1917–1981)
On Social Institutions

We have perhaps been speaking too casually about institutions and their requirements . . . it may be thought that some further account of these is called for. However, the realities for which these terms are intended to stand are thoroughly familiar, and there should be no obscurity as long as it is understood that this cluster of terms is being used very widely, that institution is meant to cover such diverse items as games like chess, the social practices that centre round the making of promises, and the thought and behavior that supports or is supported by the identity of persons through time . . .

Any institution is constituted by many people behaving in fairly regular ways, with relations between them which transmit and encourage and perhaps enforce those ways of behaving.

From: *Ethics: Inventing Right and Wrong.* J. L. Mackie. New York: Penguin Books, 1977.

Most conventional rules are habitually obeyed. In fact, most of the time, we do not even think about them but follow them quite automatically. However, there are times when we have occasion to criticize social rules, institutions, or practices. Children sometimes complain about parental authority; citizens sometimes oppose the policies of government; and university professors sometimes argue about the structure of higher education. Thus, we become aware of the role we play as makers of rules, not just followers, when we vote in elections, determine policies and procedures on our jobs, or demonstrate to win political support for some cause. Even children can be rule-makers, in making up the rules of games, in organizing clubs, or in arguing with their parents about the rules of family life.

In the case of family and friends, we often engage in the process of negotiating and renegotiating rules: who will do the dishes or mow the lawn; who is allowed to drive the family car; when we can count on time to study or work; and when or how loudly we can play our sound equipment. We also support or undermine the rules by choosing to obey or disobey them, for rules which are generally disobeyed tend to become ineffective, and rules which are obeyed tend to remain in force.

Rules and Reasoning

Because of the pervasive influence of conventional rules, we need to consider how they affect and are affected by our basic principles. We are interested in seeing how the existence of conventional rules can affect moral reasoning, and, in turn, how moral reasoning can affect them. Obviously, moral rules can affect moral reasoning by functioning as reasons for or against particular judgments and actions. Moral reasoning can affect rules by bringing moral principles to bear upon them.

Thus we pointed out earlier that we sometimes reason directly from moral principles to judgments about the rightness or wrongness of particular acts. At other times, we reason indirectly from the principles by means of rules, assuming that the rules are justified by the principles, or at least that the rules are in force. But, when there is a question about the justification of a rule, we must refer back to the principles. In other words, we must ask whether the rules serve to prevent harm or promote good, whether they curtail freedom or provide opportunities, and whether they are fair or just.

We have argued, however, that conventional moral rules cannot be deduced from moral principles alone, without taking other factors into consideration. Conventional moral rules are called "conventional" because they are made up or determined by convention or agreement, and because their force depends largely on being accepted over long periods of time. The notion of convention or agreement indicates that there is an element of choice in the selection of rules, and the time element is important to establishing consistency in application, reasonable expectation, and the stability required for teaching and learning the rules. Thus, the justification of rules depends on a background of past practices, just as it depends on existing conditions and moral principles. That is, rules or practices must be judged against the background of other rules or practices to see if they are consistent with one another, or whether they are a reasonable extension of the total set.

Thus, while our basic set of principles is meant to apply very broadly across times and places, conventional moral rules apply to a particular time and place—to a particular culture, say, a nation or a group, an institution or organization. Conventional rules differ according to times, places, and conditions, for their justification depends, in part, upon those conditions. Furthermore, there is frequently an element of choice or arbitrariness in establishing the rules, for more than one alternative may be justified by the principles. That is, it is often necessary to adopt one and only one rule when any one of a number of rules will do. As mentioned before, we seem to need a rule of the road specifying that people drive on the right or the left, but it doesn't seem to matter much initially which rule we adopt.

Once a rule has been adopted and remains in force, it then becomes a factor in moral reasoning, as a way of applying principles to cases, and as a means of determining expectations and predicting behavior.

THEORETICAL BACKING OF CONVENTIONAL RULES

Support for conventional moral rules comes from nearly all moral theories. Cultural relativism, social contract theory, and pragmatism, for example, argue directly for conventional rules, whereas natural law and natural rights theories, including Thomism and Kantianism, give more emphasis to natural, universal principles, and allocate a secondary position to social rules.

Thomists, who defend natural and even divine law, also support civil authority. Even utilitarians, who think that all actions must be justified by an appeal to consequences, have recognized the importance of social institutions and practices. The function of social rules is especially evident in rule utilitarianism, for rule utilitarians have argued that rules are needed in order to apply the utilitarian principle. Thus social rules are often thought to be "middle rules," for they are supposed to mediate between universal principles and particular judgments, enabling us to apply principles to particular cases.

We have said that each of the theories is correct in one or another point of emphasis, and hence that we cannot accept any one of them to the exclusion of all others. Thus, we may accept the claims of one theory regarding the

223

nature of first principles, or of another theory concerning the status of moral rules. Within the constraints of our general system, we may even accept a particular version of one or another theory, such as a Rawlsian claim regarding the just distribution of income or wealth. That is, we may believe that an ideal economic system should aim at maximizing the welfare of its least well-off citizens, without accepting Rawls' general theory of ethics. We may then use Rawls' principle to critique social practices that have harmful effects upon the poor. However, we should keep in mind that such special theoretical claims are not likely to win widespread agreement, and hence may not carry as much weight in argumentation as our general principles or existing social rules.

The Functions of Rules

We have already emphasized how subordinate rules are needed to supplement principles. They help to determine what specifically should be done and who has responsibility. They even help determine the meaning of the principles, or how the principles should be interpreted in particular cases. For example, our harm principle tells us to respect the property of others, but conventional rules—civil laws—determine what counts as property, or what we can legitimately claim to own.

A zoning board, composed of neighborhood citizens, may decide to limit the use of our property, and thereby diminish its value. A legislature may pass a law recognizing claims to patents and copyrights, thus limiting the use of information. Even the use of public property is governed by laws. We may be allowed to picnic in the park but not drink beer; we are allowed to drive on public highways, but only in licensed vehicles and at designated speeds.

We have seen that conventional moral rules are needed to specify the agents responsible for carrying out certain obligations. Rules may also be needed to specify the conditions under which the principles apply. Most people would probably agree that poverty should be eliminated, but we need conventional rules to tell us what counts as poverty, and who, or what agency, has the responsibility to eliminate it. Today we naturally think of the government and other social agencies as a means of eliminating injustice and poverty, but this was not always so. Under more tyrannical regimes, or even in the fabled wild west, people had to correct injustices as they could, or as they saw fit. Fair and effective government does not always exist, and there is almost always serious disagreement about the extent of the government's social responsibilities. One might try to imagine societies in which there are no institutions for creating and enforcing law, or for correcting injustices, but in a world of real, imperfect people, it is difficult to see how we could do without them.

In determining who will do what, we also need to determine how tasks will be done, and we often need to train people to do them. Thus institutions are established to accomplish specific tasks and to educate people in them. Schools provide education and train teachers. Hospitals provide medical care and train doctors and nurses. Business organizations produce and distribute goods and train workers. Rules and practices are developed in the process

---

ALFRED ADLER
(1870–1937)
On Social Bonds

Society exacts certain obligations of us which influence the norms and forms of our life, as well as the development of our mind. . . . When we observe the slow development of a child, we may be certain no evolution of human life is possible without the presence of a protecting community. The various obligations of life carry in themselves the necessity for a division of labor which not only does not separate human beings, but strengthens their bonds.

From: *Understanding Human Nature.* Alfred Adler. New York: Garden City Publishing Co., 1927.

to govern the behavior of members, but also to assign tasks and teach people how to carry them out. In smaller organizations, such as the family or local school, both adults and children will find that they have different responsibilities according to their positions in these institutions. Even in entertainment, there are rules governing the behavior of audiences and performers, determining who is allowed on the stage or playing field, or even how much noise is permitted.

In teleological ethical theory, conventional moral rules are a means to an end. They enable us to do what the principles say we should. They make it possible to do good or avoid evil more effectively than we could without them. The basic idea behind social rules, so emphasized by social contractarians from Hobbes to Rawls, is that we can become morally better persons by cooperating with one another, according to rules, than any of us could be alone, or even collectively, by uncoordinated individual action. Indeed it takes a society of considerable size and wealth to support certain kinds of institutions, such as universities and corporations, the optimal number of which, as well as the optimal size and structure of which, is an important consideration in determining their usefulness.

However, social rules may also serve to define the ends of action, for social rules characterize a way of life. That is, we want to have rules, not only because they help us produce other goods, but also because we want to live the kind of life made possible by those rules. We may believe that a society governed by certain kinds of rules is the very kind of society we want to uphold. Thus, we may speak of "the American way of life" as a way of identifying with our society, its ideals, and its way of doing things, just as members of other cultures may identify with their customs and practices. In such cases, as Mill has argued, the means become the ends.

EXERCISES

1. Explain why moral rules are sometimes necessary to supplement principles. Give examples.

2. What different sorts of jobs can be accomplished by the adoption of subordinate rules? Give examples of problems you think can be solved by adopting rules.

3. Give some reasons why conventional moral rules are likely to vary from place to place. Give examples to illustrate your points.

4. Give some reasons why, at a given time and place, there may be a justified choice between rules. Again, give examples of cases in which there may be a moral need for a rule but the choice of any one of several rules will do.

THE MORAL COMMUNITY

Social institutions and practices can become part of a person's picture of "the good life," as he or she comes to know it, in the *concrete*, and not just in principle or theory. This is one reason why people are suspicious of theory, for they tend to confront morality in the immediate and concrete— in the forms it takes in their community. This is also one of the reasons why morality often seems to be so ethnocentric and conservative. People tend to hold on to their customary ways of doing things because they find them familiar and satisfying and because the effects of change are threatening or unknown.

J. L. MACKIE
(1917–1981)
On Using and Amending Rules

What counts is rules that are actually recognized by the members of some social circle, large or small, and that thus set up expectations and claims . . . What the individual can do is to remember that there are, in different circles of relationship with which he is concerned, various fragments of a moral system which already contributes very considerably to countering specific evils which he, like others, will see as evils; that he can at once take advantage of this system and contribute to its upkeep; but that he may be able, with others, to put pressure on some fragments of the system, so that they come gradually and be more favourable to what he sees as valuable or worthwhile.

From: *Ethics: Inventing Right and Wrong.* J. L. Mackie. New York: Penguin Books, 1977.

But, of course, not all familiar things are good, and traditional ways of doing things sometimes become obsolete or are simply wrong. Slavery was an institution in early America, but we have since come to recognize that slavery is morally wrong. Hazing, an accepted practice in many fraternities and sororities, has now been banned at many universities. Medical practices and teaching practices change over the years. Thus, in recognizing the importance of rules, we need not become rule worshippers, thinking that the traditional, customary, or existing rules are necessarily good, or that disobedience to them is always wrong.

Moral rules can serve as premises in moral arguments, as we have pointed out, but the moral life is not just a matter of judging particular acts by socially accepted rules. It also involves social criticism: the examination of social policies and practices in the light of moral principles and subsequent political action aimed at producing institutional reform.

The Individual and Society

While probably all social institutions can be improved, it is doubtful that we would be better off without them. Even language depends on socially accepted rules, and, without it, communication would be practically impossible. The rules of common courtesy also facilitate communication by providing us with a silent language, so to speak, the language of sign or gesture. People who fail to learn socially accepted ways of expressing affection, appreciation, or forgiveness, often find themselves unable to perform such acts.

Our lives are in fact so permeated with rules that we hardly notice them. They constitute, as it were, the invisible social world in which we live. Like the emperor's clothes, they are nowhere to be seen, but they govern the things we do. Such rules exist in our heads, to the extent that we think about them and perhaps accept them, but they also exist in our actions, in our habits or dispositions to act, and in the buildings, tools, and other material marks of distinction we have created to express our beliefs.

G. W. F. HEGEL
(1770–1831)
On Morality and the State

Summing up what has been said of the State, we find that we have been led to call its vital principle, as actuating the individuals who compose it—Morality. The State, its laws, its arrangements, constitute the rights of its members; its natural features, its mountains, air, and waters, are *their* country, their fatherland, their outward material property; the history of this State, *their* deeds; what their ancestors have produced, belongs to them and lives in their memory. All is their possession, just as they are possessed by it; for it constitutes their existence, their being.

From: *The Philosophy of History.* G. W. F. Hegel. J. Sibree, trans. *Hegel Selections.* Jacob Lowewenberg, ed. New York: Charles Scribner's Sons, 1929.

Most everything people do is influenced by social rules, by participation in one kind of social institution or another, and the very terms in which they think of themselves and their actions are socially defined. In creating social roles, the rules determine what we can do and the kinds of persons we can be. The rules of baseball, for instance, enable us to make home runs, and they also enable us to be baseball players. These are things we could not do, or be, without those rules. Likewise the rules of government enable people to be legislators, and the rules of universities enable people to earn degrees.

Social Problems and Ideals

An important part of the moral life, therefore, consists of trying to maintain and improve a community, as well as benefitting from it. When workers or managers try to improve methods of production or forms of business organization, they are trying to improve social rules. When Congressmen vote to change the laws, one would hope that they are trying to improve society. When a couple discusses their marriage, they are trying to improve a relationship in which each of them plays a vital part.

If one thinks about it, most of the moral problems people face are a result of membership in social groups. No wonder they are so often aware of social constraints and sometimes wish to be free of them. They complain of government, job, or family, not simply because others are not doing their jobs as defined by the rules, but also because they do not like the rules. Children, for example, may complain that the family rules are unfair, or a worker may complain that there are inadequate provisions for safety.

Thus, on one level, there is a question of obeying or not obeying a socially accepted rule, but, on another level, there is a question of the justice or benefit of the rules. These issues are separable, but they are also related. Of course, generally speaking, the kinds of rules people think we should have are the kinds of rules they think everyone should obey. However, when it comes to determining moral obligations, it is important to make a distinction between actual rules and ideal rules, that is, rules that are "in force" as distinct from rules we would like to see enforced. In this connection, it is important to realize that even justified rules may have exceptions, on the one hand, and that, on the other, we may be bound to follow socially accepted rules that are not justified by the principles.

Another way of saying this is that the actual rules, or rules in force, may not be ideal rules, but that we may be bound to obey them nonetheless. In thinking of ideal rules, we may even have a concept of an ideal community in mind and hence lament the fact that our existing society falls short of the ideal. Nevertheless, we cannot sensibly ignore the positive values and the constraints of the existing system, the good it makes possible and the costs of change. We have said that there is a prima facie obligation to obey existing rules, or existing laws, and that the burden of proof is on exceptions. One reason for this is that, ex hypothesi, our ideal rules, or our ideal society, is merely ideal and not in force. Until it can be put into force, it does not have the force of actual, positive law.

EXERCISES

1. Look for examples of ways in which society's values are embodied in the external, physical world. You might begin with more obvious examples like the practices and symbols of religion and government, but consider also things of daily life, for example, tools or sporting equipment.

2. Consider cases in which activities are thought to be justified or unjustified because they conform, or fail to conform, to organizational or institutional practices or beliefs. For instance, think of the things judged to be good or bad because they are thought to be "Christian" or "non-Christian," "American" or "un-American."

3. We have argued that social practices can make things possible that would not be possible without them. Think of things we can do because

we have one or another social institution but in which we could not do without it.

4. We have argued that, although social institutions and practices are valuable, sometimes even necessary, not all institutions and practices are good. Consider examples of past social practices that have been rejected or changed, and discuss what you consider to be the value or disvalue of the change, for example, voting rights, sexual practices, employment practices, attitudes toward the use of drugs, or of specific drugs.

5. Which social practices today do you think are unjustified? Why do you think we adopted them in the first place, and how do you think they can be improved?

6. What rules do you think we could adopt in this class that would help solve some of the problems we face, or help us accomplish what we are trying to do?

ACTUAL RULES AND IDEAL RULES

By rules "in force" we mean the rules that are accepted and applied. Such rules are usually sanctioned in some way, by approval or disapproval, or by other forms of punishment or reward. Sanctions are artificial consequences, as opposed to natural consequences. In many cases the sanctions are quite definite and clearly expressed. A person who does not show up for work will lose pay; a team will be penalized if one of its players is caught breaking a rule. In other cases, people may exercise a wide range of discretion in enforcement, or in the granting of forgiveness or leniency. Parents, for instance, may scold a child or send it to its room. Judges may reduce a sentence.

There may or may not be rules about how we should enforce the rules—or about who should enforce them—but one of the functions of rules is to remove such doubts or ambiguities. A rule that is never enforced or practiced, however, may be said to be a rule in name only. It may be "on the books" so to speak, but it is not "in force." Some rules are enforced by conscience, by our beliefs or dispositions to act, and hence are enforced by being practiced. They may also be sanctioned, so to speak, by feelings of satisfaction or guilt. Thus, we may speak of "internal" sanctions, the force of conscience, as opposed to "external sanctions," the constraints which other people place upon us. In a morally mature individual, there is usually an intersection of internal and external constraints, for that person has probably internalized a large number of social rules.

A child who is told that something is wrong and yet is never prevented from doing it is not likely to learn or "internalize" the rule, unless, of course, he or she later comes to understand its justification. Even then, however, the rule may be seen as only an "ideal rule," a rule that is morally justified but not in force. When we argue about the justification of a rule, we are arguing about whether or not it is ideal, or whether or not it is a rule we

---

J. S. MILL
(1806–1873)
On External and Internal Sanctions

Sanctions are either external or internal. Of the external sanctions it is not necessary to speak at any length. They are, the hope of favor and the fear of displeasure from our fellow creatures or from the Ruler of the Universe. . . .

The internal sanction of duty, whatever our standard of duty may be, is one and the same—a feeling in our own mind; a pain, more or less intense, attendant on a violation of duty, which in properly cultivated moral natures rises, in the more serious cases, into shrinking from it as an impossibility.

From: *Utilitarianism.* J. S. Mill. 1861 (many editions).

---

should have. In so arguing, we recognize implicitly that we do not always have the rules we should. Hence we recognize a distinction between ideal and actual rules.

Workers in a factory may believe that they should be allowed more opportunity for advancement but that the rules do not allow it. They want to change the rules by substituting an ideal rule for the present actual rule, thus making the ideal rule actual. People who argue for equal rights for minorities want their ideal rules to be made actual. They want the ideal rules to be put in force by being adopted and practiced. They may say that minorities *have* these rights; but there must be a sense in which they do not have them, for the ideal rules are not enforced. They may *have* them in the sense that the rules are justified but not in the sense that they are practiced.

The grounds for making claims in the name of ideal rules are different from the grounds that support actual rules. Ideal rules are argued for and justified by direct appeal to moral principles, or to higher level rules. Actual rules, however, have only the presumptive support of principles. That is, unless obviously malevolent, they are presumed to have some justification, but such justification may be undemonstrated or incomplete. But actual rules have the additional weight of practical expectation on their side, for we can expect people to act according to them, and we can plan our actions on those expectations. Ideal rules, on the other hand, are iffy; they are based on suppositions about what the world would be like *if* people would accept a different set of standards. Of course, acting on an ideal rule may be a way of trying to win acceptance for it, just as disobedience of an actual rule may be a way of trying to defeat it.

A simple example may be helpful. Suppose Logan believes that the speed limits are too high. He reasons that if all cars traveled at 50 m.p.h. there would be fewer fatalities and billions of dollars saved on road construction, auto repairs, hospital bills, law suits, and fuel. Clearly, he has some justification for his belief. But if he decides to act on this belief and drive under 50 m.p.h., while others drive at 60 or 65, he may cause accidents. Also, there are advantages to fast driving, as indicated by the fact that people often drive above the fixed limits. For the sake of these advantages, people seem willing to take risks. So one might argue that Logan should campaign for the adoption of air bags, or DWI enforcement, instead of wanting to lower the speed limit. While the debate goes on, it seems that actual driving practices should conform to the demands of the current laws.

JUSTIFYING RULES AND ACTS

In reflecting upon ideal and actual rules, or upon obeying or disobeying one or the other, we begin to recognize that the question of justifying a rule is separable from the question of obedience or disobedience to a rule. Generally speaking, the point of having a rule is to follow it, or to try to persuade people to follow it by enforcing it in some way. One may be tempted to conclude from this that, if a rule is adopted, we should always obey it. But we have also said that an actual rule—a rule that is accepted—may not be justified, or may not be an ideal rule. In fact, we have suggested that it may sometimes be necessary to break an actual rule in order to win acceptance for an ideal rule, or in order to conform to moral principles. Thus, although we are often bound by actual rules, there are times when we are not so bound.

Thus, the difference between being bound and not being bound by an actual rule depends, one may suppose, on whether the actual rule is justified, or on whether the actual rule is also an ideal rule. But that, it seems, is too much of a burden to place on actual rules. It is almost always the case that the actual rules are imperfect and hence could be improved; but we are often bound by them nonetheless. It may also be the case, as suggested above, that we are sometimes not bound by ideal rules, simply because they are not in force, even though we may sometimes be justified in following an ideal rule—when, say, we are attempting to win acceptance for it or have it enforced.

The upshot of this discussion is simply that there is no necessary connection between the justification of a rule and the justification of an act which falls under the rule. That is, the justification of acts and the justification of rules are separable issues, even though we normally judge acts by rules. The justification of acts and rules can be separated because even justified rules can have exceptions, and also because it is sometimes better to follow unjustified actual rules than it is to break them. Thus, the following combinations are possible:

a. Justified rule and justified act conforming to it.

b. Justified rule and unjustified act conforming to it (that is, disobedience justified, perhaps even obligatory).

c. Unjustified rule and justified act conforming to it.

d. Unjustified rule and unjustified act conforming to it.

The justification of both rules and acts is often teleological; they may be justified on the grounds of doing good and avoiding evil. However, what is likely to accomplish good *as a rule*, or generally speaking, may not do so in every case, and hence what does so in a particular case may not do so as a rule. So, in addition to showing that a rule is or is not justified, according to our principles, we also need to show that an action in accordance with that rule is or is not justified. If such actions are indeed justified, as a rule, then, as a rule, we would be justified in doing them. But, we must also be alert to exceptional cases, when the rules conflict, or when the principles override the rules. A parent may know that it is usually wrong to leave a child alone, but, in an emergency, it may be necessary to do so.

EXERCISES

1. With respect to each of the following: (1) determine whether the rule is justified and (2) under what circumstances the rule should be followed or disobeyed.

    a. There is a posted rule in the dormitory which says that loud music should not be played after 10 P.M.
    b. City hospitals have adopted the rule that all patients must be admitted regardless of their ability to pay.
    c. The executives of the AAB Association declare that all factory workers must take lie detector and drug tests.
    d. The United Suburban Council declares that suburban fire departments must aid each other whenever additional fire equipment is required.
    e. The police department forbids officers to take part-time jobs that require them to wear their uniforms.
    f. A city ordinance requires that people who work for city government must live in the city.
    g. Children under eighteen years old should not watch R-rated movies.
    h. Only lawyers (not realtors) may give legal advice on real estate transactions.
    i. Only pharmacists, not physicians, can sell prescription drugs.
    j. Students are not allowed to smoke in class.

2. Of the above rules, pick out those which seem to you most "natural," and those which seem most "conventional" or arbitrary.

3. The above rules cover a wide variety of actions. Many are quite realistic, in the sense that they seem very reasonable. These rules suggest that much of our daily activity is rule-governed. By contrast, think of things we can do (are morally justified in doing) that are not rule-governed.

4. Which of the above-mentioned rules do you think are commonly followed? Do you think that any of them are not commonly obeyed but ought to be?

5. Try to think up rules which ought to be followed but are not, for example, "Women should be given the same employment opportunities as men." Of these rules, which of them do you think are "on the books," so to speak, in the sense that people acknowledge their justification, in writing or in debate, but continue to violate them nonetheless? Are these rules "ideal" rules or "actual" rules?

RULES AS HYPOTHESES

The justification of a particular rule depends upon our being able to show that more good would be accomplished by having it than by not having it; but that is not always easy to do. Rules are hypotheses that usually need to be acted upon to see how they will work, and it is difficult to compare them with untested alternatives. That is, rules exist in a hypothetical world of what might have been, or what might be, until they are tried. Even then, the fact that they succeed or fail under one set of conditions does not prove that they will also succeed or fail in another. Yet, as in any field of inquiry, we must try to learn from experience and experimentation.

We need not be limited to our own experiences, of course, for we can also observe the actions of others, and we can read histories, biographies, and novels, for example, in order to explore alternatives. We often learn more from people who break the existing rules than from people who obey them, for we may see how their lives or the lives of others are affected in the process. We may also see how the rules should be changed.

It is also possible that, in some cases, alternative sets of rules may all do the same, or at least comparable, jobs. We have said that people become attached to their ways of doing things and often find it difficult to change. For this reason, change is almost always costly. There are casualties in every revolution. However, if it were not for this cost, the alternatives might be as good, or even better than existing rules.

PATRICK DEVLIN
(1905–   )
On Moral Tolerance and Law

I return therefore to the simple and observable fact that in matters of morals the limits of tolerance shift. Laws, especially those which are based on morals, are less easily moved. It follows as another good working principle that in any new matter of morals the law should be slow to act. By the next generation the swell of indignation may have abated and the law be left without the strong backing which it needs. But it is then difficult to alter the law without giving the impression that moral judgment is being weakened . . .

From: *The Enforcement of Morals*. Patrick Devlin. Oxford: Oxford University Press, 1965.

A change in rules may be good for younger people, for example, who are just learning new sets of rules, but not for older people attached to their ways. The truth of cultural relativism is that different cultures may have different rules and that those rules may be right for those cultures. The falsity of cultural relativism is that a practice of a group is not necessarily right just for being a practice of that group. Despite justifiable variation, some practices are not justified, and some practices are better than others. However, while it may be better for people now coming up through the educational system to learn to use computers instead of typewriters, say, it may not be as good—it may even be harmful—to require older people to use them.

As it turns out, many of the problems of daily life are caused by social customs and practices, or by the rules of institutions, although people may otherwise be helped by them. Much depends, of course, on how good or bad the rules are. Laws are constantly being changed in an effort to improve them, and governments have been overthrown in an attempt to end oppression. Even religions undergo periodic reform.

Institutions that are bad in some respects, however, need not be bad in all respects, and an imperfect institution may be better than none at all. The mere intention to do good, of course, is not enough. What we need to do is try to see how our organizations and institutions actually function in order to see how they can be improved. We need to try to find the locus and causes of problems. That is, in looking at morality on the level of social practices, we need to become social analysts, social critics, and social engineers. Of course we need not do this alone, for we have the support of existing institutional apparatus—the news media, the schools, literature, and the social and political sciences.

CONCLUSION

In this chapter we have extended our basic system of morality by adding positive principles or "duals" to our negative set and by pointing up the need for subordinate social rules. The positive principles bid us to avoid harm, to help others, to ensure justice, and to provide opportunities for individual development and expression. However, because none of us can accomplish all of these things by acting alone, subordinate rules are needed to facilitate cooperation and assign responsibilities. Such rules establish expectations, for people rely upon one another to carry out their assigned tasks.

A great deal of moral reasoning is directed toward the justification or critique of social rules and institutions. That is, just as we need to justify individual acts by moral principles or rules, we also need to justify rules. Sometimes we also need to bring new rules, practices, or institutions into existence, or to modify existing rules. In the meantime, we may also need to obey the existing rules, whether or not they are justified, and whether or not the existing rules conform to our moral or social ideals.

We have also tried to illustrate that the level on which we reason about rules can be distinguished from the level of applying rules to particular acts. However, while distinguishable, these issues are not wholly separate in practice, for individual acts are also a means of establishing or undermining rules. There is an element of decision involved in determining whether or not we should have a rule, or whether or not we should enforce it, although such determinations usually require the cooperation of many individuals and cannot be accomplished by one individual acting alone. But, by our cooperation or resistance, we have said, we can serve to support or undermine existing rules.

EXERCISES

What is your opinion about the following cases? In forming your opinion, specify how moral principles bear upon your answer, and explain how, or whether, the existence of subordinate rules affects your answer.

1. Judge Jones is about to decide a case involving parents who, for religious reasons, have refused to allow their child a blood transfusion. Medical opinion has determined that the child will probably die without the transfusion. Legal precedent, according to Jones' reading, clearly requires her to order the transfusion. But Jones feels that this is an improper law, not from a legal point of view, but from her own sense of morality. Consequently, against the facts as she views them, she decides that the transfusion is not really necessary. The decision will probably be appealed, but Jones feels good about her decision, because morality has won out over law.

2. Professor Smith is chronically late for class, frequently by as much as twenty minutes. He believes that this is better for education, he says, because students cannot be expected to pay attention to a lecture for more than twenty minutes.

3. Dr. Leevers is faced with a choice between two patients, both perfectly well matched to a liver to be used for transplantation. One of the patients, Harry, is a homosexual, and the other is a young child. Dr. Leevers thinks of homosexuality as sinful, but knows he cannot argue that in front of the hospital's ethics board. Instead, he claims that, for medical reasons, the child needs the liver more urgently. Actually, he believes that Harry has a greater need, but, as the expert, he knows he can convince his colleagues that the child should receive the organ.

4. Modify Questions 1 and 3 above. Suppose that in both cases the same decisions would be made but that no lies would be involved. For example, the doctor simply does the transplantation without lying to the ethics board. Does this change affect your judgment?

5. Jane never stops for stop lights on her way to work. She works from 2 A.M. to 8 A.M. She says that it is simply stupid to stop because hers is the only car on the road.

6. Mark and Sally were disappointed with one of their sons. He had a 2.8 high school average, while his brother had a 3.5. They believed both children had about the same ability. Therefore, they decided to pay the college tuition and room and board for the child with the higher average but refused to pay for the child with the lower average. Oddly, the child with the lower high school average finally graduated from college with a higher GPA than his brother. A friend of Sally and Mark then suggested that this shows how wrong they were—that they violated the rules of good parenting.

SUPPLEMENTARY READINGS

Brandt, R. B. "Some Merits of One Form of Rule-Utilitarianism." *University of Colorado Studies.* 1967.

Diggs, B. J. "Rules and Utilitarianism." *American Philosophical Quarterly,* Vol. I, 1964: 32–44.

Dworkin, Ronald. *Taking Rights Seriously.* Cambridge: Harvard University Press, 1978.

Feinberg, Joel. "The Nature and Value of Rights." *The Journal of Value Inquiry,* Vol. 4, 1970: 243–57.

French, P., et al. *Studies in Ethical Theory.* Midwest Studies in Philosophy, Vol. 3. Minneapolis: University of Minnesota Press, 1978.

Hume, David. *A Treatise on Human Nature* (many editions).

Lomasky, Loren. *Persons, Rights and Moral Community.* New York: Oxford University Press, 1987.

MacIntyre, Alasdair. *After Virtue.* Notre Dame: University of Notre Dame Press, 1981.

Nozick, R. *Anarchy, State, and Utopia.* New York: Basic Books, 1974.

Rachels, James. *Moral Problems.* New York: Harper & Row, 1971.

Rawls, John. "Two Concepts of Rules," *Philosophical Review,* Vol. 64, 1955.

Waldron, Jeremy, ed. *Theories of Rights.* New York: Oxford University Press, 1984.

CRITIQUING AND IMPLEMENTING RULES

After considering the importance of rules and the need for their critical evaluation, how can we evaluate rules, and how can we implement them? The answers are implicit in the account we have given of the place and function of rules in moral reasoning.

SEVEN STEPS

Because rules are governed by principles, we can always (1) ask if the rules follow the principles. Because rules are supposed to be consistent with one another, we can (2) see if there is any conflict in the rules. Because rules are also subject to conflict with strongly held particular judgments, we can (3) look for counterexamples. Sometimes we will need to change a rule we are critiquing, because of its conflict with other rules, or with strongly held moral convictions, but sometimes we will need to change other rules or convictions to conform with it.

Following these tests, it is important to consider (4) whether the existing rules are effective in doing what they are supposed to do, and if not, (5) find out what can be done to make them more effective. If there appears to be good reason for amending an old rule or adopting a new one, then (6) what can we do to implement a change in the rules? Finally, before actually initiating such action, we should consider (7) the probable costs and benefits of bringing about such change, as distinct from the costs and benefits once adopted.

GERTRUDE EZORSKY
(1926–   )
A Rule Meant to Correct Injustice

"Sex discrimination is rampant in academe". . . How can such rampant discrimination be remedied? The government's answer—"affirmative action"—requires, first, "good faith" efforts to ensure that women candidates are visible at hiring time. All departments should advertise jobs, inform professional organizations, and invite women to apply. . . .

Hence, departments whose records show that they have "overlooked" qualified women are correctly required by affirmative action to do more than collect women's dossiers. Such departments are obligated to set numerical goals for women faculty.

From: "Hiring Women Faculty." *Philosophy & Public Affairs,* 7, 1977: 82–91.

These steps presuppose that rules are intended for application. Rules, we have said, mediate between principles and particular acts; they give content and specificity to the principles. However, in application, rules can also be tested for coherence and practicality.

Thus, Step 1 reminds us that rules operate on a lower level than principles, are governed by principles, and hence must be consistent with them. Step 2 reminds us that rules are also part of a system of rules which must be made to work in conjunction with one another. Steps 3 through 7 direct our attention to the connection between rules and lower-level particular acts, insisting upon the coherence of our beliefs on these two levels, but also taking account of the effectiveness of rules as they are put into practice.

For the sake of simplification, we shall talk about an existing rule and whether it should be amended or rejected, but much the same sort of criticism will apply to any new rule proposed. Sometimes, of course, we confront the problem of having to change an existing rule because it causes problems or because it seems ineffective, but sometimes we also need to devise new rules—or even new institutions—where none has existed before.

In referring to rules, we are talking about both written rules and unwritten rules. We mean to include institutions and practices in our discussion of rules, as we did in the previous chapter. We also mean to include personal rules, the rules of small groups or larger societies, of governments, or even international organizations. For example, the practice of racism can be understood as a system of harmful social rules. But other rules are entirely personal; for example, I might adopt a rule for myself requiring twenty hours of study every week. Still other rules function on an international level, such as rules governing actions on international waters. The level of the rule involved may alter the analysis somewhat, for personal rules may be subject to the demands of social organizations, and local rules are often subject to state or national regulations.

DO THE RULES FOLLOW THE PRINCIPLES?

The strongest criticism that can be brought against any rule is that it conflicts with one or more of the fundamental principles. An economic system that causes a great deal of suffering and keeps vast numbers of people in poverty, while only a few are prosperous, even wealthy, violates both the principle that bids us to do no harm and the principle of fairness. Indeed, it may also limit freedom, or at least opportunity, by making it extremely difficult for people to improve their condition.

But, it is also an important function of social rules to follow the positive prescriptions of the dual principles. We must remember that the principles apply in a prima facie sense. That is, there may be reasons which justify exceptions. In the first place, economic conditions may make it impossible for everyone to prosper, or even survive. A basically agricultural economy may suffer from periodic drought, in which case people may actually starve. Even in a society of great abundance there may be serious problems of distribution. U.S. agriculture may produce enough food to feed, not only its own poor, but even the starving peoples of other countries, but it may also be very difficult for it to distribute foods to all those people. There are transportation difficulties, political constraints, and even economic barriers, such as the low price of food, diminishing profits for farmers, and the general need to uphold the prices of agricultural products around the world.

However, it is not enough to simply excuse existing practices on the ground that, given existing conditions, a completely fair and benevolent system is practically impossible. It may be true that every system does some good and that no system is perfect, but some systems are better than others. If morally concerned, we should try to see how our institutions can be improved, by making them conform more closely to moral principles.

If transportation is a problem, we need to see what we can do to improve transportation. If there are political constraints, such as wars between or within countries, we need to see what can be done to negotiate settlements. If there are economic barriers, such as price instability, we need to see what we can do to stabilize prices. These are not things that any of us can do as individuals, acting alone, but goals we can try to reach through political action, or causes we can support in campaigning or voting for representatives in government.

In a more immediate way, we may discover that certain rules or practices in our family, in our local community, or even among our friends, cause harm, create injustice, or curtail freedom. A harmful practice such as male supremacy exhibits itself in family organization where fathers are generally considered to be the heads of families and male children are granted rights and privileges denied to females. In the community, blacks are discriminated against in housing and employment, as are other minorities. These are fairly obvious prima facie violations of principle.

Exceptions may be justified in some cases, but the burden of proof is on exceptions. "That's the way it's always been" is not a justification, although it may be a way of recognizing that conformity to principles cannot always be accomplished in a short period of time. We should at least look to see that progress is being made and that, as a means of effecting change, people are held accountable for violations.

In following Step 1, it is important to recognize that the rules we are evaluating are still quite general, although less general than our principles. The rules are also like the principles in that they, too, may have exceptions, and hence apply in a prima facie sense. It would be a mistake, therefore, to claim that a rule is unjustified just because there are unusual circumstances in which it does not apply.

R. B. BRANDT
(1910–   )
On Exceptions to Rules

Consider promises, for instance. Is it really the case that *every* promise creates *some* obligation to fulfill it? Well, consider promises made under duress, or promises made on the basis of a deliberate misrepresentation of the facts by the person to whom the promise has been made. Obviously such promises create no obligation.

From: *Ethical Theory*. R. B. Brandt. Englewood Cliffs: Prentice-Hall, 1959.

Although exceptions can be included in the statement of the rules, we do not want to overcomplicate our rules by trying to state all the exceptions, and it is usually not possible to anticipate all of them. Thus, the rule that we should stop at stop signs is not invalid just because we may be justified in running a stop sign under emergency conditions. We do not usually state such exceptions in stating the rule, but they may be understood, or left to individual discretion.

EXERCISES

Are any principles violated by the following rules? In each case, specify the principle that seems to be violated and explain how the rule violates that principle. If the rule violates one principle but conforms to another, try to determine whether the rule is a justified exception.

Note cases where the rule seems arbitrary but where, nonetheless, some rule or other seems necessary. Would just any rule do, or would some rules be better than others? Discuss the options in view of the principles.

a. Children under fourteen years of age must ride bicycles on the sidewalk.
b. Automobiles must not exceed 65 m.p.h. on open highways.
c. Students may not smoke in class.
d. Instructors must grade tests in an impartial manner.
e. Men should open doors for women.
f. Inheritance is tax free up to $500,000.
g. Only those with an above average I.Q. may serve as police.
h. Teachers must be given tenure after three years of service.
i. It is illegal to possess marijuana.
j. It is illegal for people under twenty-one to buy "hard" liquor.
k. Only men will be allowed into combat.
l. Lobbyists are always given special access to senators.
m. Only those with a 3.0 GPA will be admitted to graduate school.
n. All high school graduates must be admitted to a state university.
o. All employees receive the same pay regardless of how hard they work.

ARE THE RULES CONSISTENT?

The rules should be consistent with the principles, but they should also be consistent with one another. Consider, for instance, the role of the federal government in dealing with cigarette smoking. It regulates ads and insists on placing a health warning on cigarettes while at the same time providing subsidies for growing tobacco. The nation spends millions of dollars yearly trying to find a cure for cancer, but it also condones practices that cause the disease.

In conventional morality, people are supposed to tell the truth, but they are also supposed to refrain from telling the truth when it is harmful to others. Professions often have explicit codes intended to hold members accountable for their actions, but they also have unwritten codes that require them to "cover" for one another. Regulatory commissions, including public utility commissions, are often accused of protecting the very industries they are supposed to regulate. Such apparent conflicts as these call for resolution.

We have a variety of laws that distinguish minors from adults. People are allowed to vote and are eligible for the draft at eighteen. They can drive cars in many states at sixteen. They are not allowed to purchase alcoholic beverages until they are eighteen in some states and twenty-one in others. There is also a variety of rules relating age to trials and sentences for crimes. Thus, there is a prima facie reason for claiming that these laws are inconsistent with one another, unless, of course, there is something about the subject matter in each case that justifies the differences.

It may be the case that voting requires greater maturity than fighting in a war, or that young people who show good sense in driving may not have good sense in deciding how much to drink. The cut-off point in all such cases is arbitrary in a sense, for there is no one point at which all people become mature. Some people accept responsibility for their actions at a very young age, and some never do. But "we need to draw a line somewhere," as they say, and there may be statistics to show that people above or below a certain age have more driving accidents on average, or that one age group abuses the right to drink more than others.

BERTRAND RUSSELL
(1872–1970)
On the Aims of Government

The *primary* aims of government, I suggest, should be three: security, justice, and conservation. These are things of the utmost importance to human happiness, and they are things which only government can bring about. At the same time, no one of them is absolute; each may, in some circumstances, have to be sacrificed in some degree for the sake of a greater degree of some other good.

From: "Control and Initiative: Their Respective Spheres." Bertrand Russell. *Authority and the Individual*. Boston: Beacon Press, 1960.

Our reasoning in cases of allowing exceptions should also be consistent with our rules. We cannot reasonably exclude women from profitable employment in the marketplace, on the ground that they are not fit for physical work, say, if they are allowed and even required to do equally difficult physical work at home. Divisions of labor may be founded on differences in ability, but we should also have reasonable tests of ability and not assume that whole classes of people either are or are not qualified. The empirical evidence seems to indicate that no one group has cornered the market on strength or weakness, or on virtue or vice.

One cannot argue for the right to grant exceptions on any grounds whatever, or simply as one sees fit. An executive may promote people at one time, and not promote others at other times, because of an inconsistent application of the rules. He may argue that the cases are different, even that he must take account of special circumstances, but not every difference is a justified difference. The allowance of inconsistent unjustified applications of rules is practically equivalent to having no rules at all.

The same may be said of changing the rules as one goes along, applying one rule to one case and another rule to another. It is not inconsistent to have one set of rules at one time and another at another, for rules can change, and they can change with justification. But to change back and forth, without justification, and even without notice, is tantamount to acting on whim.

EXERCISES

1. In what ways do you think that racism, sexism, and religious and ethnic discrimination show that society has inconsistent rules?

2. Children often complain that their parents are inconsistent because parents do many of the things they tell their children not to do, for example, wear makeup, drink, smoke. Do you think that such complaints are justified?

3. Sweden has a high suicide rate, and it is often criticized for this reason. The suicide rate among college students is also high, and yet college education is not criticized on this basis. Are we inconsistent in our standards or in our application of standards?

4. Mr. Jones feels compelled to provide a very high standard of living for his family. He works about sixty hours a week and feels tired and depressed when he is not working. He worries about this because he also believes he is not being a good father to his son and two daughters. Is Jones caught between conflicting rules? If so, is there a way to resolve the conflict?

5. Doug Savino complains that less qualified people, who are members of legally "designated" minorities, have been hired ahead of him. He resents this because he knows that members of his own ethnic group have been victims of prejudice but have not been designated a minority by the law. He has been told that social policy is designed to eliminate large-scale inequities and cannot address every issue. Do you think this excuse justifies this apparent inconsistency in practice?

6. Professor Quales maintains that no distinction should be made between whites and blacks. She objects to things like "Black History Week," and she would equally object to "White History Week." As a black with a Ph.D., and a successful scholar, she believes that discrimination can be overcome only by personal success. She also believes that special programs for blacks amount to having inconsistent rules. Do you think she is right? If there is inconsistency, do you think it can be justified?

7. Jim is a socialist. Every time he tries to convince others that socialism is best, he is told that this country is great because of the system it has and that without that system he would not be free to preach his doctrines. He replies that the media of this country are completely dominated by capitalists and that there is no effective freedom of speech for people like him. He points out, for example, that the distinction between "terrorist" and "freedom fighter" is dependent on ideology and denies to socialists or communists the right to express or fight for their views. Do you think that Jim is correct in his claim that this country is inconsistent, and hence prejudiced, in this way?

8. Lisa thinks her teacher is ridiculous. The teacher says, "If you work diligently during class today, you may turn in the assignment tomorrow, but if you 'goof off' in class today, you must turn in your assignment today." Is Lisa correct in thinking that the teacher's rules are crazy?

9. Over ten million people starve to death annually. To help solve this problem, the U.S. government has agencies that sponsor foreign aid. At the same time, the U.S. government pays American farmers not to produce food. Do you think that these apparently conflicting practices can be reconciled?

10. Professor Smith hasn't written anything in years. In fact, he doesn't even read much anymore. But he has a reputation for being very demanding of his students, for he requires extensive reading and writing assignments. A young colleague complains that Smith is a hypocrite, but Smith does not think he is inconsistent. Who do you think is right?

ARE THERE ANY COUNTEREXAMPLES?

Some things strike us as intuitively wrong, even though they may seem justified by principles or are consistent with other rules in force. Of course, our moral intuitions themselves may be wrong, but some are so strong that we would be loathe to give them up. For example, in his *Republic*, Plato tries to outline the organization of a state that would be completely just. In so doing, he argues that children should be taken from their parents and raised in state nurseries. Everyone would then have equal opportunities, and favoritism or nepotism would be eliminated. But most of us would recoil at the idea of having children taken from their parents, and this feeling may persist even if we become convinced that, by and large, the state may be better off under Plato's system. We think that our intuition in this case overrides Plato's principled reasoning.

We could, of course, be wrong. Many white people in the U.S. felt "in their hearts" that white people and black people should be segregated, but many of them have since become convinced of desegregation, on grounds of justice, and also by experience.

In Plato's dialogue *Euthyphro,* Euthyphro is on his way to court to bring a charge of murder against his own father. Socrates is surprised to learn of this because Euthyphro seems so sure his father is guilty of committing this offense, when the evidence is at best ambiguous. Socrates also seems surprised that anyone would be so quick to accuse his own father, for he expects a person to be loyal to his family. But, in a way, Euthyphro seems to be an admirable person, for he seems quite willing to apply the same standards to members of his family as he would to strangers.

Many of us do not have such a strong sense of justice, for many of us would not publicly accuse members of our own families, even if we knew they were guilty of crimes. After all, how many children report their parents for cheating on their taxes? Indeed, it is the code of the streets never to tell on a friend, and we even find members of the government or other institutions protecting one another when accused of misconduct. It seems a matter of instinct to align with family, friends, or allies, when attacked from without, but it also seems unfair.

EXAMINING THE FIRST EXAMPLE

Let us examine these two examples from Plato's writings. In the first example, Plato proposes a rule about raising children that functions within a larger set of rules describing an ideal state. Although this rule is supported by a variety of arguments, it seems wrong in an almost instinctive way. How can such an opposition be resolved?

Well, in the first place, we might notice that a rule or practice that makes sense within one system of rules may not make sense in another. People who are not accustomed to playing games, or who are very business minded, may wonder why other people play games, for nothing seems to be accomplished by them. Grown people spend hours trying to hit a little ball into a hole and become upset when somebody cheats, even when no money is at stake. Yet people who play games know intuitively how important it is not to cheat, or to win by the rules, for they know that, in games, unlike business, nothing counts as winning which does not follow the rules. People can make money by violating good business practices but they cannot score at chess by violating the rules of chess.

Thus by way of analogy, Plato's rule about child care may make sense in Plato's system in a way that it does not make sense in ours. If we actually lived in a system like Plato's, his rule about child care might seem reasonable; but in our system, where so many of our rules focus on the value of family life, the practice he advocates seems out of place. In other words, the rule about child care that he wants to introduce may be consistent with other practices of his ideal state, but it would not be consistent with the practices of the society in which we live.

Of course, it is possible that even Plato's principles do not require such a practice, for there may be other ways of accomplishing the same goal. But, even if we suppose that state nurseries are an ideal solution to the problem of favoritism, it may not be possible to convince people to accept this solution—at least not yet, and perhaps not ever. Thus, even if ideal, Plato's solution may be said to be "utopian," in the sense that it is an unrealizable ideal, at least as things now appear. Indeed, given widespread feelings about the value of family life that seem to cut across space, time, and culture, one might even argue that Plato's supposed ideal runs counter to human nature, and hence is not really ideal at all.

The Second Example

In the second example from Plato, there is a conflict between justice and loyalty. This conflict arises in connection with a particular case—the case of Euthyphro's prosecuting his father—and it involves a conflict of intuitions about what he should do. But, as soon as one begins to reason about such cases, one sees them as instances of rules of one or another kind, as instances of law enforcement, for example, or of loyalty to a family member or a friend. So the conflict between our intuition, feeling, or judgment in a particular case and some rule may also be viewed as a conflict of rules. The question then is whether the same particular action should be judged by apparently contradictory rules.

One possibility, of course, is that the conflict is only apparent, or that the rules are really contradictory only if interpreted in a very general way. That is, the rules may be more carefully qualified to allow for exceptions, or to point out that each rule applies to a separate domain. Rules often apply in a special way to members of specified groups, according to the jobs people have, or the circumstances in which they find themselves. You and I may be best advised to stay out of burning buildings, but a firefighter may have an obligation to enter a burning building under given circumstances because that is his or her job. Thus, conflicts in rules, or in judgments about particular actions, may be resolved by making the rules themselves clearer and more specific.

Perhaps there is no easy resolution of the conflict between loyalty and justice, but it may be resolved by allowing uniform exceptions. That is, if we allow that everyone has a right to withhold evidence, say, in the case of his or her own family, then the rule would apply to everyone in the same way. In this way we could preserve family loyalty without sacrificing justice. We simply would not expect the cooperation of family members in criminal or even civil investigations, allowing that it is the business of others to enforce the law. Of course, the law does not always respect loyalties or confidences, in the case of a reporter who tries to conceal a source, say, or in the case of a psychiatrist who tries to protect a client. But we can make a distinction between moral responsibilities and legal responsibilities, holding that we are sometimes bound to resist the law. We can also hold that, in extreme cases, a person would be justified in breaking a trust—when, for example, the initial reason for keeping it no longer holds.

Handling the Unusual Case

Sometimes our convictions in a particular case seem to defy all rules. This may happen, for example, when, in an emergency situation, someone is suffering excruciating pain. On nationwide T.V., a Vietnam war veteran recently gave an account of a horrifying experience in which he found a tortured American soldier in great pain and close to death. He might have saved the dying soldier, but this was doubtful. He simply felt that he had to end the unspeakable horror of this other man's suffering. He did so, and he still has nightmares to remind him of his act.

It may not seem clear to all that the soldier did the right thing. All rules seem to suggest he was wrong. But even those who are generally opposed to euthanasia may allow an exception in this case. It seems that we either need better, more detailed rules to cover such cases, or we need to allow people discretion in applying the rules in extreme circumstances.

There are then several moves open to us when a given intuition or particular judgment seems to conflict with a rule. We can, of course, reject the intuition or particular judgment as wrong, or we can reject the rule. However, we can also try to reconcile the two by showing that the case in question is a justifiable exception, or that the rule governing the case applies to a different domain, class, or population than the rule with which it seems to conflict.

EXERCISES

Consider the following rules or social practices to see if they conflict with any of your moral intuitions. If they do, how would you reconcile the two?

1. Doctors should do everything they can to save a dying patient.

2. AIDS patients have a right to privacy and freedom. Therefore, the fact that they have AIDS should not be revealed, and they should be allowed to have sex with whomever they want.

3. Everyone is innocent until proven guilty. But dangerous criminals should be held without bond until they are tried.

4. Legally, many rich people pay no income tax.

5. In the name of scientific knowledge, extremely painful experimentation is conducted on countless live animals.

6. All students must pass a math requirement in order to graduate from college.

7. The rights of even vicious criminals must be carefully respected, allowing even mass murderers and rapists timely parole.

8. The law allows the slaughter of large farm animals for food but prohibits hunting endangered species.

9. As a form of punishment, parents often spank their children, and many states allow teachers to use corporal punishment.

10. An eighteen- or twenty-year-old person is often sent to prison for a crime when under similar circumstances younger persons are allowed to go free.

ARE THE RULES EFFECTIVE?

Even if our rules meet the above tests, they may not do the job they are supposed to do. That is, they may not work, or they may not work very well. Indeed, some may do more harm than good. The Prohibition Amendment to the U.S. Constitution is often cited as a case in point. The sale of intoxicating drinks was prohibited by law, but very large numbers of people simply disobeyed the law. Indeed, criminal networks began to control the manufacture, shipment, and sale of alcohol, so that, in addition to the evils of drinking, criminals prospered. This amendment was later repealed.

Many states have also had laws against the use of contraceptives, but the argument has often been put forth that we cannot assign a policeman to everyone's bedroom. In effect, the law seemed unenforceable, except by trying to prevent production or sales. But even in the case of fireworks, where their use is quite evident, the police either cannot or will not enforce the law.

Thus, laws or rules sometimes do not work because people will not accept them—even laws or rules that would otherwise be good. In this sense, people tend to get the kinds of laws or rules they deserve. Authorities simply cannot spend all of their time, energy, and resources trying to enforce unpopular rules. Rules that are accepted and practiced, we said, are "in force," whereas rules that are not accepted or practiced are not in force. However, rules may fail to be effective for reasons other than failure to win popular support. They may not do the job they are supposed to do, even if everyone supports them.

Let us suppose that the government tried to help the poor by adopting a law that ensures unemployed workers at least as much income as the guaranteed minimum wage. Well, in such a case, we may find that many people who could work will not choose to work because they can earn as much money by not working. Indeed, there are many costs incurred in taking a job that would actually reduce their income: clothes, transportation, and even babysitters, if they pay someone to care for their children. Such a law may turn out to be counterproductive in the long run, even if effectively applied—or, should we say, just because it is effectively applied.

The collective weight of rules and their enforcement may also have a negative effect. Children who are constantly told that they cannot do this and cannot do that, and are punished for practically everything they do, may become quite passive—although quite often they simply rebel or leave home. Parents may wonder why their children have no energy or spunk, but the problem may be that their rules actually destroy initiative. Too permissive an environment may have the same effect. People appear to need and even appreciate moral and social constraints, but they also need room to make a contribution of their own. All rules constrain individual freedom to some extent, but the collective weight of the rules can be overly oppressive.

The question of the effect of rules is not unrelated to the other criteria we have discussed. Rules that are inconsistent with the principles, or with one another, are also likely to be ineffective, as we have said, for they are likely to be counterproductive. That is, the effects of following one rule may be undone by the effects of following another. Conflicting rules can have the effect of causing great difficulty in people's lives by requiring them to do impossible things. One rule may prohibit what another rule requires, placing people in a no-win situation. Older children, acting as babysitters, for instance, are sometimes expected to control the behavior of younger siblings but are given no real authority over them. Thus, the babysitters are punished if the younger children misbehave, but they are also punished if they try to prevent their misbehavior! In education, students are frequently told to strive for learning and not worry about grades, yet the reward system in education seems to contradict this advice.

EXERCISES

1. Consider each of the following areas and ask yourself with respect to each of them whether it contains any rules that you regard as ineffective. Explain why you think the rule is ineffective. Is it ineffective because people refuse to obey it? Is it in conflict with some other rule? Is it defective in some other way?

    Education; medicine; criminal law; marriage; welfare; auto safety; sexual morality; foreign policy; news reporting; professional or amateur sports; for example, "amateur athletes" who are paid to play.

2. After you have identified rules that you regard as ineffective, ask yourself if you think they are otherwise justified? If so, do you think the rules can be made effective, and if so, how? Do you think these rules should be amended in some way, or abolished? Discuss.

How To Make the Rules Effective

There are several reasons why moral/social rules may be ineffective, and hence several ways in which they can be made effective. In the first place, of course, the effectiveness of a rule depends on what the rule is supposed to do, and this requires goal clarification.

GOAL CLARIFICATION

Obviously, a rule may enable someone to do something that is morally wrong, but we are not interested in "effectiveness" of this kind. In morality, we are interested in whether or not rules enable us to do what our principles say we should do, or to avoid doing what our principles say we should avoid. As obvious as this may seem, it bears mentioning, even repeating, because many rules are put into practice with no consideration of moral implications. Many of the rules people adopt are meant to make them popular, financially successful, or more powerful, but these are not specifically moral ends. They are not necessarily immoral either, but we need to keep moral principles in mind, and even call attention to them, lest we ignore the moral implications of our acts.

The need for calling attention to moral principles explains the need for moral leaders. It is easy for people to ignore moral considerations, and they sometimes even make fun of people who point them out. Yet most societies have people who function as moral leaders: priests, ministers and rabbis, parents, teachers, and even public officials. The distinction between a politician and a statesman is often made on this basis. While the former is occupied defending narrow interests, the latter is concerned with the widespread implications of government actions. A national leader can certainly do much to set the moral tone of a country, by appealing to the prejudices of the people, or by appealing to their higher, moral instincts. But, of course, everyone functions in this capacity by calling attention to violations of principle or to opportunities for doing good.

Removing Inconsistencies

Because rules can be inconsistent, even counterproductive, we can try to make them more effective by trying to remove inconsistencies. Sometimes we can do this, we said, by making the rules clearer or more specific, or by explaining why they apply differently in different cases.

In our example of rules distinguishing minors from adults, we said that some laws indicate that, for legal purposes, the age of maturity is eighteen, and others indicate that it is twenty-one. However, if we consider *why* the law specifies eighteen in one case and twenty-one in another, we may discover that there is a good reason for the apparent inconsistency. That is, people may mature in some areas faster than in others, or there may be other factors to take into consideration, such as financial liability.

In our baby-sitting example, parents may need to explain more fully just *how* the older child is expected to exercise control over the younger children—and then back her up when she follows instructions. The parents should not allow favoritism for a younger child to undermine the authority of an older child—and hence, ultimately, their own—although, ideally, everyone should be allowed a "court of appeal." There is no magical solution to family conflicts; the communication and clarification of rules may serve to reduce the number of misunderstandings.

In other cases there may be a genuine conflict between rules, in which case it may be necessary to make a choice between them. In the case of paying college athletes, for example, there seems to be a great deal of hypocracy in the behavior of college officials, and even in the rules. Some people claim that colleges should simply drop the pretense of amateurism and pay college athletes openly. Others feel that college athletes are not paid nearly

EARLE F. ZEIGLER
(1919–   )
The Effectiveness of Rules in Sport

In 1929 the Carnegie Report entitled *American College Athletics* explained that "the defects of American college athletics are two: commercialism, and a negligent attitude toward the educational opportunity for which the American college exists." Additionally, the Report stressed that the so-called amateur code was violated continually; that recruiting and subsidizing was "the darkest blot upon American college sport;" that athletic training and hygiene practices were deplorable and actually jeopardize health in many instances. . . .

In 1974, some forty-five years later, there is every indication that the only one of the above-mentioned areas of criticism showing improvement would be that of athletic training and hygiene practices!

From: *Ethics and Morality in Sport and Physical Education*. Earle F. Zeigler. Champaign, Ill.: Stipes Publishing Co., 1984.

enough for the sacrifices they make. These suggestions point to a need for changes in the rules that govern college sports, and perhaps even a change in our beliefs about the place and function of sports in our educational system.

Improving Enforcement

The problem in application may not be that a rule is a bad rule, in the sense that it violates the principles, but that the manner of enforcement is faulty. Indeed, some rules are not enforced at all, or are enforced inconsistently. But we need not discard a rule just because it fails to work, for it may be possible to improve enforcement. For years there have been laws against drunken driving, for example, but not very much was done to punish offenders. However, in reaction to the many deaths caused by drunken driving, people campaigned for heavier penalties and stricter enforcement.

If the problem is one of popular acceptance, we may need to direct our attention to winning popular support. If the problem is one of learning to develop new habits, or of "unlearning" old ones, we may need to change our methods of teaching or learning. Sometimes people do not understand the need for a rule, so a review of the reasons for the rule should be examined. Sometimes people need motivation. Many institutions fail to motivate people, it seems, because of so-called "negative reinforcement," which tends to create resentment. Such institutions may be able to engender enthusiasm by praise or reward, instead of criticism or punishment.

One strategy for introducing a new rule, or defeating an old rule, we said, is disobedience of an existing rule, or simply following a rule one would like to see enforced. Gandhi, for example, often disobeyed what he considered to be an unjust law and simply went ahead and did what he thought was just, accepting the consequences of his actions by allowing himself to be jailed. Any rule that is obeyed is to that extent practiced or enforced—even if only by one person—and any rule that is disobeyed is to that extent not in force. One person's actions may also serve as an example to others, as an example of obedience or disobedience to the rules, or as an example of resistance to unjustified authority. Revolutionaries, of course, try to enlist others in their opposition to authorities and disobedience of existing laws. However, through lawful political action, we can work to have candidates elected who will support our causes, and we can lobby to have legislation introduced.

In other words, we may need to become social critics, strategists, and even active political leaders, in order to improve social rules and institutions. The problem with many institutions, in fact, is not that their officers are morally corrupt, but that no one takes the initiative to provide moral leadership. Sometimes the policies and structure of an organization, or the habits of its members, actually punish, or at least serve to discourage, attempts at moral improvement. Thus a person may need to take risks in calling attention to the need for reform, or in organizing support for change.

EXERCISES

1. Focus on one of the problem areas mentioned in the last set of exercises. Identify a rule that is not now effectively enforced or practiced in that area and analyze what can be done to make it effective.

2. Suppose you are the Director of Volunteers in a hospital. Your job is to recruit, train, and supervise volunteers. You realize, however, that there is a problem in enforcing the rules. Paid staff are hostile to volunteers, partly because they feel that an increase in the number of volunteers threatens their jobs. On the other hand, volunteers complain that they are often expected to "fill in" for paid staff, without receiving any compensation. To make matters worse, volunteers are treated as inferiors by the employees. But the hospital administration just loves the free help, for it reduces hospital costs and enables them to pay themselves and the professional staff higher salaries. What is your assessment of this situation in *moral* terms? As a Director of Volunteers, what *would* you try to do about it? What do you think you *should* do?

3. Discuss this problem from different perspectives. Suppose you are the president of the hospital, a doctor, a nurse, an employed secretary, a volunteer. In these other capacities, do you think you would arrive at the same assessment of the existing rules, or of the need for new rules? Are the same courses of action open to you? Are the risks the same?

WEIGHING THE CONSEQUENCES

Anyone who tries to change the world, even in a minor way, must be aware of at least some of the consequences. While many of us are aware of the consequences we are trying to bring about by our actions, we are not always fully aware of probable side-effects. There is almost always a trade-off between benefits and costs. The gains may very often be well worth the costs, but sometimes the sacrifice is too great.

Overall, we need to ask ourselves whether the changes we would like to introduce are apt to make this a better world, or our society a better place in which to live. In changing rules, we should try not to undermine a respect for rules, or for law and authority; nor do we want to create the impression that rules and authorities are always right. Indeed, the more we can bring ourselves and others to pay closer attention to the actual effects of our rules and behavior, the more we will accept moral responsibility for our acts.

What Kinds of Sanctions?

We want to distinguish the costs and benefits of trying to have a rule adopted and put into practice from the costs and benefits of following a rule. For example, a consequence of everyone's obeying the law that prohibits murder is that no one will be murdered. However, in order to enforce such a law, or make it effective, society may choose to enact the death penalty, an act which causes death. So the threat of death, even actual killing, may be used to prevent killing, in which case the cost or benefit of bringing about the acceptance of a rule may be distinguished from cost or benefit of acting upon it.

In this case, in fact, society makes itself, or its agents, an exception to a rule about killing in order to enforce the rule. This is not a straightforward contradiction, for the subject changes; what is allowed to society, or to individuals acting in an official capacity, is denied to individuals in other capacities. One might object, however, that society has chosen a means of enforcement that not only causes death but also sets a bad example. By seeming to show disrespect for life, this method of enforcing the law may actually undermine respect for the law.

Sanctions, or the ways we punish or reward people for obedience or disobedience, are means of making rules effective, but the consequences of such sanctions must be weighed. Of course, the means we need to use to gain acceptance of a rule may be quite different from the means we need to enforce it after it has been adopted. Once a rule has become a habit or custom, or has been internalized, a slight reminder or gesture of disapproval is often the only thing needed to ensure obedience. However, persons who have not yet accepted a rule, or are not inclined to follow it, may need to be persuaded in other ways: by imposing a fine of some kind, or by physical restraint.

We may need to allow time for the adoption or implementation of a rule, and hence delay enforcement, because we recognize that change cannot always be brought about immediately. It may be desirable also to have only a moderate means of enforcement, or wide discretion in granting leniency, after a rule is in effect. We no longer tend to support the idea of "an eye for an eye," but oppose "cruel and unusual punishments," on the ground that they too are evil. We are, or should try to be, a civilized people. We do tend to punish serious crimes more severely than less serious crimes, but, even then, we may choose not to impose a punishment for a first offense, or if there are mitigating circumstances.

Indeed, in keeping with our principles, we should help people correct their faults instead of merely punishing them, by sending a careless driver to driving school, for example, or by sending juveniles to "correctional institutions." Of course, such institutions may turn out to be punishments as well, because they restrict a person's freedom, and they do not always work very well in correcting faults. Sometimes they are even counterproductive, when, for example, "correctional institutions" become training grounds for criminals. But the idea of helping people, not simply punishing them, is morally commendable.

These examples illustrate both the need for sanctions and the need to review and critique sanctions according to moral principles. Rules regulating punishment are subject to all of the standards we have developed for judging and implementing rules. Moral indignation does not justify revenge. Punishment always raises ethical concerns just because it involves inflicting harm, or denying freedom or opportunities to individuals. Like other exceptions to principle, punishments, and the rules or systems we have for inflicting punishments, must all meet the burden of proof.

What Can We Do?

Perhaps nothing discourages people more, when it comes to morality, or at least to politics and large scale social change, than the belief that they are unable to change the system. But, of course, some people do influence the system; in a sense, all of us do. All of us exert an influence on some part of the social structure, not only by expressing our ideas, but by our action or inaction, in obedience or opposition to socially accepted rules. We can have a direct influence on small groups or organizations by giving voice to our beliefs, by trying to persuade others, and by making it comfortable or uncomfortable for them in carrying out their will. The psychological doctrine of behavior modification reminds us that we are constantly rewarding or punishing other people for their actions, by approving or disapproving their behavior, or by supporting or opposing their acts.

JOYCE HOCKER WILMOT AND WILLIAM W. WILMOT
On Interpersonal Power

We have power over people and they over us because our social relationship means that we are interdependent—we influence one another's ability to attain goals. Furthermore, the degree of power is a function of the comparison of dependence the two parties have on one another, and the degree of dependence is a product of how invested you are in the goals the other can mediate and how many other avenues are available for the attainment of those goals.

From: *Interpersonal Conflict*. Joyce Hocker Wilmot and William C. Wilmot. Dubuque: Wm. C. Brown Co., 1978.

On a large scale, people accomplish the same results through political action, by giving speeches, by advertising, by winning the support of pressure groups, by lobbying in Congress, or simply by using their organizational strength to cooperate with or oppose other groups. Sometimes, of course, it is necessary to organize a group of people where no previous organization exists. One of the problems with social movements—for example, those involving the poor, or women—is that the people involved are scattered over a wide variety of places and are unorganized. This makes it difficult for them to identify in a common cause.

The question "What can I do?" leads us into the next chapter. There we will be concerned with the manner in which social roles and natural conditions can affect individual responsibilities by placing limitations upon, or creating opportunities for, individual action. Our duties are frequently determined by our social roles, and our ability to function in social roles is determined, partly at least, by our natural talents. Our duties are also affected by available resources, by place and time, and by interaction with other people. That is, our moral responsibility is often determined by what others do, or may be expected to do, for the effectiveness of individual action often depends on the cooperation of persons and the coordination of acts. Personal responsibility may also be determined by the failure of others to carry out their duties, for, in such cases, a duty may then fall to us.

EXERCISES

1. Look for examples from current events, or from history, to illustrate how individuals have brought about changes in the rules or laws of society.

2. In these cases, what methods did these individuals use to bring about change? Do you think their methods were justified?

3. Think of times when you yourself had an influence upon an organization or group, to the extent of changing its practices. Analyze the method you used, even if you were not conscious of choosing that method. Also ask yourself whether you were influenced by moral considerations in trying to effect this change.

4. What power do you have in this class, in your family, among your friends, in the community? How can you exercise this power?

SUPPLEMENTARY READINGS

Aristotle. *Nichomachean Ethics* (many editions).

Brandt, Richard B. *Ethical Theory*. Englewood Cliffs, N.J.: Prentice-Hall, 1959.

Churchman, C. West. *Theory of Experimental Inference*. New York: Macmillan, 1948.

Dewey, John. *Human Nature and Conduct*. New York: Carleton House, 1922.

Lyons, David. *Forms and Limits of Utilitarianism*. Oxford: The Clarendon Press, 1965.

Nowell-Smith, Patrick. *Ethics*. Baltimore: Pelican Books, 1954.

Hare, R. M. *Freedom and Reason*. Oxford: Oxford University Press, 1965.

Rosen, Bernard. *Strategies of Ethics*. Boston: Houghton Mifflin Co., 1978.

Thiroux, Jacques. *Ethics: Theory and Practice.* New York: Macmillan, 1986.

Toulmin, Stephen. *An Examination of the Place of Reason in Ethics.* Cambridge: Cambridge University Press, 1951.

Wilmot, Joyce Hocker and Wilmot, William W. *Interpersonal Conflict.* Dubuque: William C. Brown Co., 1978.

JUDGING INDIVIDUAL ACTS

In the last two chapters we examined the place and function of rules in moral reasoning. Subordinate rules help us interpret and apply moral principles, but they are also subject to critique and amendment according to moral principles. In this chapter we will consider other factors that affect the morality of particular acts. Among these are social roles and various natural determinants of moral responsibility such as natural resources, conditions of time and place, individual talents, and the numbers and dispositions of people in a position to act.

Many social rules apply only to people in particular roles or occupations, and much of moral reasoning consists of applying these rules to persons in these roles. Assuming that roles, and the rules which govern them, are justified by moral principles, we expect people to carry out the duties of their roles in life. Problems of moral reasoning can arise, however, for the duties of some roles may conflict with those of others, or role-related duties may conflict with moral principles.

The application of principles also depends on natural conditions, on opportunities and limitations provided by geography, say, or by individual talents. Actions can affect natural conditions, of course, as people can alter their environment or develop their talents, but natural conditions also determine what people can or cannot do.

Moreover, acts can support or interfere with one another. Individual acts, like social rules, are often meant to serve an instrumental function by bringing about states of affairs that will enable persons to engage in still other acts, as in ordering materials for building a house, say, or decorating a gymnasium for a dance. In such cases, the justification of an act will depend on its coordination with other acts. Social organization may help provide such coordination, but individual planning and decision are also needed. The need for action also depends on what others will do or may be expected to do. The acceptance of responsibility by someone else may relieve us of duty, but, if they do not shoulder the burden, it may then fall to us. Judging individual acts, therefore, involves not only the application of moral principles but also a consideration of roles, natural conditions, and the behavior of others. In this chapter, we shall show how these factors can affect the morality of individual acts.

SOCIAL ROLES

Although moral principles apply to everyone, not everyone has exactly the same physical limitations or opportunities, and we do not all occupy the same social positions. We do not make the same choices, nor are we affected by the decisions of others in the same ways. For these reasons, we may be said to occupy different spheres of responsibility, for our rights and duties are determined by the natural and social conditions under which we live, by the roles we play, and by what happens to us in those circumstances.

GERMAIN CRISEZ AND RUSSELL SHAW
On Social Roles and Duties

Each of us has a variety of social roles arising from membership in various communities, and each of these social roles carries with it a variety of duties . . . The fulfillment of these roles will require that the persons filling them act in certain ways. These required ways of acting are duties, and a duty may be defined as something one has a responsibility for doing or not doing by virtue of one's role in a particular community. Just as we have many social roles, so we have many duties: as a student, as a citizen, as a family member, as an employer or employee, and so on.

From: *Beyond the New Morality: The Responsibilities of Freedom.* Germain Crisez and Russell Shaw. Notre Dame: University of Notre Dame Press, 1974.

For instance, according to socially accepted rules, including the law, police are permitted to do things others are not allowed to do, but they are also subject to special constraints. They are allowed to carry handguns, and, in given circumstances, they are also required to use them. Like firefighters and soldiers, they are required to take risks that other citizens are not expected to take. The police are also aided in some ways and hindered in others by their natural talents as individuals and by natural and social conditions, including the actions of others and their other roles in life.

Various factors may aid the police or impede them in their task. Under given circumstances, their family lives may support or interfere with their performance. Thus, moral problems may be created by a conflict of roles, but problems may also be solved when roles provide mutual support. That is why we need to organize our personal lives in such a way as to prevent or reduce conflict and, if possible, achieve cooperation.

Choosing Roles

We seem to have some moral obligations whether we want them or not, but others, like the duty to keep promises, seem to follow upon choice or commitment. A person would not normally have the duties of a policeman or policewoman in the first place if he or she did not choose that kind of job. So our spheres of moral responsibility can be affected by our choices. The advantages or difficulties of having a job, or being married, follow upon a decision to take a job, or to be married. In this sense, we may be said to choose our obligations, by making promises or commitments, although we may not always understand fully the consequences of such choice.

But some roles are not chosen, or the options for choice may be severely limited. Some roles may also be difficult to change. Children, for example, have duties to parents they do not choose to have, just as parents have duties to children they cannot simply choose to ignore. Citizens have duties to their country according to its laws, and practically everyone has duties according to moral principles. Thus, we cannot always relieve ourselves of responsibilities by changing roles, as in changing jobs. Divorce does not necessarily relieve parents of responsibilities to their children, although it may relieve them of certain responsibilities to one another. Sometimes, then, we can change our obligations as individuals, and sometimes not. In any case, we are bound by the conditions in which we find ourselves, until those conditions change or are changed; that is what it means to be bound.

Roles and Principles

Social roles, such as those of police, teachers, financial analysts, or nurses, create moral responsibilities. However, in many cases, it seems that satisfying the demands of one or another of these roles conflicts with moral principles. For example, the police may believe that, in a particular case, they are doing harm by arresting a young person for the possession of drugs. Arrest and punishment, we pointed out earlier, are themselves harms that require justification as exceptions to moral principles. Individuals are not usually helped by being arrested; yet it is the duty of police to make arrests. It is their duty to enforce laws prohibiting the possession of drugs, but their duty to make an arrest in this case seems to conflict with the principle "Do no harm." Therefore, there appears to be a serious question about the moral justification of this act.

There may also be some question about the justification of the law, but we pointed out earlier that persons may be obligated to obey even unjust laws. This seems especially true in the case of police, for, in their role as police, it is their duty to enforce existing laws, not to create new laws or abolish old ones. Nor, in their role as police, are they generally allowed to determine, as a matter of personal choice, which laws they will enforce.

Moreover, arrests are not usually justified in the name of helping the persons arrested. The aim is to punish offenders, or to prevent crime by means of punishment. So, if anyone is aided by an arrest, it is likely to be persons other than the person arrested. Nonetheless, the police may know that, in this case, arrest will do little to prevent harm to others, and that it may harm the person being arrested even more than drugs.

The problem is difficult partly because other principles are involved. The justice principle requires that rules or laws be applied consistently to all cases, and the burden of proof rests on exceptions. This seems especially important in the case of law enforcement officers, for it is their specific duty to be fair in making arrests. Their failure to do so would be inconsistent with the legitimate expectations of the persons they serve, and it could undermine respect for law.

The point is that we rely on people to do their jobs, and, when they fail to do so, the fabric of society seems weakened. We have said that social rules defining roles are built on agreement, or at least acceptance, and expectations are disappointed if those agreements are not met. Indeed, as the effectiveness of one action is often dependent on another, a failure in one person's performance can undermine a whole series of acts. When a teacher does not show up for class, for instance, a large number of students may have wasted time, energy, and money they could have used to do other things. Of course, we rightly allow absences from jobs in cases of emergency, but, under normal circumstances, we also count on people to do the things they have contracted to do.

In a division of labor, we cannot expect everyone to do the same jobs. It is not the job of the police to try to solve every problem. Yet there are alternatives to making arrests. Police have some discretion, even within the law, for, in the case of minor offenses, they can sometimes issue warnings instead. Sometimes, indeed, they let known criminals go free when they serve as witnesses or informers, in order to catch other criminals.

In the performance of any role, one should not expect mindless adherence to rules. A certain range of discretion, even leniency, seems a legitimate expectation, even in law enforcement. But the roles of some people, like police, soldiers, firefighters, and doctors, say, are more clearly defined and rigorously regulated, mainly because, as a society, we need to be able to rely on these professions for the protection of basic goods. The ability of people to perform these functions also depends on highly disciplined behavior. The rules governing these roles, therefore, may allow less discretion. By contrast, the rules of family life seem to allow parents a great deal of discretion in rearing their children, or even in the ways husbands and wives relate to one another. Individual style may be a factor in professional practice, but it usually finds greater expression in personal life.

In any role, some actions are dictated by the role, and others are left to individual discretion. A teacher may try to avoid psychological harm to slow learners by slowing the pace of the class, without ever supposing this would violate teaching standards. But if, for the same reason, a teacher chose to overlook a wrong answer on a test paper, he or she would be violating a strong, basic rule of the teaching profession. There may be extreme cases which would justify such an exception—say the prevention of a suicide—but even then there may be other alternatives.

CONFLICTS BETWEEN ROLES

Sometimes, it seems, doing our duty according to one role brings us into conflict with doing our duty according to another, or even in conflict with the law. Married people who are employed outside the home frequently experience a conflict between the demands of job and family, sometimes not knowing which should come first, and feeling guilty because they are sacrificing one for the other. We also hear of cases in which a psychologist or a newspaper reporter is required to give information in court, when the ethics of their professions require confidentiality.

There is no one and only one way of resolving such conflicts, nor are they always easy to resolve. Conflicts between the demands of one role and those of another are usually solved best by planning, or by a division of labor. That is, we can set aside times to be at work and at home, say, and we can also divide work shifts or tasks among fellow employees or family members. Even then, of course, there may be times when we seem to be needed in both places at once, and there may be no way of determining once and for all which role takes precedence over the other.

Below, we will consider circumstances of space, time, and coordination, which are likely to affect such determinations. For now we wish to point out that a person's role in the family, or at work, is an important consideration in determining what he or she should do. If, say, a couple has agreed that the wife is supposed to work during the day while the husband cares for the children, and, accordingly, the husband is scheduled to work at night, then the husband should not expect his wife to miss work to help at home, except under very unusual circumstances, and the employer should not expect the husband to work during the day. Coordination of this sort is one of the great values of subordinate rules, but, unfortunately, the rules of one place and those of another are not always coordinated, and people are not always reasonable in their demands.

It may be reasonable for a court of law to seek confidential information from a professional in order to solve a crime, or to convict a criminal, but it may also be reasonable for a professional to refuse to give that information. That is, if a judge acts the way a judge should act, according to that role, and if the professional observes professional standards requiring confidentiality, it seems only reasonable for them to oppose one another. Indeed, such oppositions often lead to resolution, if not at the time, then perhaps later, when the ethics of professions, or the law itself, is modified to clarify exceptions. It is now customary for employers to make allowances for sick leave or maternity leave, and family members usually learn to make allowances for demands of the workplace. Likewise, although a judge may hold a newspaper reporter in contempt of court, the punishment is usually lenient, or even suspended, in respect of professional standards.

The Limits of Duties

The extent to which the demands of a social role are binding depends a great deal on reasonable options. A parent cannot be expected to leave a very sick and possibly dying child unless other, perhaps more competent, care is available. An employee is not likely to miss work without very good reason if its demands are pressing or the salary is badly needed. One's duty in such cases is related to the need, likelihood, and cost of replacement. Highly trained professionals are not easily or cheaply replaced, and the demands of their jobs are often pressing. In a university, for example, there is usually no provision for substitute teachers, although in primary or secondary education there usually is. In parenting, it is often possible to hire babysit-ters, but costs can be high, and qualified people are not always easy to find.

The extent of potential harm, injustice, or curtailment of freedom, of course, are primary considerations in determining whether a breach of practice is justified. If one violates the rules of a bicycle touring club by missing a Sunday meeting, the damage done is likely to be far less serious than that caused by a surgeon's failure to properly suture a wound. In the police case cited above, the seriousness of harm to the suspect must be weighed against the benefit of observing police rules.

In sum, social roles and rules can determine rights and obligations. They help realize the various kinds of goods specified by our positive, correlative principles. For example, everyone is bound by negative principles, such as the principle to avoid harm, but obligations to do specific kinds of good are often dependent on social roles and rules. The parents of the child next door have responsibilities toward that child that other people do not have. A police officer has obligations to help those in need in a way that goes beyond the moral obligations of others. A doctor, a teacher, a priest, a son, or a mother, all have positive responsibilities that go beyond the negative requirements of our basic principles and are determined by their social roles. This does not mean that our only positive duties are role-specific. We all have responsibilities to do good in times of great need. Under normal circum-stances, I may not have an obligation to help the child next door, but if I can prevent that child from being injured, I may have an obligation to do so. Often, however, our duty consists of notifying the proper authorities. If the house next door is on fire, I may be able to satisfy my obligation by calling the fire department.

We conclude, then, the rules governing roles in life are more binding on particular actions:

1. the more clearly the rules are defined.

2. the more important the goods dependent upon obedience to the rules, and

3. the greater the public acceptance and expectation of such action.

These conditions are important considerations when taken singly, and they become even more important in combination. When these conditions hold, the burden of proof placed on exceptions becomes more difficult to satisfy. Exceptions may be justified nonetheless, by serious violations of moral principles, because of conflicts between rules or roles, or because performance in a particular case is impossible or unnecessary. However, if the burden of proof is not met, persons are morally bound to follow the rules of their roles in life.

CASES IN ROLE MORALITY

Roles establish prima facie moral responsibilities. They specify who is supposed to do what and thus add specificity to the correlate principles.

But roles are not always clearly defined, as we have seen; they may often be voluntarily accepted or rejected, and they may entail actions that conflict with other roles. Actions required by role-specific rules may also conflict with moral principles. With these factors in mind, let us consider the following cases.

Case 1:   Jim agreed to babysit for his nephew. His older brother asked him to sit between 7:00 and 9:00 p.m., and Jim said this would be fine. But he told his brother that he could not stay later because he had to complete a computer program due in class the next day. Jim explained that the computer center had better turn-around time at night, so he planned to work on his program between 10:00 p.m. and 2:00 a.m. He had also promised a friend, who would be working on the same program as part of a team project, that he would arrive promptly at 10:00. But his brother did not return at 9:00 and did not call. Jim knew it would take him at least 30 minutes to travel to his college, so at 9:50 he knew he would be late. Because the children were asleep, he thought that he could leave and lock the door. He expected that his brother would be home soon, and he reasoned that, after all, his brother had broken his promise. He had not agreed to sit after 9:00. Was Jim morally justified in leaving the house?

Comment: The answer seems clear. Jim was not morally permitted to leave. The potential for harm to the children was too great. It is true that Jim's agreed upon commitment ended at 9:00. It is also true that he has other commitments dictated by his role as a student and his promise to his friend. But, in the case of babysitting, it often happens that parents are detained without fault and without ability to call ahead. Anyone stuck in a traffic jam on a highway knows this. There is a presumption that a babysitter will remain on the job until the parents come home, even if they happen to be late. Of course, Jim has the right to refuse to babysit again if he feels he has been unfairly treated, but, by accepting responsibility for the children, he has an obligation to stay.
    Of course, this does not absolve the parents of their responsibility. They should make every reasonable effort to return home on time. However, it is just because they have failed to live up to their end of the bargain that the responsibility falls on Jim. The job still needs to be done, and, presumably, Jim is the only person in a position to do it. However, there might have been other options. Jim might have attempted to call his sister who also lives in town and try to put off the programming for another hour or so. If his sister accepted, he might then have transferred the obligation to her, and if he called his friend, he might then have relieved himself of a conflicting duty.

Case 2:   Alice is a social worker. She knows that she can make three visits this afternoon, working at her normal pace, but she just doesn't feel like handling more than two. So she decides to delay, taking extra time on her second visit. She reasons that, because she is more productive than most of the other workers, she is entitled to loaf around sometimes. She doesn't believe that any great hardship will befall the third person she would have visited, and she had not made a special appointment for the visitation.

Comment: In this case it is not especially clear that any principles would be violated. The question is: has Alice violated the rules of her job? If the answer to that question is "yes," then she would not be morally permitted to take a break, all things being equal. For example, the rules of her job may require that she make a certain number of visitations each day. But, of course, there could be other circumstances which would change this answer. She may be so tired that she cannot properly fulfill her duties, or she may have important parental duties she must attend.

EXERCISES

In which of the following cases are the acts (decisions) in question justified by rules governing social roles? In any of these cases, are exceptions justified by conflicts with other roles, or with moral principles?

1. A man is having a heart attack in a theatre, but a doctor close by decides not to help. He has a dinner appointment after the show and does not want to be late. He notes that someone has gone to call an emergency unit, and he reasons that, because the person having the attack is not his patient, he has no special obligation to him. Besides, he tells his friend, many doctors get sued for helping in such circumstances, even though he knows there is a "good Samaritan" law in his state.

2. Professor Jones knows he could do a much better job teaching, but he also knows that he is rewarded, not for teaching, but for research. So he spends almost all of his time on research, often misses classes, and is poorly prepared.

3. Jimmy Jones, Professor Jones' son, is a student at a well-known state university. He often cuts classes and does very little studying. He says he would rather party instead; after all, he's a grown person and has a right to decide what he will do with his time.

4. Mary often finds it necessary to work late in order to satisfy the requirements of her job. Her husband is angry, however, for he then has the responsibility to prepare dinner and take care of the kids when they arrive home from school. He says she is not a good mother and that it is not a man's job to cook and raise kids. He arrives home early from his job, and he argues that she should do the same. To make his point, he usually leaves the house a mess and does not attend fully to the children's needs.

5. Fred was the commanding officer of a platoon fighting in the jungle. Although his platoon had suffered a great number of casualties, they had also taken large numbers of prisoners. Fred knew the rules of war governing the proper treatment of prisoners, but he also knew that he did not have enough men to guard them. Since it was his primary duty to try to win, he reasoned, he could not continue to hold the prisoners. Thus, he ordered the guards to unlock the prison gates at night and shoot any prisoner who tried to escape. In this way, he thought, he could obey the letter of the law and still accomplish his objective. The prisoners, in turn, who felt it was their duty to try to escape, were killed in the attempt.

6. Bob is doing research on voter reaction to a political debate. He believes that some of the people did not understand the questions, and so decides to throw some of the responses away. He knows that this is not acceptable practice, but he strongly believes that the results will actually be more accurate without those answers.

7. Sally knows that the math test is graded on a class curve. Her friend, Bob, requests some help. Although she has the time and the skill to give the help, she refuses. She knows that Bob has had some difficulty in receiving help at the tutoring center, but she feels that this is his problem, not hers. Besides, she tends to make sloppy errors, while Bob, once he knows the material, tends to get the answers correct. She believes that without her help Bob will earn a lower grade, but with her help he may surpass her and force her to a lower position on the curve. She knows that if she had been in a different class, she would have gladly helped her friend.

8. Harry is a political campaign organizer. This year he is working for a candidate for U.S. senator from a midwestern state, facing the incumbent. The senator voted against a bill authorizing the cleanup of a local river. This bill was defeated, and a stronger bill was eventually passed with the support of the senator. Knowing all of this, Harry decides to run an ad claiming that the senator voted against cleaning up the river. This is a locally powerful issue, so he thought that he could make political gain by the distortion. He argues that it is his job to help his candidate win the election, and that the ad is true (if not the whole truth). Besides, he says, everyone does that sort of thing.

9. Fay is a reporter for a local newspaper. The paper is going to investigate the local community college. The object of her assignment is to show that the college is not doing its job. She finds evidence to show that students are not able to transfer many of their credits to the local university. While this is true, and she believed that the community college was not doing a good job, it was also misleading. The courses in question were vocational, and these were just the sort of courses that were not intended to transfer. Courses like first year English, Math, and Logic were transferable. In fact, many students complete two years at the community college and graduate from the university two years later. Nonetheless, she writes an article criticizing the community college for its low standards.

10. Years ago an old sea captain took his young grandson on a whale hunt. Because the boy begged him, he let his grandson go out in one of the small boats with members of his crew. A storm came up and the whaling boat which had his grandson aboard did not return. Although it was one of the rules of the ship, which he himself often insisted upon, that the whole crew should not be endangered to save one man, he sent the other boats out to look for his grandson. They succeeded in the attempt, and he therefore felt vindicated in his decision. (Would your answer be the same if the other boats were also lost?)

Natural Determinants

Social roles are important factors to consider in determining moral responsibility. Roles take us beyond the general prohibitions of negative principles and specify positive duties, in keeping with the correlate positive principles. However, even within roles, people may lack the talent needed to perform an assigned task, or conditions may not be suitable for appropriate action. Thus, the extent to which role-specific duties apply to a particular case may depend on individual talents and the opportunities and limitations of time and place. Indeed, natural conditions such as these may determine responsibilities even when roles have not been assigned, or when the rules governing a person's role in life do not apply.

It is not always easy to separate natural conditions from social practices. A child, for example, stands in a certain moral relationship to its parents by virtue of the natural fact of birth, but also because of social rules and practices governing family life. The practices of family life tend to differ from one society to another, or even at different times within the same society, but natural conditions also serve to influence such practices. That is, there seem to be good reasons for having a different type of family organization in a primitive agricultural society than in modern industrial life, or in cities as opposed to rural areas. On family farms in past history children were usually an economic asset, whereas in cities they tend to become economic liabilities. Mothers and fathers normally leave home for work in the city but not on a farm. So natural conditions may affect individual duties directly, or they may do so indirectly by affecting the structure of social institutions.

Given natural tendencies, it seems reasonable to hold parents responsible for their children in a way that we do not hold others responsible. In a division of labor, it also seems reasonable to hold people responsible for the consequences of their own acts—in this case, for taking care of children they have brought into the world.

Place and Distance

Perhaps the most obvious natural conditions affecting morality are geographical variations in climate and soil, which support or limit agricultural and industrial production, and variations in population, or in the ratios of people to resources, which can affect both the distribution of goods and production. Much of the inequality of the world seems related to such variations, as people in extremely arid climates experience frequent droughts, or simply do not have enough arable land, whereas people in more temperate zones may have an overabundance of goods.

An individual person or a society may have an obligation to feed the needy in one set of circumstances but not another. Nobody can have such an obligation if there is no food to give them, or if there is no way of transporting food to persons in need. However, there may be an obligation to try to find ways of producing or distributing food.

When the principles or rules conflict, natural conditions may also deter-

NORMAN E. BOWIE
(1942–   )
On Basic Needs

In general, a need is considered basic if it is a biological need necessary for survival or physical health. The fulfillment of basic needs is a necessary condition for the fulfillment of other needs. A basic need is a function of man's biological nature. Moreover, it is commonly believed that such needs can be determined with a fair degree of objectivity. In addition, this notion of a basic need is also widely accepted in all distributive theories. Basic needs determine the welfare floor in utilitarian theories and the right to a minimum standard of living in egalitarian theories. . . . I will admit that basic needs are more urgent than others and that they should be satisfied first.

From: *A New Theory of Distributive Justice*. Norman E. Bowie. Amherst: University of Massachusetts Press, 1971.

mine orders of precedence. Under conditions of extreme hardship or poverty, for instance, mere survival is likely to be more important than freedom or equality. That is why, it seems, sick people are often willing to surrender much of their freedom by putting themselves in the hands of hospitals and health care professionals—a position of dependence they would otherwise find completely unacceptable. People will also accept extremely unpleasant and even dangerous work in order to survive, or to provide for their families. However, in times of abundance, or of health and prosperity, not much thought need be given to survival, for it may be taken for granted. It seems quite reasonable to turn our attention to other, perhaps even higher goods, when basic needs are satisfied.

These observations are especially important when considering the morality of large social issues. For example, on the subject of AIDS, many people are concerned about the apparent conflict between patients' rights and the spread of the disease—a conflict between the principles of freedom and nonmaleficence. Traditionally, people with serious communicable diseases were put under quarantine, in which case the threat to public health was judged to be a more important consideration than the limitation on freedom. In the AIDS case, however, opponents of quarantines have argued that they are not feasible, for, if cases were reported by examiners, persons would shun testing, and there is no independent way of determining carriers of the virus. In the absence of voluntary compliance, quarantines would also be impracticable, they argue, because there is no efficient way of enforcing compliance.

ACCIDENTAL CIRCUMSTANCES

When they speak of being in the right place at the right time, people are aware of the fact that luck, or accidental occurrence, often affects their lives. Among other things—and perhaps the most obvious—we do not control the circumstances of our own birth. Our careers may also be determined by an advertisement we happen to notice in a newspaper, by choosing one school rather than another, or by some person we accidentally meet. In this sense, people often do not choose but are chosen for their jobs, by other people, or by circumstances. A student who wins a scholarship is in effect chosen for a certain field of work, although he or she may refuse the offer. A young woman may become pregnant, give birth, and find herself in the role of being a mother, without ever consciously choosing that position. A young man may be drafted in the army, be sent to the front lines, and find himself facing an enemy he must kill—or be killed. At still other times we may find ourselves called upon to help someone in need because we are the only persons in a position to help.

Suppose one is standing next to a swimming pool and sees that someone else is drowning. Let us suppose also that no one else is around at the time. Under such conditions, one may have an obligation to help the other person, or at least to try to do so. One would not have this obligation if one were not in that place at that time. Or, suppose someone knocks on your door and asks for help; you may have an obligation to respond. But if the person who came to your door had chosen to go somewhere else, you would not have had that obligation. Likewise, one can incur an obligation by driving past an accident on a highway and noticing it, whereas no obligation would exist if one were not driving there or did not notice it. There are other factors, of course, such as conflicting, even overriding obligations; but, all things being equal, one may incur a particular obligation, it seems, just by being in a particular place at a particular time.

Distance is obviously an important factor because, usually, people nearby are in a better position to help others than people far away. The farther away we are, the greater the costs of helping. When costs are high, the harm we create may be greater than the harm we avoid. Moreover, distance tends to affect knowledge about the best way to address needs, for people who are closer to a problem may understand it better. Factors such as these suggest that, typically, our strongest obligations are to people close at hand. But this is not always so, for people at a greater distance may have a greater need.

DAVID HUME
(1711–1776)
On Sympathy and Distance

When the natural tendency of his passions leads him to be serviceable and useful within his sphere, we approve of his character and love his person, by a sympathy with the sentiments of those, who have a more particular connexion with him . . . The only point of view, in which our sentiments concur with those of others, is, when we consider the tendency of any passion to the advantage or harm of those, who have any immediate connexion or intercourse with the person possess'd of it. And tho' this advantage or harm be often very remote from ourselves, yet sometimes 'tis very near us, and interests us strongly by sympathy. This concern we readily extend to other cases, that are resembling; and when these are very remote, our sympathy is proportionably weaker, and our praise or blame fainter and more doubtful . . .

From: *Treatise on Human Nature*. David Hume. L. A. Selby-Bigge, ed. Oxford: The Clarendon Press, 1888.

Sometimes, it seems, people try to put distance between themselves and others as a way of escaping responsibilities and gaining an easier life for themselves. Of course, generally speaking, there is nothing morally wrong with desiring an easier life, or even acting according to that desire. On the other hand, there is nothing morally praiseworthy in avoiding responsibilities or running away from problems.

THE FACTOR OF TIME

Time is also an important factor, of course, because we may be in different places at different times, and hence stand in relation to different people and problems. For example, we have different obligations at different stages in life. Young people do not have the same responsibilities as older people. Very young children are simply unable to perform adult acts, while older children are often excused from other duties in order to attend school. Very old people may also be excused from responsibility because they are infirm, or because they have done their share. Thus, time of life is an important consideration in applying principles. Placing excessive obligations on very young children can curtail freedom and development and create harmful stress. Even if a young person has the capacity to perform the action of an adult, that youth may not be required to do so, because of his or her time of life.

It also takes time to do things—sometimes a great deal of time. It takes time to eat a meal, build a house, or earn a degree. It is therefore necessary to plan our use of time in order to perform such acts. Indeed, many acts not only involve time but require timing. If the right time has passed, it may not be possible to perform an act, or it may be ineffective or even harmful. Human learning, for example, is dependent on maturation; if the optimal time for learning a skill has passed, it may be difficult, even impossible, to learn it at all.

Time, like distance, can affect moral responsibility by affecting our ability to cause or prevent harm or injustice, or our ability to create or curtail opportunities. The longer it takes to prevent a harm, the longer the harm is likely to last. The longer it takes to bring about a desired effect, the greater the cost. Again, like distance, time is often used as an excuse; not having time is frequently cited as a reason for inaction, but we can often make time if we choose to do so. But, again, we have only so much time, and that is why it is important to use time wisely, and to coordinate our actions.

NUMBERS AND COORDINATION

Natural factors are obviously related. In some of the above examples, it was not just the time or place that was important, but also the numbers of people involved. When a person is alone, he or she may have no obligations toward anyone; the question of violating a principle may not even arise, except in prospect, say, as one is planning a course of action. Obviously, a person cannot have an obligation to save another, say, if there is no other to save, or if others are not in need. In our example of saving a drowning person, the duty was predicated on the assumption that only one person was in a position to help. But suppose more than one person could do the job. In such a case, it becomes less clear who has the obligation—if indeed anyone does. Other factors, it seems, must be taken into account, such as ability, social roles, or other pressing concerns.

Where more than one person is in a position to help, some decision may need to be made about where the responsibility lies. That determination cannot always be made on the basis of moral principles alone. That is often why, in times of emergency, crowds of people are ineffective, because they may have no way of knowing on whom the obligation falls. If, in the case of a medical emergency, a doctor is present, the duty may fall to the doctor, because of his or her expertise, or because of his or her social role. But where no role has been assigned, people may not know how to act, or what each of them ought to do. Because they do not know what others will do, or what others are expected to do, they do not know what their own obligation is. Thus we often consider actions in such situations to be heroic, or above and beyond the call of duty, just because no duty has been assigned.

SOREN KIERKEGAARD
(1813–1855)
The Crowd is Untruth

A crowd—not this crowd or that, the crowd now living or deceased, a crowd of humble people or superior people, of rich or of poor, etc.—a crowd in its very concept is the untruth, by reason of the fact that it renders the individual completely impenitent and irresponsible, or at least weakens his sense of responsibility by reducing it to a fraction.

From: *The Point of View for My Work as An Author*. Soren Kierkegaard. New York: Harper Torchbooks, 1962.

In more ordinary circumstances, however, where helpful actions do not require special training or ability, each person may share responsibility for acting or initiating action. We hear of cases, like Kitty Genovese in Queens, New York, who cried for help while being attacked, yet not one of thirty-eight people hearing her bothered to call the police. Calling the police is a very simple act that requires little effort, talent, or courage. The persons involved might have supposed that someone else would call for help, but they could also have inquired to make sure, and any one of them might have tried to organize the others in an attempt to prevent the crime. That is, even if it is not one's assigned duty to solve a problem, or one is unable to solve it alone, it may be one's duty to try to bring about a solution by contacting others who do have such a duty or ability, or even to assume leadership in trying to persuade others to cooperate in reaching a solution.

Again, this sort of problem is often solved by adopting rules, and where there are rules, the situation changes. For example, at public beaches or pools, lifeguards are usually appointed the job of saving people and of regulating behavior to ensure safety. Under such conditions, other people can assume they are relieved from responsibility. In fact, others are obligated not to interfere with those who have this responsibility—even if they are better qualified to do the job. So a person may be prohibited from trying to save a drowning person because his or her action might interfere with the actions of lifeguards. However, if a lifeguard is not doing his or her duty, leaves the beach or pool momentarily, or becomes disabled descending from the lifeguard stand, others may then be called upon, so to speak, to do the lifeguard's job.

A conjunction of acts requires coordination, as when a team of doctors is performing an operation, for instance, or when a football team is trying to execute a play. A cook must learn to do many things at once, or in the right sequence, in order to make the meal turn out right. Thus, the appropriateness of an act, or our duty to perform it, may depend on how it is related to a number of other acts. This is especially true when many people, or many agencies, must coordinate their actions, as in running a circus or an army, or in the activities of economic life, involving the manufacture, transportation, storage, and distribution of goods.

Thus social rules, institutions, and roles are often created to solve the problem of determining where responsibility lies. They can bring about greater efficiency in action by eliminating the kind of confusion and conflict that arises from not knowing who should do what, and they also enable people to specialize in assigned tasks. They even make it possible to do jobs that could not otherwise be done, because of the need to coordinate behavior. If, say, in a very simple case, the drowning person is very large and the lifesavers are rather small, it may require two or more people to pull the drowning person from the water. Several people may also be needed to coordinate the actions of lifeguards, ambulance drivers, paramedics, doctors, and nurses. Indeed, it usually takes large numbers of people, each doing his or her own job, to carry out institutional tasks. Thus, the numbers of people available may determine whether a job can be done at all, and hence whether anyone has the responsibility to do it.

An individual would not have an obligation to perform an act if he or she could not do it alone. However, as we have said, given individuals may have obligations to try to organize others, or to try to cooperate with them in attempting to get a job done. Morally speaking, it seems that we must stand ready to cooperate with others in performing acts that require assistance or in creating rules and institutions that can solve problems that none of us can solve alone. We should also stand ready to do our share by cooperating with others in those institutions, as is consistent with moral principles and our other roles in life.

Americans may have obligations toward starving people on the other side of the earth, but it is highly unlikely that many of them, as individuals, could do much to solve that problem. However, world hunger, involving the starvation of some twelve million people annually, suggests that individuals have an obligation to become informed of such needs and to engage in appropriate political action. Even then, not everyone can be expected to actively support every cause, for there is a limit to the number of things any individual can effectively do. Different agencies are needed to address different issues so that the people working in those agencies can direct appropriate attention to them.

RESOURCES, TALENTS, AND TOOLS

People frequently talk of expressing themselves, developing their talents or "potential," or of simply being creative—meaning, it seems, that, as individuals, they want to make their mark upon the world. There is certainly room for such expression in morality. In fact, the aim of moral principles is to allow people such freedom of action, as is consistent with the freedom and general welfare of others as well. On the other hand, in attempting to achieve their goals, people are also limited by their talent or lack of talent, and by the talents or limitations of others.

Talent, therefore, is not only related to the kinds of things we would like to do with our lives; it also conditions the kinds of things we are morally required to do. In the case of saving the drowning person, one's ability to swim may determine whether one has a responsibility to act—especially when the other people standing by cannot swim. In other words, who gets the job, sometimes an unpleasant and unrewarding job, often depends on who can do it, or on what abilities or expertise a person has. If, in the case of an accident, a surgeon is standing by, he or she may have an obligation to perform surgery, but an untrained person may have no obligation, or even be prohibited from such performance. One reason for developing social institutions is that raw talent is often not enough to get the job done. People often need to be trained for their jobs, and they may also need the proper tools to do them.

The moral relevance of talent is dependent upon the positions, resources, and tools available. If one is born into a rather primitive, agricultural economy where there are no schools, or where music is limited to playing a flute, it makes little difference whether one has the talent to become a mathematical genius or a world class violinist. On the other hand, even where both talent and opportunity exist, one may choose to use one's talents elsewhere in order to do more good.

In keeping with positive moral principles, it is desirable for people to develop their talents, but they cannot develop one talent fully without neglecting other talents, and hence cannot have an obligation to fully develop each and every talent. That is one reason why people are usually allowed a wide range of discretion in choosing which talents they will develop or in their choice of careers. But there also seems to be a hierarchy of more or less general abilities such that some of them are common and even essential to others. Speaking, reading, and writing, for example, are important to most everything we do. People also seem to have a general obligation to develop their reasoning abilities, and their understanding of and sensitivity to moral situations, so they can become morally better people. We at least seem to have an obligation not to impede such learning.

According to positive moral principles, societies support the development of individual talents and provide training in language, reasoning, and computational skills by funding formal education and occupational training. Indeed, in most countries, a minimum level of such education is expected. It is necessary to develop talents in order to promote the general welfare, to provide opportunities for individual expression, and to satisfy the demands of social roles.

THE DISTRIBUTION OF DUTIES

People often speak of the distribution of the benefits of action, of the distribution of goods; but perhaps they do not speak as often of the distribution of responsibilities, or the fairness or unfairness of the division of tasks. Yet, it is not unusual to hear people complain that they have too much to do. Because some people are where the action is, so to speak, they may find themselves saddled with many more responsibilities than people who are far removed. People who are more ambitious usually take on more tasks than others. On the other hand, one of the benefits of wealth is that it can serve to remove a person from the many distasteful tasks of daily life that affect people who perform menial work, or who are simply poor. It also removes them from the poor who need help, so they are not frequently called upon to respond in a personal way. Indeed, as we have noted, many people spend much of their lives trying to escape responsibility by removing themselves from conditions in which they may be required to respond. It is certainly not always wrong to do so, for a person's job may be much too difficult, or a person may be carrying an unfair share of responsibility. It may also be the case that a person can use his or her talents better in other ways.

Escaping to a desert island may or may not be immoral, depending on what one proposes to do there and on what obligations one has left behind. As we have said, numbers and talents may be important, for we may be morally permitted to leave a job if someone else is there to do it, but we may not be morally permitted if there is no one to take our place. The freedom we have to change employment or careers is not absolute, for our freedom to do anything is always limited by moral principles and social rules. However, it is a matter of moral concern that tasks or duties be distributed as fairly as possible, given the limitations of natural conditions and the talents of the people involved.

In an advanced industrial society where life is to a large extent institutionalized and even impersonal, much of the responsibility for welfare, safety, and education is in the hands of the state, or of social organizations and individuals who occupy official positions. Thus, our moral responsibility to help feed or educate other people may be satisfied by supporting such social organizations by paying taxes, for example, and by voting in favor of issues that provide funding for schools, hospitals, or other forms of social welfare. In this century, the graded income tax has been used as a way of distributing the burden of taxation, or the burden of social responsibility, while, at the same time, governments have also assumed greater responsibility for the equitable distribution of goods.

CASES INVOLVING NATURAL DETERMINANTS

Case 1:   Sam is a skilled auto mechanic. He is driving home from work, late at night, and sees a car at the side of the road with its hood up. No other cars are in sight, and he knows that the road is only infrequently patrolled. A major snow storm is expected. It occurs to Sam that this person may be in serious trouble, but he also thinks it may be a trick and that he may be in danger if he stops. He drives on without stopping, but his conscience bothers him. He fears the person with car trouble may be stuck in the storm, but he consoles himself in thinking that it is not his job to help everyone in need.

Comment: We should note that, by not stopping to help, Sam does not violate any fundamental negative principles. It is also not his duty as a mechanic to help every person with car problems. However, he is in a special position to help, and no one else is. The person in trouble faces potentially serious danger, and it would not require a great effort from Sam to be of assistance. The danger Sam imagines is pure conjecture. Of course, there is always some risk, but if he were really afraid, he could at least call for help at the nearest gas station or telephone. It seems then that Sam fails to do what he ought to do, morally speaking. His duty would be a duty of charity, but a very specific duty nonetheless. The action called for in this case requires sensitivity to the needs of others, but it does not require great heroism or saintliness.

Sam's duty might be different if, as part of his job, he were indeed answering another call and felt he had no time to stop, if he felt fairly certain that other cars would be along soon, or if he actually saw a police car on the way or someone else stopping to help. Note that his special talent is relevant but it is not crucial. Even if he were not a mechanic, he could still stop to give the person a ride, or he could call for help. It is also important that no one else may be expected to help in this case and that the consequences appear serious. If Sam were in a hurry and if there were a phone or houses nearby, the person in need might reasonably be expected to help himself.

Case 2:   While Sandra was on a city bus, two youths held a knife to the driver and demanded all his money. There were at least twenty other people on the bus, and Sandra thought that somebody should do something. She did not feel that she could stop the youths from robbing the driver, and she was afraid that she and other passengers, as well as the driver, might get hurt. She did nothing. In fact nobody did anything to stop the attack. The youths took the money and ran out the door, but the driver was not injured.

Comment: This case is significantly different from the first. Sandra has no special talent that would enable her to be of help. There are in fact many other people who are in a position to help, some of whom may be better equipped to do the job. The risk is again potentially serious, but there seems to be no point in risking lives to prevent a theft. Any action on Sandra's part would be heroic—indeed, it might even be foolish, for it might provoke more harm than it prevents. In some cases, the leadership of one person will encourage others, but in this case, there would seem to be little opportunity to communicate with and organize the other passengers. Such initiative might be called for, however, if the robbers began to threaten or kill people on the bus.

Notice that we have distinguished between duties of charity and actions that are heroic or above and beyond the call of duty. In the first case, Sam appeared to have a *duty* of charity. In failing, he appeared to be at fault. But, in the second case, Sandra did not appear to have a duty. Any action on her part would appear to have been above and beyond the call. She was not at fault. The point is that, under appropriate circumstances, we can have positive duties that go beyond our specific roles in life. However, not every opportunity for doing good is a duty, even if commendable.

274

EXERCISES

In each of the following cases, determine responsibility based on talents, time, place, resources, and so on, as well as the moral principles and the roles involved. Ask yourself whether the persons in question have a moral duty or whether the action involved is above and beyond the call of duty. Also consider factors not mentioned that might alter your answer. If, in your judgment, a particular individual is not responsible for a particular act, is there anything else that individual might do to help solve the problem?

1. Pete sees a robber flee from a building across the street. Although he knows who the person is, he decides not to tell the police because he doesn't want to get involved.

2. Ann wonders how much she should give to charity. She recently found out the average family gives about 2.5 percent of their income to charity. She gives about $300 a year, which is 1 percent of her salary. She wonders whether she has a responsibility to give more. But she knows that the extra money for charity might mean that she either would have to give up the family's trip to visit her parents or else her daughter's piano lessons.

3. Mary strongly believes that a nearby uranium production plant is unsafe. She thinks that a letter to her representative may help solve the problem. But she hates to write letters and is very busy. She wonders whether she has a moral responsibility to write. If she does, she wonders whether this means that she will have a responsibility to write a large number of letters, because she has strong beliefs about issues ranging from gun control to acid rain.

4. Some high school friends of Sally and Harry are making fun of an unpopular student in the school. While their friends are enjoying the moment, it occurs to Sally that it is wrong and that she and Harry should try to stop them. Harry argues that it is not their responsibility to interfere.

5. Chris, who lives in Kansas, decides to go to Israel to work on a Kibbutz for one year. She believes that this is a moral responsibility. She has had a good life and feels obliged to give something back. She believes that because of her social and occupational background (in agriculture), this task would be the best one that she could perform.

6. Peter wants to help the IRA. He believes that his background and talents could be useful to the task. Besides, his father was once imprisoned by the British. Peter lives in the Bronx, and his friends tell him that he doesn't know enough about the IRA to commit himself to the cause. Some other friends tell him that they believe that some of what the IRA does is immoral, and that he should not get involved.

7. Joe is a teacher. An adult on his block is illiterate. He asks Joe to teach him how to read. It is clear to Joe that the neighbor does not intend to pay him and that he expects about two hours per week of Joe's time and skill. Joe refuses because he knows that the man could afford a paid tutor. But Joe worries that the man may remain illiterate, so he feels guilty about his decision.

8. Frank and Mabel live on the corner of an intersection where, in the winter, cars are frequently stuck in the snow. Because there are no other houses on this corner, they find that they are frequently called upon to help by letting drivers use the telephone or by actually helping them out of a ditch. But Frank is growing tired of all this. On a cold winter's evening when Frank is in his robe and slippers watching his favorite TV show, Mabel tells him there is a car stuck in the ditch outside. He responds by saying, "It's not my responsibility. After all, haven't we done enough already?"

9. Harry lives in a crime-ridden neighborhood. He has several times tried to prevent attacks on people by running out of his house to frighten thieves and muggers away. One time, however, he himself was beaten badly in an attempt to help others. As a result, he vows never to try to help anyone again. Instead, he adds additional locks to his doors and turns up the radio when he is at home so he cannot hear cries for help. He reasons that he is not a policeman, that he cannot by himself stop crime anyway, and that his own life is in danger.

10. Nancy lives in the country with her husband Fred. She reads the newspaper and finds that a neighbor's barn was burned to the ground. She also learns that the barn was just purchased by a black man, the first black person to move into her community, and that a swastika and racial slurs were painted on his barn the night before the fire. Later she also finds that the mayor, police chief, and fire chief make no public announcements about the incident except that they will investigate it. She thinks this is an outrage and that somebody in the community should publicly condemn the act and offer friendship and assistance to the victims. Fred says to her that it is none of their business and that they will incur hostility from the neighbors if they speak out against the incident. The best thing, he says, is to remain quiet.

CONCLUSION

In this chapter we have tried to show that the rightness or wrongness of individual acts is dependent on a number of factors including social roles and natural conditions. Among natural conditions, we discussed the factors of place, distance, time, talent, and numbers, and how these, in turn, can affect the need for action, as well as opportunity. Previously we said that, in simpler cases, the morality of acts may be determined directly by moral principles or social rules. Indeed, in this chapter we emphasized the point that our moral duty is often determined directly by social role, and that a role, in turn, is governed by social rules and practices. But we also pointed out that the requirements of a social role may conflict with a moral principle, another role, or even the law. In such cases, we said, there is not always a clear or certain answer, but it is helpful to look back to the principles and reconsider the purpose of the rules. That is why, in cases of moral uncertainty, it is important to have a firm grasp of principles.

In view of these factors, we have called attention to the following considerations. First, with respect to the way roles affect acts:

1. How is my (his or her) action in this case affected by my (his or her) role or position? Relative to a particular case:

   a. What role or position do I (does he or she) occupy that is relevant to this issue?
   b. Is there an explicit rule governing the role in this kind of case? Is some rule assumed or implicit? If so, what is the rule?
   c. Does the rule clearly apply? Is there an exception to it in this case, and if so, why? If an exception is claimed, can the exception be generalized to cover similar cases?

2. In considering a particular case, there may be reason to question a rule. The question then moves to a higher level.

   a. Is this a good rule to have? Is there an intuitive counterexample to the rule? Does it conflict with a moral principle or some other rule?
   b. Should the rule be changed, and if so, should I work toward change? If the rule cannot be changed immediately, am I bound by the rule, that is, go back to Step 1c.

3. The choice of roles is also a particular act, or a series of acts. Therefore, we can ask:

   a. Should I accept this particular role? Do I have a moral choice in this?

   Or, with respect to the future:

   b. What sorts of jobs or careers should I choose? How does the cost of training, in time, effort, and money affect my other responsibilities? How is my choice affected by my talents, interests, and educational resources? Is there a need, and is this need adequately satisfied by others?

   For example, should I marry, or, if married, divorce? Should I have children? The considerations include a couple's ability to help one another to meet the challenges of life and develop their potentialities. They should consider their ability to support one another, financially and emotionally, and to support their children. A person's decision to marry also affects his or her ability to pursue other goals in life, or to fulfill other obligations. It may be the case that people who expect to devote themselves fully to a particular career other than marriage really should not get married, or, if they do choose marriage, they should recognize that they are no longer free to devote themselves fully to other careers.

   c. In choosing a role, one should ask: What contributions can I make to society? Am I prepared to accept my fair share of responsibility? How will the role I choose contribute to the welfare of others, as well as myself?

These latter, more general questions, place individual actions in a broader context, within the framework of "all things considered," instead of looking at individual actions in isolation, as if they had no bearing on anything else, or as if nothing else had any bearing on them. As we look beyond our immediate circumstances to broader spatial, temporal, and social considerations, we become, to that extent, more responsible and mature. We claimed that our most pressing moral obligations are usually more immediate, for they are determined by proximity in space, time, and social position. However, we also argued that our responsibilities extend outward to persons beyond our immediate families, friends, neighbors, or associates, to include fellow citizens, and even persons in distant lands. In special cases of need, we may also be expected to fill in for others, or to come forth when they are unable to do so, or to take charge when no one else has been assigned.

Thus, we have concluded that there are several guidelines that may be followed in determining personal responsibility:

1. Primary responsibility rests with those who have been assigned the responsibility.

   Very often such responsibility is direct and clear, as in the case of the lifeguard at the beach. At other times it may not be clear. Suppose a student suffers a heart attack in class. The teacher may have the primary responsibility to seek aid, but one of the other students may be a health care professional—say, a nurse. In this case, both the teacher and the nurse may have a responsibility to aid the other student. Given a willingness to act and cooperate, rapid communication should enable them to address the problem.

2. If responsibility is diffused (there is no clear rule or role), then each person involved is under a general moral obligation to perform simple, ordinary actions, as needed, to prevent harm, ensure justice, or protect freedom.

   This rule suggests that people are not under a general moral obligation to perform unusual or heroic actions; but, of course, it does not prohibit them. However, as the harm to be avoided becomes greater, the greater the obligation to prevent it. Let us say that an engineer knows that telling the news media the truth about an injurious company project will get her fired. She may not be obligated to tell the truth in this case if the consequences of withholding the information are not serious. However, if by telling the truth she could avoid extremely harmful consequences, she would seem obligated to tell the truth—unless, of course, those consequences could be avoided by other morally acceptable means—say, by discussing the matter with company officials.

3. When, in order to solve a problem, it becomes necessary to assign responsibility, the parties involved have a prima facie responsibility to make that assignment (by adopting a rule, say, according to moral principles).

   This rule relates to present circumstances as well as the future, , for it may be necessary to cooperate in assigning and accepting tasks in order to solve an immediate problem. When a car is stuck, the driver might say, "You push and I'll steer," and if the parties involved accept and act upon this advice, the problem may be solved. If they continue to argue about it, however, or if both refuse to push, the car may remain stuck. But often such assignment or reassignment of responsibility pertains to the future. A nurse, for example, may not be permitted to defy a doctor's orders, even when doing so would be beneficial to a patient, but the nurse may have a moral responsibility to try to change hospital or professional policies pertaining to the assignment of authority and responsibility.

So-called "whistle blowing" cases are often like this. We do not normally expect people to be heroic, risking jobs and future employment, in order to report wrongdoing by their employers, but we should expect them to try to change the policies or practices of the institutions in which they work in order to prevent harmful practices. This also means that morally responsible organizations should try to provide procedures for reporting and correcting harmful practices so that heroic measures will not be required. In a just organization, or a just society, people should be encouraged, not punished, for being socially responsible.

EXERCISES

1. Use Steps 1 through 3 presented above to help resolve the following problems:

    a. You have been offered a job that will take you to another state. The job is very good; it seems like a once-in-a-lifetime opportunity. Yet your mother is ill and depends on your care. You believe that your aunt would help, but you know that your mother would become upset if you left home.

    b. You would like to go to college to become a teacher, partly because you enjoy working with children, partly because you think a long summer vacation is good, and partly because you like the security. But you can work for your father in his insurance business without going to college. You hate the thought of being without money, and even taking a loan to pay for college. You also hate the thought of working in your father's office.

    c. You believe that you have a religious calling and that there is a need for religious vocations. You are hesitant, however, for you have doubts about your ability to do a good job.

2. Discuss the following questions:

    a. Why do roles create prima facie moral responsibilities?

    b. Can you think of roles that are sexist or racist? Suppose a role is sexist or racist; would that role create moral responsibilities? Do we have a moral obligation to change such roles? Would such a responsibility depend on the role we occupy?

    c. Discuss the ways talents can affect moral responsibility. Consider whether persons are ever justified in accepting positions for which they are not fully qualified. Consider also whether persons should accept positions for which they are overqualified. How, in turn, are these considerations related to social needs or the job market? Given these considerations, do you think people are ever obligated to accept a given role, or do you think they are always morally free to accept or reject it?

    d. Identify and discuss roles that seem to be more general, those which many people share, such as of citizenship. Try to specify some of the rights and obligations that attend these roles. Then discuss more specific roles and the duties that belong to these.

SUPPLEMENTARY READINGS

Aristotle. *Nichomachean Ethics* (many editions).

Austin, J. "A Plea for Excuses." *Proceedings of the Aristotelian Society,* 57, 1956.

Bierman, A. K. *Life and Morals.* New York: Harcourt, Brace and Jovanovich, 1980.

Bowie, Norman. *Towards a New Theory of Distributive Justice.* Amherst: University of Massachusetts Press, 1971.

Brandt, Richard B. *Ethical Theory.* Englewood Cliffs: Prentice-Hall, 1959.

Dewey, John. *Human Nature and Conduct.* New York: Holt, Rinehart and Winston, 1922.

Grisez, Germain and Shaw, Russell. *Beyond the New Morality.* Notre Dame: Notre Dame University Press, 1974.

Hare, R. M. *Freedom and Reason.* Oxford: Oxford University Press, 1963.

Lyons, David. *Forms and Limits of Utilitarianism.* Oxford: The Clarendon Press, 1965.

Mandelbaum, M. *The Phenomenology of Moral Experience.* New York: Free Press, 1955.

Nowell-Smith, P. *Ethics.* New York: Penguin Books, 1954.

Regan, Donald. *Utilitarianism and Cooperation.* Oxford: The Clarendon Press, 1980.

CASE STUDIES

In this part we examine and attempt to resolve a number of moral problems according to the system developed in Part Three. There we defended a set of moral principles we could use in judging social practices and individual acts. We also gave examples of how the principles can be applied, and we included exercises to help the reader gain practice in application. However, the examples and exercises previously considered were limited in number, and they were chosen to illustrate specific points in the text. The case studies in this section will add to the number and complexity of the examples previously studied, and they will also provide practice using the system as a whole. Instead of beginning with parts of the system and then illustrating them, we will begin with the cases and then look to the system to see how it can help us find the answers.

The case studies in the following chapters have been taken from several areas, including medical ethics and business ethics, and from personal life. Some in fact are examples of well-publicized controversial issues. Thus, in addition to improving our ability to reason in ethics, an examination of these subjects should enable the reader to gain a better understanding of the issues. Indeed, to the extent that the system enables persons to actually find answers, it may add to substantive moral knowledge as well.

The reader should gain greater familiarity with the system by using it, but it may be helpful at this point to review the system in outline so that it may be kept in mind when cases are being examined.

THE BASIC STEPS OF MORAL REASONING

The steps of moral reasoning need not always be followed in the order presented, and it is not always necessary to include all of them. Many judgments can be made by referring directly to roles in life, or to rules governing roles. There may be no occasion to consult moral principles unless role-specific duties are unclear, or if there seem to be exceptions to rules, or if the rules themselves seem questionable. Sometimes an action is not covered by a rule, in which case one may need to refer directly to the principles. Thus, the order in which the following steps are followed need not always be the same. One can always begin with principles and then consider subordinate rules and roles, or one might begin with one's intuitions about particular acts and then check those intuitions against rules and principles. One can also test the universalizability of a rule by seeing if one is willing to apply it consistently to all cases.

STEP ONE: ARE ANY MORAL PRINCIPLES VIOLATED?

The basic principles are:

1. Do no harm.

2. Do not be unfair.

3. Do not violate another's freedom.

These negative principles, we said, are the basis of our most fundamental obligations, for, even though they may have exceptions, they are applicable to all persons all of the time. The dual, correlative principles that correspond to each of these bid us to try to avoid harm and even do good, to try to prevent injustice, and to try to create opportunities. The positive principles are less definite in application, for it is not clear when or how often we should do what they say, or for whom. We said that a morally good person is always open to opportunities for doing positive good, but doing such good is not a fundamental obligation. In fact, doing good for others is often considered an act of charity, above and beyond the call of duty, unless it is a duty that attaches to one's role in life. Thus, as indicated below, positive duties are usually specified by subordinate rules governing social roles. The dual principles, therefore, may also be used to critique subordinate rules, to see if the rules of society are effective in preventing harm, fostering justice, and enhancing human freedom.

STEP TWO: ARE ANY MORAL RULES VIOLATED?

There are a number of well known and widely accepted moral rules that seem to follow directly from our principles: "Do not lie," for example, "Do not kill," or "Do not steal." "Do not break promises" or "Do not betray a friend" are other examples. These rules govern human behavior in the same way as moral principles, for they apply to all cases in a prima facie sense. There are also laws and practices, enacted by legislatures or determined by custom, which give greater detail to these rules. Criminal law, for example, will make distinctions about different types of homicide, and civil law will specify procedures for obtaining permits or licenses. Thus, one of our subordinate principles specifies that we have a prima facie obligation to obey such laws or rules.

But there are still other rules, mentioned above, that govern particular walks of life—rules governing medical practice, rules governing business practice, or rules governing family life. Thus, practically everyone has special duties that correspond to his or her social roles. Role-specific duties tend to give our dual principles determinate shape, for they specify who has positive obligations, to whom, and even under what circumstances. Thus, under Step 2, we should consider whether a person is fulfilling the duties of his or her role in life. To do so, we may need to explicate and clarify the rules that govern his or her role.

Step Three: Is This Case an Exception?

Principles and rules apply in a prima facie sense. This means that they can have exceptions, but the exceptions must be justified. The burden of proof, we said, rests on exceptions. This means that we must show that there is a good, overriding reason for allowing an exception. Exceptions may be necessary if there is a conflict between principles or rules. So one good reason for allowing an exception is that, in a given case, it is impossible to follow all the principles or rules at once. One way of testing an exception is to generalize the exception, by asking ourselves if we would allow the same sort of exception in relevantly similar cases. In this way we can test our position to see if it is just or fair.

Step Four: Are the Rules Justified?

In some cases, the problem we face in applying a rule is that we believe the rule itself is not justified, either because it is actually harmful, or because it could be improved in some way. The same question applies to laws, institutions, or practices, for it may be the case that the accepted way of doing things—even the official way—is morally wrong. Therefore, when it comes to applying rules, one can always question whether a rule under consideration is a good rule. If a rule violates moral principles, it is morally wrong, at least in a prima facie sense, although, upon inspection, there may be good reasons for allowing it as an exception.

In questioning moral rules, we said, one is reasoning on a higher level than if one were trying to justify a particular act. It is important to distinguish judging rules from judging acts because, in practice, one may be bound by a rule, even if that rule is not a good rule. That is, one may be bound by a rule until it can be changed, and it may not be possible to change a rule very easily or soon. Because changes in existing rules often involve social or political action, we may need to become concerned with how better rules can be formulated and brought into existence. Thus, Step 5 consists in asking:

Step Five: How Can the Rules Be Changed?

The answer to this question is one of applied psychology and/or social engineering. If the rules are personal rules or family rules, we may simply need to review the alternatives or enter into direct negotiation. Other changes, we said, may require political action in the form of campaigning for candidates for political office or demonstrating for a cause. Thus ethics is not only concerned with what we should do, ideally speaking, or with judging practices to be right or wrong, but also with seeing what we can do to change those practices and create a better world.

In the meantime, however, we also need to see what we can do in view of the existing rules and practices, for they provide both opportunities and constraints. While we may question and try to change the rules, therefore, we need to move back to Step 3 to see what we are justified in doing given the rules that exist. We will find that sometimes we are justified in breaking an existing rule in order to bring about a change, and that sometimes we must follow an existing rule.

XIV

STUDIES IN BIOETHICS

Bioethics literally means "life ethics," but the term is usually used to refer to ethical issues and practices in the life sciences, including medicine and biology. Directly or indirectly, our physical health is affected by these fields. It is directly affected by the quality of medical care we receive when ill—the expertise of doctors, for example, and the efficacy of medical technology. We are also indirectly affected by the standards of health care developed in these professions, and we support the health care system, by taxes and insurance, whether we use it or not.

Of course, matters of life and health are not limited to medical and scientific practices. Persons can contribute to or detract from their own health by diet and exercise, for instance, or by smoking and drinking, and they may be helped or harmed by persons other than health care professionals. Improper waste disposal contributes to the pollution of our environment, but efficient economic practices in the production and distribution of food supports our physical well-being. Although bioethics overlaps with these areas of concern, it is usually treated in a much narrower sense, and hence distinguished from environmental ethics, on the one hand, or business ethics, on the other.

On the level of individual actions, cases in bioethics tend to deal with issues involving the day-to-day decisions of health care professionals and patients and their families. The word "patient" itself connotes a social role where people place themselves in the hands of others and are acted upon, so to speak, instead of being "agents" who do things for themselves. Thus, problems of autonomy and authority arise. Who has the right to decide whether treatment should be initiated or continued? How much information are health care professionals required to give patients? When should a patient's right to confidentiality be violated? Indeed, when, if ever, is euthanasia, suicide, or abortion justified, and who has the right to decide these issues?

These matters, involving individual actions, also raise questions of policy, professional ethics, and even law. Many of the duties of doctors and nurses are determined by the rules and regulations of the medical profession, but questions may arise concerning exceptions, or about the justification of the rules and practices themselves.

FIRST CODE OF MEDICAL ETHICS
American Medical Association

Veracity, so requisite in all the relations of life, is a jewel of inestimable value in medical description and narrative, the lustre of which ought never to be tainted for a moment, by even the breath of suspicion. Physicians are peculiarly enjoined, by every consideration of honour and of conscientious regard for the health and lives of their fellow beings, not to advance any statement unsupported by positive facts, nor to hazard an opinion or hypothesis that is not the result of deliberate inquiry into all the data and bearings of which the subject is capable.

From: Proceedings of the National Medical Convention, 1846–1847.

It is important to realize that, in bioethics, as well as other areas of morality, the actual rights of people are determined by what other people—including society and the government—will allow them to do. Medical practice is a social institution, and medical practitioners are granted special rights in being licensed by the state. They have, by and large, exclusive rights to such practice, and these rights carry with them correlative obligations. Such obligations are determined partly by history, or by traditional medical practice, and the stated or implied objectives of the field, such as dedication to saving lives and the relief of suffering. When acting as professionals, practitioners are expected to subordinate their personal interests in the pursuit of these goals. But traditional practices, as well as individual actions, are always subject to review according to higher level ethical principles and according to the changing demands of place and time. We shall therefore discuss examples of such obligations in this chapter. We will begin by seeing how individual judgments may be justified by principles or rules and then proceed to examine questions of public policy or institutional practice. We shall also begin with relatively simple cases and then proceed to the more complex.

TWO BRANCHES OF BIOETHICS

Two branches of bioethics are clinical ethics and health care policy. Though there is an overlap between branches, each branch has its own special problems.

Clinical ethics deals mainly with interaction between health care professionals and patients. It assumes the existing organization of the health care delivery system, including the organization of hospitals, the type of training given physicians, levels of government support, and private health insurance. For example, in clinical ethics, a doctor may be concerned about which of her patients should receive an organ transplant, but conducting a campaign to improve the system of organ collection or distribution would take her out of the area of clinical ethics into the area of health care policy.

The ethics of health care policy is concerned with general rules and regulations governing medical practice and the organization of the health care system. In advanced nations, vast amounts of money are spent on health care, but it is not clear how much money should be spent, how a system of health care should be organized, or how the benefits of such a system should be distributed. Some of these are questions of government and politics; others involve business practices. The government, for example, spends tax dollars for social welfare and medical research, and hospitals are run as businesses. The operation of hospitals is affected by interaction with the government, drug manufacturers, and insurance companies, as well as patients. Medical practitioners are also affected by the traditional practices of hospitals and medical schools, as well as financial pressures and public needs.

CASES IN CLINICAL ETHICS

THE ROLE OF THE HEALTH CARE PROFESSIONAL

Problems in clinical ethics should be addressed by application of the principles contained in our basic and extended systems, but they also involve a consideration of the special goals of medical practice and the rules governing medical practitioners. We may assume that the main function of medical practitioners is to cure, to rehabilitate, to promote health and safety, and to comfort and relieve pain. They ought to perform in accordance with reasonable skill and care, according to the standards of the profession. They should treat people with respect, and not overcharge them or other agencies for services.

As to rules, health care professionals are expected to: (1) respect confidentiality, (2) provide medical information, (3) respect patients' preferences, and (4) provide care according to medical indications, without prejudice. The first rule helps to encourage openness in sharing information and protects the patient against harmful uses of medical knowledge. The second is intended to provide patients with the knowledge they need to make important decisions about their lives, and the third requires the practitioner to respect those decisions. The fourth specifies that health care should not be denied on the basis of race, creed, sex, or even the supposed moral character of the patient. Thus, the first is justified mainly by the harm principle, the second and third by the freedom principle, and the fourth by the justice principle.

TYPES OF ISSUES

There are mainly three types of issues in clinical ethics: problems of confidentiality, decisions regarding treatment, and questions of truthfulness. The first has to do with justifiable exceptions to the confidentiality rule; the second with whether, because of unusual conditions, a person should not be treated; and the third with whether information should be withheld. Notice that all these issues involve the presumption of rules governing standard practice on the one hand, and an awareness of possible exceptions on the other.

We shall first take up an example of the first type of case and illustrate how it can be analyzed according to our system of principles and the relevant rules. We will then discuss the types of cases that arise in health care policy. Following these discussions, we will include a number of cases for the reader to solve.

A Case of Confidentiality

A fifty-three-year-old man was brought into a hospital by an emergency medical unit. He was diagnosed as having a heart attack and treated immediately. When the doctor told him that his condition was serious and that there was a likelihood of future attacks, he told the doctor not to inform his wife. The problem is: should the doctor violate the confidentiality rule?

We said that cases can be addressed by first considering our basic set of negative principles and our extended set of correlative positive principles. We could then consider relevant social rules and practices. We are here concerned with possible exceptions to such principles or practices, and we should remember that the burden of proof is on exceptions. We may also wish to question the justification of a practice, but that would move us to a higher level more appropriately considered under questions of health care policy.

Because the basic principles are essentially negative, the doctor would not violate any of them by not informing the wife. For example, she would not be doing anything to harm the wife or to violate her freedom. However, when we consider the positive correlates, the doctor might avoid harm and even help the wife by giving her information she could use. How weighty is this consideration, given the special rule that requires confidentiality?

The doctor's special professional duty is to her patient, and to the rules of her profession. We may suppose there is no question in her mind that the confidentiality rule is a good rule. The mere supposition that somebody might benefit from breaking the rule is not by itself a good reason for breaking it. To allow exceptions on such grounds would be tantamount to having no rule at all. In the absence of unusual considerations, then, the burden of proof placed on exceptions does not seem to be met. We conclude that the physician's duty in this case is to keep the confidence, especially as the patient has insisted she do so.

Discussion

Part of the problem in this case, as in others, is that it is often difficult to know what kind of harm may be caused by either commiting or omitting the act in question. The doctor is not privy to the patient's personal life and marital affairs. After all, the man may have good reason for not wanting to inform his wife. A husband may be expected to know more about his wife and his relationship with her than the doctor does. Moreover, any obligation to inform her must fall to him in his role as her husband. It does not fall to the doctor. A doctor cannot be expected to become involved in every patient's personal problems, especially those that are not medical. Such involvement could interfere with good medical practice.

However, the doctor might have knowledge of special circumstances. She might know that the wife would be seriously harmed by not having information about her husband's health. Telling the wife might also be beneficial to the patient. But the doctor has options other than those mentioned in the description of this case. For example, she could try to persuade the patient to tell his wife, or win permission to tell her. If the patient waived his right to confidentiality, the doctor would then be permitted to release the information.

EXERCISES

Solve the following cases by applying our system. In each case, take account of the aims and practices of the profession, including the rule of confidentiality. In your answer, explain why this case is or is not an exception to the rule.

1. The circumstances in this case are similar to the one analyzed above, except the patient is diagnosed as having the AIDS virus instead of a heart condition. Would the doctor be permitted, even required, to tell the man's wife?

2. According to a certain hospital rule, nurses are required to have a physical examination every year. When conducting such an exam, a doctor discovers that a nurse has a low grade infection he is supposed to report. However, he thinks there is little chance the nurse will spread the infection. She says she will have it treated and asks him not to report her case. Should he report it?

3. A psychiatrist is asked by the police to release information about one of his patients who is suspected of murder. The police believe that information about the patient's criminal tendencies would be helpful to them in making their case. On the contrary, the doctor believes that psychiatric predictions are unreliable evidence. Should the doctor withhold the information?

DECIDING TO WITHHOLD TREATMENT

Some cases in medical ethics raise questions about whether to treat or withhold treatment. Such questions may arise when medical indications do not clearly support treatment, or when a patient does not or cannot consent to treatment. There are also questions about whether persons should be treated when they are in extreme suffering, or are severely incapacitated, or if the disease is incurable. Questions of cost and the allocation of time, space, and special equipment may also arise.

Many such cases are covered by law. Licensed hospitals are prohibited by federal law from refusing treatment to the poor, and active euthanasia is regularly judged by the courts to be unjustifiable homicide. Laws differ from state to state, but the rise in lawsuits against doctors has led to an increase in the number of procedures ordered to protect doctors against claims of malpractice. On the other hand, doctors are less likely to intervene or continue treatment against the express will of the patient than they were only a few years ago. In fact, it is not uncommon for doctors to write "do not resuscitate" or "no code" orders. Such withholding of treatment is sometimes considered to be "passive euthanasia." Special problems arise when the patients are children, say, and are unable to express themselves, or are judged to be incompetent, or when an adult patient is in a coma or unable to communicate.

We should note that the withholding of treatment does not violate our basic negative principles. That is why we can make a distinction between killing and allowing to die. But withholding treatment does appear to oppose both the goal and code of medical practice. Doctors are trained to intervene and tend to regard cases of withholding treatment as exceptions. Yet, as noted, there are other goals in medicine other than saving lives, and other rules than those requiring treatment.

EXERCISES

Try to resolve the following cases by applying our system. In each case, take account of the aims and practices of the profession. In your answer, explain why this case is or is not an exception to the rule.

1. A local dentist finds that he has many delinquent accounts and that he is also losing patients. Thus, as a matter of policy, he requires evidence of dental insurance or money up front before providing service. A young man who has been in a fight comes to his office for emergency dental work but does not have cash or insurance. Would the dentist be justified in refusing treatment? What additional information do you think might be relevant to this case?

2. A seventy-three-year-old male patient has been suffering from lung cancer and there is virtually no prospect of recovery. Other organs are functioning poorly. The doctor warns of a possible heart attack. The patient's family asks that in the event of a heart attack, the patient be allowed to die. In that event, should the doctor write a "do not resuscitate" or "no code" order?

3. A teenage female patient has been in a coma for six months as a result of brain damage caused by an automobile accident. She is being kept alive and is apparently not suffering, but the doctors believe she will never regain consciousness. The girl's parents want the doctors to withdraw artificial means of life support. Should the doctors follow the parents' decision?

4. Suppose in Case 3 that the parents wanted treatment to continue. Would this alter your judgment?

DECIDING TO WITHHOLD INFORMATION

Health care professionals, like others, are generally bound not to lie or to impede the process of discovering truth, and they have a special obligation to inform patients of their condition. Lies to patients can deprive them of useful information, undermine confidence in the therapeutic relationship, and suggest a lack of respect for patient autonomy. There is, of course, a limit to the amount of information that can be given in any particular case, but patients have a right to understand their condition and to make decisions accordingly. Thus, even the withholding of information may be wrong. However, there are cases in which either lying or withholding information seems beneficial to the patient, or when a patient may not be able to understand the implications of his or her case.

AMERICAN HOSPITAL ASSOCIATION
A Patient's Bill of Rights

The patient has the right to receive from his physician information necessary to give informed consent prior to the start of any procedure and/or treatment. Except in emergencies, such information for informed consent should include but not necessarily be limited to the specific procedure and/or treatment, the medically significant risks involved, and the probable duration of incapacitation.

From: *Hospital,* Vol 47, February 1973.

EXERCISES

Try to resolve the following cases by applying our system. In each case, take account of the aims and practices of the profession. In your answer, explain why this case is or is not an exception to the rule.

1. A ninety-five-year-old man is confined to a nursing home. He has lapses of memory and has broken his hip. In his better moments, he realizes he is recovering and wants to go home. However, the doctors believe that he is incapable of caring for himself, and that if he returns home his insurance benefits will cease paying for his care. Should they tell him the truth or invent reasons for keeping him in the institution?

2. An adult patient has an incurable disease and is expected to die within six months. However, he is expected to be able to live a normal life for much of that time. The doctors believe they should tell him he is progressing nicely, so as not to upset him during the short time he has left. They feel they can tell his wife of his condition, so she can plan their life together accordingly. Should they lie or withhold information?

3. A woman is diagnosed as having breast cancer. The doctors believe that a biopsy would confirm their diagnosis and that, if positive, they should perform a radical mastectomy immediately. The woman has

expressed doubts about the need for surgery. Should they tell her that, in their opinion, the surgery is mandated, but not make it clear that she has a choice to refuse?

CASES IN HEALTH CARE POLICY

Many important issues of health care policy tend to fall under four closely related heads: access and cost, promotion of health, allocation of resources, and organization.

Access to medical care currently depends on a number of factors: income, for example, or insurance, or ability to pay; on location, or proximity to or remoteness from medical personnel and facilities; on need, for patients may be accepted or denied access on the basis of the severity of illness—or on the likelihood of successful treatment; and on information, for people may not be aware of the extent of illness or of opportunities for medical care.

Thus, people who are too poor, who live too far away from health care centers, or who are not properly informed about needs or opportunities, are in effect denied access to the health care system. Is this fair? Should personal wealth be a factor? Should all people have access to minimal care? Variously, how high a level of care should hospitals or societies provide, and *for whom?* Such questions obviously raise questions of cost and of who should pay. Should the government pay? Should individuals pay? Who should provide insurance?

There are also questions of improving access by providing more hospitals or medical care centers, more doctors and nurses, and more and better emergency equipment. Attempts have been made to encourage doctors to practice in rural areas, for instance, where they are not as likely to earn as much money. There has also been an increase in the number of medical centers or clinics located in suburban areas. These are nearer to suburban residents than city hospitals are, but they also tend to have less adequate facilities. In the meantime, insurance companies are trying to contain costs, the government is trying to reduce deficits, and individuals resist paying more taxes.

Remember that, on the level of social rules, we should be concerned about the generalizability of our conclusions, not only whether cases are being decided in the same way according to a rule, but also whether a rule in one area is consistent with rules we have in other, similar areas. For example, many attempts to extend benefits through a tax-supported welfare system are criticized on grounds of "socialism," and socialism, in turn, is often held to be both inefficient and a limitation on individual freedom. But many existing institutions are socialistic in the sense of being tax-supported, and even regulated or run by the government. Consider the public school system, or even the government itself, including police, firefighters, and the courts. Thus, we cannot settle issues by labelling them "socialistic." We need to see if they violate principles, or whether they are indeed more or less efficient than other alternatives. When there is an apparent inconsistency in practices, exceptions need to be justified by appealing to special features of the practices themselves.

A Case of Apparent Conflict

The announced aim of a national cancer association is to wipe out cancer. It collects millions of dollars annually and devotes a large percentage of that money to cancer research aimed at finding a cure. That same agency, however, devotes little money to cancer prevention. It makes little signs that say "Please do not smoke," for example, but it does little to attack the tobacco industry or to lobby for legislation aimed at prohibiting the sale of tobacco. The president of the association argues that they do not want to interfere with free enterprise. Besides, he adds that members of the tobacco industry contribute large amounts of money for cancer research, and nobody has really proved that smoking causes cancer. Is the cancer association justified in its position?

We assume that an association dedicated to eliminating cancer should do all that it can to achieve that end, excepting the use of immoral means. There is, of course, a factual assumption about the extent to which smoking contributes to cancer, but the connection has been well documented, and health professionals are in general agreement that smoking is a major cause. It seems unreasonable to argue that a prohibition on the sale of tobacco limits free enterprise; the regulation and prohibition of other drugs, or of prostitution, has the same effect. If one supports free use in this case, then it seems one should support it in other cases as well. The same holds for the argument of throwing people out of work. However, the association could lobby for a law that would phase out tobacco production and sales, allowing time for economic adjustment. The fact that the tobacco industry is a large contributor to the association should not be a major consideration, for, in this case, it is the practical equivalent of a bribe.

A case may be made for distinguishing abuse from justified use. In the case of other drugs, we allow them for therapeutic purposes but not simply for enjoyment, and certainly not when the effects are clearly harmful. The use of tobacco might be justified if it could be shown to be therapeutic, or at least harmless in small doses. But, because tobacco is addictive, few people can control its use. Indeed, if it harmed only the individual user, one might yield to freedom of choice. However, smoking in public places can hurt other people, and caring for cancer cases caused by smoking is a burden on hospitals, insurance companies, the welfare system, and ultimately all citizens. Our conclusion is that anyone seriously interested in eliminating cancer cannot reasonably ignore a major cause. Tobacco should not be treated differently from other harmful substances, practices, or industries.

A case may be made for claiming that prohibition will not work. It does not seem to work very well in preventing the use of other drugs. Indeed, one might argue that illegal industry flourishes and that profits are larger because of prohibition. Thus, not only do we wish to protect human freedom; we need to recognize that there is a limit to what the government can do. In the final analysis, the effectiveness of public policy depends on social acceptance and individual habits. No law will work if large numbers of people choose to disobey it. There is, therefore, a need to try to raise the moral consciousness of society. However, legislation and enforcement are themselves means of consciousness raising. Consider recent laws against drunk driving, for example. It is difficult but not impossible to combat socially approved substance abuse by outlawing such abuse and by showing how harmful it can be. A national association dedicated to cancer prevention, one would suppose, should engage in such an educational effort.

EXERCISES

Try to determine whether the policies discussed below are justified by moral principles. Would the proposed policies conflict with any other generally accepted policies or practices?

1. The federal government is being pressured by a medical lobby to raise the tax on cigarettes by $1.25 per package. This tax would do two things, they argue. (1) Based on reliable findings of economists, it would discourage smoking because of the increase in price. And (2) the revenues could be used to finance educational efforts designed to curtail smoking. Because smoking is one of the main causes of early loss of life in this society, this tax would have extremely beneficial results. Some of those in Congress agree; but they claim that the economic loss to states like Virginia would be enormous. Besides, they believe that tobacco manufacturers have a good deal of political power.

2. The poor in the inner cities are burdened with a much higher than average infant mortality rate. Some "equal access" advocates argue for local support for prenatal clinics. They argue that this is more important than using equal funds to support a domed stadium in the city. The city already has a fine stadium, but infants are dying and are born deformed due to poor prenatal care.

3. It is known that during large snowstorms several people each year in a certain city die of heart attacks while shoveling snow. A city councilman proposes that the city provide the service of clearing sidewalks, as they do in one of the wealthier suburbs. He argues that this is a matter of life and death, and, therefore, as an ethical matter, must be done by the city.

4. Medical training directs an enormous amount of talent to surgery. It is claimed that this training discourages equal access to medical care because local physicians are becoming scarce in many rural areas; surgeons typically work in city and suburban hospitals. It is also argued that because of the supply of surgeons, too much unnecessary surgery is performed. The solution proposed is to have the federal government put pressure on medical schools to limit the training of surgeons.

SUPPLEMENTARY READINGS

Bayles, Michael. *Professional Ethics*. Belmont, Calif.: Wadsworth Publishing Co., 1989.

Beauchamp, T. L. & Childress, James. *Principles of Biomedical Ethics*. Oxford: Oxford University Press, 1979.

Brody, Howard. *Ethical Decisions in Medicine.* Boston: Little, Brown and Company, 1976.

Garrett, Thomas et al. *Health Care Ethics.* Englewood Cliffs, N.J.: Prentice-Hall, 1989.

Gorovitz, Samuel et al., eds. *Moral Problems in Medicine.* Englewood Cliffs, N.J.: Prentice-Hall, 1976.

Humber, James and Almeder, Robert, eds. *Biomedical Ethics and the Law.* New York: Plenum Press, 1976.

Jonson, Albert et al. *Clinical Ethics.* New York: Macmillan, 1981.

Reiser, Joel, Dyck, Arthur J., and Curran, William J., eds. *Ethics in Medicine.* Cambridge, Mass.: The MIT Press, 1977.

Veatch, Robert M. *Case Studies in Medical Ethics.* Cambridge, Mass.: Harvard University Press, 1977.

STUDIES IN BUSINESS ETHICS

T he expression "business ethics" is sometimes said to be a contradiction in terms. Business, as often conducted, appears to ignore ethical considerations altogether, and the professed object of business, as many understand it, is to make a profit in competition with and at the expense of others. But this conception of business seems rather primative, for it tends to ignore the fact that legitimate business, unlike crime, operates within a complex set of laws and social practices that defines and regulates the use of property and money, determining what constitutes a legal contract or fair exchange. The laws and practices that govern business also protect it by making it possible to exchange goods and money in an orderly way, to own property, or to make and keep a profit. Thus, business ethics, like medical ethics, or professional ethics generally, presupposes a set of customs, laws, and expectations.

Indeed, the operation of business greatly affects the economic welfare of nations, as well as of individuals and groups within nations, and, for this reason, it is a matter of foremost moral concern. Because the operation of business creates profits for owners, jobs for workers, and goods for consumers, its moral justification depends not simply on its benefit to one or another of these groups, but on the welfare of all who are affected by it. Business, like any other human activity, must ultimately be judged by moral principles, and not simply by the interests of some limited group.

However, to say that business practices are governed by special rules, customs, and laws, means that moral problems can arise in business contexts that are different from problems in other areas. It also means that the solutions to such problems, or moral judgments regarding appropriate behavior, may be different in the conduct of business than elsewhere. Consider, for example, the justification of lying in the following two cases.

1. John is asked an embarrassing question about his conduct last night in a singles bar. He figures the information is nobody's business, so, to avoid embarrassment, he tells a lie.

2. John is an auto salesman. A customer asks him an embarrassing question about the condition of the car he is trying to sell. John figures it is his business as a salesperson to make sales, so he lies about the car in order to make a sale.

In the first case, it might well be true that the person asking the question has no right to an answer, in which case John would have no obligation to give it. In the latter case, however, there is good reason to believe that the customer does have a right to an answer and that the salesperson does have an obligation to give it. That is, the role-relationship of salesperson and customer carries with it certain correlative rights and duties that may be ignored, of course, but not with moral justification. Even the law specifies that businesses are required to make certain kinds of fair disclosure. This is not to say that customers need not be cautious, for salespersons may be tempted to lie, or to hide information, even when it is immoral or illegal to do so. Both law and custom may also permit certain types of misleading advertising, such as exaggerating quality when promoting products.

GENE JAMES
(1934–   )
On Whistle Blowing

The reason most often given for the relative infrequency of whistle blowing is loyalty to the organization. I do not doubt that this is sometimes a deterrent to whistle blowing. Daniel Ellsberg, e.g., mentions it as the main obstacle he had to overcome in deciding to make the Pentagon Papers public. But by far the greatest deterrent, in my opinion, is self-interest. People are afraid that they will lose their job, be demoted, suspended, transferred, given less interesting or more demanding work, fail to obtain a bonus, salary increase, promotion, etc. This deterrent alone is sufficient to keep most people from speaking out even when they see great wrongdoing going on around them.

From: "Whistle Blowing: Its Nature and Justification." Gene James. *Philosophy in Context*, Vol. 10, 1980: 99–117.

In the above example, John the salesperson would be bound by a general obligation to tell the truth, or at least not to lie, by moral principles, and also by a special duty that attaches to his role. But salespersons, and employees generally, are often faced with moral dilemmas, not always because they themselves are tempted by immoral practices, but because employers sometimes require them to perform immoral acts in order to keep their jobs. Thus, persons selling appliances, for instance, may be required to try to sell expensive maintenance agreements with each product, even if such agreements are poor bargains for customers. Or salespersons may find that, because of the immoral practices of competitors, the only way they can make sales is by engaging in such practices themselves. It is just these kinds of pressures that make many people feel that, although ideally it would be good for businesses to be moral, "the real world is not like that!"

Business persons, therefore, may be torn between loyalty to their company and loyalty to the principles and rules of ethical business practice, for, in order to be ethical, businesses may need to sacrifice profits, just as persons may need to sacrifice individual goods. However, unlike professionals in medicine, education, or law, business people are often taught that their primary duty is to their company rather than to the clients or customers they serve. Thus, people trained in business are not as likely to be aware of ethical standards as are people trained in other professional fields, unless, perchance, they learn them elsewhere. So business, unlike medicine or law, say, is not a field in which ethical standards have been developed and taught as a matter of professional pride. Although certainly there are many ethical businesses and businesspersons, the absence of a widely accepted business ethic leaves many without the moral guidance or moral support that comes from conscious membership in and allegiance to a broader moral community.

BUSINESS–CUSTOMER RELATIONS

The problems that arise in business ethics may be catalogued in a variety of ways. Some types of problems, for instance, tend to arise in large corporations but not small businesses, or in some industries but not others. Negotiations between business managers and labor union representatives are typical of employer-employee relations in large companies but not in family stores. Pollution may be a real danger that concerns a company manufacturing or using hazardous chemicals, but not other types of companies. Instead of using these categories, however, we will classify problems in business ethics according to the relationships between persons or groups within companies, between companies, or between companies and customers, the larger community, and even international trade.

When a business sells goods to a customer, whether directly or indirectly, there is a contractual relationship in which, typically, goods are exchanged for money. Such exchanges are usually unproblematic if fair, free of deception, and voluntary, and if they are not harmful to either of the parties to the exchange or to others. An exchange raises moral issues, however, if it violates any of these conditions—if it causes harm, say, even if it is voluntary and fair.

On the basis of moral principles, one might question the justice of a profit economy, but that problem arises on a higher level, for it has to do with the justification of an economic system and not with the justification of actions within a system. The level we are now considering involves the interactions between businesses or businesspersons and customers within a capitalistic system. Such problems are likely to occur when there is a defective product or service, when a business overcharges, when deception or fraud is involved, when people are pressured or forced to buy, or when a product or service is dangerous. Let us briefly work through a couple of sample cases before presenting other cases for the reader to solve.

> Case 1:   An aircraft manufacturer under contract with the federal government produced a jet airplane with defective brakes. In redesigning the plane, company executives thought they could correct the problem without quite satisfying the more costly government specifications, so they decided to falsify the records to make it look like the specifications were met. A year later, a pilot was killed because he could not bring his plane to a stop at the end of a runway, and brake failure was thought to be the cause. The company managers denied this, pointing out that many other planes with the same brakes did not have this problem, and they complained that government standards were overdemanding.

> Case 2:   A car salesperson knows that the four-cylinder models she sells have poor pick up. They have slower acceleration than competitive models of other companies, but she reasons that all such cars are rather slow, so it doesn't really matter if she tells customers that the cars she sells are better than the competition. If her customers want a high performance car, she says, then, obviously, this is not the car for them.

These two cases are considered together because of their similarity. In both cases clients are given false information or are simply lied to by people in business. Thus, the actions in both cases appear to be morally wrong. In both cases, because of false information, there is potential if not actual harm, there is unfairness, and there is a limitation on freedom of choice. Yet there also appear to be dissimilarities. In the first case, the potential for harm seems greater because defective brakes may fail without notice, while a car's poor acceleration is not likely to escape a driver's attention for very long. In the first case, the plane manufacturer actually fails to meet the government's specifications, but, in the case of the car salesperson, there is no explicit violation of law or contract. Indeed, the salesperson may know that the car does meet the government's specifications, even though those specifications are not very high. Finally, client expectations in the two cases are likely to be different, for, in the first case, the company agreed to meet very exact standards held to be important for safety, while, in the second case, customers were asking for a salesperson's personal judgment and might well have expected exaggeration, even deception.

In general, society's specifications and expectations for airplane manufacture and performance are more demanding than for cars. Perhaps this should not be so, but because it is so, we let people in the automobile industry know that, as a society, we do not hold them to the same high standards. Some people in the auto industry may have high standards, but they are not held to such standards by their socially defined role. The moral problem then is not so much one of correcting individual salespeople as it is one of improving the industry itself by stricter legislation and enforcement. Even though, on general moral grounds, salespersons, as anyone else, should not lie, we cannot expect them, as part of their job performance, to tell people the faults of a product they are trying to sell. We should not place on individuals the whole moral weight of a defective social policy.

EXERCISES

What principle or principles, if any, are violated in the following cases? Are any of the actions discussed in these cases justifiable exceptions?

Case 1:   A prominent producer of baby food sold bottles of beverages labelled "apple juice" which contained only colored water and sugar. Although not correctly labelled, this "apple juice" was not harmful to babies, and the substitution netted the company greater profits.

Case 2:   A washing machine manufacturer uses plastic gears instead of more durable metal gears. This change reduces the life expectancy of a machine from about ten years to about eight years. Top management believes the substitution is good for the industry. The newer machines are good for the consumer because they are cheaper; they also create more work for employees and greater profits for the company. But the company keeps the life expectancy of the machine a secret; if people knew of the reduced life, they might not buy it.

Case 3:   Years ago companies producing asbestos realized that it was harmful, even deadly, for workers who produced and installed it, and even that it was an environmental hazard in buildings. Yet they reasoned that, because the government did not prohibit its manufacture or sale, they were not breaking the law. They argued that everything in life involves risk and hence that it was unnecessary for them to warn the public of possible danger.

RELATIONSHIPS WITHIN BUSINESS

There is a wide variety of problems that arise in relations between people in a business. These often have to do with the treatment of people in lower positions in the company—with working conditions, for example, pay, promotion, or even freedom of expression. But problems also arise among people on the same level, having to do with respect, smoking, sexual harassment, lack of cooperation, or inadequate performance (which shifts the workload to someone else). There are also the responsibilities of workers toward the company; these involve doing an adequate day's work for a day's pay, protecting company property and secrets, and cooperating with company leaders in promoting the company's interests.

The mistreatment of employees by exposing them to unnecessary risk, for the sake of added profit, may be immoral in a very straightforward way. But there may be complications that make judgments more difficult. As mentioned above, a firm with a competitive disadvantage may not be able to survive, and the elimination of a risk from the workplace may be a costly disadvantage. It seems unfair to ask some firms to be moral when others are not, or when the law does not require it. There are also questions about the extent of possible harm, about its likelihood, and about warnings to employees that will enable them to recognize dangers and make choices accordingly. In the asbestos example mentioned above, not only were customers kept in the dark, employees were not told of the possible harm, safeguards were not used, and compensation was not paid to workers who became ill.

Consider the following two cases:

Case 1: John runs a small factory that cleans metals. The job is dangerous, tedious, and strenuous, but John prides himself on running one of the safest metal cleaning operations in the country. Yet, in the last five years, two workers out of forty were permanently disabled. John is constantly preaching safety and reminds workers of the dangers of the job. He also worries about working conditions, but he knows that newer equipment, which will make the job less tedious and less physically demanding, would be expensive. It would also not reduce the danger significantly. Thus, he chooses not to buy new equipment in order to reduce costs and thereby keep his plant competitive. Otherwise, he believes, the plant would be forced to close and workers would lose their jobs.

Case 2: Smith knows that dangerous chemicals in his plant could be harming his employees, but full containment of those chemicals would be very costly. He is violating OSHA specifications, but OSHA has not noticed the violations, and even if he is caught, the penalties would not be serious. He wants his plant to survive and believes that costly safety equipment would put him in an unfavorable competitive position relative to Japanese imports. The chemicals are supposed to be a potential cause of death, but Smith reasons that, because he is not sure of any direct, actual harm, he is justified in having his employees take the risk. In any case, the employees are not aware of any danger and are therefore not worried about it.

Again, these two cases are similar but contain important differences. In both cases, the plant managers allow harmful conditions in order to reduce costs and keep their companies in business. In the former case, however, John does everything he can to reduce harm and to inform workers of the danger, whereas, in the second case, Smith seems to rely on their ignorance in order to carry on the company's deceptive practices. Because OSHA standards are being violated, the second case also involves a violation of law. Thus, John is trying his best to reduce harm and to give workers a choice in determining their own welfare, whereas Smith is not trying to avoid harm, for he denies workers information, preventing them from protecting themselves.

In both these cases, the seriousness and probability of harm are important considerations. It may turn out that new laws need to be enacted, or present laws need to be more strictly enforced, in order to solve these problems. There is also a consideration of justice, for society should not demand that employers make sacrifices in one case if it does not ask other employers to make the same sorts of sacrifices in similar cases. Good laws and good law enforcement would impose the cost of safety on everyone alike, and hence not make compliance a competitive disadvantage.

EXERCISES

What principle or principles, if any, are violated in the following cases? Are any of the actions discussed in these cases justifiable exceptions?

Case 1: The officers of a large bank know that huge loses in the banking industry are a result of white collar crime, that is, theft by employees. They also learn that such theft is usually committed by employees of lesser rank, such as tellers, cashiers, or loan officers, although sometimes, certainly, top executives have been known to steal large amounts of money. So they institute a policy requiring lie detector tests of applicants for lower-level jobs but not for company executives. Most job applicants will tolerate such tests, they reason, because they need the job, but they do not think that top executives would tolerate such questioning of their integrity, or such intrusion on their privacy. Although the tests are not wholly reliable, the company executives believe the tests will serve as a deterrent to crime.

Case 2: JPM Inc. has a set of standards for raises and promotions that are rather vague. It also turns out that, under those standards, women are not promoted or rewarded with raises as often as men are: women are often said to be lacking in some particular respect, according to the standards, but such failures are not often noted in men. However, the charge of favoritism is not easy to prove because the standards are cited in denying promotions or raises to women and in giving them to men. The company also keeps discussions of raises or promotions confidential, it says, so as not to embarass anyone.

Case 3: Alice, a salesperson at a department store, has developed a "profile" for detecting big spenders. She carefully watches for such people and makes sure she waits on them whenever possible. As a result, she makes more money in commissions than anyone else in her department, even though some of them make more sales. She does not tell anyone about her method, for she is able to win sales contests and keep her job while others fail to meet quotas.

Case 4: Bob is an inspector for the city. He knows that a good inspection usually takes about four hours, but he does one in less than two, gets a "bonus" from the builder for failing to notice problems, and is able to spend half his working day on personal affairs. Others, he knows, follow the same practice, so, he asks, why should he accept the same pay for more work?

BUSINESS–BUSINESS RELATIONSHIPS

Ethical problems in the relation of businesses to one another usually arise because of unfair competition, although, in some cases, it may be difficult to determine whether a practice is unfair. Companies, or their agents, can make untrue statements about other companies, steal secrets, or even influence government officials to force competitors out of business. Monopolistic practices, such as takeovers, may not be as clearly immoral or illegal. Larger firms sometimes engage in price wars to drive smaller companies out of business. The larger firms may be able to absorb their losses and then make greater profits when the smaller firms have closed. This serves to eliminate competition and raise prices.

EXERCISES

Which of the following cases involve morally unjustified business practices? In each case, explain why you think the practice is justified or unjustified.

Case 1:   In bidding for a government contract for road construction, other companies try to figure their true costs and make their bids accordingly, allowing for what they take to be a reasonable profit. However, a larger company with more experience in bidding realizes it can bid low, win the contract, and then make up the apparent loss with cost overruns; in other words, it plans to request more money later in order to finish the job. In the past, it has always been able to win such awards from the government, for the government cannot allow jobs to go unfinished.

Case 2:   A small guitar manufacturer makes a guitar that looks exactly like a famous, very expensive, Spanish guitar. He makes a number of minor changes in it that he believes will protect him legally but that are also unnoticeable. He sells his guitars without labels and creates the impression, but never actually says, that they are surplus stock from the famous maker. He charges about half the price of the more famous brands, but his guitars, if known to be copies, would be worth only about one fifth. The manufacturer of the more famous brand feels frustrated, especially as the market is small and sales have fallen by 20 percent since the imitation has appeared.

Case 3:   KEM Ltd. knows that its rival has developed a process that will allow them to produce their product more cheaply, and hence take away needed business. Therefore, KEM decides to offer a job to their competitor's project manager, in order to use her knowledge of the process. Because the high salary they offer her is contingent on her willingness to use the knowledge she has gained, the project manager points out that she previously signed a contract with the other company promising not to use such information for at least a year after leaving. However, to gain her consent, KEM Ltd. assures her that such contracts will not stand up in court.

Case 4:   A large food retailer seeks a greater share of a big city market. To accomplish this, it seeks concessions from the grocery workers union in the form of lower wages and fewer job benefits. If it fails to win the concessions, it threatens to sell its store and move to an area of the country where real estate is less expensive and labor is cheaper. Workers argue that the executives of the company have no social conscience, for the workers cannot afford a cut in wages, and relocation of the company would throw many of them out of work. Company executives argue that they can no longer compete if wages and benefits are high.

RELATIONSHIPS BETWEEN BUSINESS AND SOCIETY

In this category, we move into public policy issues. For example, to what extent should businesses be taxed or regulated by society? Currently there is a wide variety of laws regulating and taxing businesses. There are even laws that prohibit certain types of business organization, because of monopolistic practices, for example, or because of the socially undesirable nature of a product or service. Gambling, for instance, is illegal in many places, as is prostitution. Regulation of business is often meant to prevent harm, but it may also require certain types of positive contribution to society. Laws governing waste disposal are meant to prevent harm, but businesses may also be expected to beautify plants or stores, or to contribute to social welfare by forced payments to pension plans or health insurance.

TIME MAGAZINE
On the Effects of Deregulation

"What do I think of deregulation, you ask me?" muses Joe Sixpack as he takes a break from mowing the lawn. "Frankly, I love it and I hate it! Take the airlines. I can get a great bargain fare to Miami, but you can be sure my flight will be delayed for two hours because of air-traffic congestion. As for the bank, it now gives me interest on my checking account, which is nice, but then sticks me with a fee every time I drop below my minimum balance. Our family's long-distance bill has gone down, but somehow the total phone charges have gone way up."

From: "Rolling Back Regulation." Stephen Koepp. *Time*, July 6, 1987: 50.

Taxes on business are a means of distributing profits to the community. In times of emergency, such as war, the government may also intervene directly in the economy, by requiring certain types of production, or by freezing wages or prices. Certain benefits may also be granted to companies in order to encourage their expansion. The U.S. government has granted land to railroads, and cities often grant companies tax abatements. Low interest loans are available to encourage minorities and women to start new businesses.

EXERCISES

Which of the following actions are justified or unjustified? In defending your answer, appeal to moral principles and accepted social practices.

Case 1:   The federal government recently decided to deregulate the nation's airlines in order to increase competition and lower fares. But some argue that, by cutting costs, the airlines have become less responsive to passenger needs. Baggage is lost, planes are late, people are bumped for "reserved" seats. But even more importantly, the critics argue, the airlines are becoming unsafe because of less frequent maintenance and inspection and because the skies are more crowded. The number of near misses has gone up. Critics of deregulation conclude that the government has a moral responsibility to use its powers of regulation to avoid these problems. Defenders point out that rates have never been so low and that the benefits are worth the costs. Competition, they claim, will also correct the faults.

Case 2: In view of world competition, observers have noted that there are two things wrong with American industry: (1) It is not progressive or innovative enough, and (2) it involves too large a separation between managers and workers, in money and prestige, which creates conflict and hostility. Companies in some foreign countries do not seem to suffer from these flaws. They have a partnership between business and government in which the government rewards innovation, and business, in turn, shares profits with workers. Defenders of this practice argue that government support of business, on the one hand, and the sharing of profits on the other, provides greater incentive for managers and workers alike because both profit from increased production. Opponents of this practice argue against it because they say it is socialistic.

Case 3: Large manufacturers of military equipment regularly hire a large number of retired military officers who have connections at the Pentagon and use them. This not only enables the companies to win contracts with the government but tends to insulate them from penalties for overcharging and other contract violations. At the same time, government agencies intended to act as "watchdogs" of government spending have also been dismantled or underfunded. The findings of such agencies, in fact, are often ignored. Yet the Administration keeps asking for more money for national defense, while complaining that the national budget is out of hand. In the meantime, allocations for social programs such as education are being cut.

INTERNATIONAL RELATIONS

Many businesses today have offices and plants in foreign countries, and many more are engaged in commerce with foreign governments and foreign companies. Such transnational corporations can do a great deal of good, investing money in other countries, providing jobs, and improving goods, services, and skills. They can, however, also cause problems, by exploiting poor people, corrupting government officials, destroying natural resources, or diverting profits and goods. The protection of business interests is often an important consideration in making treaties between governments, or in fighting wars. Jobs, prices—even the national debt—are affected by international economic practices, involving the importation of goods from other countries and the exportation of goods to foreign markets. Some international business practices are regulated, but, generally speaking, there is relatively little control of transnational firms.

EXERCISES

Try to determine whether the actions described in the following cases are morally justified or unjustified. How do moral principles and rules bear upon your judgment?

Case 1:   American and French environmentalists are seeking national laws and international trade agreements to prevent the killing of whales. Some countries, however, more dependent on the whaling industry, argue that they cannot afford the luxury of protecting animals. They are trying to protect jobs. In rebuttal, the environmentalists note that the killing has increased and that, at the present rate, there will soon be no whales left. The solution they propose is international regulation of the number and types of whales killed.

Case 2:   An American automobile manufacturer advertises its product by telling people to "Buy American," because the sale of foreign cars, it says, is putting Americans out of work. The same firm also lobbies Congress for higher tariffs so that foreign cars will cost more. Yet most of its parts are manufactured in other countries, and some of the cars are assembled in foreign plants where labor is cheaper, even though the cars bear an American name. The company tries to keep this information secret but argues that it could not make a profit if it had to rely exclusively on higher-paid American workers.

Case 3:   A multinational firm is unhappy with the political structure of a South American country. Although still democratic, the country is controlled by an elected socialist government that wants to nationalize many of its industries. However, the firm thinks it can use its influence in the U.S. government to encourage a military coup in the South American country and create a military junta that will protect and defend private business. The executives of the firm and members of the CIA reason that it would be wrong for the U.S. to tolerate (in this hemisphere) a socialist regime hostile to capitalist interests.

SUPPLEMENTARY READINGS

Barnet, Richard and Mueller, Ronald. *Global Reach: The Power of Multinational Corporations.* New York: Simon and Schuster, 1974.

Bok, Sissela. *Moral Choice in Public and Private Life.* New York: Pantheon Books, 1978.

DeGeorge, R. T. *Business Ethics.* New York: Macmillan, 1982.

DeGeorge, Richard and Pichler, Joseph, eds. *Ethics, Free Enterprise & Public Policy.* New York: Oxford University Press, 1978.

Donaldson, Thomas. *Corporations and Morality.* Englewood Cliffs, N.J.: Prentice-Hall, 1982.

Donaldson, Thomas and Wehane, Patricia. *Ethical Issues in Business.* Englewood Cliffs, N.J.: Prentice-Hall, 1979.

Gibson, Mary. *Worker's Rights.* Totawa, N.J.: Roman and Allenhead, 1983.

Goldman, Alan. *Justice and Reverse Discrimination.* Princeton, N.J.: Princeton University Press, 1979.

Luthans, Fred et al. *Social Issues in Business.* New York: Macmillan, 1980.

Manne, Henry and Wallich, Henry. *The Modern Corporation and Social Responsibility.* Washington, D.C.: American Institute for Public Policy Research, 1972.

XVI

PERSONAL ETHICS

What is "personal" is often distinguished from what is "impersonal." To be treated "impersonally" is to be treated as if one were not a person, a mere object or thing, a statistic or a number. When a person is treated as a person, his or her individual feelings, beliefs, and welfare are respected and taken into consideration. In this sense, the personal point of view is practically equivalent to the moral point of view, for morality is founded upon a respect for persons. In morality, persons are regarded as ends in themselves and not as means only. Their subjective concerns are the concerns of morality.

The notion of "personal ethics," however, also carries with it the idea of one's own personal or individual morality, as distinct from the morality of other persons. In common use, the idea that people have their own personal ethics recognizes the fact that they do not always agree with one another, hence "my morality" means my set of beliefs on moral issues and "your morality" means your set of beliefs. We argued in Part I of this book that my moral beliefs are not true just because they are mine, nor are yours true just because they are yours. Indeed, it is just such conflicts of beliefs, between individuals or groups, that moral reasoning is meant to resolve. Such conflicts or "issues," we said, can be resolved only by reference to moral principles or rules.

Nonetheless, we have noted that there is room for individual variation or "style," even within the framework of principles and rules, depending upon a person's choice of role in life and the manner in which he or she chooses to fulfill the duties of that role. This involves self-concepts of the kinds of persons we want to be and the kinds of goals we seek to achieve. Some persons, for example, will dedicate themselves almost exclusively to doing their jobs as well as they possibly can, to the exclusion of other alternatives, while others will limit the time or energy they spend on their jobs in order to pursue other goals. For instance, in order to win a promotion, one person may spend sixty or seventy hours a week on a job that requires only forty hours of work, while another may serve only forty hours in order to have more time for family life, to pursue a hobby, or to contribute time to a charitable cause. Neither is necessarily a better or worse person, morally speaking, for one person may do more good by doing his or her job extremely well, and the other by becoming active in family or community affairs.

We sometimes distinguish our private lives from our public lives, thinking perhaps that our private lives are nobody's business. Indeed, it has become fashionable these days to speak of a right to privacy. When we speak of a private life, in this sense, we often mean the life we lead with our families and friends, as distinct from our jobs, say, or our roles as citizens. However, even our relations with family and friends are governed by moral principles and rules, even if such rules are not always as clearly defined or as strictly enforced. Marriage, for example, is a way of "going public" with what might otherwise be considered a purely private affair, and it brings with it attending legal and moral responsibilities. But even the rules of married life allow for considerable variation in lifestyle. With moral justification, both husband and wife may work outside the home, or one of them may stay at home to care for the children.

Thus, in speaking of "personal ethics," we do not mean to suggest that persons are ever exempt from moral principles or social rules. However, the rules governing our private lives—our relations with family and friends—often allow for more variation than public roles. The morality of actions is not always determined by a person's social role, or by that role alone. In such cases it is often necessary to appeal directly to moral principles.

Personal Ethics and Social Issues

As previously suggested, questions of personal ethics can become social issues, for they can become matters of widespread concern. The answers to them may also have far reaching consequences, affecting society as a whole. The abortion issue, for example, is certainly a question of personal ethics, but it is widely debated, and the manner in which persons answer it affects other people. The issue is of such concern that it has been addressed by the U.S. Supreme Court, by national and international religious organizations, by state legislatures, and by women's rights groups. The Supreme Court's recent decisions regarding abortion have affected the attitudes and practices of millions of people.

In a sense, all moral questions are questions of personal ethics in that they involve individual moral decisions. Moral questions, we said, are also concerned with the manner in which persons are affected. The decisions of doctors and business persons, for instance, are personal decisions although they may be decisions on issues which arise in medical or business settings. They are also questions about how patients, say, or clients, are affected. We said that personal ethics differs from other areas of ethics in the sense that our private lives may be distinguished from our public lives, but the boundaries are not always clear. Sex and marriage, for example, may seem like wholly private matters, but sexual practices can affect others as well as one's self. Sexual practices within a marriage can affect a person's marriage partner, children, and even relatives and friends. Sex can invade the workplace when persons working together are sexually attracted or when they use the power of their positions to gain sexual favors. For these sorts of reasons, sexual practices, including marriage, have been regulated by law, and marriage has traditionally been recognized as an institution that serves social as well as individual needs.

Questions of personal ethics are thus conjoined with social issues in this chapter to emphasize (1) that questions of individual behavior may be matters of general concern, such that some of them become social issues, and (2) that questions of individual behavior cannot be isolated from the effects of individual actions on other people. To say that a decision is one's own personal decision does not exempt it from evaluation according to moral principles and rules. One has a right to one's own decisions, so to speak, or a right to decide what one wishes, but only when all of the alternatives under consideration are morally permitted. That is, no one has a moral right to do morally wrong things. However, it is often the case that the alternatives under consideration are morally permitted, in which case a person may very well have a right to choose among them. Choices of a career, a marriage partner, a friend, a hobby, a house, a car, or a meal, are examples of actions that are usually permitted, all things being equal, although there may be circumstances that restrict such choices, or even rule them out.

A career may be ruled out on moral grounds because one lacks talent. The strain of trying to perform beyond one's capabilities may be too great, and one may not be able to serve others in even a minimally competent way. A particular marriage may be ruled out, even by persons who are sexually attracted to one another, because one or the other is married to someone else, or because of kinship or other forms of incompatibility. It may be morally wrong to buy a new car if the purchase puts excessive strains on the family budget. Past choices can also limit future choices to the extent that promises or commitments create duties and to the extent that past actions have consequences that must now be faced. Thus, marriage limits one's freedom to choose sexual partners, and people who choose to have children have a duty to raise them.

DUTIES TO SELF AND OTHERS

We have emphasized the point that people do not live in a vacuum, and hence that, by and large, our moral obligations depend on relations with others. But we do have obligations to ourselves as well—not to do ourselves harm, for example, not to treat ourselves unfairly, or not to restrict our own freedom as our moral principles dictate. We might harm ourselves by misusing drugs or intoxicating drinks, or we might be unfair to ourselves by minimizing our own worth, or we might violate our own freedom by allowing ourselves to be used by others, in an attempt, perhaps, to win their approval. In view of our correlative principles, we also have a general obligation to help ourselves, by eating or by seeking medical care, for instance; to be fair to ourselves, by allowing, say, that we cannot be perfect, and by expressing our freedom and developing our talents. Of course, the manner in which we do these things will be affected by our personal circumstances, our ability, and our style.

One reason it may be morally wrong to act in a certain way, therefore, is because it would be harmful to us, or not appropriately expressive of us as persons. Addiction to drugs, for instance, is usually regarded as an instance of self-abuse, and hence immoral, aside from any harm it may bring to others. Such abuse may not only harm a person physically, it may also greatly restrict his or her powers to act in a rational and efficient way. Such faults are more serious, however, when others are affected, as they often are. In fact, problems of personal ethics usually reveal themselves as questions of responsibility to others, according to our relationships to them, or according to the need or desirability of entering such relationships. In the former sort of case, we may question how we should behave toward a friend or relative, and, in the latter, whether we should enter into or encourage a friendship, or whether we should get married or have children. As discussed in the last section of this book, these are questions about the duties of our roles in life, or about whether we should accept such responsibilities.

Personal ethics also includes duties to others that extend beyond positions in social institutions or ongoing role-relationships, for we have obligations to others by virtue of promises made or debts unpaid, or by simply being in a position to provide a service that perhaps only we can give. Personal ethics also includes opportunities to rise above our minimal obligations by volunteering or by performing acts that are above and beyond the call of duty. Heroics aside, we have many opportunities in our personal lives to try to do good, even in small ways, by being kind, polite, or thoughtful— or simply by being more pleasant than we are normally inclined to be. We can also attend more carefully to the ways we manage our affairs so that we may become more cooperative and efficient in the things we do.

Personal ethics can include hobbies and sports, personal habits such as eating or bathing, our manner of dress or of speaking. Practically everything we do affects others in some way, but sometimes in ways that are quite minor. Indeed, because not everybody is always affected in the same way, the ways in which people will be affected cannot always be predicted. Predictability depends largely on knowledge of the habits and customs of the people involved. Much has to do with expectations or with what people regard as socially appropriate or inappropriate behavior. A person in a bathing suit may not be shocking to others at the beach, but, so dressed, that same person would probably shock people at a business meeting. Inviting somebody to dinner, or accepting such an invitation, is tantamount to a wedding engagement in some cultures but not in others. We cannot become concerned with every nuance of human behavior, but we should not be wholly indifferent to such considerations. To purposely oppose conventional practices or expectations, for no good reason, is to show disrespect for the feelings of others.

Two Cases in Personal Ethics

Case 1: Jim is overweight, has high blood cholesterol, and high blood pressure. He is not very active. One day he is asked to play on a local softball team. He would like to play, but he is somewhat afraid because he is not in good physical condition and he has been having mild chest pains. Yet he feels that, at his age, this might be his last chance to do something he really enjoys. His wife asks him not to play, reminding him of his family responsibilities and physical condition. She not only loves him but is financially dependent on him, so she asks him to see a doctor for a checkup before deciding to play. However, he reasons that it is his right to choose his own form of recreation, so he decides to play without seeing a doctor. After playing several games his chest pains disappear and he tells his wife that all of her worrying was for nothing.

Comment: In this case, one might note that there are no general, moral prohibitions against playing softball. Participation in sports, recreation, or hobbies is not excluded by the marriage contract. Nonetheless, moral principles are involved. Jim has a responsibility to care for himself. Given his physical symptoms and general physical condition, he has good reason to see a doctor before engaging in strenuous activity. He also has obligations to his wife who is dependent on him. The mere fact that he no longer has symptoms does not by itself justify his behavior, for there was and still is probability of physical harm. By continuing to play, he may also be a cause of anxiety to his family.

Case 2: Harriet wants to change jobs. She is now a secretary, but she has always wanted to be a kindergarten teacher. She has had some trouble adjusting to college and quit after two years, but now she believes she can do much better. By returning to school, she thinks she can earn a teaching degree in two more years. But her boss, who is against the move, reminds her that college is expensive, that she will lose two years of pay, and that she will probably make less money as a new teacher. Harriet's mother, with whom she lives, is also against the change. She tells her that she will need all the money she can get, and that if she marries, her family will depend on that money. She also believes that she will not like teaching as much as her current job, which she does enjoy. In effect, both her boss and her mother have suggested that she has a moral responsibility to retain her present position.

Comment: Of course, money is sometimes crucially important, but nothing in this case suggests that money alone should be the primary consideration. Harriet's opportunity to do what she has always wanted to do and to realize her potential as a person seems to far outweigh any temporary financial loss. The arguments of her mother and her boss may themselves constitute immoral acts, for they may be trying to restrict her freedom, without good reason, in their own interests. Even if they are acting in good faith, according to their own personal beliefs, they may be exerting undue pressure on her to conform to their ways. If so, they also fail to respect her wishes and aspirations, or her importance as a person.

315

EXERCISES

Which actions described in the following cases do you think are morally justified or unjustified? In determining your answer, explain how moral principles and social practices bear upon your answer.

Case 1: Frank has great enthusiasm for everything he does. In fact, he finds it hard to understand why other people do things differently. He always talks about himself, his work, and his accomplishments, but he fails to appreciate the activities or achievements of others and often criticizes them openly. In fact, he thinks he is quite clever and that he is entertaining and impressing people with his accounts of himself. As a matter of fact, he actually bores people and they avoid him, but that only makes him try harder to impress them.

Case 2: Bob, who is fifteen years old, wants to have his ear pierced so that he can wear an earring. But his mother and father are very upset at the prospect. They put a great deal of pressure on him, arguing that this will embarrass them among their friends and that he will have difficulties getting a job. They say he is morally obliged, as their son, to follow their strong wishes in this regard; if he wants to have an earring, he should wait, they say, until he is living on his own.

Case 3: Louise is an atheist. She thinks that religion is irrational and that it has caused great evil. On every possible occasion, she argues with friends, acquaintances, and relatives against their religious views. She doesn't let up easily, and she usually makes people angry.

Case 4: Winston is committed to a religion that aggressively solicits new members. When he meets people, or sees relatives or friends, he constantly tries to pursuade them to join his religion. His friends tell him to stop it. They argue that they all have strong beliefs about religion and that if they all did what he does their friendships would soon cease. As a matter of fact, one of his friends now refuses to see him.

Case 5: In Case 4, suppose that Winston only does this occasionally. Would this affect your evaluation?

Case 6: Suppose that Case 4 were about politics. Winston is now similarly committed to a minor political party and acts similarly. Would this affect your evaluation? 1

Case 7: Leslie works full time in a factory job. When not working, Leslie either eats, sleeps, or watches cable T.V. Leslie's friend claims that this blocks opportunities for growth and is thereby morally wrong.

Case 8: Mary promised her friends that she would attend their monthly club meeting on Friday night. She attends regularly and enjoys the meeting very much. Her husband normally works on Friday nights, but he says that this Friday he would like the two of them to go out to the theatre and have dinner. She is faced with a dilemma. If she doesn't attend the meeting, her friends will be disappointed, but if she refuses her husband, he will not understand. He thinks she could miss a meeting once in a while, and she thinks it would be no great inconvenience to him to postpone their evening out. However, because he becomes angry with her, she calls her friends and says that she is going to have to break her promise.

Case 9: Hank, a teacher of mathematics, always holds the better students in his class up as examples to the poorer students. In fact, he has the bright students come to the board to show the slow learners how it should be done. Sometimes, in fact, he actually humiliates students who can't do the work. When parents complain, he tells them that he has been teaching for twenty years and knows what he is doing. Besides, he says, that's his style. He's doing his job as well as he knows how, and if the poor students can't learn the material, that's not his fault.

Case 10: Maria is a highly accomplished figure skater. She practices six hours a day before and after school, and she often travels to tournaments on weekends. She believes she can be a national champion and hopes to make the Olympic team. But she worries because her grades in school are not as high as they could be and she hopes to be accepted in medical school. Her parents also make great sacrifices in time and money, and they have in fact taken a second mortgage on their house to pay her expenses. But Maria reasons that she has the talent and that this is a once in a lifetime opportunity.

Sexual Ethics

Various topics can be included under the heading of sexual ethics. For example, there is the question: when is sexual intercourse morally permitted? Or, is sexual intercourse the only form of "normal" sex, or are other forms of sex, such as homosexuality, sexual perversions? Indeed, are so-called perverted or abnormal sexual acts morally wrong? Related to sexual ethics are questions about the morality of pornography and even women's rights. The abortion issue may also be included in sexual ethics, because children are normally conceived by sexual intercourse, and attitudes toward having and rearing children can greatly affect sexual practices.

Sex and Marriage

In sexual ethics, as in any other topic in ethics, it is necessary to keep in mind moral principles and rules. Every society has taboos regarding sex, but it would be wrong to simply accept or reject social practices for no good reason. Some such practices may be irrational or superstitious, but others may be founded on good reasons. Therefore, as in any subject, it is important to consider reasons for supporting or rejecting sexual practices.

Traditionally sexual practices have been regulated by marriage, although, certainly, sexual activity has taken place outside marriage, with or without social approval. Almost every society tries to regulate sex by upholding the institution of marriage, even though marital customs vary somewhat from one society to another. Various forms of sexual activity, such as masturbation

317

or even premarital intercourse, may be tolerated outside of marriage, but marriage itself is usually celebrated and protected. Marriage is in fact usually idealized and encouraged, whereas extramarital sex tends to be discouraged, or to be looked down upon as being immature or irresponsible. And, just as sexual intercourse has been supposed to find its proper place in marriage, it has also been taken to be the paradigm of normal sexual activity. Sex acts other than intercourse were generally held to be abnormal.

The reasons for these traditional attitudes toward sex and marriage are not difficult to find. According to the traditional view, one of the primary purposes of marriage is to provide for the procreation and rearing of children. Because, biologically, a normal result of sexual intercourse is pregnancy, sex has naturally been linked with procreation; and because children need care in order to survive and develop as persons, biological parents have been expected to fill this role. A continuing and lasting relationship between the caretakers has also seemed important to this purpose, because it takes so long for human offspring to mature.

A stable family structure was also the basis of tribes or clans, the primary form of social organization. Just as it has always seemed unrealistic to suppose that persons other than parents and relatives would provide child care, it also seemed important for married people to help one another, and to receive support from relatives. Thus, marriage has also been supposed to benefit the parties to a marriage, by providing a lasting sexual relationship, of course, but also by providing mutual care and support in meeting the challenges of life. Because this kind of security depends largely on trust and loyalty, these have been upheld as important family virtues.

As an argument for fidelity and against promiscuity, one can always cite the threat of venereal disease. Other physical dangers associated with so-called "casual" sex are those likely to be caused by jealousy or unrequited love, for people are frequently beaten and even killed for such reasons. These kinds of actions, in turn, point up the powerful psychological aspects of sex, for the desire for sex and love is a basic human drive. Ideally, these desires for love and romance were supposed to be satisfied in marriage, for the ideal of romantic love was thought to be both eternal and exclusive. Thus, the commitment between lovers was also supposed to be total, as expressed in the traditional marriage vows.

NORMAN L. GEISLER
On the Power of Sex

Of course, sex is not only a power to procreate; it is also a power for pleasure. But whatever kind of power sex is, it needs to be controlled. No passion should go unbridled. Rape and sadistic sexual crimes cannot be justified on the mere grounds that they bring pleasure to the abuser.

From: "The Christian and Sex." Norman L. Geisler. *Ethics: Alternatives and Issues.* Grand Rapids: Zondervan Publishing House, 1970.

But, of course, actual marriages did not always measure up to the ideal, and some people have come to believe that they never do. In fact, today, some aspects of traditional forms of marriage are looked upon as not only unrealistic but oppressive. People still seem to want love, but many do not think it can be guaranteed for life, and others do not seem to even want lifelong commitments. At least the idea of easy divorce has become widely accepted as a means of escaping unhappy marriages. Drunkenness, drug addiction, spouse-beating and child-beating, and even rape and incest within the home, have pointed up the fact that the dangers of sex are not automatically excluded from marriage or family life. Indeed, marriage has been, to some extent, a means of preserving male dominance in our society and legalizing tyranny over women and children.

The nature of marriage and family life has also changed somewhat over the years because they have been affected by other social conditions. As the economy has changed from being basically agrarian to industrial, and the vast majority of people live and work in cities, married couples are usually separated from one another during the day. When they meet in the evening they often have quite different expectations. They also enter marriage with little preparation and unrealistic beliefs. Most people seem to want children, but children have become an economic liability and a restriction on the freedom of parents. Because of economic and social mobility, the backgrounds of married couples are often significantly different, and family ties are difficult to sustain. Indeed, most young people seem to want to break free of traditions and family obligations, but they may be torn between their desire for freedom on the one hand and security on the other.

Thus, today, we find that sexual attitudes reflect a conflict in moral principles, a conflict between a desire for greater freedom and a desire for love and security. There is also a widespread movement in society for greater justice in sexual affairs, in the laws governing marriage, and in the enforcement of laws against rape, for example, or child abuse. However, many widely accepted sexual attitudes also seem antithetical to a fair and just society. The media, for example, celebrate male dominance and female submission by featuring sexual violence and sado-masochistic relations. Thus, our society seems to teach on the one hand what it condemns on the other.

There are then many good things to be said about both traditional practices and modern reforms, but both have also produced large numbers of casualties. While tyranny was often tolerated in traditional marriages and family life, more liberal attitudes toward sex and divorce have also produced loneliness, rejection, and even poverty, not only for unmarried or divorced adults but for children as well. These problems may be blamed on traditional or modern ways, but, in both cases, they often reveal personal immorality and failure as a society to teach moral principles. Just as people in the past have been hypocritical in hiding the faults of the traditional family, people today may be hypocritical in pretending that casual sex is simply innocent fun. In neither case, however, should we confuse actual practices with ideals, or the proper use of sex with its abuse. The proper use of sex is sex in accordance with moral principles and justified rules governing sexual acts, and the improper use of sex is sex that violates such principles or rules. The solution to bad marriages is better marriages—not the abolition of marriage—just as the solution to bad sexual relations is good sexual relations, not the abandonment or prohibition of sex.

APPLYING PRINCIPLES AND RULES TO SEX

Some sexual practices are so obviously wrong that they require little discussion or analysis. Rape, for example, is wrong because it causes harm, because it violates freedom, and because it is unfair. In a word, it violates all of the principles. The immorality of other sex acts may not be quite so obvious because, perhaps, only one principle is violated. Many people feel that sexual contact requires informed consent, and this is in keeping with our freedom principle, but it is possible that consenting persons may harm themselves or others, or that their actions are unfair. A person who commits adultery, for example, may be unfair to a husband or wife, for he or she may be bound by marriage vows and rules that govern married life. According to social practice, promises create duties, and the rules governing marriage are binding on married couples.

Even dating and courtship are governed by social practices. It would be wrong to make a date, for example, and then break it at the last minute for no good reason, or not show up because one has made another date in the meantime. To keep a date is to keep an appointment, and not taking appointments seriously is tantamount to lying. In the case of dating, one can certainly disappoint another's expectations. To pretend to love someone is a form of deception, and it is unfair for a mature person to take advantage of a person who is naive.

Thus, in sexual relations, as elsewhere, we need to consider whether moral principles are violated and whether the acts in question are covered by social rules. On a higher level, we may also want to consider whether the rules themselves are justified. Concerning so-called "perverted" acts, for example, we should want to know if anyone is being harmed, whether the relationship is unfair to anyone, and whether anyone's freedom is being violated. In the case of consenting adults no principles may be violated, but when children are seduced some of them certainly are.

In considering exceptions to principles or rules, we need to consider viable alternatives. Many problems that arise in sexual affairs are created by immoral behavior, and hence might be avoided by correcting that behavior. Teenage pregnancy, for example, is recognized as an important social issue, but it seems possible to reduce teenage pregnancies by discouraging sexual intercourse among very young people. Abortions are sometimes also regarded as a solution to the problem of unwanted pregnancies, but there are alternatives to abortion as well. There are effective methods of birth control, and there is the possibility of putting children up for adoption, especially as so many people desperately want babies.

Of course, today's teenagers grow up in a society that not only tolerates but encourages sex before marriage. There are peer pressures to engage in sexual intercourse, and individuals themselves usually have strong romantic or sexual desires. Without social support—and sometimes even parental guidance—it is difficult for young people to resist such pressures and delay sexual gratification. From their point of view, they may simply be doing "the done thing." Therefore, to a large extent, the individuals involved may be innocent victims of immoral social practices. Given the likely consequences of encourag-

ing promiscuity—including pregnancy—which are known to practically everyone, it seems morally insensitive to encourage unbridled sexual expression.

Two Cases

The following two cases may illustrate how, in matters of personal ethics,
accepted social practices may conflict with moral principles. In the first case,
what is condoned by a widely accepted practice seems opposed to moral
principles, and, in the second case, what is condemned by social practice
seems in accord with principles.

Case 1:   Bob knows that Joan is emotionally involved with him. She considers
him the love of her life and wants to marry him. Bob does not share these
feelings, but because he enjoys sex with Joan, he does not discourage her
romantic ideas. In fact, he does not intend to date her much longer because
he feels she is becoming too serious. He knows she will be hurt, but he
says to his friends, "All is fair in love and war."

Comment: Deceiving other people in order to win sexual favors seems to
be a commonly accepted practice, but it is deception, and great harm can
be caused by it. Sexual exploitation of this seemingly innocent sort, as in
more obvious examples, shows a disrespect for other persons and their
feelings and welfare. This is not to say that persons can always become
disengaged without harming or being harmed, and it is true that some people
do not know how to take "no" for an answer. In those cases it may be the
rejected person who is at fault for not respecting the other person's freedom
of choice.

Case 2:   Jim and Harold are homosexuals. They love each other and live
together as roommates. As far as anyone knows, they are not harming
themselves or anyone else in any way. They are both adults and both consent
to the relationship. They simply ask to be treated fairly by being left alone.
Their parents disown them, however, because they are thought to be a
scandal to the family, and neighbors and co-workers discriminate against
them, thinking they are "abnormal." In fact, because of harassment, they
are forced to leave their jobs and move.

Comment: Discrimination against homosexuals is widespread, but, in
justice, they should be judged by the same standards as anyone else. As
described, the actions of Jim and Harold do not seem to violate any moral
principles. By violating a commonly accepted practice, however, they
disappoint and embarass their parents, and they irritate neighbors and co-
workers. Should this latter consideration be overriding? It could be, depending
on the consequences, not only to others, but to Jim and Harold as well. In
a very bigoted environment, it might be impossible for them to live together
openly as homosexuals. However, in today's world, it seems that prejudice
against homosexuality should not be accepted as a sufficient reason for
prohibiting homosexual relations. Indeed, in the light of moral principles,
it seems that people should try to overcome their prejudices against
homosexuals and try to modify traditional beliefs.

EXERCISES

Which actions described in the following cases do you think are morally justified or unjustified? In determining your answer, explain how moral principles and social practices bear upon your answer.

Case 1:   Bob and Alice have decided to live together without getting married. Their families disapprove, but they argue that, because they are both over twenty-one, they have a right to decide such matters for themselves. They do not want a marriage contract, they say, for they want to stay together only as long as they love one another and not because they are obligated to do so.

Case 2:   John and Mary are high school students who plan to marry after graduation. Mary wants to sleep with John, but John argues that they should wait until they are married; he believes that premarital sex is wrong. Mary thinks that sex itself is healthy and innocent and that it would be good for them to find out if they are sexually compatible before marrying. John, in turn, thinks that sexual compatibility is a matter of working at it, and that people who accept extramarital sex cannot be trusted as marriage partners.

Case 3:   Sue is quite lonely. She uses frequent sex with many partners as a way to feel wanted, but that feeling lasts only a short time. As a result, she is becoming more and more depressed. She also worries about contracting a sexually transmitted disease, but, nonetheless, she feels that her actions are not morally wrong. After all, she reasons, she is not harming anyone else.

Case 4:   Lee, a hard-working college student, looks at sexually explicit magazines and masturbates several times a week. He claims that this relieves tension, is healthy, and harms no one.

Case 5:   Butch has engaged in homosexual practices and prefers these to heterosexual acts. However, he is afraid of discovery and social rejection. Therefore, he thinks he ought to "go straight" in order to avoid being labelled "gay." His homosexual friends claim he is a coward for "not coming out of the closet."

Case 6:   Faith, sixteen, feels pressured into having sex. However, her religion and parental teaching prohibit sex before marriage, so she constantly feels guilty about her behavior. Her friends tell her that her feelings of guilt are irrational and that liberated women today should not worry about such things.

Case 7:   Amartya was recently divorced after eighteen years of marriage. After dating for six months, she believes it is morally permissible to have sex. Her children, however, are horrified even by the thought of her dating, for they would like to see their parents united again. Their father, however, has always cheated on his wife and this was the cause of their divorce.

Case 8:   Arnold and Beth are involved in an ongoing sexual relationship, but they sometimes have sex with other partners as well. In their love for each other, they say, they allow each other the freedom to do what they like. Both refuse to use contraceptives. They argue that abortion can always solve the problem of pregnancy and that sexually transmitted disease is just a risk they have to take, like the risk of driving a car.

Case 9:   Harold is a divorced man of forty-five who supervises a sales office that employs many single women. He frequently flirts with them and sometimes even tells dirty jokes. Some of the women complain, however, that he is too familiar with them. They also hesitate to criticize his behavior because he is their boss. When his personal secretary brings this matter to his attention, he tells her to mind her own business. He's just trying to have a little fun, he says, and if they can't take a joke they should quit. Besides, he adds, where is he supposed to find women to date if not on the job.

Case 10:   Betty is having a hard time with Tom. She loves him but he is not very reliable. He often breaks dates and fails to show up on time. He also plays around with other women, and when she challenges him about this he becomes angry and sometimes beats her. Nonetheless, she wants to marry him because she thinks she can't live without him. Her friends tell her she is crazy, but she hopes that marriage will change him. Besides, she says, that's what love is all about.

THE ABORTION ISSUE

It would be impossible to cover the abortion issue in this short space, and it is certainly not easy to settle all of the issues. We may point out, here at the beginning, that, until the Supreme Court decision in the case of Roe vs. Wade, the public attitude, including the law and religious teaching, was generally anti-abortion. After that decision, there was soon widespread public acceptance, although, certainly, a large number of people today still oppose abortion. In fact, public debate and demonstration has become quite heated, and there seems to be little chance of reconciliation between the so-called "pro-life" and "pro-choice" groups. Many people in the pro-life group seem to think that abortions are always wrong, and many people in the pro-choice group seem to think that abortions are always permitted. The former tend to believe that abortion is outright murder, and the latter seem to believe that a fetus has no rights whatsoever.

JAMES P. STERBA
Generalizing Arguments on Abortion

Those who favor a liberal view on abortion and thus tend to support abortion on demand are just as likely to support the rights of distant peoples to basic economic assistance and the rights of future generations to a fair share of the world's resources. Yet, as I shall argue, many of the arguments offered in support of abortion on demand by those who favor a liberal view of abortion are actually inconsistent with a workable defense of these other social goals.

From: "Abortion, Distant Peoples, and Future Generations." James P. Sterba. *The Journal of Philosophy*, vol. LXXVII, no. 7, 424–440.

However, we have argued with respect to other types of acts that they are sometimes permitted and sometimes prohibited, depending on a number of conditions. Even if abortion is killing, and also the killing of a person, it may sometimes be permitted, for the killing of a person is sometimes permitted in other types of cases, as in self-defense, for example, or even in some cases of euthanasia. On the other hand, even if abortion can be justified in some cases, it is unlikely that it will be justified in all cases—when, for example, the fetus is in the latter stages of pregnancy and well developed, and there is no additional compelling reason for an abortion.

These appear to be fairly obvious cases of exceptions on either side, but, of course, there are more difficult cases in between, and it is difficult to determine for all cases just where to draw the line. Recent decisions of the Supreme Court have upheld a woman's right to abortion during the first term of pregnancy, but they allow restrictions on abortions performed during the second and third trimesters. These decisions have taken into account traditionally accepted practices according to which "quickening," the time when a mother begins to experience fetal life in her body, was thought to be the time beyond which abortions should not be performed except for very serious reasons. However, "viability" seems to have gained widespread acceptance as a more precise point of distinction, the point at which a fetus is capable of surviving outside the womb. But even the time of viability cannot be permanently fixed, since improvements in medical technology will continue to make it possible for infants to survive at earlier and earlier stages of development.

The answers in the abortion issue are often thought to depend on whether the fetus is or is not a person, but there appears to be no decisive way of answering this question. Many people believe the fetus has a soul at the time of conception and hence is a person with a right to life. Other people, of course, do not think that anyone has a soul and hence that rights, or personhood, must be determined using some other basis. But there are no universally accepted criteria for distinguishing persons from nonpersons, and the criteria actually used tend to shift from one context to another.

Even though there are no universal standards for determining personhood, some writers have argued that we should at least be consistent in applying whatever standards we use. They have argued, for example, that if we have a social policy which recognizes premature babies to be persons, requiring even that heroic measures be taken to save them, we should also recognize that fetuses at the same stages of development are persons who have a right to live. Although pro-choice advocates often distinguish between fetuses that are not wanted and premature babies that are wanted, the wanted/not wanted distinction is irrelevant to whether or not a fetus is a person. If being wanted by others did determine either personhood or the right to live, then, in consistency, all unwanted people should cease to be considered persons or cease to have rights.

Likewise, if we suppose that a fetus is not a person, and hence can be killed with moral justification—because a fetus does not have one or another characteristic of normal adult persons—then should we allow that others, already born, who also lack that characteristic, may also be killed? For example, are we justified in killing the severely retarded on the ground that they are not persons? It has also been argued that because we have obligations to future generations of people not yet born, by caring for the world's environment, for instance, we must also have obligations to those already conceived but not yet born. These kinds of arguments are meant to place a strain on any list of characteristics that may be said to determine personhood, for if they prove anything, they may prove too much. That is, they may also justify infanticide or the killing of disabled or unwanted people.

There is also the question of burden of proof. When in doubt, where does the burden of proof lie? Well, one may argue that if there is no clear obligation not to do something, then one is morally permitted to do it. However, in cases other than abortion where there is a serious question as to whether a person will be killed or even seriously harmed, we often feel that we should not take the risk. If one were about to shoot a gun at a target and then saw or heard what seemed to be a person behind the target, it seems that one would not be justified in shooting unless certain that no one was there. By analogy, the burden of proof would then rest on those who want to justify abortion to show that the fetus is not a person or to show that there are overriding reasons for taking the risk.

The pro-choice group sometimes argues that a woman has a right to her own body, and hence a right to abortion. There are considerations in favor of this position, for, in principle, persons are prohibited from harming one another and are justified in defending themselves. In this sense, they have a right to their own bodies or lives. It is also important to recognize that pregnant women must bear the burdens of pregnancy, and, in our culture, it is women primarily who must bear the burden of raising children. Pregnancy and motherhood can be serious limitations on a person's ability to pursue other goals in life.

However, in the first place, a fetus is not part of a woman's body in the same sense that her bodily parts are—say her arms or legs. In the second place, persons do not have a general right to destroy parts of their own bodies, for they would then be harming themselves. Anti-abortionists also point out that pro-choice arguments such as this take into consideration only the rights of the pregnant woman: they fail to take into account any rights the fetus may have. Inconvenience, even hardship, do not necessarily relieve persons of moral responsibility, for persons are often required to make sacrifices in order to do the morally right thing.

Finally, however, we should point out again that there may be a real difference between moral and legal justification. Even if an abortion is morally wrong, there may be good reasons for not making it illegal. For example, it may be next to impossible to enforce such a law—or to enforce it equitably. That is, people may continue to choose illegal abortions in any case, and the poor may turn out to be penalized more than the rich. Pro-choice advocates argue that poor women would return to "back alley" abortions while the rich would find doctors willing to perform illegal abortions for a high enough price. In any case, it would be difficult to subject pregnant women to any judicial process for the sake of distinguishing justified from unjustified abortions, for such a process is likely to be too slow to allow a decision to be rendered in time. Because the law currently distinguishes only between early and later stages of pregnancy, it must rely largely on medical staff to make that determination. Enforcement, therefore, is likely to focus on practitioners rather than on clients. The vast majority of people also seem to accept abortion, at least in some cases, and it would be difficult to win support for laws that prohibit abortions in all cases.

Which actions described in the following cases do you think are morally justified or unjustified? In determining your answer, explain how moral principles and social practices bear upon your answer.

Case 1:   Francine is a young career woman who became accidentally pregnant. Her boyfriend insists that she have an abortion. He reasons that having a baby would interrupt her career and his, greatly complicating their relationship. Her married sister, who has been unable to have children, volunteers to adopt and raise the baby; in fact, she begs Francine to let her have it. Francine is very emotional about facing pregnancy and feels that, once the baby is born, she would find it difficult to give it up. She reasons that, after all, it is her life and body anyway, so she decides to have the abortion.

Case 2:   Virginia and Fred, who have been trying to have a baby for years, were pleased by the news of Virginia's pregnancy. However, tests revealed that the fetus was deformed and would be born with incurable defects. They were told that the baby might be kept alive for a short time after birth but that this would require several operations and almost constant hospitalization. Although the decision was painful, they decided to have an abortion during the first trimester.

Case 3:   Helen, a fifteen-year-old girl, discovered she was pregnant. When her parents and relatives discovered this, they insisted she have an abortion. They said she would be foolish to give up her life to raising a baby, and they said that they certainly would not raise it for her. Instead, they insisted, she should plan to go to college and have fun. Helen herself was inclined to have the baby, but she consented to having an abortion in order to make everyone happy.

Case 4:   Dorothy's mother advised her to "save herself for marriage," because, if she engaged in premarital sex, she might become pregnant. Dorothy told her mother she was old fashioned because there are effective means of birth control and that, if birth control fails, she can always have an abortion. Several of her friends have had an abortion, she pointed out, and there's nothing to it.

Case 5:   Joan and Sam believe that abortion is murder. They cannot stand knowing that so many abortions are performed each day in their neighborhood. They decide to burn down the abortion clinic. They have planned this for several weeks and believe that they can do it without being caught. They believe no one will be hurt because the building is not occupied at night and is not close to other buildings.

Case 6:   After burning down the clinic, Joan and Sam feel depressed. The clinic reopened five days later in a new location, and when it was closed other clinics in the city performed more abortions than usual. A firefighter was also seriously injured in the blaze. He will probably be disabled for life. Joan and Sam now believe that their action was morally wrong. They have decided to organize politically and seek a constitutional amendment against abortions.

Case 7:   Roger believes that much social misery is caused by unwanted children and that many people have children they are poorly suited to raise. He believes that he has studied the problem carefully and that the best way around the problem is to encourage abortions. He believes that high schools should teach about abortions, explain how to get them, and that the government should set up a large number of abortion clinics. When told about the effort on the part of some people to foster a constitutional amendment against abortion, he argues that they have no right to force their morality on others.

Case 8:   Dr. Chin wants to use aborted fetuses in experiments relating to Alzheimer's disease. Some people on the hospital's board of ethics are concerned that such use of a fetus will lead people to have abortions in order to sell fetuses to researchers. This, they argue, is clearly immoral. Dr. Chin responds by claiming that abortions happen frequently, with or without the research. The disease, he adds, is so terrible that any improvement would compensate for the potential harm of using aborted fetuses. The ethics board decides to prohibit the experiments.

Case 9:   Practitioners in an abortion clinic are pro-choice advocates who believe that there should be no restrictions on abortions. However, they know that the law requires them to conduct tests to determine the stage of fetal development. They conduct the tests but generally ignore the results. Why should a woman be denied an abortion, they argue, simply because she discovers her pregnancy too late, or because she failed to make her decision on time. Besides, they note, the law is not strictly enforced in any case.

Case 10:   Senator Fencerider is against abortion but also wants to win the pro-choice vote. Thus, in his speeches, he admits that he, personally, is anti-abortion, but he also claims that women have a right to choose for themselves. In a freedom-loving country such as this, he says, everyone is entitled to his or her own views, and he would not want to impose his beliefs on anyone else.

FAMILY RELATIONSHIPS

There are many obligations involved in being a family member. Children and parents have duties to one another, as do husbands and wifes. Children are supposed to be obedient to their parents, for example, and married couples are supposed to be faithful to one another. Parents are also supposed to care for their children, and couples are supposed to help one another. Thus, family members may fail in their duties by not being helpful to other members, or by not consulting them in making decisions, or by not being considerate of their feelings.

The family is often said to be the most fundamental social unit. The larger community depends on the family for rearing and, to a large extent, educating its future citizens. It is in the family primarily that people receive their moral educations, although religious organizations, schools, and peers also play an important part. Thus, interaction among family members provides a training ground for moral life. While some of the responsibilities of family members are fairly well defined by their roles in the family, not all questions of family responsibility can be answered by appealing to the roles of father, mother, or child. Relations with the outside community must also be considered, and it is often necessary to appeal directly to moral principles.

Two Cases of Ethics in Family Life

Case 1: Andy works as a postal clerk. He finds his job tiring. His wife, Jenny, sells shoes in a local department store. Her job is part-time, but she works nearly thirty-three hours per week, mainly nights and weekends. They have two children, nine and six. Andy sits with the children while Jenny is working. But he does not help with any of the day-to-day jobs around the house, takes a minor part in raising the children, and is often out with his friends, usually playing ball. He claims that housework is not for men, and that, after all, he repairs the plumbing and takes the car to the garage when it needs to be fixed. Jenny believes that Andy is taking advantage of her but feels there is little she can do about it.

Comment: Andy is being unfair. At work, Jenny puts in nearly as many hours as Andy, but Andy does little at home. His actions violate moral principles, and they also oppose contemporary attitudes about the roles of husbands and wives when both work. It is not clear what Jenny should do about this, but she might begin by telling Andy that he is being unfair.

Case 2: Beth and Brian have almost complete control over their children. Angela, their oldest daughter, eighteen, is not allowed to date or to see boys. She wants to date very much and has been asked out frequently. She obeys her parents because she has been taught that this is her moral responsibility. She tries to avoid talking to boys. Her friends make fun of her and she is upset about not having dates. But she believes that her parents are right. They have more experience than she, and she knows that some of her friends have been hurt by boys or have gotten into trouble by dating. But she hopes that in several years she will be allowed to date.

Comment: Being a parent is difficult. It is hard to know how much control of a child is too much. Too little control or too much control may result in harm. Conventional practice may be too strict or too lax. But in this case it appears that Beth and Brian have gone too far. Dating before eighteen is a well-entrenched practice. Refusing to allow their daughter to date deprives her of opportunity and freedom. It may result in harm. The control they have over their daughter also appears to be extreme.

EXERCISES

Which actions described in the following cases do you think are morally justified or unjustified? In determining your answer, explain how moral principles and social practices bear upon your answer.

Case 1: Ted frequently goes hunting and fishing. He stays away from home sometimes for entire weekends and, on special occasions, for a week at a time. He never takes his wife and children with him, but he asked his wife to come along on one or two occasions and she refused. She in turn complains of his being gone and of spending the family money, but he claims he has earned the money and that, as a man, it is his right to do what he wants. If she doesn't like it, he says, let her try to find someone else.

Case 2: Bev's father died recently, and her mother is lonely and wants to live with Bev and her family. But Bev is afraid that if her mother moves in it will disrupt her family life. Her husband and mother do not get along very well and her mother is critical of the children. Bev feels guilty and thinks her mother should move into her house, even though her mother is healthy and financially independent. Bev's husband argues that her guilt is unjustified; it would be better for everyone, he says, if her mother lived alone.

Case 3: Steve and Nora regarded themselves as swingers when they were first married, so they both agreed they would "sleep around" even after marriage. This they thought would even strengthen their marriage, for they would then not have to worry about giving up other sexual affairs. However, they found that they became jealous of one another and frequently argued about it. Nora thought that, to save their marriage, they should give up their original pact, but Steve argued that they should stick to their original agreement, for it would be unfair to expect him to change. Unable to settle their dispute, Steve secretly continued to play around.

Case 4: Nancy is divorced and has two children, ages fourteen and eight. She has to work at the beauty shop in order to support them, so her older daughter, Clare, has to take care of her younger daughter, Sue, after school. Clare also has to cook the meals and clean the house before her mother comes home. Clare complains that she can never spend time with her friends after school or engage in extracurricular activities. "You must do your share," Nancy tells her, but Clare argues that Sue can take care of herself till Nancy gets home.

Case 5: Sally is a junior in high school and wants to go to college. But her dad says they can't afford it; he and Sally's mother have waited all these years so they could do all the things they were unable to do when Sally was growing up. If they give her money for school, he says, they'll be stuck for another four years. Being a girl, he feels, she will only get married and waste her education anyway. If she wants college so badly, she can borrow the money and then pay it back when she gets a job.

Case 6: Frank lived with his parents when he started working after high school, and he still lives with them now, five years later. His parents desperately want him to move out, because he eats their food, uses their car, and never cleans up after himself. He argues that he doesn't make enough money to pay for his own apartment and that he would be unhappy if he had to rent a small room or take a bus. His father wants to throw him out, but his mother thinks it would be immoral to put him out on the street. Frank, in turn, thinks it is their duty as parents to give him a place to live.

Case 7:   Diane has children in school, finally, after years of caring for them at home. Because she is college educated, she thinks she should now pursue a career, but this means that she and her husband must hire a sitter to watch the children after school. Her husband argues that Diane should stay at home, or only work part time so that she can be at home for the children after school. He also says that you can never be sure a baby sitter is reliable. But Diane decides to take a full-time job anyway. She tells her husband that he can stay home and babysit if he can't find anyone else.

Case 8:   Herman drinks and swears around the house. He also criticizes his wife openly and often remarks about the beauty of other women. In restaurants, when he flirts with the waitresses, his wife becomes embarrassed. She tells him that, even if he can't respect her, he should at least be a good example for the children. But he argues that he loves his children, provides for them, and sends them to good schools. Besides, he is only acting like a man, and it is the job of the church and schools to provide moral education.

Case 9:   Betty is a divorced woman who lives with her two children, eight and thirteen. She sometimes has men friends over for dinner and drinks and even spends the night with them in her house. She wants to set a good example for her children, but she also does not want to be deprived of sexual relationships. She and her friends could go to motels, but she thinks that is beneath her dignity. In any case, being a mature woman, she thinks it would be immature to hide. Her children, however, are truly shocked by their mother's behavior and ask her to stop it. They think she is not behaving like a mother and they are embarrassed to have strange men in the house.

SUPPLEMENTARY READINGS

Bayles, Michael and Henley, Kenneth. *Right Conduct.* New York: Random House, 1983.

Clark, Ralph. *Introduction to Moral Reasoning.* St. Paul, Minn.: West Publishing Co., 1986.

Kierkegaard, Soren. *Either/Or.* Princeton, N.J.: Princeton University Press, 1946.

Leiser, Burton M. *Liberty, Justice and Morals: Contemporary Value Conflicts.* New York: Macmillan, 1973.

Martin, Mike W. *Everyday Morality: An Introduction to Applied Ethics.* Belmont, Calif.: Wadsworth Publishing Co., 1989.

Pope Paul VI. *Humanae Vitae,* 1968.

Purtill, Richard L. *Moral Dilemmas.* Belmont, Calif.: Wadsworth Publishing Co., 1985.

Rachels, James. *Moral Problems.* New York: Harper & Row, 1971.

Wellman, Carl. *Morals and Ethics,* Englewood Cliffs, N.J.: Prentice-Hall, 1975.

White, James. *Contemporary Moral Problems.* St. Paul, Minn.: West Publishing Co., 1985.

ACCIDENT, FALLACY OF:

The fallacy of arguing from a general rule to an exceptional case. Exceptional factors were called "accidents" in medieval logic. These are especially common in moral reasoning, e.g.: "Lying is wrong; therefore I should not tell a lie in order to save my grandmother from the Nazis."

ACT DEONTOLOGY/RULE DEONTOLOGY:

See deontology. Rule deontologists hold that particular acts are right or wrong in and of themselves, just because they are acts of a certain kind, or because they conform to moral rules. Act deontologists hold that particular acts are right or wrong in and of themselves, but not because of the kinds of acts they are, or because they conform to moral rules. Thus, rule deontologists believe we can find out what is right or wrong by appealing to rules, but act deontologists think that we must intuit the rightness or wrongness of each particular act.

AD HOMINEM ARGUMENT:

An argument that attempts to show that an opinion is wrong by attacking the person who holds it. This is a fallacy, because the opinion may be correct even if the accusation against the person is true.

ALTRUISM:

An interest in other people's welfare for their own sake, and not motivated by gain to one's self. The opposite of egoism.

ANTECEDENT:

See conditional.

ARGUMENTATION:

The process of showing that some beliefs are true on the basis of other beliefs; deriving conclusions from premises.

AUTHENTIC:

Being honest with one's self and not pretending to be something else. People are sometimes inauthentic in pretending to be something they are not, in order to win approval from others, or they may act out or play a role that they think is expected of them. Authentic persons recognize that they are the authors of their own choices and are responsible for them, as opposed to inauthentic persons who blame others for their behavior.

AUTHORITY, FALLACY OF:

Appealing to an authority (rather than to evidence and reasoning) to settle a disputed fact. A fallacy, because even if the authority is a recognized one and all parties are bound to accept her decision, she may still be wrong.

AUTONOMY (OF THE WILL):

In Kantian ethics, the will realizes its autonomy when it acts from its own inner principle, or gives its law to itself, rather than acting upon a principle imposed on it from outside.

BEGGING THE QUESTION, FALLACY OF (CIRCULAR REASONING):

The fallacy of assuming in the premises what one is attempting to prove, or taking for granted in one's argument precisely what is in dispute.

BIOETHICS:

A branch of ethics that concerns itself with the ethical problems arising in biological science and health care practice.

CATEGORICAL:

Unconditionally necessary; opposed in Kantian ethics to the hypothetically necessary, or necessary if a particular end is to be reached.

CATEGORICAL PROPOSITION:

A proposition that makes an assertion of truth unconditionally or without qualification, as opposed to a hypothetical or conditional proposition.

CLINICAL ETHICS:

A branch of bioethics that concerns itself with the ethical problems arising from the interaction of patients and health care professionals in the existing health care system.

COMMISSION (ACT OF):

An act by which a person does something morally wrong, as opposed to an act of omission, or a failure to do what is right or good.

COMPOSSIBILITY:

The possibility that two or more things could be in existence at the same time; as opposed to the case in which the existence of one rules out the existence of the others.

GLOSSARY

CONCLUSION:

The proposition that, in argumentation, a person is trying to prove.

CONDITIONAL PROPOSITION:

A conditional proposition has the form: "If A then B," where A and B are component propositions. The component A is the antecedent and B is the consequent. Example: "If it is raining outside, then I will get wet." This is a conditional proposition: "It is raining outside" is the antecedent, and "I will get wet" is the consequent.

CONSEQUENT:

See conditional.

CONSEQUENTIALIST:

Any ethical theory which holds that the rightness or wrongness of an action depends solely on consequences. Utilitarianism is a consequentialist theory.

CONTRACTARIAN (CONTRACTUALIST):

A philosopher who believes the moral basis of society may be explained by reference to a social contract.

CONTRADICTION:

A statement that is held to be both true and false at the same time and in the same way. While it is never possible, logically, for a contradiction to be true, people may believe contradictions without realizing that they do.

CONVENTIONAL MORAL RULES:

Rules that define institutions and social roles, and govern behavior, which are determined by agreement among members of a group, and which derive their force from having been accepted over a period of time. These may vary from time to time and place to place, but are considered to be binding on members of society.

CULTURAL RELATIVISM:

The position in ethics which holds that morality is determined by the customs of cultures or societies. Cultural relativism also holds that there are no universal principles binding on all persons at all times, but that morality differs from culture to culture and time to time.

DECISIONALISM:

An ethical theory which holds that morality is a matter of subjective choice. Decisionalists

believe that reasoning is never sufficient to reach moral conclusions; each of us must at some point choose for ourselves what is morally right or wrong.

DEDUCTIVE REASONING/INDUCTIVE REASONING:

Deductive reasoning usually proceeds from more general premises to more specific conclusions. In a valid deductive argument, conclusions must be true (are necessarily true) if the premises are true. Inductive reasoning proceeds from more specific premises to more general conclusions. It can only establish that conclusions are probably true.

DEONTOLOGY:

A general term for those forms of ethics that base morality on duty and obligation. Deontological theories hold that actions are right or wrong in and of themselves, regardless of consequences; thus they are often contrasted with teleological theories. Deontic logic formalizes our understanding of the rules of permission, prohibition, and obligation.

DESCRIPTIVE/PRESCRIPTIVE:

Descriptive approaches to human behavior state what people do in fact believe and how they actually behave. Prescriptive approaches, in contrast, tell us how people ought to think and act.

DIALECTICAL REASONING:

Reasoning that follows the pattern of a conversation in which questions are proposed and answers tested against other beliefs we hold.

DILEMMA:

An argument that combines hypothetical and categorical propositions in the following form: If A then B; if C then D. Either A or C; therefore either B or D. The word is often used for a situation in which a choice must be made between two unpleasant alternatives.

DISJUNCTION (OR DISJUNCTIVE PROPOSITION):

A disjunction asserts that one or the other of two statements is true. An exclusive disjunction asserts that one or the other, but not both, is true; an inclusive disjunction asserts that at least one of the statements is true, leaving open the possibility that both may be.

DIVINE COMMAND THEORY:

An ethical theory that rests all of ethics upon the will of God. If God has commanded an action, it is right; if He has forbidden it, it is wrong. We are not entitled to ask whether His commands are themselves right or wrong; there is no independent standard to which we can appeal.

DOGMATISM:

The claim that certain (moral) doctrines are known to be true (often without adequate evidence), and hence are not subject to critical examination. Dogmatism in ethics holds that moral reasoning is unnecessary, because the answers are already known.

DOUBLE EFFECT:

Given an action that has two consequences, one morally permissible or praiseworthy, and the other morally blameworthy, this Thomist principle holds that (at least in certain cases) it may be permissible to choose that action, if the morally acceptable consequence is intended, and the morally blameworthy consequence is not intended. Example: If I happen to kill someone who is threatening my life, but do not choose to do so, I would not be on this account guilty of murder, if I acted with the intention of defending myself, rather than with the intention of killing the other person.

DUAL:

The dual of a negative moral principle is the principle that prescribes a correlative positive course of action.

EGOISM:

In ethics, the position that morality can ultimately be explained entirely in terms of self-interest. On the egoistic view, altruism, or concern for others, is ultimately only enlightened self-interest.

EMOTIVIST:

Emotivists in ethics believe that ethical utterances are noncognitive. That is, they believe that ethical utterances are not statements of fact and do not give information about the world. Ethical utterances cannot be true or false. Instead, they may express our moral feelings about our own or others' actions; or they may attempt to arouse feelings similar to ours in others and thus influence their actions. Thus, emotivists claim, no one is really right or wrong in moral disputes; the parties simply have different feelings about the situation.

ENDS MEANS CONTINUUM:

The view that there is no absolute distinction between ends and means: What is an end in one context may be a means in another.

EQUIVOCATION, FALLACY OF:

The fallacy committed when a word is used in more than one sense in an argument, in order to establish a conclusion that depends on a confusion between the senses of the word.

FORCE, FALLACY OF APPEALING TO:

The fallacy committed when force or threats are used to get one's opponent to accept one's conclusion.

HARMONY:

For the ancient Greek philosophers, a state in which reason has ordered our own and others' actions in such a way as to secure greater cooperation and prevent conflict. Reason does this by allotting different tasks to different persons and different times to different activities, coordinating this diversity into an ordered whole.

HASTY GENERALIZATION, FALLACY OF:

The fallacy of generalizing from too few cases, or from atypical cases, to a rule meant to hold for all cases; e.g., "Some persons abuse alcohol; therefore society should totally prohibit its use."

HEALTH CARE POLICY ETHICS:

A branch of bioethics concerned with the organization and administration of a nation's health care system, and the ethical problems that arise when health care resources must be administered and allocated in a fair, but cost-effective manner.

HEDONISM:

Ethical hedonism is the position in ethics that pleasure is the highest, or the only, good in life, and that we should aim, in our actions, at producing the greatest amount of pleasure. Psychological hedonism is the position that human beings always do, as a matter of fact, aim at producing pleasure and avoiding pain and that no one ever acts otherwise. Psychological hedonism makes a statement about what human beings in fact do; ethical hedonism makes a statement about what they ought to do.

HEDONISTIC CALCULUS:

A means, proposed by the utilitarian Jeremy Bentham, of measuring, comparing, and summing up the total of pains and pleasures which each of our actions causes in all persons affected. Bentham attempts to make it possible to calculate which of several possible courses of action would produce the "greatest good [and the least evil] for the greatest number."

HIERARCHY OF GOODS:

The belief that goods (or ends) can be rank-ordered. Some goods are higher or nobler than others, and therefore more desirable.

HYPOTHETICAL PROPOSITION:

A proposition which asserts that something is true *if* something else is true. Also called a conditional proposition.

HYPOTHETICAL SYLLOGISM:

An argument that has two premises and a conclusion and in which both premises and conclusion have the form of conditional propositions.

IDEAL RULES:

Rules that are not actually in force in a given society at a given time, but that can be justified on the basis of moral principles.

IMPERATIVE:

An imperative sentence, in grammar, expresses a command. It is distinguished from an interrogative sentence (which expresses a question); a hortative sentence (which expresses a wish or a request); and a declarative or indicative sentence (which states a matter of fact).

INCONSISTENT:

Two beliefs are inconsistent if they contradict one another. Contradictory beliefs cannot both be true at the same time and they cannot both be false.

INSUBORDINATION:

The failure of some person to maintain his or her proper rank. Interestingly, insubordination covers cases in which a higher-ranking person fails to maintain his or her high rank and sinks to a lower place than is appropriate.

INTRINSICALLY GOOD:

That which is good in itself, without regard to its effects or consequences.

MAXIM:

In Kantian ethics, a rule according to which a person acts, or proposes to act, which may or may not be a moral law according to Kant's principle of universalizability.

METAETHICS:

A division of ethics that analyzes the logic of moral reasoning and the meanings of the words (such as "ought," "good," "right," and the like) used in ethical statements. It attempts to clarify the meaning and force of such statements and the conditions under which it is appropriate to make them. Thus, where normative ethics would ask "Is it wrong to tell a lie?" or perhaps, "Is it wrong for me to tell this lie?," metaethics would ask "What does it mean to say 'It is wrong to tell a lie,' and how could someone argue for or against that belief?"

MODALITY:

A way in which a proposition may be held to be true. For example, instead of saying a proposition is true, we may say that it is *necessarily* true; or, instead of saying that it is false, that it is impossible for it to be true. In ethics, when we speak of performing acts, we may say that it is possible or impossible to do so, or that the acts are obligatory, permitted, or prohibited.

MONISM:

In ethics, a theory which holds that there is only one ultimate principle.

MORAL SIGNIFICANCE:

The moral significance of an action is determined by considering the ways in which it affects persons and other sentient beings, not only in some limited respect but "all things considered," according to moral principles and rules.

MORALLY NECESSARY:

A term used for actions that people are duty-bound or obligated to do (or not to do).

NATURAL LAW:

In some systems of ethics, a basic system of moral principles or rules that is given by nature and binding on all persons. "Natural" is here opposed to merely customary or conventional. The natural law is taken to be superior to the laws of a society and serves as a test of their validity.

NONCOGNITIVE:

As the word is used by emotivists, a noncognitive utterance does not make a statement about a matter of fact, and so cannot be said to be true or false. An example would be an imperative.

NORMATIVE ETHICS:

A branch of ethics that uses ethical language and moral reasoning to make moral judgments about particular actions or classes of actions. Also called substantive ethics.

NORMATIVE STATEMENT:

A statement that expresses a person's standards about the way people ought to act (rather than what they in fact do), or about which actions are right or wrong.

OMISSION (ACT OF):

The non-performance or neglect of an action or duty.

PARTICULAR PROPOSITION:

A categorical proposition that contains a quantifier making reference to some (at least one) member of a given subject-class. It does not specify which particular members of the subject-class are being referred to.

PITY, FALLACY OF APPEALING TO:

The fallacy committed when one is asked to accept a given conclusion, not on the basis of evidence, but on the basis of sympathy or pity. Whether or not Jean Valjean stole a loaf of bread is a matter of fact and should not be decided by an appeal to pity. However, if he were starving, sympathy for his situation might be a reason to mitigate his penalty.

PLURALISM:

In ethics, a theory which holds that there is more than one ultimate kind of principle.

POSITIVE DUTIES:

Duties that exist only because they are imposed by the laws, customs, regulations (and so forth) of the society in which we live, and that are relative to those institutions and that society.

PRACTICE RULES:

One of two types of rules distinguished by John Rawls in his 1955 article "Two Concepts of Rules." Practice rules define a practice and determine which kinds of acts conform to that practice. See summary rules.

PRAGMATISM:

A late nineteenth-, early twentieth-century form of philosophy, which appears as a theory of meaning (Peirce) and as a theory of truth (James, Dewey). William James stated: "Ideas become true just so far as they help us get into satisfactory relations with other parts of our experience." Dewey likewise emphasized the problem-solving character of thinking, believing it to be a tool used to achieve practical results, rather than an abstract activity undertaken for its own sake. No ends are absolutes (see means end continuum), and reasoning must adapt itself to changing circumstances. Pragmatism emphasizes pluralism, relativism, creativity, and teleology.

PREMISE:

A proposition in an argument that serves as a reason for the conclusion. Premises may be spoken of as evidence for the conclusion.

PRIMA FACIE:

A Latin phrase meaning "at first look" or "on the face of it." It contrasts with the notion of "on balance," or "all things considered."

PRINCIPLE:

A principle is a "high level" rule that justifies other rules. A moral principle is a person's highest or most general moral belief.

PROPOSITION:

A statement that is either true or false. Declarative sentences typically express propositions. Example: "It is raining outside."

QUANTIFIER:

The words "all," "some," or "no" are called quantifiers, when they are used in a categorical proposition to indicate how many things in a given subject-class are referred to by the proposition.

RETRIBUTIVIST:

Used of those moral theories which hold that legal penalties are or should be inflicted on wrongdoers as punishment (retribution) for the wrongs they have done. There are two other common opinions about the purpose of legal penalties. One holds that their aim is or should be the rehabilitation of offenders; the other, that penalties inflicted on offenders should aim at deterring other persons from committing similar offenses.

RIDICULE, FALLACY OF APPEALING TO:

A type of ad hominem argument in which the fallacy consists in making fun of one's opponent rather than attempting to answer her arguments.

RULE DEONTOLOGY:

See act deontology.

SELF-REALIZATION THEORIES:

Ethical theories that make the realization of human potential the ultimate goal of life.

SINGULAR PROPOSITION:

A categorical proposition that makes reference to one unique, specified individual.

SOCIAL CONTRACT (THEORIES):

Theories which hold that moral principles or rules are brought into existence by a contract. In some variants (e.g., Locke), the making of the contract was considered an actual historical event; in others (e.g., Rawls), it is not claimed that any such contracts were ever made. Rather, the social contract serves as a theoretical model, a justification, and a test of validity for laws and social institutions.

SOUND ARGUMENT:

A sound argument is a valid argument that has true premises. Thus, the conclusion of a sound argument must be true.

STATE OF NATURE:

The original position in which persons either did or would exist in the absence of a social contract. No persons have given up any of their individual liberties, and no law or authority has power over any of them.

STOICISM:

Term for a group of ancient philosophical theories of the Hellenistic-Roman period (from about the end of the fourth century B.C. to about the end of the third century A.D.). Stoic ethical theories held that each person should accept his or her situation in the world, seeing in it a reflection of the universal power of reason that governed the world. They believed that persons should simplify their lives, maintain rational control over their passions, and attempt to achieve only that which is in their power, gaining by this peace of mind.

SUBJECT-CLASS/PREDICATE-CLASS:

The subject-class of a proposition is the collection of things referred to by the grammatical subject of the proposition. The predicate-class is the collection of things referred to by the grammatical predicate. In "All horses are animals" the subject-class is all the horses in the world, and the predicate-class is all the animals in the world.

SUBJECTIVE/OBJECTIVE/INTERSUBJECTIVE:

Subjective may mean what exists for me, in my own consciousness, as opposed to objective, which means what exists outside consciousness. Beliefs or attitudes are intersubjective if shared by two or more persons.

SUBSTANTIVE ETHICS:

See normative ethics.

SUMMARY RULES:

One of two forms of rules distinguished by John Rawls in his 1955 article, "Two Concepts of Rules." Summary rules are summaries of previous particular judgments about the rightness or wrongness of acts which may be used to predict what kinds of acts are likely to be right or wrong in the future. They are merely inductive generalizations; acts are not right or wrong because they conform to summary rules. See practice rules.

SUPEREROGATORY ACTS:

Acts "above and beyond the call of duty." We are permitted to do such acts, and are praiseworthy if we do so, but we are not obligated to perform them.

SYLLOGISM:

A kind of deductive argument that contains two categorical propositions as its premises and one as its conclusion.

TELEOLOGICAL:

Concerning the end or purpose toward which a process or action is directed. In ethics, a theory that the moral value of an action should be determined by its purpose or results.

UNIVERSAL PROPOSITION:

A categorical proposition that contains a quantifier making reference to all members of a given subject-class.

UNIVERSALIZABILITY:

The ability to generalize a particular moral judgment in an individual case, so as to make it apply, as a universal judgment, to every such case. In Kantian ethics, a test of the validity of the judgment being applied in the particular case.

UTILITARIANISM:

A consequentialist theory concerned with all persons who are affected by an action and not just the interests of the agent. According to John Stuart Mill, "The creed which accepts as the foundation of morals, Utility, or the Greatest Happiness Principle, [and] holds that actions are right in proportion as they tend to promote happiness, wrong as they tend to promote the reverse of happiness. By happiness is intended pleasure and the absence of pain; by unhappiness pain and the privation of pleasure." Act utilitarianism believes that each action should be judged by the "greatest happiness" criterion. Whether an individual action is right or wrong depends on whether that individual action promotes happiness or the reverse. Rule utilitarianism does not apply the "greatest happiness" criterion to individual actions, but rather to classes of actions. An individual action on a specific occasion may be right, even if it promotes less happiness than its alternatives, if that sort of action will in most cases tend to promote a greater happiness.

VALID ARGUMENT:

A valid argument is one whose conclusion must be true if its premises are true. (A valid argument need not have premises which are true.) See sound argument.

VALUES/FACTS:

Values are the qualities of things that make them desirable, as opposed to facts, which are properties of things considered independently of their desirability.

INDEX

Prichard, H. A., 145
prima facie, 142, 143, 170, 171, 186, 335
principles, 15–17, 51–55, 58–60, 335
    affirmative, 174
    development of, 169–192
    do no harm, 176–179, 220
    do not be unfair, 180–183
    do not violate another's freedom, 184–187
    legality, 188–189
    opportunity, 190, 191
    ordering of, 209–213
    steps used in applying, 195–215
    subordinate, 187–191
proposition, 29, 335
Purtill, Richard, 330

Rachels, James, 236, 330
Rand, Ayn, 83
Rawls, John, 127, 135–138, 140, 149, 165, 181, 193
Raz, Joseph, 193
reasoning, 19, 23–48, *see also* moral reasoning
    fallacies in, 73–82
    levels of, 47–61
    obstacles to, 63–72
    steps in, 283–286
    types of, 41–44
Regan, Donald, 108
Reiser, Joel, 297
relativism, 8–11, 65–67, 332
retributivism, 253, 335
Richards, David, 193
Roe *v* Wade, 56
roles, 257–264
Rosen, Bernard, 45, 61, 216
Ross, Steven, 22
Ross, W. D., 19, 108, 142–144
Rousseau, Jean-Jacques, 140
rule deontology, 142–144, 331
rule utilitarianism, 147–151
rules, 15, 37–39, 49–51, 56–60
    actual and ideal, 229–230
    conflict of, 92, 93
    conventional, 221–225, 332
    critiquing, 237–254
    subordinate, 217–235
    two kinds of, 149, 150
Russell, Bertrand, 241

Salmon, Wesley, 45
sanctions, 252
Sartre, Jean-Paul, 67, 83, 162, 165
Scanlon, Thomas, 209
Scheffler, Israel, 193
self-realization theory, 109–117, 335
Sellers, W., 83
sexual ethics, 317–321

Shaw, Russell, 258, 280
Shirk, Evelyn, 22
Sidgewick, Henry, 108
Simco, Nancy, 45
Singer, Marcus, 108
skepticism, 64, 65
Smart, J. J. C., 101, 103, 105, 108, 148, 165
social contract theory, 127–138
social issues, 312, 313
Socrates, 75, 202
sound argument, 28, 336
state of nature, 127, 336
Stebbings, Susan, 45
Stevenson, C. L., 83
Stirner, Max, 110
stoicism, 118–120, 336
subordinate moral rules, 217–234
substantive ethics, 53, 336
summary rules, 149, 336
Sumner, Graham, 8
syllogism, 29–34, 336
    hypothetical, 32, 33, 34, 35

Taylor, Richard, 193
teleology, 115, 336
theory, ethical, 52–53, 87–165
Thiroux, Jacques, 22
Thomistic ethics, 120–123
Thrasymachus, 77
Time, 307
Toulman, Stephen, 45, 165
Tufts, James, 61

universality, 145
universalizability, 88, 89, 94
Urmson, J. O., 83, 219
utilitarianism, 97–106, 115, 214, 336
    act and rule, 104, 105, 147–151

valid argument, 28, 336

Waldron, Jeremy, 236
Wall, George, 22
Wallich, Henry, 309
Warnock, G. J., 22, 83, 177
Wehane, Patricia, 309
Wellman, Carl, 330
White, James, 330
Williams, Bernard, 61, 66, 83, 108
Wilmot, Joyce and William, 253
Wippel, John, 126
withholding
    information, 293
    treatment, 291–292
Wolter, Alan, 126

Zeigler, Earle, 250